高等职业教育装备制造大类专业系列教材

汽车构造

Automobile Structure

闫云敬　邓　宁　主　编

中国建筑工业出版社

图书在版编目（CIP）数据

汽车构造：汉英对照/闫云敬，邓宁主编. —北京：中国建筑工业出版社，2019.2（2024.8重印）

高等职业教育装备制造大类专业系列教材

ISBN 978-7-112-24621-2

Ⅰ. ①汽… Ⅱ. ①闫… ②邓… Ⅲ. ①汽车-构造-高等职业教育-教材-汉、英 Ⅳ. ①U463

中国版本图书馆 CIP 数据核字（2020）第 011057 号

本教材是以职业教育伴随企业"走出去"的国际化项目"上汽通用五菱—印尼"项目"中印 SGMW 汽车学院"以及"东风柳州汽车有限公司服务培训中心"为载体，根据培养海内外学生和企业员工培训需求而编制的双语教材。本教材共有 5 个模块，内容包括：总论、汽车发动机、汽车底盘、汽车车身、汽车电气系统等。

本教材为高等职业教育装备制造大类专业系列教材，可作为高职高专院校汽车检测与维修技术和汽车营销与服务专业的教材用书及指导书，也可以供从事汽车维修行业或其他相关行业的国内外技术人员参考。

责任编辑：司　汉
责任校对：焦　乐

高等职业教育装备制造大类专业系列教材
汽车构造

闫云敬　邓　宁　主　编

*

中国建筑工业出版社出版、发行（北京海淀三里河路 9 号）

各地新华书店、建筑书店经销

北京科地亚盟图文设计有限公司制版

北京凌奇印刷有限责任公司印刷

*

开本：880×1230 毫米　1/16　印张：14¼　字数：439 千字

2020 年 5 月第一版　2024 年 8 月第五次印刷

定价：**40.00** 元

ISBN 978-7-112-24621-2

（35255）

本书编委会

主　编：闫云敬　邓　宁

副主编：覃京翎　彭定文　吴津宇　杨永贵
　　　　董志辉

编　委：朱炳耀　黄　彧　侯庆愉　韦淇淋
　　　　韦东辉　韦雪薇　曾云生　吴　铭
　　　　范　涛

前 言
Preface

随着"一带一路"倡议的提出，越来越多的中国企业走出国门投资建厂，企业对机电、电气类国际化高技能人才的需求也快速增长。为了建设推动与中国企业和产品"走出去"相配套的职业教育发展模式，加强国际交流与合作，满足国际学生学习现代汽车检测与维修、汽车营销与服务的需求，编写本教材。

With the introduction of the Belt and Road initiative, more and more Chinese enterprises have gone abroad to invest and build factories, and the demand for international high skilled talents of electromechanical and electrical majors has also increased rapidly. In order to build a development mode of vocational education matching with the Chinese enterprises and products abroad, strengthen international exchanges and cooperation, and meet the needs of international students to learn modern automobile detection and maintenance, automobile marketing and service, this textbook has been compiled.

本教材是国际、国内现代学徒制教学模式改革的建设成果之一，是围绕首批现代学徒制试点项目建设过程中，学校与地方龙头企业——上汽通用五菱汽车股份有限公司、广西汽车集团、上汽汽车变速器有限公司柳东分公司等企业，开展校企合作共同培养具备国际竞争力的高素质复合型新工科人才，在实践教学过程中校企共同开发的专业教材。教材以职业教育伴随企业"走出去"的国际化项目"上汽通用五菱—印尼"项目"中印 SGMW 汽车学院"为载体，根据海内外学生和企业员工培训需求而编制的双语教材。

This textbook is one of the achievements of the international and domestic modern apprenticeship teaching mode reform. During the construction of the first group of modern apprenticeship pilot projects, the schools and local leading enterprises, such as SAIC-GM-Wuling Automobile Co., Ltd., Guangxi Automobile Group, Liudong branch of SAIC automobile transmission Co., Ltd., carry out school-enterprise cooperation to jointly cultivate high-quality composite new engineering talents with international competitiveness. It is a professional textbook jointly developed by the school-enterprise cooperation in the practice teaching process. This book is based on China and Indonesia SGMW automobile College of international project called SAIC-GM-Wuling Automobile in Indonesia, with the purpose of vocational education accompanying enterprises abroad. It is a bilingual teaching material compiled for training students at home and abroad and the training needs of enterprises' employees.

本教材以读者够学够用为原则，对《汽车发动机结构与原理》《汽车底盘结构与原理》《汽车车身》《汽车电气系统》等课程的知识点进行了整合，运用任务驱动的教学模式编写，降低学习的难度。教材中所有中文的内容皆有与之相对应的英文，有利于我国职业教育课程的国际化。教材内容主要包含总论、汽车发动机、汽车底盘、汽车车身、汽车电气系统五部分，主要从组成、作用、分类、工作原理等方面进行阐述。

Based on the principle of sufficiency, this textbook integrates the knowledge points of Automobile Engine Structure and Principle, Automobile Chassis Structure and Principle, Automobile Body, Automobile Electrical System and other courses, and uses the task-driven teaching mode to compile, so as to reduce the difficulty of learning. All Chinese contents in this book have corresponding English, which is conducive to the internationalization of vocational education curriculums of China. The content of the textbook mainly includes five parts: general introduction, automobile engine, automobile chassis, automobile body, automobile electrical system, which mainly expounds the composition, function, classification, working principle, etc.

本教材注重落实立德树人根本任务，促进学生成为德智体美劳全面发展的社会主义建设者和接班人。教材内容融入思想政治教育，宣扬大国工匠精神，推进中华民族文化自信自强。

This textbook focuses on implementing the fundamental task of building morality and cultivating people. Promote students to become socialist builders and successors with all-round development of morality, intelligence, physique, beauty and labor. The contents of the textbooks are integrated into ideological and political education, publicize the craftsmanship spirit of a great country and promote the self-confidence and self-improvement of the Chinese culture.

本教材的主要特点如下：

The main characteristics of this textbook are as follows:

（1）适用于理论教学与实训相结合的模块一体化教学模式。每个章节都将理论教学与实训内容相结合，将社会上已经实用化的教学结构纳入教材，实现理论与实践的有机结合，提高学生分析问题、解决问题的综合能力。

（1）It is applicable to the module integration teaching mode combining theory teaching and practice training. Each chapter combines the theoretical teaching with the practical training contents, and brings the practical teaching structure in society into the teaching materials, which realizes the organic combination of theory and practice, and improves the comprehensive ability of students to analyze and solve problems.

（2）集成了汽车发动机、底盘、车身、电器这四大核心系统的构造和工作原理进行讲解。

（2）The structure and working principle of the four core systems of automobile engine, chassis, body and electrical appliances are integrated for explanation.

（3）该书全文应用了汉英对照模式，既能学习汽车构造也能对汽车专业英文术语进行了解和学习。

（3）The Chinese-English mode is applied in the full text of this book, which is helpful to learn the automobile structure as well as the automobile professional English terms.

本教材为高等职业教育装备制造大类专业系列教材，可作为高职高专院校汽车检测与维修技术和汽车营销与服务专业的教材用书及指导书，也可以供从事汽车维修行业或其他相关行业的国内外技术人员参考。本书突出能力培养，注重实用为原则，将理论知识和实际应用结合起来，是一本实用而全面的教材。

This textbook is a series of textbook for equiprnent manufacturing category in higher vocational education, and can be used as a teaching material and guide book for both automobile detection and maintenance technology major and automobile marketing and service major in higher vocational colleges, and can also be used as a reference for domestic and foreign technical personnel engaged in automobile maintenance industry or other related industries. This book is a practical and comprehensive textbook, which emphasizes the cultivation of ability, the principle of practicality and the combination of theoretical knowledge and practical application.

本教材由柳州城市职业学院的闫云敬、邓宁担任主编，覃京翎、彭定文、吴津宇、杨永贵、董志辉担任副主编，闫云敬负责统稿并校对。

Yan Yunjing and Deng Ning at Liuzhou City Vocational College are chief editors of this textbook, with Qin Jingling, Peng Dingwen, Wu Jinyu, Yang Yonggui and Dong Zhihui as associate editors, and Yan Yunjing is responsible for compiling and proofreading.

由于编者的经验、水平有限，加之时间仓促，书中难免在内容和文字上存在不足和缺陷，敬请广大读者批评指正。

Due to the limited experiences and level of the editor, as well as the short time, there are inevitably deficiencies and defects in the content and words of the book. The editor hopes to get the criticism and suggestion from readers.

目　录

Contents

项目一 总论
Item 1 General Introduction of Automobile

任务一 汽车定义

Task 1 Automobile Definition

汽车通常是指由动力装置驱动，具有 4 个或 4 个以上车轮的非轨道承载的车辆，主要用于载运人员或货物、牵引载运人员或货物的车辆以及特殊用途的车辆，其中包括与电力线相连的车辆（无轨电车）和整车装备质量超过 400kg 的三轮车辆。

An automobile usually refers to a non-rail carrying vehicle that is driven by a power device with four or more wheels, which is mainly used to carry or drag people or goods, and vehicles for special purposes, including vehicles connected to power lines (trolleybus) and tricycles with a complete vehicle mass of more than 400 kg.

任务二 汽车组成

Task 2 Automobile Composition

汽车整体结构组成 Working Principle of Automotive

燃料汽车通常由发动机、底盘、车身和电气与电子设备四部分组成（图 1.2.1）。发动机是汽车的心脏，为汽车提供动力，一般为汽油机或柴油机；底盘，包括传动系统、行驶系统、制动系统、转向系统和安全系统等；车身，一般来说轿车和客车分别采用承载式车身和非承载式车身，载货汽车车身包括驾驶室和车厢；电器与电子设备，包括电源、照明与信号设备、仪表、电气与电子系统、取暖及通风和刮水器等。这 4 个部分相互关联，组成统一的整体。

In general, a fuel automobile consists of four components: engine, chassis, body and electrical and electronic equipment. The engine is the "heart" of the automobile, providing power for the automobile, which is usually a gasoline engine or a diesel engine. The chassis is composed of the transmission system, driving system, brake system, steering system and security system. In regard of body, the car and the bus generally have a load-bearing body and a non-load-bearing body respectively. The body of a truck includes cab and trunk. Electrical and electronic equipment is composed of the power supply, lighting and signal equipment, instrumentation, electrical and electronic systems, heating, ventilation and wipers, etc. These four parts are interrelated and form a unified whole.

纯电动汽车主要由电力驱动系统、汽车底盘、汽车车身和其他电子、电气设备等组成（图 1.2.2）。纯电动汽车采用电力驱动电机代替了传统的燃油内燃发动机，车辆的驱动系统作了变更，动力驱动装置作了较大调整，动力源由燃油（汽油或柴油）改变为电能，动力传动系统也随之作相应的调整与改进。

Electric battery automobiles are mainly composed of an electrical driving system, automobile chassis, automobile body and other electronic and electrical equipment，etc. Electric vehicles use an electric drive motor instead of a traditional fuel internal combustion engine. The driving system of the automobile has been changed and the power drive device has been greatly altered. The source of power is changed from fuel oil (gasoline or diesel) to electricity，and the power transmission system is adjusted and improved accordingly.

图 1.2.1 燃料汽车的组成

Figure 1.2.1 Composition of fuel automobile

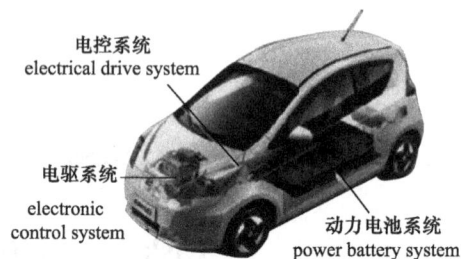

图 1.2.2 纯电动汽车组成

Figure 1.2.2 Composition of electric battery automobiles

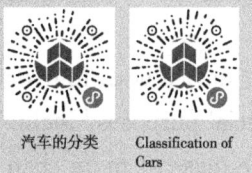

任务三 汽车分类

Task 3 Automobile Classification

按照《汽车和挂车类型的术语和定义》GB/T 3730.1—2001 的分类方法，汽车分为乘用车和商用车等。

According to the classification method in *Terminology and Definition of Automobile and Trailer Types* of GB/T 3730.1—2001，automobiles are divided into passenger automobiles and commercial ones，etc.

乘用车用于载运乘客及随身行李和临时物品，包括驾驶员座位在内不超过 9 个座位，部分车型可以牵引一辆挂车。其主要包括普通乘用车（图 1.3.1）、活顶乘用车（图 1.3.2）、高级乘用车（图 1.3.3）、小型乘用车（图 1.3.4）、敞篷车（图 1.3.5）、商务车（图 1.3.6）、越野车（图 1.3.7）、专用车（图 1.3.8）等。

Passenger automobiles are used to carry passengers, carry-on luggage and temporary items, which have no more than nine seats, including the driver's seat，and some are allowed to tow a trailer. They mainly include ordinary passenger automobiles, convertible top passenger automobiles, advanced passenger automobiles, micro passenger automobiles, convertibles, commercial automobiles, off-road automobiles and special automobiles，etc.

图 1.3.1 普通乘用车

Figure 1.3.1 Ordinary passenger automobile

图 1.3.2 活顶乘用车

Figure 1.3.2 Convertible top passenger automobile

图 1.3.3　高级乘用车

Figure 1.3.3　Advanced passenger automobile

图 1.3.4　小型乘用车

Figure 1.3.4　Micro passenger automobile

图 1.3.5　敞篷车

Figure 1.3.5　Convertible

图 1.3.6　商务车

Figure 1.3.6　Commercial automobile

图 1.3.7　越野车

Figure 1.3.7　Off-road automobile

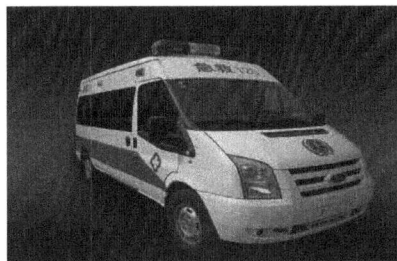

图 1.3.8　专用车

Figure 1.3.8　Special automobile

商用车用于运送人员和货物的汽车，可牵引挂车（乘用车不包含在内）。主要包括客车（图 1.3.9）、货车（图 1.3.10）和半挂牵引车（图 1.3.11）。

Commercial automobiles are used to transport people and goods, which can drag trailers (except the passenger automobiles). They mainly include buses, trucks and semi-trailer towing vehicles.

图 1.3.9　客车

Figure 1.3.9　Bus

图 1.3.10　货车

Figure 1.3.10　Truck

3

图 1.3.11　半挂牵引车

Figure 1.3.11　Semi-trailer towing vehicle

按动力装置不同分为汽油机汽车（图 1.3.12）、柴油机汽车（图 1.3.13）、天然气汽车（图 1.3.14）、纯电动汽车（图 1.3.15）、混合动力汽车（图 1.3.16）、燃料电池汽车（图 1.3.17）。

According to the different power devices, they can be divided into gasoline automobiles, diesel automobiles, natural gas automobiles, electric battery automobiles, hybrid automobiles and fuel cell automobiles.

图 1.3.12　汽油机汽车

Figure 1.3.12　Gasoline automobile

图 1.3.13　柴油机汽车

Figure 1.3.13　Diesel automobile

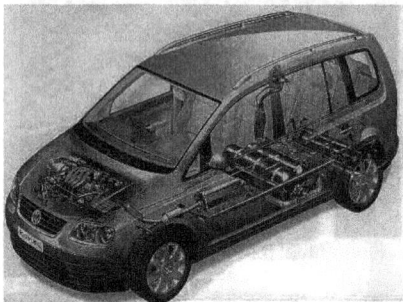

图 1.3.14　天然气汽车

Figure 1.3.14　Natural gas automobile

图 1.3.15　纯电动汽车

Figure 1.3.15　Electric battery automobile

图 1.3.16　混合动力汽车

Figure 1.3.16　Hybrid automobile

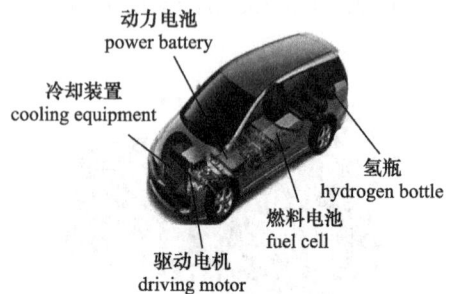

图 1.3.17　氢燃料电池汽车

Figure 1.3.17　Hydrogen fuel cell automobile

任务四　车辆识别代码（VIN）

Task 4　Vehicle Identification Number

车辆识别代号（VIN），也称17位编码，是国际上通行的标识机动车辆的代码，是车辆制造厂为该车辆指定的一组字码，一车一码，具有在世界范围内对一辆车的唯一识别性。

Vehicle Identification Number（VIN），which is known as a 17-digit code，is an internationally accepted code for identifying motor vehicles. It is a set of codes designated by the vehicle manufacturer for the vehicle. One vehicle has one code，which has a unique identification of a vehicle worldwide.

4.1　VIN 所在位置（Location of VIN）

汽车VIN码的识读　How to Read Automobile VIN Code

图 1.4.1　VIN 所在位置

Figure 1.4.1　Location of VIN

4.2　VIN 的组成（Composition of VIN）

《道路车辆　车辆识别代号（VIN）》GB 16735—2004 规定，车辆识别代号（VIN）由世界制造厂识别代号（WMI）、车辆说明部分（VDS）、车辆指示部分（VIS）三部分组成，共17位字码（图1.4.2）。

Vehicle Identification Number（VIN）*in Road Vehicles* GB 16735—2004 stipulates that the Vehicle Identification Number（VIN）consists of World Manufacturing Plant Identification Code（WMI），Vehicle Descriptor Section（VDS）and Vehicle Indicator Section（VIS），a total of 17 digit codes，as shown in Figure 1.4.2.

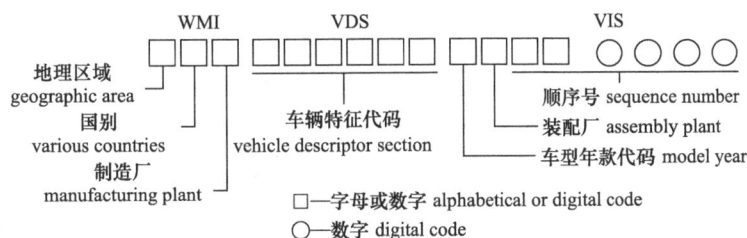

图 1.4.2　VIN 的组成

Figure 1.4.2　Composition of VIN

WMI 代号的第一位字码是由国际代理机构分配的、用以标明一个地理区域的一个字母或数字字码，国际代理机构已经根据预期的需要为某一个地理区域分配了几个字码。例如：1～5是北美洲；S～Z是欧洲；A～H是非洲；J～R是亚洲；6、7是大洋洲；8、9和0是南美洲等。

The first character code of WMI is an alphabetical or digital code assigned by an international agency to indicate a geographic area. The agency has allocated several codes to a geographic area for the expected requirement. For example：1-5 is North America；S-Z is Europe；A-H is Africa；J-R is Asia；6-7 is Oceania；8, 9 and 0 are South America, etc.

WMI 代号的第二位字码是由国际代理机构分配的、用以标明一个特定地区内的一个国家的一个字母或数字字码，国际代理机构已经根据预期的需要为某一个国家分配了几个字码。WMI 代号应通过第一位和第二位字码的组合保证国家识别标志的唯一性。例如：10～19、1A～1Z 是美国；W0～W9、WA～WZ 是德国；L0～L9、LA～LZ 是中国等。

The second character code of the WMI codes is an alphabetical or digital code assigned by an international agency to indicate a country in a particular region, which has distributed several codes to a country on the basis of expected need. The WMI codes should ensure the uniqueness of national identification marks through the combination of the first and second character codes. For example：10-19, 1A-1Z is the United States；W0-W9, WA-WZ is Germany；L0-L9 and LA-LZ are China, etc.

WMI 代号和第三位字码是由国家机构指定的、用以标明某个特定的制造厂的一个字母或数字字码，WMI 代号应通过第一位、第二位、第三位字码的组合保证制造厂识别标志的唯一性。例如：LFV 是一汽-大众汽车有限公司；LSG 是上海通用汽车有限公司；JHM 是日本本田技研工业股份有限公司；WDB 是德国戴姆勒-奔驰公司；WBA 是德国宝马汽车公司；KMH 是韩国现代汽车公司等。

The third character code of the WMI codes is an alphabetical or digital code designated by a national institution to indicate a particular manufacturer. The WMI codes should be combined with the first, second and third codes to ensure the uniqueness of the factory identification marks. For example：LFV is FAW-Volkswagen Automobile Co. , Ltd；LSG is Shanghai General Motors Co. , Ltd；JHM is Honda Technology Research and Development Industry Co. , Ltd. of Japan；WDB is Daimler-Benz Company of Germany；WBA is BMW Company of Germany；KMH is Hyundai Automobile Company of Korea, etc.

例如：上海大众汽车有限公司车辆识别代码（表 1.4.1）

For instance, vehicle identification number of Shanghai Volkswagen Automobile Co. , Ltd. is shown in Table 1.4.1.

上海大众汽车有限公司车辆识别代码　表 1.4.1

位置	说明	位置	说明
1～3	全球制造识别，即上海大众汽车有限公司（LSV）	7、8	车辆等级
		9	检查位
4	车身/底盘形式	10	生产年份
5	发动机/变速器	11	装配厂
6	乘员保护系统	12～17	生产厂序号

Vehicle Identification Number produced by Shanghai Volkswagen Automobile Co. , Ltd.（VIN）　Table 1.4.1

DIGIT	EXPLANATION	DIGIT	EXPLANATION
1～3	Global Manufacturing Identification；LSV-Shanghai Volkswagen Automobile Co. , Ltd.	7、8	Vehicle grade
		9	Check digit
4	Body /chassis type	10	Vehicle model year
5	Engine/ transmission	11	Assembly plant
6	Restrain System	12～17	Serial number

任务五 汽车的总体布置形式

Task 5 General Layout of Automobiles

为满足不同的使用要求，汽车的总体构造和布置形式可以各不相同。按照发动机和各个总成的相对位置不同，现代汽车的布置形式通常有发动机前置前轮驱动（FF）、发动机前置后轮驱动（FR）、发动机后置后轮驱动（RR）、发动机中置后轮驱动（MR）、四轮驱动（4WD）五种。

In order to meet different requirements, the general structure and layout of automobiles can be different. According to the position of the engine and each assembly, the layout of modern automobiles usually includes five types: front engine and front-wheel drive (FF), front engine and rear-wheel drive (FR), rear-engine and rear-wheel drive (RR), middle-engine and rear-wheel drive (MR) and four-wheel drive (4WD).

5.1 发动机前置前轮驱动（Front engine and front-wheel drive）（FF）

发动机前置前轮驱动是现代大多数轿车盛行的布置形式（图 1.5.1）。该形式具有结构紧凑、质量轻等特点，由于没有传动轴，故乘员室内宽敞、舒适。

The front-engine and front-wheel drive is the prevalent layout of most modern cars. This layout has the characteristics of compact structure and light weight, etc. Because there is no transmission shaft, the occupants' room is spacious and comfortable.

图 1.5.1 发动机前置前轮驱动

Figure 1.5.1 Front engine and front-wheel drive

5.2 发动机前置后轮驱动（Front engine and rear-wheel drive）（FR）

发动机前置后轮驱动布置形式具有很好的重平衡，控制性和稳定性好，其构造包括：发动机、变速器、传动轴、后差速器、半轴（图 1.5.2）。

The layout of FR has good weight balance, control ability and stability, it includes engine, transmission, propeller shaft, rear differential and half axle(Figure 1.5.2).

5.3 发动机后置后轮驱动（Rear-engine and rear-wheel drive）（RR）

发动机后置后轮驱动布置形式具有室内噪声小和空间利用率高等优点（图 1.5.3）。

The layout of RR has the advantages of low indoor noise and high space utilization, etc.

5.4 发动机中置后轮驱动（Middle-engine and rear-wheel drive）（MR）

发动机中置后轮驱动布置形式是方程式赛车和大多数跑车采用的布置形式（图 1.5.4）。该形式将功率和尺寸很大的发动机布置在驾驶员座椅和后轴之间，使前桥和后桥上有很好的重平衡，易于控制。

The layout is adopted by formula racing cars and most sports cars. For this layout, the engine with large power and size is arranged between the driver's seat and the rear axle，which makes the front axle and the rear axle have good weight balances and control ability.

Front engine Rear wheel
drive,简称FR。

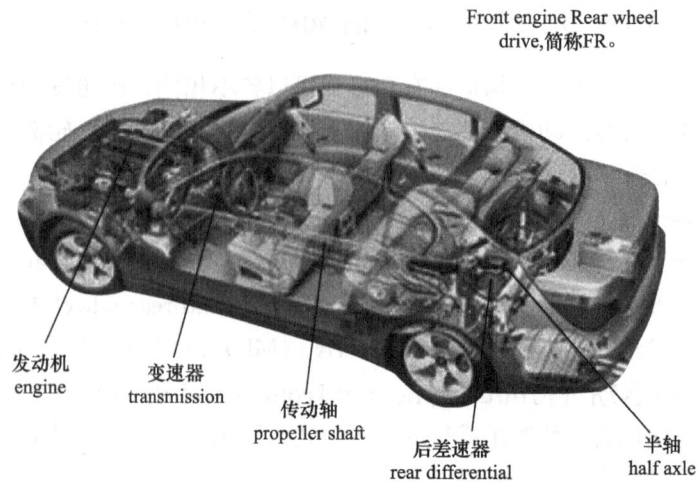

发动机
engine

变速器
transmission

传动轴
propeller shaft

后差速器
rear differential

半轴
half axle

图 1.5.2　前置后驱汽车构造图

Figure 1.5.2　The structure diagram of FR

图 1.5.3　发动机后置后轮驱动

Figure 1.5.3　Rear-engine and rear-wheel drive

图 1.5.4　发动机中置后轮驱动

Figure 1.5.4　Middle-engine and rear-wheel drive

5.5 四轮驱动（Four-wheel drive）（4WD）

四轮驱动布置形式是指汽车 4 个车轮都是驱动轮（图 1.5.5），可以在路况不理想的状况下保持稳定行驶，通常越野汽车采用这种布置形式。

The layout of 4WD means that all four wheels of a vehicle are driving wheels, which can maintain stable driving under unsatisfactory road conditions. Off-road vehicles usually adopt this layout.

图 1.5.5 四轮驱动

Figure 1.5.5 Four-wheel drive

任务六 汽车的主要技术参数

Task 6 Main Technical Parameters of Automobiles

6.1 汽车的主要外部尺寸（Main exterior dimensions of automobiles）

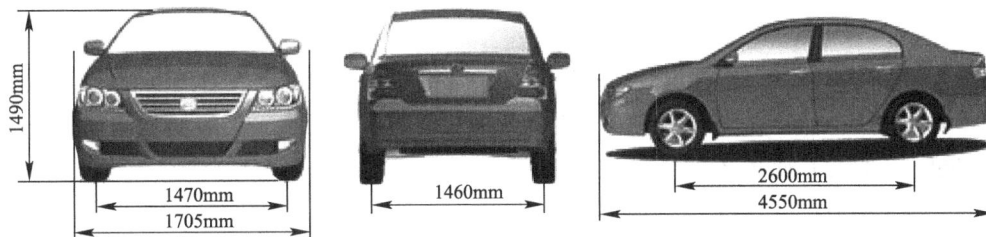

图 1.6.1 汽车的主要外部尺寸

Figure 1.6.1 Main exterior dimensions of automobiles

车长：垂直于车辆纵向对称平面并分别抵靠在汽车前、后最外端突出部位的两垂直面间的距离，简单地说是汽车长度方向两极端点间的距离。

车宽：平行于车辆纵向对称平面并分别抵靠车辆两侧最外刚性固定突出部位（除后视镜、侧面标志灯、方位灯、转向指示灯等）的两平面之间的距离。

车高：车辆最高点与车辆支承平面之间的距离。

轴距：车辆同侧相邻前后两个车轮的中心点间的距离。

轮距：在支承平面上，同轴左右车轮两轨迹中心间的距离（轴两端为双轮时，为左右两条双轨迹的中线间的距离）。

前悬：汽车最前端至前轴中心的水平距离。

后悬：汽车最后端至后轴中心的水平距离。

Vehicle length：the distance between the two vertical planes perpendicular to the longitudinal symmetrical plane of the vehicle and against the protruding parts of the front and rear extremities of the vehicle, which is simply the distance between the two extreme points of the vehicle's length direction.

Vehicle width：the distance between the two planes parallel to the longitudinal symmetrical plane of the vehicle and against the outermost rigid fixed protrusion (except rear view mirrors, side marker lamps, position lamps and turn signals, etc.) on both sides of the vehicle.

Vehicle height：The distance between the highest point of the vehicle and the supporting plane of the vehicle.

Wheelbase：The distance between the center points of the two adjacent wheels in the front and rear of the same side of the vehicle.

Tread：on the bearing surface, the distance between the two track centers of coaxial left and right wheels (if both ends of the shaft have double wheels, it is the distance between the center lines of left and right double tracks).

Front overhang：the horizontal distance from the foremost end of the vehicle to the center of the front axle.

Rear overhang：the horizontal distance from the rearmost end of the vehicle to the center of the rear axle.

6.2 汽车的质量参数 (Mass parameters of automobiles)

图 1.6.2 汽车的质量参数

Figure 1.6.2 Mass parameters of automobiles

整车干质量：指装备有车身、全部电气设备和车辆正常行驶所需的辅助设备的完整车辆的质量。

整车装备质量：整车干质量、冷却液质量、燃料（不少于整个油箱的 90%）质量和随车件（备胎、灭火器、标准备件和随车工具等）质量之和。

最大总质量：汽车满载时的质量。

最大装载质量：最大总质量与整车装备质量之差。

最大轴载质量：汽车单轴所承载的最大总质量。

The dry mass of the whole vehicle：the quality of whole vehicles equipped with body, all electrical equipment and auxiliary equipment required for normal driving of vehicles.

The equipment mass of the whole vehicle：the sum of the dry mass of the whole vehicle, coolant mass, fuel (not less than 90% of the whole tank) mass and parts along with the vehicle(spare tires, fire extinguishers, standard spare parts and tools, etc.).

The maximum total mass：the mass of the vehicle fully loaded.

The maximum loading mass：the difference between the maximum total mass and the equipment mass of the whole vehicle.

The maximum axle load mass：the maximum total mass loaded by a single axle.

思考与练习

（Reflection and Exercises）

1. 汽车由哪几部分组成？简要说明各部分的功用。

2. 举例说明汽车的分类。

3. 电动汽车和燃料汽车有什么区别？

1. What parts does a car consist of? Give a brief description of the functions of each part.

2. Illustrate the classification of automobiles.

3. What's the difference between an electric automobile and a fuel automobile?

项目二　汽车发动机
Item 2　Automobile Engines

任务一　汽车发动机概述

Task1　Overview

教学目标

1. 知识目标

（1）了解发动机的总体结构；

（2）掌握发动机的基本术语；

（3）理解四冲程发动机的工作原理。

2. 能力目标

（1）具有分析发动机的性能指标的能力；

（2）具有区分汽油发动机和柴油发动机的能力。

汽车发动机将化学燃料与空气进行混合在气缸体内燃烧，将化学能转化为热能，再将热能转变为机械能并对外输出动力。

3. 情感和素养目标

（1）培养学生的团结合作、善于人际交往沟通的意识；

（2）培养学生责任感、使命感，树立远大理想，弘扬爱国精神。

Teaching objectives

1. Knowledge objectives

（1）Understanding the overall structure of engines；

（2）Mastering basic terminology of engine；

（3）Principle of four-stroke engine.

2. Ability objectives

（1）The ability to analyze performance indicators of engines；

（2）The ability to distinguish between gasoline engines and diesel engines.

Automobile engines mix the chemical fuel and air, and the mixture is burnt in the cylinder body, which converts chemical energy into thermal energy, and then transforms thermal energy into mechanical energy to output power, which is provided for the automobiles.

3. Emotion and quality goals

（1）Cultivate students' awareness of being united and cooperative and being good at interpersonal communication;

（2）Cultivate students′sense of responsibility and mission，establish great ideals and promote patriotism.

发动机是一种能够把其他形式的能转化为机械能的机器，汽车发动机主要以内燃机为主，内燃机的发展源于18世纪的法国、德国，中国在这方面发展较晚，但是经过先辈历尽艰辛、艰苦奋斗，终于在1949年上海吴淞制造总厂自行设计试制成功第一台中速柴油机。中华人民共和国成立后，兴建大批柴油机厂等大型企业，同时以柳州机械厂、常州柴油机厂等中国内燃机第一批骨干企业如雨后春笋般发展。在中国内燃机的百年征程中，涌现一大批大国工匠，他们技艺精湛、爱岗敬业，值得同学们学习，未来的工作学习中，我们要传承工匠精神和钻研科技，专注技术改进与磨砺大国工匠品质。

An engine is a machine that can convert other forms of energy into mechanical energy. Automobile engines are mainly internal combustion engines originated in France and Germany in the 18th century. China developed late in this regard，but thanks to the arduous struggle and hard work of the ancestors，the first medium-speed diesel engine was designed and manufactured successfully at Shanghai Wusong Manufacturing General Factory in 1949. After the founding of the People′s Republic of China，a large number of diesel engine factories and other large enterprises have been built. At the same time，the first batch of backbone companies that produced internal combustion engines such as Liuzhou Machinery Factory and Changzhou Diesel Machinery Factory have sprung up like mushrooms. In the century-long journey of the development of China′s internal combustion engine，there are a large number of artisans who are skilled and dedicated to their jobs，which is well worth learning. Students are supposed to learn from them and carry forward the craftsmanship spirit，study science and technology，focus on improvement in technology and develop the craftsman spirit.

1.1　发动机的基本术语（Basic terminology of engines）

1. 上止点（top dead center）

活塞顶离曲轴中心最大距离时的位置称为上止点（TDC）（图2.1.1）。

The position of the piston head at the maximum distance from the center of the crankshaft is called the top dead center（TDC）.

2. 下止点（bottom dead center）

活塞顶离曲轴中心最小距离时的位置称为下止点（BDC）（图2.1.2）。

The position of the piston head at the minimum distance from the center of the crankshaft is called the bottom dead center（BDC）.

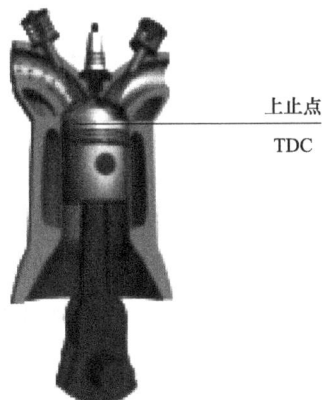

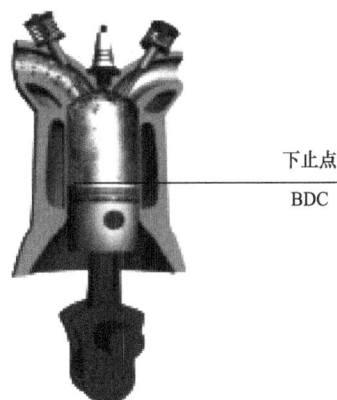

图2.1.1　上止点位置　　　　　　　图2.1.2　下止点位置
Figure 2.1.1　Top dead center　　　Figure 2.1.2　Bottom dead center

3. 活塞行程（piston stroke）

活塞运行在上下两个止点间的距离称为活塞行程（图2.1.3），一般用 S 表示。

The distance between TDC and BDC is called piston stroke，which is generally denoted by S.

4. 曲柄半径（crank radius）

曲轴旋转中心到曲柄销中心之间的距离称为曲柄半径（图2.1.4），一般用 R 表示。

The distance between the rotating center of crankshaft and the center of crank pin is called crank radius，which is generally denoted by R.

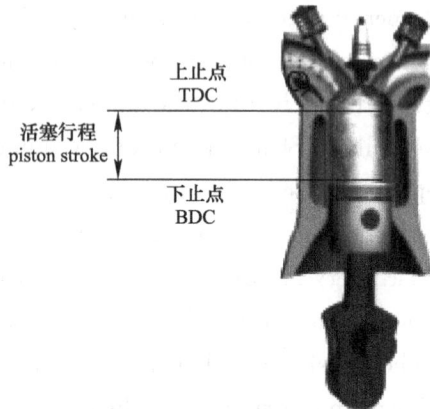 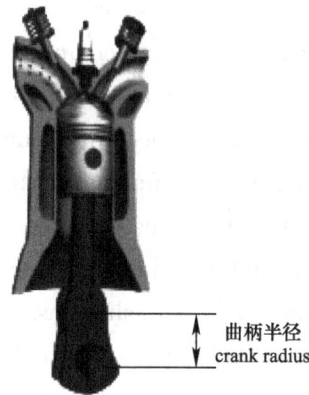

图2.1.3　活塞行程

Figure 2.1.3　Piston stroke

图2.1.4　曲柄半径

Figure 2.1.4　Crank radius

5. 燃烧室容积（combustion chamber volume）（图2.1.5）

活塞位于上止点时，活塞顶上方的空间，一般用 V_C 表示。工作容积：活塞从上止点运行到下止点所让出的容积，一般用 V_H 表示。

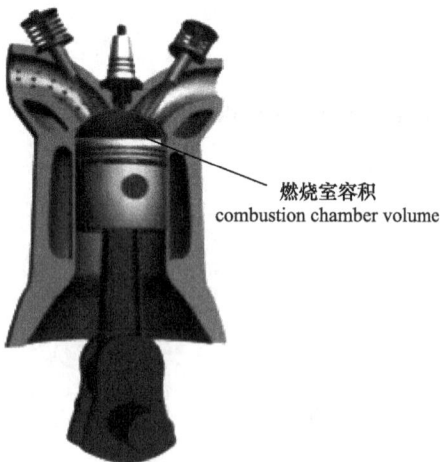

图2.1.5　燃烧室容积

Figure 2.1.5　Combustion chamber volume

$$V_H = \frac{\pi}{4} \cdot D^2 \cdot S \times 10^{-6} (L)$$

式中　D——气缸直径，mm；

　　　S——活塞行程，mm。

When the piston is located at the top dead center, the space above the piston head is called combustion chamber volume，which is usually expressed by V_C. Working volume：The volume of piston from top dead center to bottom dead center is called Working volume，which is usually expressed by V_H.

Where，D—cylinder diameter，mm；S—Piston stroke，mm.

6. 气缸工作容积（cylinder working volume）（V_h）（图2.1.6）

活塞从上止点到下止点所让出的空间容积（L）。

The volume of piston from top dead center to bottom dead center (L).

7. 发动机排量（engine displacement）

多气缸发动机，各气缸工作容积之和，叫发动机排量，一般用 V_L 表示：

$$V_L = V_H \times i$$

式中　i——气缸数目。

For the multi-cylinder engine, the sum of the working volumes of each cylinder is called engine displacement, which is generally denoted by V_L:

$$V_L = V_H \times i$$

Where, i —— Number of cylinders.

8. 总容积 (total volume)

活塞位于下止点时，活塞顶上方的容积，一般用 V_A 表示，$V_A = V_C + V_H$。

The volume above the piston head when the piston is at the lower dead center, which is usually denoted by V_A, $V_A = V_C + V_H$.

9. 压缩比 (compression ratio)

气缸总容积与燃烧室容积的比值。压缩比表示进入气缸内的气体被压缩的程度，它是发动机的一个重要参数。在一定范围内适当提高压缩比，可以改善发动机的经济性和动力性。汽油发动机的压缩比一般为 6～10，柴油发动机的压缩比一般为 16～22。

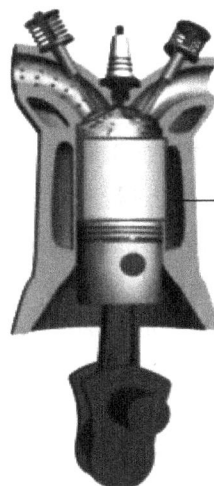

图 2.1.6　气缸工作容积

Figure 2.1.6　Cylinder working volume

气缸工作容积
cylinder working volume

The ratio of total cylinder volume to combustion chamber volume. Compression ratio represents the degreeof compression for gas entering the cylinder, which is an important parameter of the engine. Increasing the compression ratio properly in a certain range can improve the economy and power performance of the engine. Usually, the compression ratio of gasoline engine is 6-10, and that of diesel engine is 16-22.

10. 工作循环 (working cycle)

汽车的每一个工作循环包括进气、压缩、做功和排气过程四个过程（图 2.1.7）。

Every working cycle of the automobile includes the process of intake, compression, power and exhaust (Figure 2.1.7).

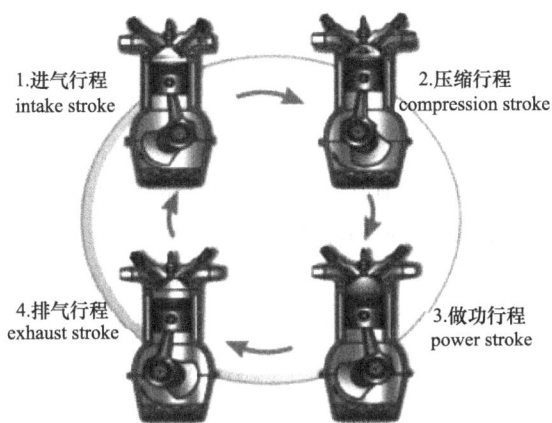

1.进气行程
intake stroke

2.压缩行程
compression stroke

4.排气行程
exhaust stroke

3.做功行程
power stroke

图 2.1.7　工作循环

Figure 2.1.7　Working cycle

1.2　发动机的基本工作原理 (Basic working principle of engines)

发动机每个工作循环是由进气行程、压缩行程、做功行程和排气行程等四个过程组成，即四冲程。四冲程发动机又分为四冲程汽油机和四冲程柴油机，两者的主要区别是点火方式不同，汽油机采用点燃方式，而柴油机是压燃方式。

Each working cycle of the engine consists of four processes: intake stroke, compression stroke, power stroke and exhaust stroke. That is four-stroke. The four-stroke engine is divided into four-stroke gasoline engine and four-stroke diesel engine. The main difference between them is that the ignition mode. The ignition mode is used for gasoline engines, while the compression ignition mode is used for diesel engines.

1.2.1　四冲程汽油机的工作原理 (Working principle of four-stroke gasoline engine)

四冲程汽油机的运转是按进气行程、压缩行程、做功行程和排气行程的顺序不断循环反复的。单缸四冲程汽油发动机工作循环（图 2.1.8）。

The operation of a four-stroke gasoline engine is repeated in the order of intake

汽车发动机的工作原理

Working Principle of Automotive Engine

stroke, compression stroke, power stroke and exhaust stroke. The working cycle of a single-cylinder, four-stroke gasoline engine is shown in Figure 2. 1. 8.

（1）进气行程（intake stroke）

在进气行程中，活塞在曲轴和连杆的带动下由上止点向下止点运行，这时进气门开启，排气门关闭。在活塞由上止点向下止点运动过程中，由于活塞上方气缸容积逐渐增大，形成一定的真空度。这样，可燃混合气通过进气门被吸入气缸，直到活塞到达下止点时，进气行程结束。

During the intake stroke, the piston is driven by the crankshaft and connecting rod and moves from the top dead center to the bottom dead center. At this moment, the intake valve opens and the exhaust valve closes. In the process of piston moving from top dead center to bottom dead center, a certain degree of vacuum is formed because the volume of cylinder above piston increases gradually. In this way, the combustible mixed gas is sucked into the cylinder through the intake valve until the piston reaches the bottom dead point and the intake stroke ends.

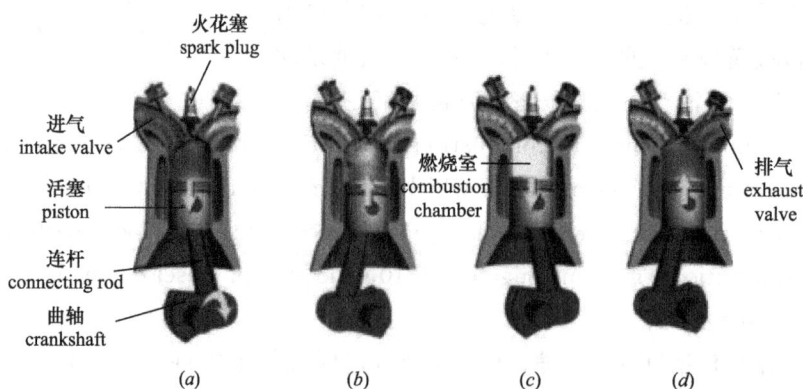

图 2. 1. 8　单缸四冲程汽油发动机工作循环

Figure 2. 1. 8　Working cycle of single-cylinder four-stroke gasoline engine

(a) 进气行程（intake stroke）；(b) 压缩行程（compression stroke）；(c) 做功行程（power stroke）；(d) 排气行程（exhaust stroke）

（2）压缩行程（compression stroke）

活塞在曲轴和连杆的带动下由下止点向上止点运动，此时进排气门处于关闭状态。由于活塞上方气缸容积逐渐减小，进入气缸内的可燃混合气被压缩，温度和压力不断升高，直到活塞到达上止点时，压缩行程结束。

Driven by crankshaft and connecting rod, the piston moves from the lower dead center to the upper dead center, at which time the intake and exhaust valves are both closed. As the cylinder volume above the piston decreases gradually, the combustible mixed gas entering the cylinder is compressed, and the temperature and pressure increase continuously until the piston reaches the top dead center, and the compression stroke ends.

（3）做功行程（power stroke）

当活塞运动到接近压缩行程上止点附近时，火花塞跳火点燃气缸内的可燃混合气。这时由于进气门和排气门均处于关闭状态，使缸内气体温度和压力同时升高，高温高压的气体膨胀，推动活塞由上止点向下止点运动，并通过连杆带动曲轴旋转输出机械能，直到活塞到达下止点时，做功行程结束。

When the piston moves near the top dead center of the compression stroke, the spark plug ignites the combustible mixture in the cylinder by spark over. At this time, because the intake and exhaust valves are closed, the temperature and pressure of the gas in the cylinder rise simultaneously. The gas at high temperature and high pressure expands, pushing the piston to move from the top dead point to the bottom dead point, and driving the crankshaft through the connecting rod to rotate and output mechanical energy until the piston reaches the bottom dead point，and the power stroke ends.

（4）排气行程（exhaust stroke）

在做功行程结束后，气缸内的可燃混合气通过燃烧转变成废气。此时排气门开启，进气门处于关闭状态，活塞在曲轴和连杆的带动下由下止点向上止点运动，气缸内的废气经排气门排出，直到活塞到达上止点时排气行程结束。

At the end of the working stroke, the combustible mixture in the cylinder is converted into burned gases by combustion. At this time, the exhaust valve opens and the intake valve is closed. The piston moves from the bottom dead point to the top dead point driven by the crankshaft and connecting rod. The burned gas in the cylinder is discharged through the exhaust valve until the piston reaches the top dead point，and the exhaust stroke ends.

排气行程结束后，进气门再次开启，又开始下一个工作循环，如此周而复始，发动机就连续运转。发动机工作时，需要连续不断地进行循环，在每个循环中都是依次完成进气、压缩、做功和排气四个活塞行程。

When the exhaust stroke is over, the intake valve is opened again and the next working cycle begins. In this way, the cycle repeats itself. The engine runs continuously. When the engine is working, it needs to be continuously circulated. In each cycle, four piston strokes of intake, compression, power and exhaust are completed successively.

1.2.2 四冲程柴油机的工作原理（Working principle of four-stroke diesel engine）

四冲程柴油机的工作原理与四冲程汽油机一样，四冲程柴油机每个工作循环也是由进气、压缩、做功和排气四个活塞行程组成。但由于柴油和汽油使用性能的不同，柴油机在可燃混合气的形成方式、着火方式等方面与汽油机有较大的区别。单缸四冲程汽油发动机工作循环（图2.1.9）。

The working principle of a four-stroke diesel engine is the same as that of a four-stroke gasoline engine. Each working cycle of a four-stroke diesel engine consists of four piston strokes：intake, compression, work and exhaust. However, due to the different performance of diesel and gasoline, diesel engine is quite different from gasoline engine in the ways of formation and ignition of combustible mixture. The working cycle of a single-cylinder four-stroke gasoline engine is shown in Figure 2.1.9.

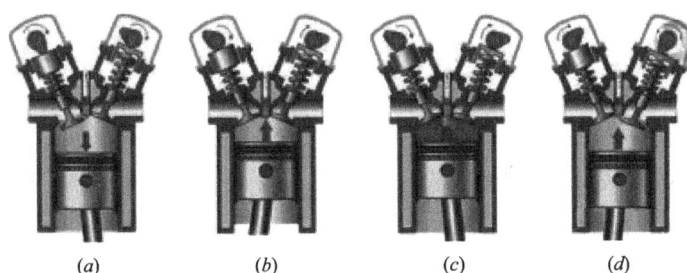

（a）（b）（c）（d）

图2.1.9 单缸四冲程柴油发动机工作循环

Figure 2.1.9 Working cycle of single-cylinder four-stroke diesel engine

（a）进气（intake）；（b）压缩（compression）；（c）做功（power）；（d）排气（exhaust）

（1）进气冲程（intake stoke）

进入气缸的是纯空气。由于柴油机进气系统阻力较小，进气终点压力 P_a＝（0.85～0.95）MPa，比汽油机高。进气终点温度 T_a＝300～340K，比汽油机低。

Pure air enters the cylinder. Because the resistance of intake system of diesel engine is low, the intake terminal pressure P_a＝(0.85～0.95) MPa is higher than that of gasoline engine. The intake terminal temperature T_a＝300～340K, which is lower than that of gasoline engine.

（2）压缩冲程（compression stroke）

柴油机的压缩比比汽油机高（一般为＝16～22）。压缩终点的压力为 3000～5000kPa，压缩终点的温度为 750～1000K，大大超过柴油的自燃温度（约 520K）。

The compression ratio of diesel engine is higher than that of gasoline engine（generally＝16～22）. The compression terminal pressure is 3000-5000kPa, and the temperature at the end of compression is 750-1000K, which is much higher than the spontaneous combustion temperature of diesel oil（about 520K）.

（3）做功冲程（power stroke）

当压缩冲程接近终了时，在高压油泵作用下，将柴油以 100MPa 左右的高压通过喷油器喷入气缸燃烧室中，在很短的时间内与空气混合后立即自行发火燃烧。气缸内气体的压力急速上升，最高达 5000～9000kPa，最高温度达 1800～2000K。由于柴油机是靠压缩自行着火燃烧，故称柴油机为压燃式发动机。

When the compression stroke is close to the end, under the action of high pressure oil pump, diesel oil is injected into the cylinder combustion chamber at high pressure of about 100 MPa through the injector, which combusts spontaneously after mixing with air in a short time. The gas pressure in the cylinder rises rapidly, reaching 5000-9000 kPa and the highest temperature reaching 1800-2000K. Because the diesel engine is self-ignited by compression, it is called compression-ignition engine.

（4）排气冲程（exhaust stroke）

柴油机的排气与汽油机基本相同，只是排气温度比汽油机低。

The exhaust stroke of diesel engine is basically the same as that of gasoline engine, but the exhaust temperature is lower than that of gasoline engine.

1.3 发动机的总体构造（Overall structure of engines）

发动机又称内燃机，是将液体燃料或气体燃料与空气混合后直接输入机器内部燃烧产生热能，热能再转变为机械能的机器。常见的车用发动机有汽油发动机和柴油发动机两种。

汽油发动机通常由两大机构和五大系统组成，即由曲柄连杆机构、配气机构，燃料供给系统、点火系统、起动系统、冷却系统和润滑系统组成。

汽车发动机的组成

The Composition of Automobile Engine

Engine, also known as internal combustion engine, is a machine that combines liquid fuel or gas fuel with air, which enter directly into inside of machine to generate heat energy, which is then converted into mechanical energy. The common automobile engines are gasoline engines and diesel engines.

A gasoline engine usually consists of two main mechanisms and five major systems, which are crankshaft and connecting rod mechanism, valve mechanism, fuel supply system, ignition system, starting system, cooling system and lubrication system.

1.3.1 曲柄连杆机构（Crankshaft and connecting rod mechanism）

曲柄连杆机构是将活塞的往复直线运动转变为旋转运动而输出动力的机构。

曲柄连杆机构由机体组、活塞连杆组和曲轴飞轮组三部分组成（图 2.1.10）。在做功行程中，活塞承受燃气压力在气缸内做直线运动，通过连杆转换成曲轴的旋转运动，并从曲轴对外输出动力。而在进气、压缩和排气行程中，飞轮释放能量又把曲轴的旋转运动转化成活塞的直线运动。

The crankshaft and connecting rod mechanism converts the reciprocating linear motion of the piston into rotary motion and outputs power. Its components are shown in Figure 2.1.10.

The crankshaft and connecting rod mechanism is composed of three parts: engine block group, piston-connecting rod group, and crankshaft-flywheel group. During the power stroke, the piston moves in a straight line bearing the gas pressure in the cylinder, which is converted into the rotary motion of the crankshaft through the connecting rod, and the power is output from the crankshaft. While in the intake, compression and exhaust strokes, the flywheel releases energy and converts the rotation of crankshaft into the linear motion of piston.

1.3.2 配气机构 (Valve mechanism)

配气机构是根据发动机的工作顺序和各缸工作循环的要求，及时地开启和关闭进、排气门，使可燃混合气（汽油发动机）或新鲜空气（柴油发动机）进入气缸，并将废气排出。

Valve mechanism is to open and close the intake and exhaust valves timely according to the working order of the engine and the requirements of the working cycle of each cylinder, so that the combustible mixture (gasoline engine) or fresh air (diesel engine) can enter the cylinder and exhaust the burned gases.

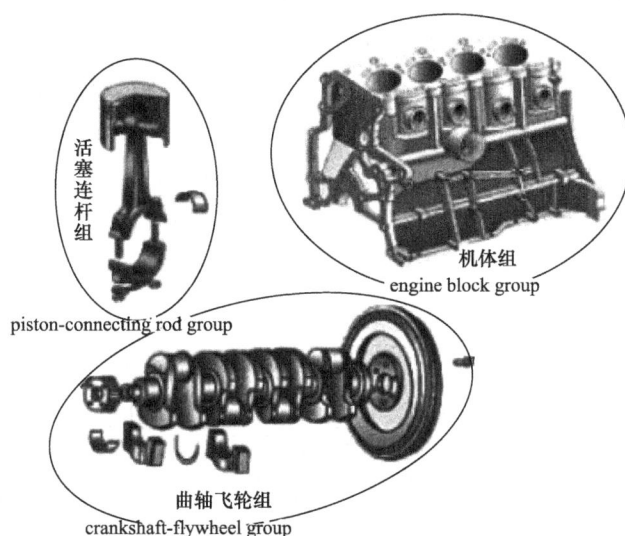

图 2.1.10 曲柄连杆机构组成部分

Figure 2.1.10 Components of crankshaft and connecting rod mechanism

配气机构主要由气门组和气门传动组组成。气门组包括气门、气门导管、气门座及气门弹簧等部件；气门传动组主要包括凸轮轴、正时齿轮、挺柱及其导杆、推杆、摇臂和摇臂轴等部件（图 2.1.11）。

Valve mechanism is mainly composed of valve group and valve transmission group. Valve group includes valves, valve guide, valve seat and valve spring, etc. Valve transmission group mainly includes camshaft, timing gear, tappet and its guide rod, push rod, rocker arm and rocker arm shaft, etc. Its component composition is shown in Figure 2.1.11.

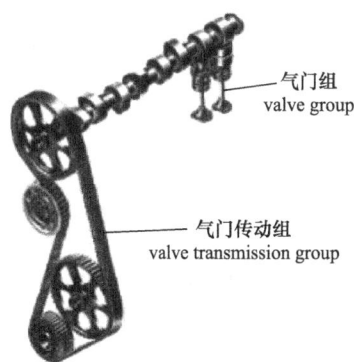

图 2.1.11 配气机构组成部分

Figure 2.1.11 The components of valve mechanism

1.3.3 燃料供给系统 (Fuel supply system)

汽油机燃料供给系统是根据发动机的要求，配制出一定数量和浓度的混合气，供入气缸，并将燃烧后的废气从气缸内排出到大气中。汽油机燃料供给系由燃油箱、燃油滤清器、燃油泵、节气门体和喷油器等组成。其在车辆中的示意位置（图 2.1.12）。

The fuel supply system of gasoline engine is based on the requirement of the engine. A certain amount and concentration of mixture is prepared to feed into the air cylinder and the burned gases after combustion is exhausted into the atmosphere from the cylinder. The fuel supply system of gasoline engine consists of fuel tank,

图 2.1.12　燃油供给系统位置示意图

Figure 2. 1. 12　The composition diagram of the fuel supply system's location

fuel filter, fuel pump, throttle body and injector, etc. Its schematic position in the vehicle is shown in Figure 2. 1. 12.

1.3.4　点火系统（Ignition system）

汽油机点火系统能够适时、准确、可靠地在气缸内产生火花，以点燃可燃混合气，使汽油机实现做功。

发动机 ECU（电子控制单元）根据各个传感器发来的信号，进行控制点火线圈，得到最佳的点火提前角，进而达到最佳的点火正时。点火系统通常由蓄电池、发电机、点火线圈、火花塞和电子控制系统等组成。其组件组成示意图（图 2.1.13）。

The ignition system of gasoline engine can generate sparks in the cylinder timely, accurately and reliably to ignite the combustible mixture and make the gasoline engine work.

The engine ECU (electronic control unit) controls the ignition system according to the signals from each sensor to achieve the best ignition timing. The ignition system is usually composed of battery, generator, ignition coil, spark plug and electronic control system, etc. Its composition diagram of the ignition system is shown in Figure 2. 1. 13.

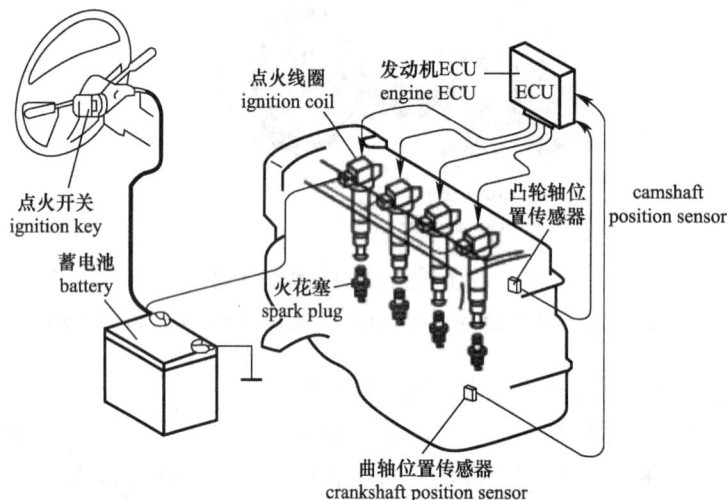

图 2. 1. 13　点火系统组成示意图

Figure 2. 1. 13　The composition diagram of the ignition system

1.3.5　启动系统（Starting system）

要使发动机由静止状态过渡到工作状态，必须先用外力转动发动机的曲轴，才能使发动机工作。起动系统就是通过起动机将蓄电池的电能转换成机械能，起动发动机运转。起动系统由蓄电池、点火开关、起动继电器和起动机等组成。其组件组成示意图（图 2.1.14）。

In order to make the engine transit from static state to working state, the crankshaft of the engine must be rotated by external force before the engine can work. Starting system is to convert the battery energy into mechanical energy through a starter motor to start the engine running. Starting system consists of battery, ignition switch, starting relay and starter, etc. Its component composition diagram is shown in Figure 2. 1. 14.

1.3.6　冷却系统（Cooling system）

发动机冷却系统的作用是使发动机温度升到正常工作温度后保持工作温度，从而保证发动机的正常工作。一般发动机的冷却系统组成大体相同，主要由水泵、水套、散热器、节温器和冷却风扇等组成。其安装位置示意图（图 2.1.15）。

The function of the engine cooling system is to keep the working temperature after the engine temperature rises to the normal working temperature, so as to ensure the normal operation of the engine. Generally, the cooling system of engine is composed of water pump, water jacket, radiator, thermostat and cooling fan, etc. The diagram of the installation position is shown in Figure 2.1.15.

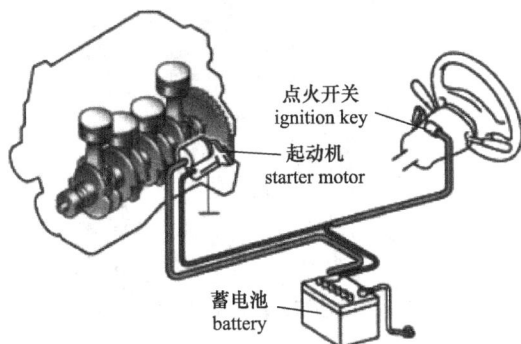

图 2.1.14　启动系统组成示意图
Figure 2.1.14　The composition diagram of the starting system

图 2.1.15　冷却系统安装位置示意图
Figure 2.1.15　The installation composition diagram of the cooling system

1.3.7　润滑系统（Lubrication system）

润滑系统是在发动机工作时连续不断地将足够数量、适当温度的清洁机油供给发动机各摩擦表面，从而减小阻力、降低功率消耗、减轻机件磨损，以达到提高发动机工作可靠性和耐久性的目的。润滑系统一般由油底壳、机油泵、机油滤清器、主油道、限压阀、旁通阀、传感器和机油压力报警指示灯等组成。其组件组成示意图（图 2.1.16）。

The lubrication system continuously supplies enough and clean engine oil with appropriate temperature to the friction surfaces of the engine when the engine is working to reduce the resistance, power consumption and wear of the engine parts and improve the reliability and durability of the engine. The lubrication system is generally composed of oil pan, oil pump, oil filter, main oil gallery, pressure limiting valve, bypass valve, sensor and oil pressure alarm indicator lamp, etc. The component composition diagram is shown in Figure 2.1.16.

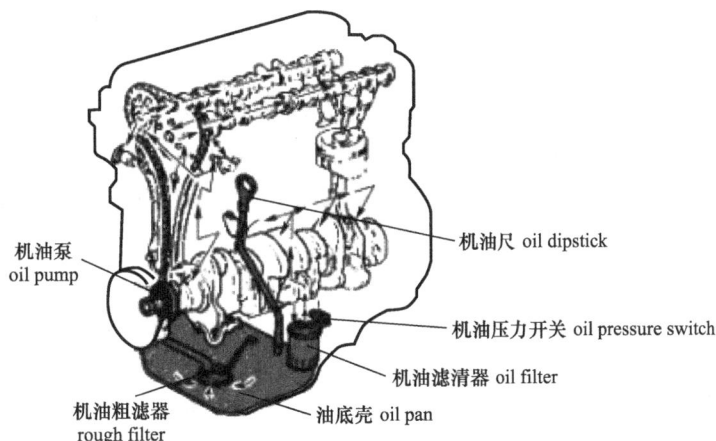

图 2.1.16　润滑系统组成示意图
Figure 2.1.16　The composition diagram of the lubrication system

1.4 发动机的分类 (Classification of engines)
1.4.1 按活塞的运动方式分类 (Classification by motion mode of pistons)

图 2.1.17　往复活塞式发动机
Figure 2.1.17　Reciprocating piston engine

图 2.1.18　转子活塞式发动机
Figure 2.1.18　Rotor-piston engine

1.4.2 按所用燃料分类 (Classification by fuels)

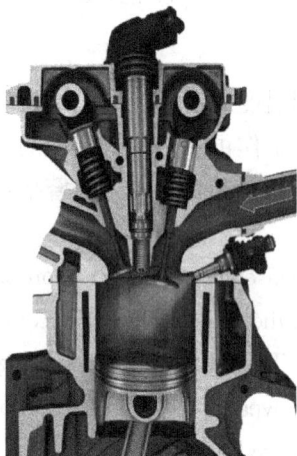

图 2.1.19　汽油机
Figure 2.1.19　Gasoline engine

图 2.1.20　柴油机
Figure 2.1.20　Diesel engine

1.4.3 按冲程数分类 (Classification by stroke number)

内燃机按照完成一个工作循环所需的冲程数可分为四冲程内燃机和二冲程内燃机。把曲轴转两圈（720°），活塞在气缸内上下往复运动四个冲程，完成一个工作循环的内燃机称为四冲程内燃机。而把曲轴转一圈（360°），活塞在气缸内上下往复运动两个冲程，完成一个工作循环的内燃机称为二冲程内燃机。汽车发动机广泛使用四冲程内燃机。

The internal combustion engine can be divided into four-stroke internal combustion engine and two-stroke internal combustion engine according to the number of strokes required to complete a working cycle. The internal combustion engine whose crankshaft rotates twice (720 degrees) and the piston moves up and down four strokes in the cylinder to complete a working cycle is called a four-stroke internal combustion engine. While the engine whose crankshaft turns a round(360 degrees) with two stroke of the piston reciprocating movement in the cylinder to complete a work cycle is called the two- stroke internal combustion engine. Four-stroke internal combustion engines are widely used in automobile engines.

1.4.4 按点火方式分类（Classification by ignition method）

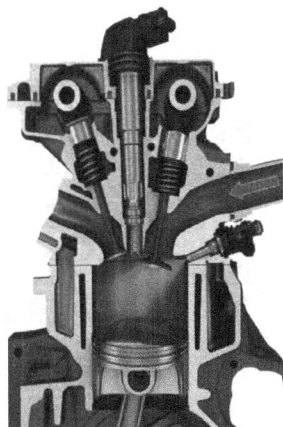

图 2.1.21　点燃式
Figure 2.1.21　Spark ignition

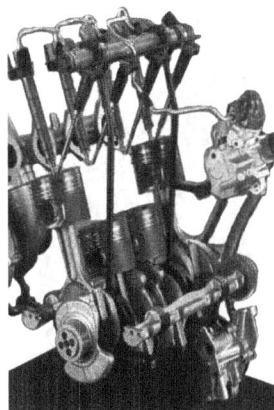

图 2.1.22　压燃式
Figure 2.1.22　Compression ignition

1.4.5 按冷却方式分类（Classification by cooling mode）

图 2.1.23　水冷发动机
Figure 2.1.23　Water cooling engine

图 2.1.24　风冷发动机
Figure 2.1.24　Air cooling engine

1.4.6 按气缸数分类（Classification by number of cylinders）

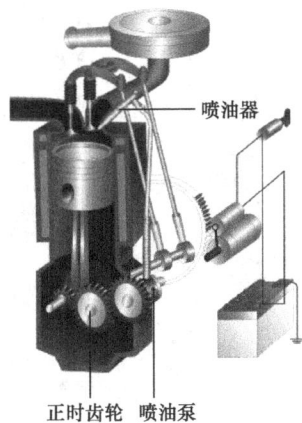

图 2.1.25　单缸发动机
Figure 2.1.25　Single-cylinder Engine

图 2.1.26　多缸发动机
Figure 2.1.26　Multi-cylinder Engine

1.4.7 按气缸的排列形式分类 (Classification by arrangement of cylinders)

图 2.1.27　直列发动机
Figure 2.1.27　In-line engine

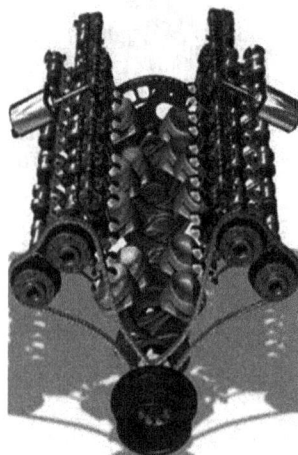

图 2.1.28　V 形发动机
Figure 2.1.28　V-type engines

图 2.1.29　水平对置发动机
Figure 2.1.29　Horizontally opposed engine

图 2.1.30　辐射式发动机
Figure 2.1.30　Radial engine

1.4.8 按进气系统是否采用增压方式分类 (Classification according to whether supercharging is adopted or not)

图 2.1.31　自然吸气式发动机
Figure 2.1.31　Naturally aspirated engine

图 2.1.32　强制进气式发动机
Figure 2.1.32　Forced intake engine

思考与练习

（Reflection and Exercises）

1. 什么是热机、外燃机与内燃机、热机工作循环、二冲程与四冲程发动机？

2. 试述四冲程往复活塞式发动机的基本结构及主要部件。

3. 什么是发动机的理论压缩比与实际压缩比？

4. 什么是发动机的排量？

5. 试述四冲程往复活塞式汽油机与四冲程往复活塞式柴油机的工作原理。

1. What are heat engines, external combustion engines and internal combustion engines, working cycle of heat engines, two-stroke and four-stroke engines?

2. Describe the basic structure and main components of a four-stroke reciprocating piston engine.

3. What are the theoretical compression ratio and the actual compression ratio of the engine?

4. What is the engine displacement?

5. Describe the working principles of four-stroke reciprocating piston gasoline engines and four-stroke reciprocating piston diesel engines.

任务二 曲柄连杆机构

Task 2 Crankshaft and Connecting Rod Mechanism

教学目标

1. 知识目标

（1）了解机体组的结构；

（2）了解曲柄连杆机构的结构；

（3）知道曲柄连杆机构的工作原理。

2. 能力目标

（1）具有识别曲柄连杆机构部件能力；

（2）具有分析曲柄连杆机构的结构和工作原理的能力。

3. 情感和素养目标

（1）培养学生良好的职业道德和注重产品的品质意识；

（2）培养学生吃苦耐劳，精益求精的思想意识。

Teaching objectives

1. knowledge objectives

（1）Understanding the structure of the body group；

（2）Understanding the structure of crankshaft and connecting rod mechanism；

（3）Knowing the working principle of crankshaft and connecting rod mechanism.

2. Ability objectives

（1）The ability to identify the components of crankshaft and connecting rod mechanism；

（2）The ability to analyze the structure and working principle of crankshaft and connecting rod mechanism.

3. Emotion and quality goals

（1）Cultivate students' professional ethics and awareness of paying attention to the quality of products；

(2) Cultivate students' ideological consciousness of being hard—working and striving for excellence.

2.1 曲柄连杆机构的作用与组成 (Function and composition of crankshaft and connecting rod mechanism)

曲柄连杆机构是内燃机完成工作循环、实现能量转换的传动机构。它的作用是将燃料燃烧时产生的热能转变为活塞往复运动的机械能,通过连杆将活塞的往复运动变为曲轴的旋转运动而对外输出做功。

曲柄连杆机构由机体组、活塞连杆组和曲轴飞轮组三部分组成。

The crankshaft and connecting rod mechanism is the transmission mechanism for the internal combustion engine to complete the work cycle and achieve the energy conversion. Its function is to transform the heat energy generated during fuel combustion into the mechanical energy of reciprocating motion of piston. The reciprocating motion of piston is changed into the rotating motion of crankshaft by connecting rod to output work.

The crankshaft connecting rod mechanism is composed of three parts: body group, piston-connecting rod group and crankshaft-flywheel group.

2.2 机体组 (Engine block group)

机体组是发动机的骨架,也是发动机各机构和各系统的安装基础。其内、外安装着发动机的所有主要零件和附件,承受各种载荷。如图 2.2.1 所示,机体组主要由气缸体、曲轴箱、油底壳、气缸套、气缸盖和气缸垫等组成。

The engine block is the framework of the engine, and also the installed foundation for all parts pf an engine. All the main parts and accessories of the engine are installed inside and outside, and bear various loads. As shown in Figure 2.2.1, the engine block group is mainly composed of cylinder block, crankcase, oil pan, cylinder liner, cylinder head and cylinder gasket, etc.

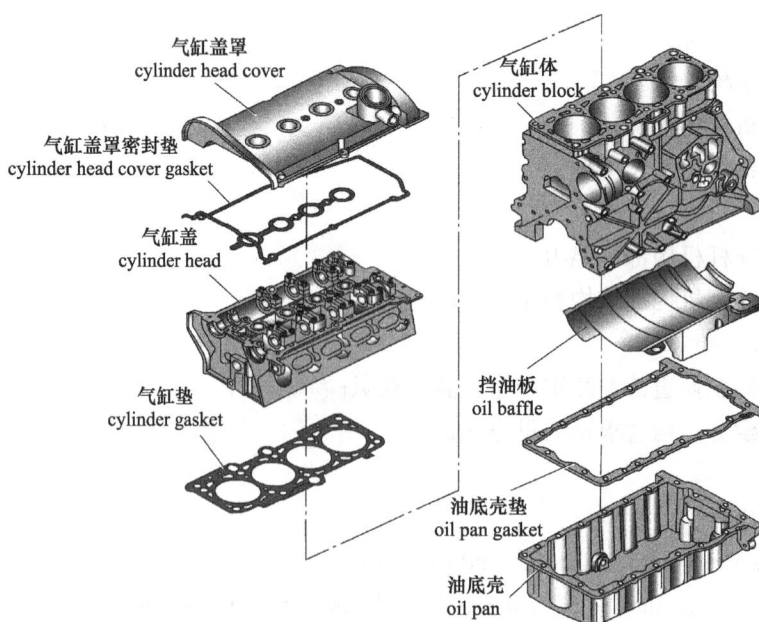

图 2.2.1　机体组

Figure 2.2.1　The engine block group

2.2.1 气缸体 (Cylinder block)

气缸体的结构如图 2.2.2 所示,水冷式发动机的气缸体和曲轴箱常使用铸铁或铝合金铸成一体,通称为气缸体。气缸体是发动机各个机构和系统的装配机体,活塞、曲轴、气缸盖、油底壳等零部件都安装在气缸体上，并由它来保持发动机各运动件相互之间准确位置关系。气缸体上半部有若干个为活塞在其中运动导向的圆柱形空腔，称为气缸。下半部为支撑曲轴的曲轴箱。其内腔为曲轴运动的空间，在气缸体内部铸有许多加强筋，以增加缸体的刚度。在缸体内铸有冷却水套和润滑油道等。

The structure of the cylinder block is shown in Figure 2.2.2. The cylinder block and crankcase of a water-cooling engine are usually cast together with cast iron or aluminum alloy, commonly known as the cylinder block. The cylinder block is the assembly body of each engine mechanism and system. Piston, crankshaft, cylinder head, oil pan and other parts are all installed on the cylinder block, and it can maintain the accurate position relationship between the engine moving parts. There are several cylindrical cavities in the upper half of the cylinder block, which guide the motion of pistons, known as cylinders. In the lower half, there is a crankcase supporting the crankshaft, whose inner cavity is the space for the motion of the crankshaft, and many strengthening ribs are cast inside the cylinder block to increase the rigidity of the cylinder block. Cooling water jackets and lubricating oil galleries as well as other parts are cast in the cylinder block.

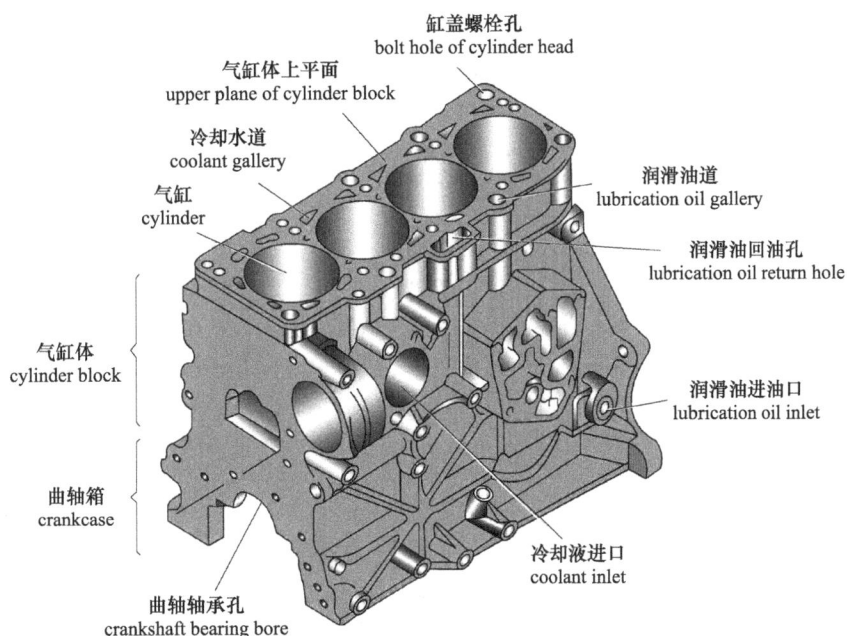

图 2.2.2 气缸体
Figure 2.2.2 Engine block

在多缸发动机中，气缸的排列形式决定了发动机的外形尺寸和结构特点，并影响汽车的总体布置。气缸的排列形式有直列式、V形式和水平对置式三种。如图 2.2.3 所示。

In a multi-cylinder engine, the arrangement of cylinders determines the shape, size and structural characteristics of the engine, and affects the overall layout of the automobile. There are three types of cylinder arrangement: in-line type, V type and horizontal opposite type, as shown in Figure 2.2.3.

2.2.2 气缸套 (Cylinder liners)

气缸套按照是否与冷却液直接接触可分为干式气缸套和湿式气缸套两种。

Cylinder liner can be divided into dry cylinder liner and wet cylinder liner according to whether it comes in direct contact with coolant or not.

1. 干式气缸套 (Dry cylinder liner)

如图 2.2.4 所示，干式气缸套的外表面不直接与冷却液接触。其壁厚一般为 1~3mm。为了保证散热效果和缸套的定位，缸套的外表面与气缸体的缸套孔内表面均有较高的加工精度，并采用一定的过盈量将气缸套装到缸套孔中。

As shown in Figure 2.2.4, the outer surface of the dry cylinder liner does not come in direct contact with the coolant, whose wall thickness is generally 1～3 mm. In order to ensure the effect of heat radiation and the positioning of the cylinder liner, both the outside surface of cylinder liner.

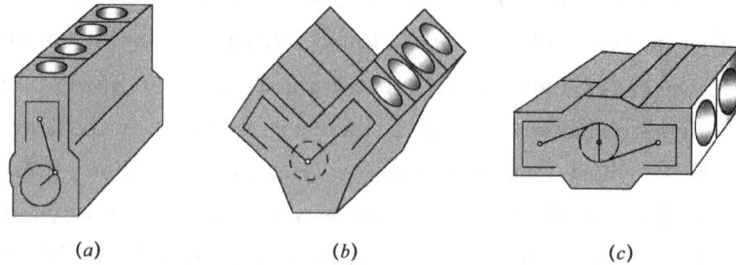

图 2.2.3　气缸的排列形式

Figure 2.2.3　Arrangements of cylinders

(a) 直列四缸（in-line type with four cylinders）；(b) V 形八缸（V-type with eight cylinders）；

(c) 对置四缸（opposed type with four cylinders）

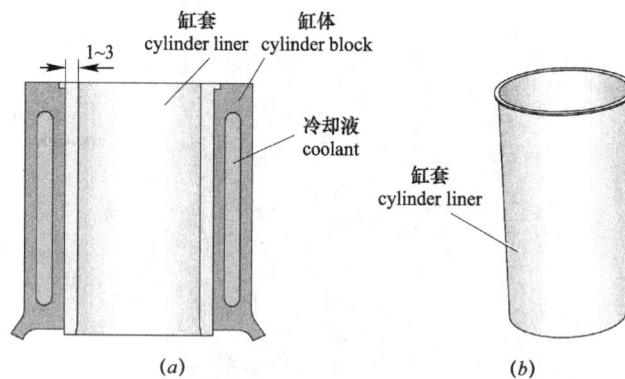

图 2.2.4　干式气缸套

Figure 2.2.4　Dry cylinder liner

(a) 装配示意图（assembly diagram）；(b) 干式气缸套（dry cylinder liner）

干式气缸套的优点是不易漏水、漏气。缸心距小，结构紧凑，缸体结构刚度好。缺点是散热效果差，维修、更换不便。

The advantage of dry cylinder liner is that it is not easy to leak water andgas. In addition, small cylinder center distance, compact structure and good structural stiffness of the cylinder block are other advantages. The disadvantage is that the effect of heat radiation is poor, and the maintenance and replacement are inconvenient.

2. 湿式气缸套（Wet cylinder liners）

湿式气缸套的结构如图 2.2.5 所示，其外表面与冷水直接接触。壁厚一般为 5～9mm。湿式气缸套利用缸套上部凸缘的下平面 C 为轴向定位，以外圆柱表面上的圆环凸台 A 和 B 为径向定位。上支承圆环凸台 A 直径略大，与缸套座孔配合较紧密。下支承圆环凸台 B 与缸套座孔配合较松，缸套装入座孔后，缸套顶面略高出气缸体上平面 0.05～0.15mm，这样在拧紧缸盖螺栓时，使缸套凸出部分与气缸垫压得更紧，起到防止气缸漏气和水套漏水的作用。为防止漏气、漏水，有的缸套凸缘下平面 C 处还加装有金属垫片。为了防止漏水，在缸套的下部装有 1～3 道耐油、耐热的橡胶密封圈，用以密封。

The structure of the wet cylinder liner is shown in Figure 2.2.5. The outside surface of the wet cylinder liner is in direct contact with cold water with the wall thickness of about 5-9 mm. As shown in Figure 2.2.5, the wet cylinder liner is positioned axially by the lower plane C of the upper flange of the cylinder liner and positioned radially by the ring boss A and B on the outer cylindrical surface. The diameter of the upper supporting ring boss A is slightly larger, and it fits closely with the cylinder liner seat hole. The lower supporting ring boss B is loosely matched with the cylinder liner seat hole. After the cylin-

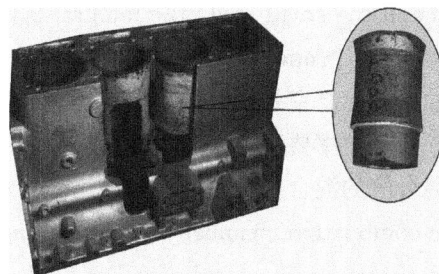

图 2.2.5 湿式气缸套的结构

Figure 2.2.5 The structure of the wet cylinder liner

der liner is installed into the seat hole, the top surface of the cylinder liner is slightly higher than that of the upper surface of the cylinder block by 0.05-0.15 mm. In this way, when bolts of the cylinder head are tightened, the protruding part of the cylinder liner and the cylinder gasket are pressed more tightly, thus preventing the leakage of gas and water from the cylinder liner. In order to prevent the leakage of gas and water a, some cylinder liners are also equipped with metal gaskets at the lower plane C of the flange. To prevent leakage of water, there are 1 to 3 oil-resistant and heat-resistant rubber sealing rings at the lower part of the cylinder liner for sealing.

湿式气缸套的优点是在气缸体上没有封闭的水套，铸造较容易，便于修理更换，且散热效果较好。缺点是气缸体的刚度差，易产生穴蚀，易漏气、漏水等。

The advantage of wet cylinder liner is that there is no closed water jacket on the cylinder block, so it is easy to cast, repair and replace, and the effect of heat radiation is better. The disadvantages are that the poor stiffness of the cylinder block, cavitation, leakage of gas and water, etc.

2.2.3 气缸盖 (Cylinder head)

气缸盖安装在气缸体的上面。其主要作用是密封气缸，并于活塞顶部和气缸壁一起构成燃烧室。

The cylinder head is mounted on the top of the cylinder block. Its main function is to seal the cylinder and form a combustion chamber with the top of the piston and the cylinder wall.

如图 2.2.6 所示，气缸盖的结构随气门的布置、冷却方式以及燃烧室的形状而异。气缸盖上设有进、排气通道。气门座、气门导管孔、火花塞（汽油机）座孔或喷油器（柴油机）座孔、缸盖螺栓孔以及供混合气燃烧的燃烧室等，凸轮轴上置式发动机的气缸盖上还有凸轮轴轴承孔，用以安装凸轮轴。为了润滑凸轮轴，在缸盖上设有与气缸体相通的润滑油道。

As shown in Figure 2.2.6, the structure of the cylinder head varies with valve arrangement, cooling mode and the shape of the combustion chamber. The cylinder head has intake and exhaust passages, valve seat, valve guide hole, spark plug (gasoline engine) seat hole or injector (diesel engine) seat hole, cylinder head bolt holes, and combustion chamber for mixed gas combustion, etc. The cylinder head of the camshaft mounted engine also has a camshaft bearing hole for mounting the camshaft. Additionally, the cylinder head of the overhang camshaft type engine also has a camshaft bearing hole for mounting the camshaft. In order to lubricate the camshaft, lubricating oil galleries connected with the cylinder block are arranged on the cylinder head.

1. 气缸盖的形式 (Type of cylinder head)

为了便于制造和维修，减少气缸盖受力和受热后变形对密封性的影响，功率较大的柴油机和部分汽油机多采用分体式气缸盖。而汽油机因缸径较小，气缸盖结构轻巧，负荷较小，故多采用整体式缸盖。

For ease of manufacture and maintenance, and reducing the influence of cylinder head stress and deformation after heating on sealing, a separate cylinder head is mostly used in high power diesel engines and some gasoline engines. While due to the small cylinder diameter of gasoline engine, the light structure of the cylinder head and the small load, the integral cylinder head is mostly adopted.

2. 燃烧室 (Combustion chamber)

汽油机的燃烧室是由活塞顶部及缸盖上相应的凹部空间组成。对燃烧室有如下基本要求：一是结构尽可能紧凑，充气效率要高，以减小热量损失及缩短火焰行程；二是使混合气在压缩终了时具有一定压缩涡流，以提高混合气的混合质量，保证混合气得到及时和充分燃烧；三是表面要光滑，不易积炭。

The combustion chamber of gasoline engine contains the space between the top of piston and the corresponding concave part of cylinder head. The basic requirements for the combustor chamber are as follows: first, the structure should be as compact as possible, and the charging efficiency should be high, so as to reduce the heat loss and shorten the flame journey; the second is to make the mixture have a certain compressed turbulence at the end of compression, so as to improve the mixing quality of the mixture and ensure the timely and full combustion of the mixture; the third is to make the surface smooth and not easy to deposit carbon.

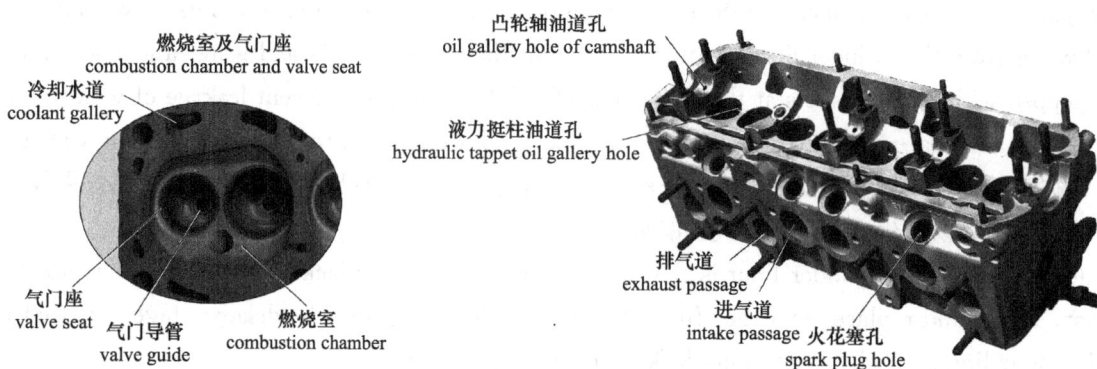

燃烧室及气门座
combustion chamber and valve seat

凸轮轴油道孔
oil gallery hole of camshaft

冷却水道
coolant gallery

液力挺柱油道孔
hydraulic tappet oil gallery hole

气门座
valve seat

气门导管
valve guide

燃烧室
combustion chamber

排气道
exhaust passage

进气道
intake passage

火花塞孔
spark plug hole

图 2.2.6 气缸盖

Figure 2.2.6 Cylinder Head

汽油机常用燃烧室形状有以下几种，如图 2.2.7 所示。

There are several shapes of combustion chambers commonly used in gasoline engines, as shown in Figure 2.2.7.

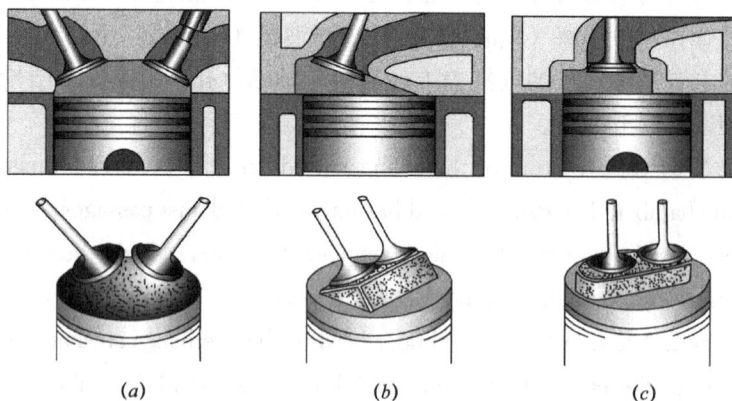

(a)　　　　　　　　(b)　　　　　　　　(c)

图 2.2.7 汽油机的燃烧室形状

Figure 2.2.7 Combustor chamber shapes of gasoline engine

(a) 半球形燃烧室 (hemispherical combustion chamber); (b) 楔形燃烧室 (wedge-shaped combustion chamber);

(c) 盆形燃烧室 (basin-shaped combustion chamber)

(1) 半球形燃烧室 [图 2.2.7 (a)] (Hemispherical combustion chamber, as shown in Figure 2.2.7a)

断面形状为半球形，结构较后两种更紧凑，气门成横向 V 形排列，其配气机构比较复杂。但由于其散热面积小，有利于促进燃料的完全燃烧和减少排气中的有害气体，对排气净化有利，轿车发动机多采用这种燃烧室。

The section shape is hemispherical, and the structure is more compact than the latter two. The valves are arranged in a transverse V-shape. The valve mechanism is more complex. However, due to its small heatradiation area, it is conducive to promoting the complete combustion of fuel and reducing harmful gases in exhaust, and is conducive to exhaust purification. Car engines mostly use this kind of combustion chamber.

（2）楔形燃烧室 ［图2.2.7 (*b*)］（Wedge-shaped combustion chamber, as shown in Figure 2.2.7*b*）

断面形状为楔形，结构较简单、紧凑。在压缩终了时能形成挤气涡流，可产生高压缩比。因而燃烧速度较快，经济性和动力性较好，是20世纪60年代的主流之一，其燃烧室面大，可以防止异常燃烧，但热损失较大。

The section is wedge-shaped, and the structure is simple and compact. At the end of compression, the squish turbulence can be formed and the high compression ratio can be produced. As a result, the combustion speed is faster, and the economy and dynamic performance are better. It is one of the mainstreams in the 1960s. Its combustion chamber surface is large, which can prevent abnormal combustion, but the heat loss is large.

（3）盆形燃烧室 ［图2.2.7 (*c*)］（Basin-shaped combustion chamber, as shown in Figure 2.2.7*c*）

断面形状为盆状，结构也较简单、紧凑。弯曲的进气歧管和排气管，容易产生进气涡流，但进气效率低。

The section is basin-shaped, and the structure is simple and compact. The curved intake manifold and exhaust pipe are prone to generate intake swirl, but the intake efficiency is low.

2.2.4 气缸垫 (Cylinder head gasket)

气缸盖与气缸体之间置有气缸盖垫（图2.2.8）。其功用是填补气缸体与缸盖接合面上的微观孔隙，保证接合面处有良好的密封性，进而保证燃烧室的密封，防止气缸漏气和水套漏水。

A cylinder head gasket is arranged between the cylinder head and the cylinder block. Its function is to fill the microscopic pores on the joint surface of cylinder block and cylinder head, to ensure good sealing at the joint surface, and then ensure the sealing of combustion chamber, and prevent air leakage and of the cylinder and water leakage of the water jacket.

图2.2.8 气缸垫

Figure 2.2.8 Cylinder head gasket

目前应用较多的有以下几种气缸垫：金属-石棉气缸垫、实心金属片制成的气缸垫、中心用编织的钢丝网或有孔钢板（冲有带毛刺小孔的钢板）为骨架，两面用石棉及橡胶黏结剂压成的气缸盖衬垫、加强型无石棉气缸垫结构等。

At present, the following kinds of cylinder gaskets are widely used: metal-asbestos cylinder gaskets, solid sheet metal cylinder gaskets, woven steel wire gauze or perforated steel plate (Steel plate punched with burred holes) as framework, cylinder head gaskets made of asbestos and rubber binder on both sides, reinforced asbestos-free cylinder gasket structure, etc.

气缸盖用螺栓紧固在气缸体上，拧紧螺栓有两种方法：一种是力矩法；另一种是转角法。

The cylinder head is fastened to the cylinder block with bolts. There are two ways to tighten the bolts: one is the torque method, the other is the angle method.

2.2.5 油底壳 (Oil pan)

油底壳 (图 2.2.9) 的主要功用是储存和冷却机油并封闭曲轴箱。在最低处设有放油螺塞，以便放出润滑油。有的放油螺塞还带有磁性，可以吸附润滑油中的铁屑，以减小发动机的磨损。为了防止汽车振动时油底壳油面产生较大的波动，在油底壳的内部设有稳油挡板。由于油底壳受力很小，一般用薄钢板冲压而成。有些铝合金油底壳还带有散热片。曲轴箱与油底壳之间为了防止漏油，其之间装有软木衬垫，也有涂密封胶的。

The main function of the oil pan (Figure 2.2.9) is to store and cool the oil and seal the crankcase. In the lowest position, it is equipped with a drain plug for draining lubricating oil. Some drain plugs are also magnetic, which can absorb iron filings in lubricating oil to reduce engine wear. In order to prevent the oil surface of the oil pan from fluctuating greatly when the vehicle vibrates, a Stabilizing oil baffle is installed inside the oil pan. The oil pan is usually stamped with thin steel plates because of its small load. Some aluminum alloy oil pans also have heat sinks. In order to prevent oil leakage between crankcase and oil pan, there are cork gaskets between them, while some adopt sealant.

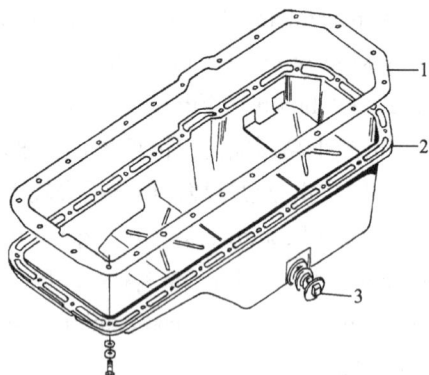

图 2.2.9 油底壳
Figure 2.2.9 Oil pan

1—衬垫 (gasket)；2—油底壳 (oil pan)；
3—放油螺塞 (drain plug)

2.3 活塞连杆组 (Piston and connecting rod group)

活塞连杆组的功用是将活塞的往复运动转变为曲轴旋转运动，同时将作用于活塞上的力转变为曲轴对外输出的转矩，以驱动汽车车轮转动。它由活塞、活塞环、活塞销和连杆等主要机件组成 (图 2.2.10)。

The function of piston connecting rod group is to change the reciprocating motion of piston into the rotating motion of crankshaft. At the same time, the force acting on piston is transformed into the output torque of crankshaft to drive the wheels of the automobile. It consists of piston, piston ring, piston pin and connecting rod, etc. (Figure 2.2.10).

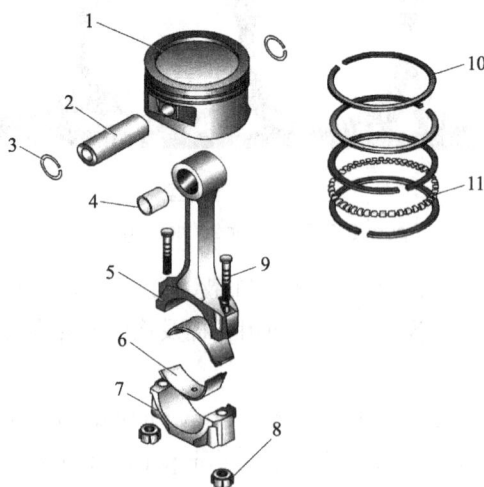

图 2.2.10 活塞连杆组
Figure 2.2.10 Piston and connecting rod group

1—连杆 (connecting rod)；2—连杆螺栓 (connecting rod bolt)；3—卡环 (snap ring)；4—连杆轴瓦 (connecting rod bearing)；
5—活塞环 (piston ring)；6—活塞环槽 (piston ring groove)；7—活塞裙部 (piston skirt)；8—活塞销 (piston pin)；
9—卡簧 (clip spring)；10—压缩环 (compression ring)；11—油环衬簧 (cushion spring of oil control ring)

2.3.1 活塞（Piston）

活塞的功用是与气缸盖、气缸壁等共同组成燃烧室，承受气体压力，并将此力通过活塞销传给连杆，以推动曲轴旋转。汽车发动机目前广泛采用的活塞材料是铝合金，近年来柴油机活塞有采用灰铸铁材料。

The function of the piston is to form a combustion chamber with the cylinder head, cylinder wall and other parts, to withstand the gas pressure, and transfer this force to the connecting rod through the piston pin to rotate the crankshaft. Aluminum alloy is widely used as piston material in automobile engines. In recent years, grey cast iron is used as piston material of diesel engines.

活塞的基本构造可分为顶部、环槽部、裙部和活塞销座四部分（图2.2.11），其中顶部和环槽部也统称头部。

The basic structure of a piston can be divided into four parts: head, ring grooves, skirt and piston pin boss (Figure 2.2.11). The head and ring grooves are also collectively called head.

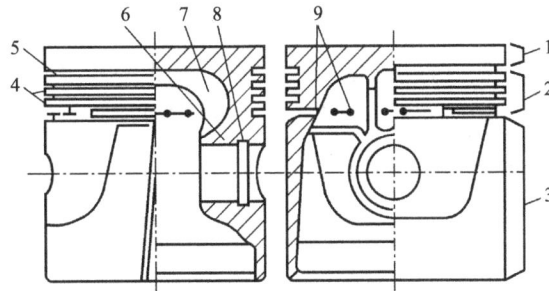

图 2.2.11 活塞

Figure 2.2.11 Piston

1—顶部（head）；2—环槽部（ring grooves）；3—裙部（skirt）；4—环岸（ring lands）；5—环槽（ring grooves）；6—销座（pin boss）；7—加强筋（strengthening rib）；8—卡环槽（snap ring groove）；9—泄油孔及泄油槽（oil drain hole and oil drain pan）

1. 活塞顶部（Piston head）

活塞顶部是燃烧室的组成部分，用来承受气体压力。为了提高刚度和强度，并加强散热能力，背面多有加强筋。根据不同的目的和要求，活塞顶部制成各种不同的形状，汽油机活塞顶部的几种常见形状如图2.2.12所示。

The piston head is part of the combustion chamber, which is used to withstand gas pressure. In order to improve the stiffness and strength, and reinforce the heat-sinking capability, there are many strengthening ribs behind. According to different purposes and requirements, the piston head is made into various shapes. There are several common shapes of piston heads of gasoline engines, as shown in Figure 2.2.12.

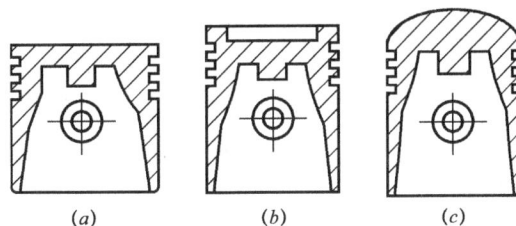

(a)　(b)　(c)

图 2.2.12 活塞顶部形状

Figure 2.2.12 Shapes of piston heads

(a) 平顶（flat head）；(b) 凹顶（concave head）；(c) 凸顶（convex head）

2. 环槽部（Ring groove）

活塞的环槽部切有若干环槽，用以安装活塞环。它是活塞的防漏部分，两环槽之间称为环岸。环槽的形状与活塞环断面形状相适应，通常为矩形或梯形。靠顶部的环槽装压缩环（气环），一般为2～3道，下面的环槽装油环，一般为1～2道。油环槽的槽底圆周上制有若干贯通的泄油孔或泄油槽，以便油环从缸壁上刮下的多余润滑油经此流回油底壳。

The ring groove section of the piston is cut with several ring grooves to install piston rings. It is the leakproof part of the piston, and the sections between ring grooves are called ring lands. The shape of the groove is usually rectangular or trapezoidal, which corresponds to the shape of the piston ring section. Compression rings (gaseous rings) are installed in the top ring grooves, generally 2-3 channels, and oil rings are installed in the bottom ring grooves, generally 1-2 channels. A number of connecting oil drain holes or oil drain pans are arranged on the circumference of oil ring grooves' bottom so that the excess lubricating oil scraped from the cylinder wall can flow back to the oil pan through them.

3. 裙部（Skirt）

活塞的裙部指从油环下端面起至活塞最下端的部分，其形状为一薄壁圆筒。裙部要有一定的长度，以保证可靠的导向，又要有足够的面积，以防止活塞对气缸壁的单位面积压力过大，破坏润滑油膜、加大磨损。

The piston skirt refers to the part from the lower end surface of the oil ring to the lowest end of the piston, which is in the shape of a thin-walled cylinder. Skirt should have a certain length to ensure reliable guidance, but also have enough area to prevent the big pressure of unit area on the cylinder wall by the piston, which damages the lubrication oil film and increases wear and tear.

4. 活塞销座（Piston pin boss）

活塞销座是活塞通过活塞销与连杆的连接部分。位于活塞裙部的上部，为厚壁圆筒结构，用以安装活塞销。活塞销座的作用是将活塞顶部气体作用力经活塞销传给连杆。销座通常有筋片与活塞内壁相连，以提高其刚度。销座孔内接近外端面处，车有安放弹性卡环的卡环槽，卡环用来防止活塞销在工作中发生轴向窜动。

The piston pin boss is the connecting part between the piston and the connecting rod through the piston pin, which is located at the upper part of the piston skirt with a thick-walled cylinder structure for installing piston pins. The function of the piston pin boss is to transfer the gas force acting on the top of the piston to the connecting rod through the piston pin. The piston pin boss usually has strengthening ribs connected to the inner wall of the piston to improve its stiffness. In the hole of the piston pin boss near the end face, there are snap ring grooves made by turning to contain snap ring, which is used to prevent the piston pin from moving axially at work.

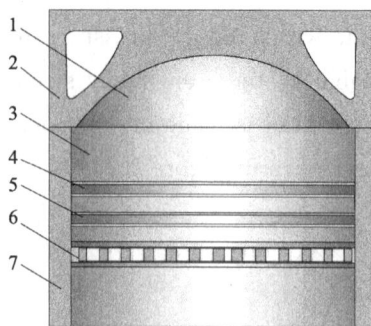

图 2.2.13　活塞环的作用

Figure 2.2.13　Function of piston rings

1—燃烧室（combustion chamber）；2—气缸套（cylinder liner）；
3—活塞（piston）；4—第一道气环（top compression ring）；
5—第二道气环（second compression ring）；
6—组合式油环（combinedtype oil ring）；7—气缸（cylinder）

2.3.2　活塞环（Piston rings）

活塞环是具有一定弹性的金属密封环，它装配在活塞环槽中，与活塞一起密封气缸。如图2.2.13所示。活塞环按用途不同分为气环和油环两种环。

The piston ring is a metal seal ring with certain elasticity. It is assembled in the groove of the piston ring to seal the cylinder with the piston. As shown in Figure 2.2.13. Piston rings are divided into compression rings and oil rings according to their different purposes.

1. 气环 (Gas ring)

气环又称压缩环，作用是保证活塞与气缸间的密封，防止气缸中高温、高压燃气窜入曲轴箱，并将活塞头部的大部分热量传给气缸壁，避免活塞过热。气环密封效果一般与气环数量有关，汽油机一般采用 2 道气环，柴油机一般多采用 3 道气环。

Gas ring, also known as compression ring, ensures the seal between the piston and the cylinder, prevents gas with high temperature and high pressure in cylinder from entering the crankcase, and transfers most of the heat of the piston head to the cylinder wall to avoid overheating of the piston. The sealing effect of gas rings is generally related to the number of gas rings. Generally, gasoline engines use two gas rings, while diesel engines use three gas rings.

(1) 气环的密封原理 (Sealing principle of gas ring)

如图 2.2.14 所示，活塞环在自由状态下其直径略大于气缸直径。当气环随活塞装入气缸后，在自身弹力的作用下气环紧贴在气缸壁上，形成第一密封面，防止了气缸与活塞环之间漏气。当少量气体窜入环槽内，在背隙处形成背压力，使气环与缸壁间的贴合更可靠，再次提高了密封性能。当活塞带动活塞环移动时，活塞环抵靠在环槽上，形成第二密封面，防止了活塞与活塞环之间漏气。而气体的压力使气环压紧在环槽侧面上，使第二密封面更加密封。几道气环的开口相互错开一定角度。形成"迷宫式"漏气通道，延长了漏气途径，从而对气缸中的高压燃气进行有效地密封。

As shown in Figure 2.2.14, the diameter of the piston ring is slightly larger than that of the cylinder in a free state. When the gas ring is placed into the cylinder with the piston, under the action of its own elasticity, the gas ring is closely attached to the cylinder wall, forming the first sealing surface, which prevents the leakage between the cylinder and the piston ring. When a small amount of gas enters the ring groove, the back pressure is formed at the back gap, which makes the fit between the ring and the cylinder wall more reliable and improves the sealing performance again. When the piston drives the piston ring to move, the piston ring rests on the ring groove to form a second sealing surface, which prevents the leakage between the piston and the piston ring. The pressure of the gas makes the gas ring pressed on the side of the ring groove, which makes the second sealing face more sealed. The openings of several air rings are staggered at a certain angle. The "labyrinth" leak passage is formed, which lengthens the leak passage and effectively seals the high-pressure gas in the cylinder.

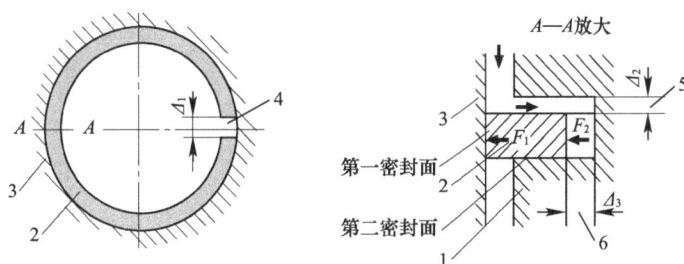

图 2.2.14　气环的密封

Figure 2.2.14　Sealing of Gas Ring

1—活塞 (piston)；2—活塞环 (piston ring)；3—气缸 (cylinder)；4—端隙 (end clearance)；

5—侧隙 (side clearance)；6—背隙 (back clearance)

F_1—自身弹力 (self-elasticity)；F_2—气体背压力 (gas back pressure)

(2) 气环的断面 (Sections of gas ring)

气环的断面形状多种多样，选择不同断面形状的气环组合，可以得到较好的密封效果和使用性能。常见的气环断面形状有如图 2.2.15 所示。

The section shapes of the gas rings are various. Choosing the combination of the gas rings with different sectional shapes can obtain better sealing effect and service performance. The common sectional shapes of gas rings are as follows：

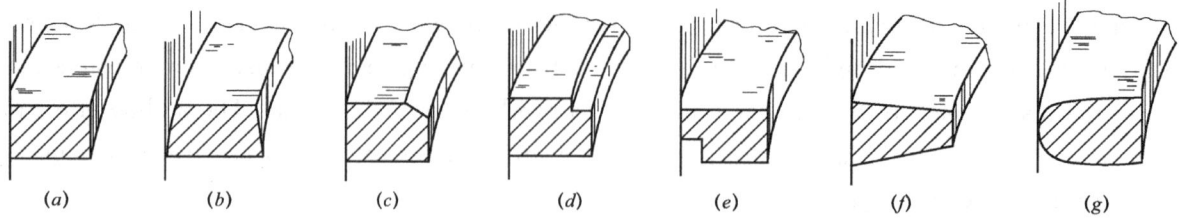

图 2.2.15　气环断面的形状

Figure 2.2.15　Sectional shapes of gas rings

(a) 矩形环 (rectangular ring)；(b) 锥形环 (conical ring)；(c、d) 内切口扭曲 (inner incision twist ring)；
(e) 外切口扭曲环 (outer incision twist ring)；(f) 梯形环 (keystone ring)；(g) 桶形环 (barrel ring)

（3）活塞环的安装间隙 （Installation gap）

发动机工作时，活塞、活塞环等都会发生热膨胀，活塞环既要相对于气缸上下运动，活塞环又要相对于活塞横向移动。因此活塞在安装时应留有端隙、侧隙、背隙三处间隙（图 2.2.16），以防止胀死于槽内，卡死于缸内，以保证其密封性能。

When the engine works，the piston，heat expansion occurs for the piston，piston rings and other parts. The piston rings not only move up and down relative to the cylinder，but also move transversely relative to the piston. Therefore，the piston should be installed with three clearances that are end clearance，side clearance and back clearance，in order to prevent rings from bursting in the grooves and binding in the cylinder due to expansion，so as to ensure its sealing performance.

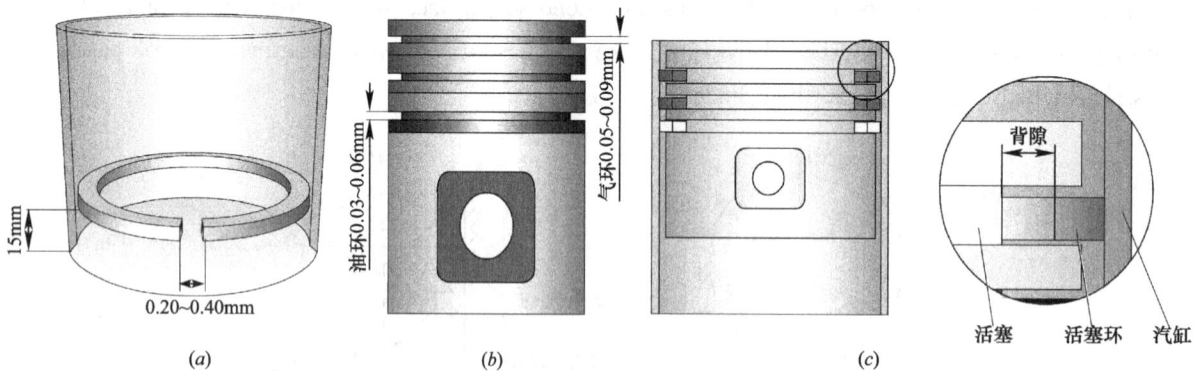

图 2.2.16　活塞环的间隙

Figure 2.2.16　Clearance of piston ring

(a) 端隙 (end clearance)；(b) 侧隙 (side clearance)；(c) 背隙 (back clearance)

2. 油环 （Oil control ring）

油环的作用是活塞上行时，使飞溅在气缸壁上的润滑油均匀分布，有利于活塞、活塞环和气缸壁的润滑。活塞下行时，刮除气缸壁上多余的润滑油，防止润滑油窜入燃烧室燃烧。如图 2.2.17 所示，油环按结构形式不同可分为普通油环和组合式油环两种。

The function of the oil-control ring is to make the oil splashed on the cylinder wall uniformly distributed when the piston goes up, which is beneficial to the lubrication of the piston, the piston ring and the cylinder wall. When the piston goes down, the oil-control ring scrapes the excess lubrication oil off the cylinder wall to prevent the lubrication oil from entering the combustion chamber. As shown in Figure 2.2.17, the oil rings can be divided into two types according to their different structures: ordinary oil control rings and combined oil control rings.

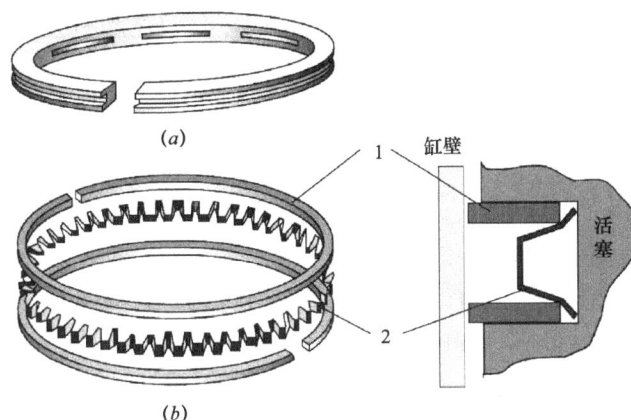

图 2.2.17 油环

Figure 2.2.17 Oil control Rings

(a) 普通油环 (ordinary oil control ring); (b) 组合式油环 (combined oil control ring)

1—刮片 (scraper); 2—衬簧 (cushion spring)

普通油环的结构如图 2.2.17 (a) 所示,一般是用合金铸铁制造的。其外圆面的中间切有一道凹槽。在凹槽底部加工出很多穿通的排油小孔或狭缝。

The structure of common oil ring is shown in Fig. 2.2.17 (a). It is usually made of alloy cast iron. A groove is cut in the middle of the ex-circle face. Many connected oil drainage holes or slits are machined at the bottom of the groove.

组合式油环如图 2.2.17 (b) 由上、下两片刮片与中间衬簧组成。刮片用镀铬钢片制成,在自由状态下,安装到衬簧的刮片外径比气缸直径略大一些。两刮片之间的距离也比环槽宽度略大。当组合油环及活塞安装到气缸后。衬簧在轴向和径向都受到压缩,在衬簧弹力的作用下,可使刮片紧紧压向气缸壁,提高了刮油效果。同时两刮片也紧紧地抵靠在环槽上。组合式油环没有侧隙,这样就减少了活塞环的泵油作用。这种油环的接触压力高,对气缸壁面适应性好,而且回油通路大、质量小,刮油效果明显。

The combined oil control ring Fig. 2.2.17(b)consists of upper and lower scrapers and intermediate cushion spring. The scraper is made of chromium-plated steel sheet. Under a free state, the outer diameter of the scraper mounted to the cushion spring is slightly larger than that of the cylinder. The distance between the two scrapers is also slightly larger than the width of the ring groove. When the combined oil control ring and piston are installed in the cylinder, the cushion spring is compressed in both axial and radial directions. Under the action of the elasticity of the cushion spring, the scraper can be pressed tightly against the cylinder wall, thus improving the oil scraping effect. At the same time, the two scrapers are tightly against the ring groove. The combined oil ring has no backlash, which reduces the pumping effect of the piston ring. This kind of oil ring has high contact pressure, good adaptability to cylinder wall, large oil return path, small quality and obvious oil scraping effect.

2.3.3 活塞销 (Piston pin)

活塞销 (图 2.2.18) 用来连接活塞和连杆小头，并把活塞所受的气体压力传给连杆。

The piston pin (Fig. 2.2.18) is used to connect the piston and the connecting rod small end, and transmit the gas pressure on the piston to the connecting rod.

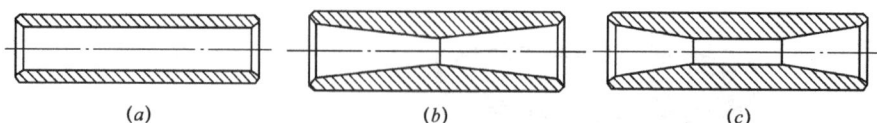

(a) (b) (c)

图 2.2.18 活塞销

Figure 2.2.18 Piston Pin

活塞销与活塞销座孔和连杆小头衬套一般多采用全浮式连接配合，即在发动机运转过程中，活塞销不仅可以在连杆小头衬套孔内缓慢地转动，还可以在销座孔内缓慢地转动。如图 2.2.19 所示。

The piston pin and piston pin boss, and the liner of connecting rod small end usually adopt full floating connection. In the process of engine operation, the piston pin can not only rotate slowly in the hole of liner of connecting rod small end, but also rotate slowly in the hole of the pin boss. As shown in Figure 2.2.19.

半浮式连接方式指的是活塞销与活塞销座孔和连杆小头两处，一处固定，一处浮动。销座孔内无卡环，连杆小头处无衬套。其中大部分是采用销与连杆小头固定的方式，这种固定方式有两种：一种是用螺栓将活塞销夹紧在连杆小头孔内，如图 2.2.19 (b) 所示；另一种是活塞销与连杆小头孔以过盈配合的方式固定，如图 2.2.19 (c) 所示。

There are two connections of the piston pin and the hole of the piston pin boss, and connecting rod small head. Semi-floating connection means that one of them is fixed, and another is floating. There is no snap ring in the hole of pin boss and no liner at connecting rod small end. Most of them are fixed by the connection of the pin and the connecting rod small end. There are two ways: one is to clamp the piston pin in the hole of the connecting rod small end with bolts, as shown in Figure 2.2.19 (b); the other is to fix the piston pin and the hole of connecting rod small end with interference fit, as shown in Figure 2.2.19 (c).

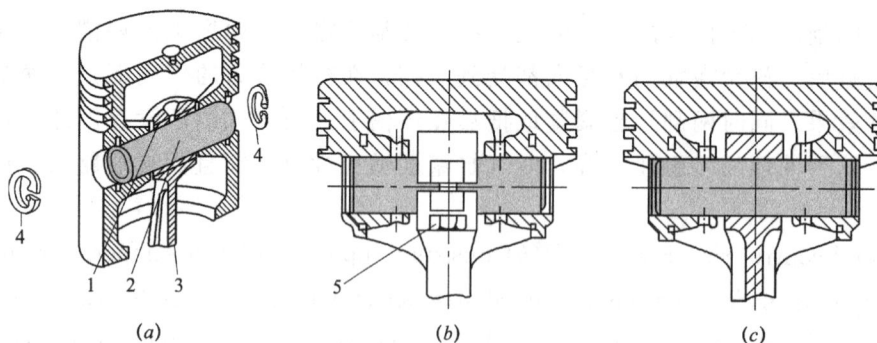

(a) (b) (c)

图 2.2.19 活塞销连接方式

Figure 2.2.19 Connected mode of the piston pin

(a) 全浮式 (full floating); (b、c) 半浮式 (semi-floating)

1—连杆小头衬套 (liner of connecting rod small end); 2—活塞销 (piston pin); 3—连杆 (connecting rod);

4—卡环 (snap ring); 5—小头紧固螺栓 (fastening bolt of small end)

2.3.4　连杆（Connecting rod）

连杆的功用是连接活塞与曲轴，将活塞承受的力传给曲轴，把活塞的往复运动变为曲轴的旋转运动。连杆可分为小头、杆身和大头三部分，如图2.2.20所示。

The function of the connecting rod is to connect the piston and the crankshaft，transferring the force acting on the piston to the crankshaft，and change the reciprocating motion of the piston into the rotating motion of the crankshaft. The connecting rod can be divided into three parts：small end，connecting rod shank and big end，as shown in Figure 2.2.20.

（1）连杆小头用来安装活塞销，以连接活塞。

（2）杆身：杆身通常做成"工"字形断面。以求在强度和刚度足够的前提下减小质量。

（3）大头：连杆大头与曲轴的连杆轴颈相连，为便于安装，连杆大头一般做成剖分式的。连杆大头按剖分面的方向可分为平切口和斜切口两种。

（1）The connecting rod small end is used to install the piston pin to connect the piston.

（2）The connecting rod shank：it is usually made into "I" shaped section，in order to reduce the mass in the premise of sufficient strength and stiffness.

（3）Big end：The connecting rod big end is connected with the connecting rod journal of the crankshaft. For ease of installation, the connecting rod big end is generally split. The connecting rod big end can be divided into two kinds according to the direction of splits：flat split and oblique split.

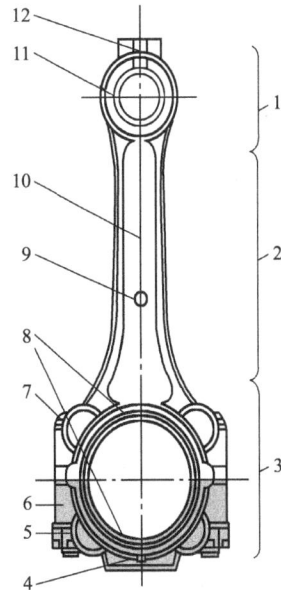

图2.2.20　连杆
Figure 2.2.20　Connecting rod

1—小头（small end）；2—杆身（connecting rod shank）；3—大头（big end）；
4、9—装配记号（朝前）（assembly mark (forward)）；5—螺母（nut）；
6—连杆盖（connecting rod cap r）；7—连杆螺栓（connecting rod bolt）；
8—轴瓦（bearing inserts）；10—连杆体（connecting rod body）；
11—衬套（bush）；12—集油孔

2.4　曲轴飞轮组（Crankshaft and flywheel group）

曲轴飞轮组主要由曲轴、飞轮、扭转减振器、带轮、正时齿轮（或链条）等组成。如图2.2.21所示。

The crankshaft flywheel group is mainly composed of crankshaft, flywheel, torsion damper, pulley, timing gear (or chain), etc. As shown in Figure 2.2.21.

2.4.1　曲轴（Crankshaft）

曲轴是发动机中最重要的机件之一，其功用是承受活塞连杆组传来的气体压力转变为曲轴的转矩并对外输出。另外，曲轴还用来驱动发动机的配气机构及其他辅助装置。

Crankshaft is one of the most important parts of engines. Its function is to change the gas pressure from the piston and connecting rod group into the torque of crankshaft and output it. In addition，the crankshaft is also used to drive the valve mechanism and other auxiliary devices of the engine.

1. 曲轴的结构（Structure of crankshaft）

如图2.2.22所示，曲轴一般由前端、主轴颈、曲柄、平衡重、连杆轴颈和后端组成。由一个连杆轴颈和它左右主轴颈组成一个曲拐。

As shown in Figure 2.2.22，the crankshaft generally consists of the front end，the main journal，the crank，the counter balanced weight，the connecting rod journal and the rear end. A crank throw consists of a connecting rod journal and its left and right main journals.

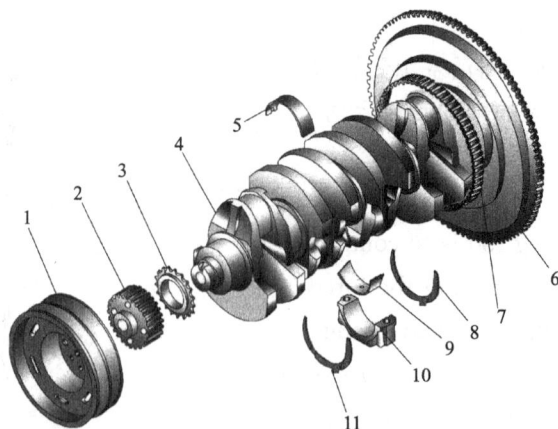

图 2.2.21　曲轴飞轮组

Figure 2.2.21　Crankshaft flywheel group

1—带轮（pulley）；2—曲轴正时齿形带轮（crankshaft timing toothed pulley）；3—曲轴链轮（crankshaft sprocket）；4—曲轴（crankshaft）；5—曲轴主轴承（上）（crankshaft main bearing (upper)）；6—飞轮（flywheel）；7—转速传感器信号发生器（signal generator of speed sensor）；8、11—止推垫（thrust pad）；9—曲轴主轴承（下）（crankshaft main bearing (lower)）；10—曲轴主轴承盖（crankshaft main bearing cap）

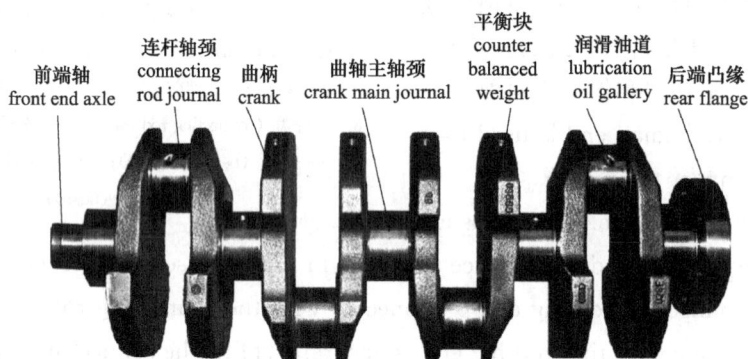

图 2.2.22　曲轴的结构

Figure 2.2.22　Structure of crankshaft

2. 曲拐的布置原则（Layout principle of crank throw）

曲轴的形状和各曲拐的相对位置主要取决于气缸数、气缸的排列形式和各缸的工作顺序，在安排发动机工作顺序时应尽量遵循如下规则：

The shape of the crank throw and the relative position of each one mainly depend on the number of cylinders, the arrangement of cylinders and the work sequence of each cylinder. When arranging the work sequence of the engine, the following rules should be followed as far as possible:

（1）使连续做功的两缸尽可能相距远些，以减轻主轴承的负荷，避免在进气过程中发生相连两气门同时开启，出现"抢气"现象，影响发动机的充气效率。

（1）The two continuous working cylinders should be arranged as far apart as possible to reduce the load of the main bearing and avoid the simultaneous opening of two connected valves in the process of intake, which will lead to the phenomenon of "grabbing air" and affect the charge efficiency of the engine.

（2）各气缸的做功间隔角应该相等，以利于发动机运转平稳，在发动机完成一个工作循环的曲轴转角内，每个气缸都应做功一次。对气缸数为 i 的四冲程发动机而言，做功间隔角为 $720°/i$，即曲轴每转 $720°/i$，就应有一个缸做功，以保证发动机运转平稳。

(2) The working angular interval of each cylinder should be equal to ensure the smooth running of the engine. Within the crankshaft angle of the engine which completes a working cycle, each cylinder should do work once. For a four-stroke engine with cylinder number i, the working angular interval is $720/i$. That is to say, for every $720°/i$ rotation of crankshaft, it should have a cylinder to do work to ensure that the engine runs smoothly.

（3）如果是 V 形发动机，则左右两列气缸应交替做功。

(3) If it is a V-shaped engine, the left and right cylinders should work alternately.

3. 常见的多缸发动机曲拐布置形式与工作顺序（Common layout and work sequence of the crank throw of multi-cylinder engine）

（1）直列四冲程发动机曲轴曲拐的布置（The arrangement of crankshaft and crank throw for in-line four-stroke engine）

直列四缸四冲程发动机做功间隔角是 $720°/4=180°$，四个曲拐布置在同一个平面内，发动机工作顺序（或点火顺序）为 1→3→4→2 或 1→2→4→3 两种，其工作循环见表 2.2.1。

The working angular interval of the in-line, four-cylinder, four-stroke engine is $720°/4=180°$. Four crank throws are arranged in the same plane. There are two kinds of the work sequence(or ignition sequence) of the engine , which is 1→3→4→2 or 1→2→4→3. The working cycle of the engine is shown in tables 2.2.1.

直列四缸四冲程发动机工作循环表   表 2.2.1

The working cycle table of the in-line, four-cylinder, four-stroke engine   Table 2.2.1

直列四冲程四缸发动机工作循环表（工作顺序 1→3→4→2）

曲轴转角（°）	第一缸	第二缸	第三缸	第四缸
0~180	做功	排气	压缩	进气
180~360	排气	进气	做功	压缩
360~540	进气	压缩	排气	做功
540~720	压缩	做功	进气	排气

直列四冲程四缸发动机工作循环表（工作顺序 1→2→4→3）

曲轴转角（°）	第一缸	第二缸	第三缸	第四缸
0~180	做功	压缩	排气	进气
180~360	排气	做功	进气	压缩
360~540	进气	排气	压缩	做功
540~720	压缩	进气	做功	排气

注：工作顺序-work sequence；曲轴转角-crankshaft angle；第一缸-the first cylinder；第二缸-the second cylinder；第三缸-the third cylinder；第四缸-the fourth cylinder；进气-intake；压缩-compression；做功-power；排气-exhaust.

直列六缸四冲程发动机：做功间隔角为 $720°/6=120°$，六个曲拐布置在互成 $120°$ 夹角的三个平面内，发动机工作顺序（或点火顺序）为 1→5→3→6→2→4 或 1→4→2→6→3→5，前者应用较为普遍，其工作循环表见表 2.2.2。

The in-line , six-cylinder , four-stroke engine：the working angular interval is $720°/6=120°$, and the six crank throws are arranged in three planes with 120-degree angle between each other. The work sequence (or ignition sequence) of the engine is 1→5→3→6→2→4 or 1→4→2→6→3→5. The former is widely used, whose working cycle table is shown in Table 2.2.2.

直列四冲程六缸发动机工作循环表 表 2.2.2
The working cycle table of in-line, four-stroke, six-cylinder engine Table 2.2.2

直列四冲程六缸发动机工作循环表（工作顺序 1→5→3→6→2→4）

曲轴转角（°）		第一缸	第二缸	第三缸	第四缸	第五缸	第六缸
0～180	0 / 60	做功	排气	进气	做功	压缩	进气
	120	做功	排气	压缩	排气	压缩	进气
180～360	180 / 240	排气	进气	压缩	排气	做功	压缩
	300	排气	进气	做功	进气	做功	压缩
360～540	360 / 420	进气	压缩	做功	进气	排气	做功
	480	进气	压缩	排气	压缩	排气	做功
540～720	540 / 600	压缩	做功	排气	压缩	进气	排气
	660	压缩	做功	进气	做功	进气	排气
	720	压缩	排气	进气	做功	压缩	排气

注：工作顺序-work sequence；曲轴转角-crankshaft angle；第一缸-the first cylinder；第二缸-the second cylinder；第三缸-the third cylinder；第四缸-the fourth cylinder；第五缸-the fifth cylinder；第六缸-the sixth cylinder；进气-intake；压缩-compression；做功-power；排气-exhaust.

（2）V 形排列四冲程发动机曲轴曲拐的布置（Arrangement of crankshaft and crank throws of the v-type, four-stroke engine）

V 形排列八缸四冲程发动机：做功间隔为 720°/8＝90°。曲拐的布置形式有两种：一种是四个曲拐布置在同一个平面内，与直列四缸发动机的曲拐布置形式完全一样；另一种是四个曲拐布置在互成 90°夹角的两个平面内。发动机的工作顺序（或点火顺序）为 1→8→4→3→6→5→7→2，这样的布置有利于发动机的平衡，其工作循环见表 2.2.3。

For the V-type, eight-cylinder, four-stroke engine, working angular interval is 720°/8＝90°. There are two kinds of arrangement of crank throws: one is that four crank throws are arranged in the same plane, which is exactly the same as that of in-line four-cylinder engine; the other is that four crank throws are arranged in two planes with 90 degrees angle. The work sequence (or ignition sequence) of the engine is 1→8→4→3→6→5→7→2. This arrangement is beneficial to the balance of the engine, whose working cycle of the engine is shown in Table 2.2.3.

V 形四冲程八缸发动机工作循环表 表 2.2.3
The working cycle table of the V-shaped, four-stroke, eight-cylinder engine Table 2.2.3

V 形四冲程八缸发动机工作循环表（工作顺序 1→8→4→3→6→5→7→2）

曲轴转角（°）		第一缸	第二缸	第三缸	第四缸	第五缸	第六缸	第七缸	第八缸
0～180	0 / 90	做功	做功	进气	压缩	排气	进气	排气	压缩
	180	做功	排气	压缩	压缩	进气	进气	排气	做功
180～360	270	排气	排气	压缩	做功	进气	压缩	进气	做功
	360	排气	进气	做功	做功	压缩	压缩	进气	排气
360～540	450	进气	进气	做功	排气	做功	做功	压缩	排气
	540	进气	压缩	排气	排气	做功	做功	压缩	进气
540～720	630	压缩	压缩	排气	进气	排气	排气	做功	进气
	720	压缩	做功	进气	进气	排气	排气	做功	压缩

注：工作顺序-work sequence；曲轴转角-crankshaft angle；第一缸-the first cylinder；第二缸-the second cylinder；第三缸-the third cylinder；第四缸-the fourth cylinder；第五缸-the fifth cylinder；第六缸-the sixth cylinder；第七缸-the seventh cylinder；第八缸-the eighth cylinder；进气-intake；压缩-compression；做功-power；排气-exhaust.

4. 曲轴的轴向定位 (Axial positioning of crankshaft)

采取轴向限位措施来保证曲轴的轴向位移量，使曲轴既有受热膨胀的余地，又不至于产生过大的轴向位移量。曲轴轴向限位措施通常用止推装置来实现的，且只能有一处设置轴向限位装置，止推装置常用的有：单面制有减摩合金层的半圆形的止推垫、带有翻边的曲轴主轴承和圆形的止推环三种形式。

The axial displacement amount of crankshaft can be limited by adopting the measure of axial limited location, so that the crankshaft has the space for thermal expansion and does not produce excessive axial displacement amount. The measure of crankshaft axial limited location is usually realized by thrust device, and only one axial limiting device can be installed. There are three kinds of thrust devices commonly used: semi-circular thrust pad with anti-friction alloy layer on one side, crankshaft main bearing with flanging and circular thrust ring.

5. 曲轴径向密封 (Radical seal of crankshaft)

曲轴径向密封环安放在曲轴的自由端（前端）和飞轮端（功率输出端）。其作用是防止发动机机体内的机油外溢和水（汽）与灰尘进入机体内。

The crankshaft radial sealing ring is located at the free end (front end) of the crankshaft and the flywheel end (power output end). Its function is to prevent engine oil from spilling over and water (steam) and dust from entering the engine block.

2.4.2 曲轴扭转减振器 (Vibration damper of crankshaft)

在发动机运转时，由于各缸气体压力和往复运动的惯性力周期性的作用在曲轴的连杆轴颈上，使曲轴转速变得忽快忽慢，从而产生曲轴对于飞轮的扭转摆动，这种扭转摆动在产生共振时就更加剧烈，会产生功率损失，加速驱动齿轮、链轮、链条磨损增加，严重时甚至将曲轴扭断。为了消减曲轴的扭转振动，有的发动机在曲轴前端装有扭转减振器。曲轴常用摩擦式扭转减振器，按其减振元件不同其可分为橡胶式扭转减振器和硅油式扭转减振器两类。

When the engine is running, the crankshaft speeds up and down due to the periodic action of cylinder gas pressure and inertia force of reciprocating motion on the connecting rod journal of the crankshaft, resulting in the torsional swing of the crankshaft relative to the flywheel. This kind of torsional swing is violent when resonance occurs, which will cause power loss, accelerating the wear and tear of driving gears, sprockets and chains, and even twist the crankshaft off in serious cases. In order to reduce the torsional vibration of crankshaft, some engines are equipped with torsional vibration dampers at the front of crankshaft. The friction torsional vibration dampers commonly used in crankshafts can be divided into rubber torsional vibration dampers and silicone oil torsional vibration dampers according to their different damping components.

2.4.3 飞轮 (Flywheel)

飞轮的主要功用是通过储存和释放能量，协助发动机完成进气、压缩和排气行程，并能提高发动机运转的均匀性。同时，它又是离合器的主动盘，将发动机的动力传递给离合器的从动盘。

The main function of flywheel is to assist the engine to complete the intake, compression and exhaust strokes by storing and releasing energy, and to improve the running uniformity of engines. At the same time, it is the driving disk of the clutch, which transfers the power of the engine to the driven disk of the clutch.

思考与练习

(Reflection and Exercises)

1. 为什么有的发动机在曲轴的每个曲拐臂上都设有平衡块，有的则没有，有的还专门设置有一根或两根平衡轴？

2. 试述多缸发动机气缸体的结构及气缸排列方式。

3. 为什么有些发动机采用有缸套结构，而有些发动机却采用无缸套结构？

4. 什么是干缸套与湿缸套？采用湿缸套时如何防止漏水？

5. 汽油机的燃烧室通常有几种？什么才是较好的燃烧室？

6. 柴油机的燃烧室通常有几种？为什么柴油机的主燃烧室通常都在活塞顶内？

1. Why do some engines have balancing blocks on each crank throw arm of the crankshaft，others do not，and some have one or two special balancing shafts?

2. Describe the structure of cylinder block and cylinder arrangement of multi-cylinder engines.

3. Why do some engines adopt cylinder-liner structure while others adopt cylinder-liner-free structure?

4. What are dry cylinder liners and wet cylinder liners? How to prevent water leakage when using wet cylinder liners?

5. How many kinds of combustion chambers are there in gasoline engines? What is a better combustion chamber?

6. How many kinds of combustion chambers are there in diesel engines? Why is the main combustion chamber of a diesel engine usually located in the piston head?

任务三 配气机构

Task 3　Valve Mechanism

教学目标

1. 知识目标

（1）了解配气机构的组成；

（2）掌握配气机构的工作原理；

（3）掌握曲柄连杆机构的工作原理。

2. 能力目标

（1）具有分析配气机构原理的能力；

（2）具有区别不同类型的配气机构的能力。

3. 情感和素养目标

（1）培养学生具备良好的职业素养、严谨的工作态度；

（2）培养学生具备高度的责任心、吃苦耐劳的精神。

Teaching objectives

1. Knowledge objectives

（1）Understanding the composition of valve mechanism；

（2）Master the working principle of valve mechanism；

（3）Master the working principle of crankshaft and connecting rod mechanism.

2. Ability objectives

（1）Ability to analyze the principle of valve mechanism；

（2）Ability to distinguish different types of valve mechanism.

3. Emotion and quality goals

（1）Cultivate students to have good occupational quality and a rigorous work attitude；

（2）Cultivate students to have a strong sense of responsibility and work hard.

3.1 概述 (Outline)

3.1.1 配气机构的作用与分类 (Function and classification of valve mechanism)

1. 配气机构的作用 (The function of valve mechanism)

配气机构的作用是按照发动机各缸工作循环的要求，适时开启和关闭进、排气门。在进气行程中及时打开进气门，使混合气（汽油机）或新鲜空气（柴油机）进入气缸。在排气行程中及时打开排气门，将燃烧后的废气及时从气缸内排出。而在压缩行程和做功行程中，进、排气门均关闭，从而使气缸具有良好的密封性。

The function of the valve mechanism is to open and close the intake and exhaust valves at definite moments according to the requirements of working cycle of each cylinder of the engine. It opens the intake valve in time during the intake stroke to let the mixture (gasoline engine) or fresh air (diesel engine) enters the cylinder. In the exhaust stroke, the exhaust valve is opened timely, and the burned gas after combustion is discharged from the cylinder in time. While in compression stroke and work stroke, the intake and exhaust valves are both closed, so that the cylinder has a good seal.

可燃混合气或空气充满气缸的程度，常用充气效率表示，也称充气系数。对于一定工作容积的发动机而言，充气效率与进气终了时气缸内的压力和温度有关，进气终了压力越高，温度越低，则一定容积的气体质量就越大，充气效率越高。充气效率总是小于1，一般为0.8～0.9。

The degree of the combustible mixture or air filling the cylinder is usually expressed by the charging efficiency, also known as the charging coefficient. For an engine with a certain working volume, the charging efficiency is related to the pressure and temperature in the cylinder at the end of intake. The higher the final intake pressure is, and the lower the temperature is, then the larger the mass of a certain volume of gas is, and the higher the charging efficiency is. Charging efficiency is always less than 1, which is usually 0.8-0.9.

2. 配气机构的分类 (Classification of valve mechanism)

四冲程车用发动机大都采用气门式配气机构，其机构形式多种多样。按每缸气门数目不同分为二气门式和多气门式两种。其中多气门式发动机又分为三气门式、四气门式和五气门式几种。按凸轮轴布置位置不同分为凸轮轴下置式配气机构、凸轮轴中置式配气机构和凸轮轴上置式配气机构。按曲轴和凸轮轴的传动方式不同分为齿轮传动式、链传动式和齿形带传动式三种形式。

Valve-type valve mechanism is mostly used in four-stroke vehicle engines with various mechanism forms. According to the number of valves per cylinder, it can be divided into two-valve type and multi-valve type. And the multi-valve engine is divided into three-valve, four-valve and five-valve types. According to the location of camshaft, it can be divided into three types: underneath camshaft valve mechanism, medial camshaft valve mechanism and overhead camshaft valve mechanism. According to the transmission mode of crankshaft and camshaft, it can be divided into three types: gear drive, chain drive and toothed belt drive.

3.1.2 凸轮轴下置式配气机构组成及工作原理 (Composition and working principle of downward camshaft valve mechanism)

如图 2.3.1 所示，凸轮轴下置式配气机构由气门组和气门传动组两部分组成。

As shown in Figure 2.3.1, the downward camshaft valve mechanism consists of two parts.

凸轮轴下置式配气机构工作原理示意图如图2.3.2所示，发动机工作时，曲轴通过正时齿轮16驱动凸轮轴正时齿轮1旋转。当凸轮的凸起顶起挺柱3时，挺柱3推动推杆4一起上行。作用于摇臂8上的推力使摇臂绕摇臂轴6转动。摇臂的另一端下移，压缩气门弹簧11，打开气门14。凸轮轴继续转动时，凸轮的凸起部分离开挺柱时，在气门弹簧张力的作用下，气门上升而落座，使气门关闭。

The diagram of the working principle of the underneath camshaft valve mechanism is shown in Fig. 2.3.2. When the engine works, the crankshaft drives the camshaft timing gear 1 to rotate through the

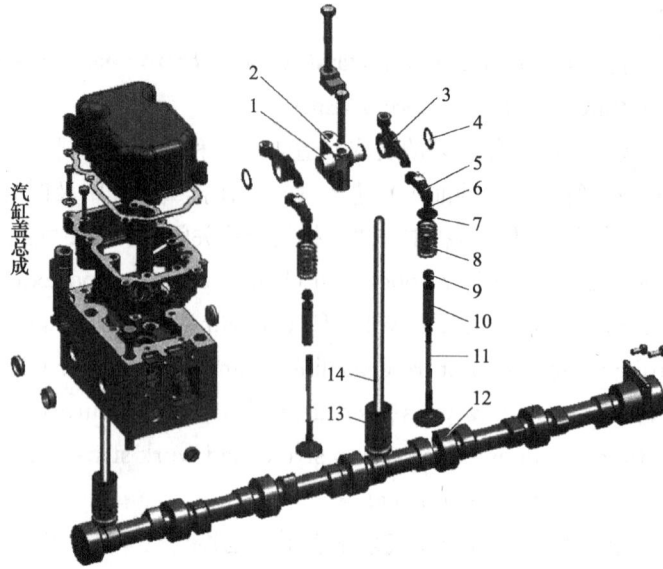

图 2.3.1　凸轮轴下置式配气机构组成

Figure 2.3.1　Composition of underneath camshaft valve mechanism

1—摇臂轴（rocker arm shaft）；2—摇臂轴支座（rocker shaft support）；3—摇臂（rocker arm）；4—卡环（snap ring）；5—气门桥（valve bridge）；6—气门锁片（valve keys）；7—气门弹簧座（valve spring seat）；8—气门弹簧（valve spring）；9—气门油封（valve oil seal）；10—气门导管（valve guides）；11—气门（valve）；12—凸轮轴（camshaft）；13—挺柱（tappet）；14—推杆（push rod）

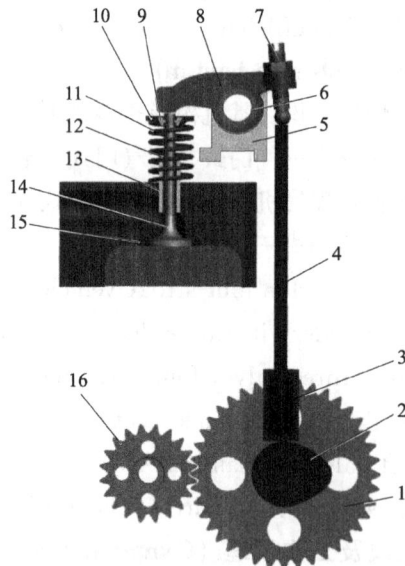

图 2.3.2　凸轮轴下置式配气机构工作原理

Figure 2.3.2　Working principle of underneath camshaft valve mechanism

1—凸轮轴正时齿轮（camshaft timing gear）；2—凸轮轴（camshaft）；3—挺柱（tappet）；4—推杆（push rod）；5—摇臂轴支架（rocker shaft bracket）；6—摇臂轴（rocker shaft）；7—调整螺钉及锁紧螺母（adjusting screw and lock nut）；8—摇臂（rocker arm）；9—气门锁片（valve keys）；10—气门弹簧座（valve spring seat）；11—气门弹簧（valve spring）；12—气门油封（valve oil seal）；13—气门导管（valve guide）；14—气门（valve）；15—气门座（valve seat）；16—曲轴正时齿轮（crankshaft timing gear）

timing gear 16. When the protruding part of the cam bumps up the tappet 3, the tappet 3 pushes the push rod 4 upward together. The thrust acting on the rocker arm 8 causes the rocker arm to rotate around the rocker arm shaft 6. The other end of the rocker arm moves down, compressing the valve spring 11 and opens the valve 14. With continuous rotation of the camshaft, the protruding part of the cam leaves the tappet, and under the action of the tension of the valve spring, the valve rises and sits, so that the valve is closed.

凸轮轴上置式配气机构组成及工作原理如图 2.3.3 所示，凸轮轴上置式配气机构由气门组和气门传动组两部分组成。气门组包括气门锁片 7、气门弹簧座 8、气门弹簧 9、气门油封 10、气门导管 11、气门 12、气门座 13 等。气门传动组包括曲轴正时齿形带轮 1、正时齿形带 2、张紧轮 3、凸轮轴 4、凸轮轴正时齿形带轮 5、液力挺柱总成 6 等。

The composition and working principle of overhead camshaft valve mechanism are shown in Fig. 2.3.3, which consists of valve group and valve transmission group. Valve group includes valve keys 7, valve spring seat 8, valve spring 9, valve oil seal 10, valve guide 11, valve 12 and valve seat 13, etc. Valve transmission group includes crankshaft timing gear pulley 1, timing gear belt 2, tensioner 3, camshaft 4, camshaft timing gear pulley 5 and hydraulic tappet assembly 6, etc.

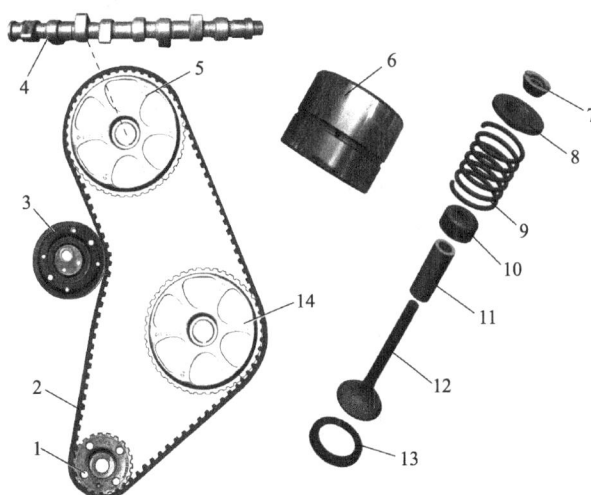

图 2.3.3　凸轮轴上置式配气机构组成

Figure 2.3.3　Composition of overhead camshaft valve mechanism

1—曲轴正时齿形带轮（crankshaft timing toothed pulley）；2—正时齿形带（timing toothed belt）；3—张紧轮（tensioner）；

4—凸轮轴（camshaft）；5—凸轮轴正时齿形带轮（camshaft timing toothed pulley）；6—液力挺柱总成（hydraulic tappet assembly）；

7—气门锁片（valve keys）；8—气门弹簧座（valve spring seat）；9—气门弹簧（valve spring）；10—气门油封（valve oil seal）；

11—气门导管（valve guide）；12—气门（valve）；13—气门座圈（valve retainer）；14—中间轴带轮（intermediate shaft pulley）

凸轮轴上置式配气机构工作原理如图 2.3.4 所示，如发动机在做进气行程时，要求配气机构将进气门打开，此时曲轴带动曲轴正时齿形带轮转动，通过正时齿形带带动凸轮轴正时齿形带轮转动，凸轮轴正时齿形带轮带动凸轮轴转动。当凸轮轴上的凸轮转过基圆部分后，凸轮的凸起部分将驱动液力挺柱下移，克服进气门弹簧的弹力使进气门下移，打开进气通道，混合气通过进气门进入气缸。随着凸轮的凸起部分的顶点转过液力挺柱以后，凸轮对液力挺柱的推力逐渐减小，进气门在弹簧张力的作用下上移，逐渐关闭进气道。当凸轮转到基圆部分时，凸轮对液力挺柱的推力消失，气门完全关闭时，进气行程结束。

The working principle of the overhead camshaft valve mechanism is shown in Fig. 2.3.4. For example, when the engine is working on the intake stroke, the valve mechanism is required to open the intake valve. At this time, the crankshaft drives the crankshaft toothed pulley to rotate, and the timing toothed belt drives the camshaft timing toothed pulley to rotate, and the camshaft timing toothed pulley drives the camshaft to rotate. When the cam on the camshaft rotates the base circle part, the protruding part of the cam will drive the hydraulic tappet downward, overcome the elasticity of the intake valve spring to make the intake valve downward, which opens the intake passage, and the mixture will enter the cylinder through the intake valve. With the vertex of the cam's protruding part turning to pass by the hydraulic tappet, the thrust of the cam acting on the hydraulic tappet decreases gradually, and the intake valve moves upward under the action of the spring tension and closes the intake port gradually. When the cam turns to the base circle, the thrust of the cam on the hydraulic tappet disappears and the valve closes completely, and the intake stroke ends.

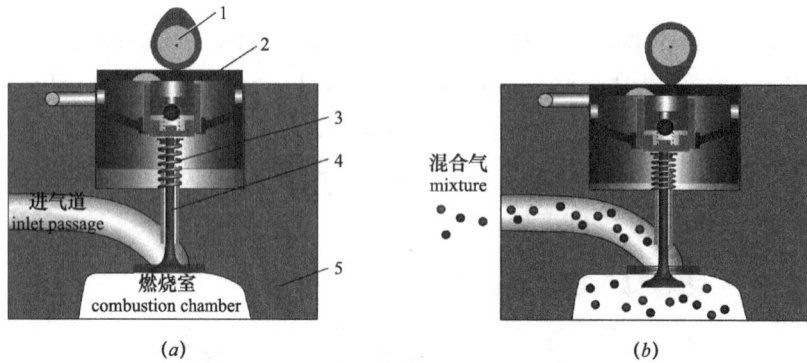

图 2.3.4　凸轮轴上置式配气机构工作原理示意图

Figure 2.3.4　Diagram of working principle of overhead camshaft valve mechanism

(a) 气门关闭 (valve-closing)；(b) 气门开启 (valve-opening)

1—凸轮轴 (camshaft)；2—液力挺柱总成 (hydraulic tappet assembly)；3—气门弹簧 (valve spring)；4—气门 (valve)；5—气缸盖 (cylinder head)

3.1.3　气门的布置形式 (Arrangement of valves)

如图 2.3.5 所示，一般发动机每个气缸有两个气门，即一个进气门和一个排气门。三气门式发动机配气机构，其每缸有两个进气门和一个排气门，如图 2.3.6 所示。与二气门式发动机相比，进气量有明显增加，发动机功率及排放有所改善。

As shown in Figure 2.3.5, an engine usually has two valves per cylinder, an intake valve and an exhaust valve. The valve mechanism of a three-valve engine has two intake valves and one exhaust valve per cylinder, as shown in Figure 2.3.6. Compared with the two-valve engine, the intake volume has increased significantly, and the engine power and discharge have been improved.

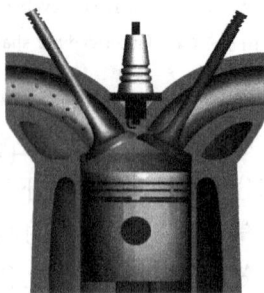

图 2.3.5　两气门配气机构

Figure 2.3.5　Two-valve valve mechanism

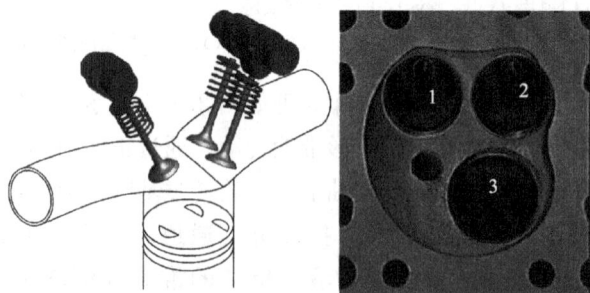

图 2.3.6　三气门配气机构

Figure 2.3.6　Three-valve valve mechanism

四气门式是最完善使用最广泛的配气机构，目前在许多发动机上采用。其结构如图 2.3.7 所示。四气门式发动机配气机构一般采用顶置双凸轮轴式结构的驱动方式。其主要优点是进、排气门数量增加，进、排气通道截面积随之增大，提高了发动机的进、排气效率。单个气门的尺寸缩小使质量减轻，满足了发动机高速化的要求。火花塞可布置在燃烧室的中心位置，改善了可燃混合气的燃烧过程和燃烧质量，有利于提高发动机的功率和降低燃油消耗量，气缸盖的结构布局更为合理。

Four-valve valve mechanism is the most perfect and widely used type, which is currently used in many engines. Its structure is shown in Figure 2.3.7. The valve mechanism of four-valve engine is usually adopted a driving method with the structure of overhead double camshafts. Its main advantage is that the number of intake and exhaust valves increases, and the sectional area of intake and exhaust passages increases, and the efficiency of intake and exhaust are improved. Reducing the size of a single valve reduces the mass and meets the requirement of high-speed engines. The spark plug can be arranged in the center of the combustion chamber, which improves the combustion process and quality of the combustible mixture, and improves the engine power and reduces fuel consumption, and makes the cylinder head structure layout more reasonable.

四气门式发动机中，气门的排列方式有两种：一种是同名气门排成两列；另一种是同名气门排成一列，如图 2.3.8 所示。

In a four-valve engine, there are two kinds of valve arrangement: one is in two rows with the same name valves, and the other is in one row with the same name valves.

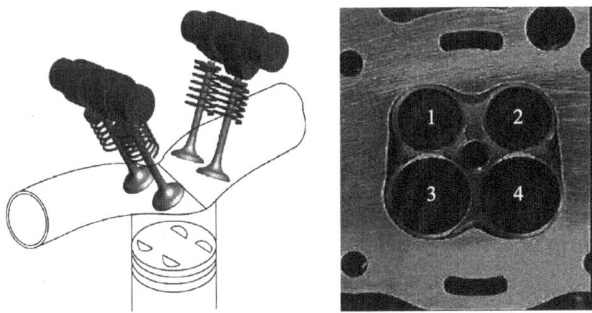

图 2.3.7　四气门配气机构
Figure 2.3.7　Four-valve valve mechanism

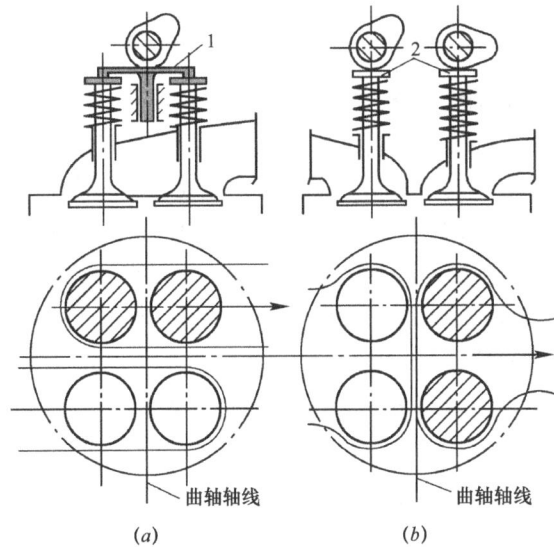

图 2.3.8　四气门的气门布置
Figure 2.3.8　Valve layout of four valves
(a) 同名气门排成两列 (Valves of the same name in two rows);
(b) 同名气门排成一列 (Valves of the same name in a row)
1—T形杆 (T rod); 2—气门尾端的从动盘 (driven plate at the end of the valve)

五气门式发动机配气机构．其每缸有三个进气门和两个排气门。如图 2.3.9 所示，气门数目的增加，使发动机的进、排气通道截面积增大，明显提高了发动机的充气效率，改善了发动机的性能。因此每缸采用五个气门，为满足高性能指标要求提供了机会，可以实现燃油消耗低、转矩大及排污少，比四气门发动机达到的性能指标更好。

The valve mechanism of a five-valve engine has three intake valves and two exhaust valves per cylinder, as shown in Figure 2.3.9. With the increase of the number of valves, the sectional area of the intake and exhaust passages of the engine is increased, and the charging efficiency of the engine is obviously improved, which improved the performance of the engine. Therefore, the utilization of five valves per cylinder provides an opportunity to meet the requirements of high performance, which can achieve low fuel consumption, high torque and less emission. It achieves better performance than a four-valve engine.

当每缸采用五气门时，气门排列的方案通常是同名气门排成一列，分别用进气凸轮轴和排气凸轮轴驱动。

When five valves are used in each cylinder, the layout of valves is usually in a row of valves with the same name, driven by intake camshaft and exhaust camshaft respectively.

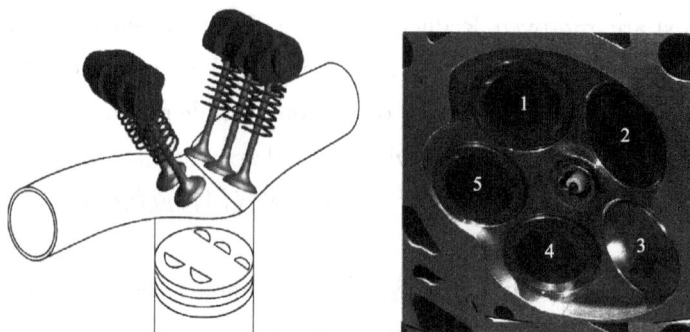

图 2.3.9　五气门配气机构

Figure 2.3.9　Five-valve valve mechanism

3.1.4　配气机构的传动（Transmission of valve mechanism）

曲轴通过齿轮副或链传动或齿形带传动来驱动凸轮轴，凸轮轴再带动摇臂或直接推动进、排气门。由于曲轴与凸轮轴之间驱动方式不同，配气机构的传动有齿轮驱动、链驱动和齿形带驱动三种。

The crankshaft drives the camshaft through gear pair or chain drive or toothed belt drive, and the camshaft drives the rocker arm or directly pushes the intake and exhaust valves. Because of the different driving modes between crankshaft and camshaft, there are three driving modes of valve mechanism: gear drive, chain drive and toothed belt drive.

1. 齿轮驱动形式（Gear drive form）

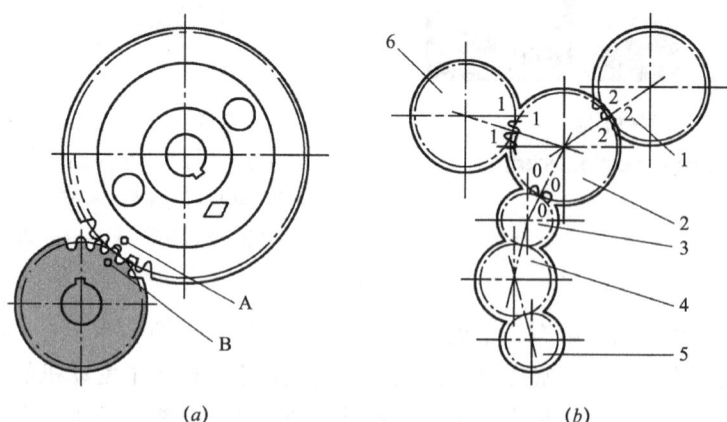

(a)　　　　　　　　　　　(b)

图 2.3.10　齿轮传动及正时记号

Figure 2.3.10　Gear drive and timing mark

（a）一对正时齿轮的传动（transmission of a pair of timing gears）；（b）加惰轮的齿轮传动（transmission of gears with idle gear）

1—喷油泵正时齿轮（fuel injection pump timing gear）；2、4—惰轮（idle gear）；3—曲轴正时齿轮（crankshaft timing gear）；

5—机油泵传动齿轮（oil pump transmission gear）；6—凸轮轴正时齿轮（camshaft timing gear）；

A—凸轮轴正时齿轮记号（camshaft timing gear mark）；B—曲轴正时齿轮记号（crankshaft timing gear mark）

2. 链驱动形式（Chain drive form）

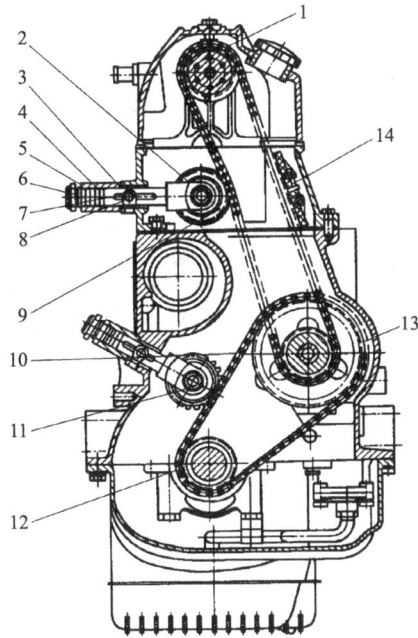

图 2.3.11 链驱动形式

Figure 2.3.11 Chain drive form

1—凸轮轴链轮（camshaft sprocket）；2—上链条张紧轮（upper chain tensioner）；3—张紧轮导向套筒（tensioner guide sleeve）；4—压紧弹簧（pressed spring）；5—锁紧螺母（lock nut）；6—张力调整螺钉（tensioning screw）；7—张紧轮导向销（tensioner guide pin）；8—导向销锁紧螺母（guide pin lock nut）；9—上链条（Upper Chain）；10—下链条（lower Chain）；11—下链条张紧轮（lower Chain Tensioner）；12—曲轴链轮（crankshaft sprocket）；13—中间链轮（intermediate sprocket）；14—导链板（Guide chain plate）

3. 齿形带驱动形式（Toothed belt drive form）

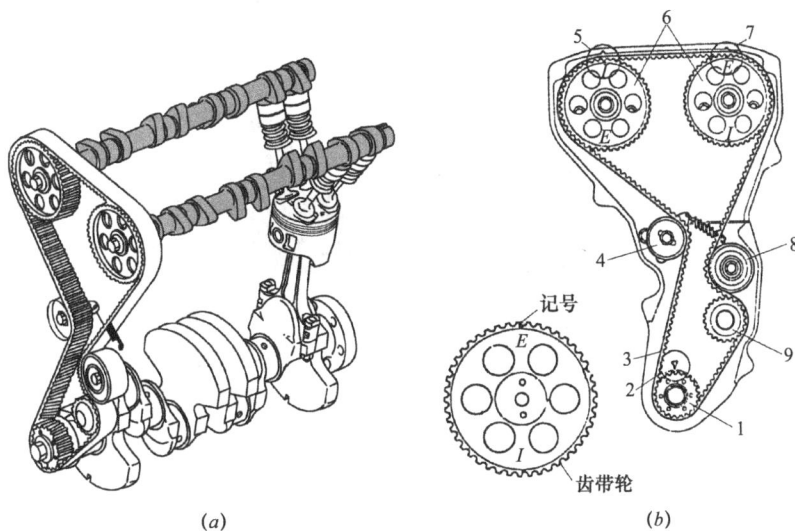

图 2.3.12 双顶置凸轮轴的传动布置图（一）

Figure 2.3.12 Transmission layout of double overhead camshafts（1）

（a）空间布置图（Space layout plan）；（b）平面布置图（Plane layout plan）

1—曲轴正时齿带轮（crankshaft timing toothed pulley）；2—正时对正记号（timing alignment mark）；3—齿形带（Toothed Belt）；4—张紧轮（Tensioner）；5—进气凸轮正时记号（Intake Cam Timing Mark）；6—凸轮轴正时齿形带轮（Camshaft Timing Toothed pulley）；7—排气侧正时记号（Exhaust Side Timing Mark）；8—导向轮（Guide Wheel）；9—水泵齿形带轮（Pump Toothed pulley）

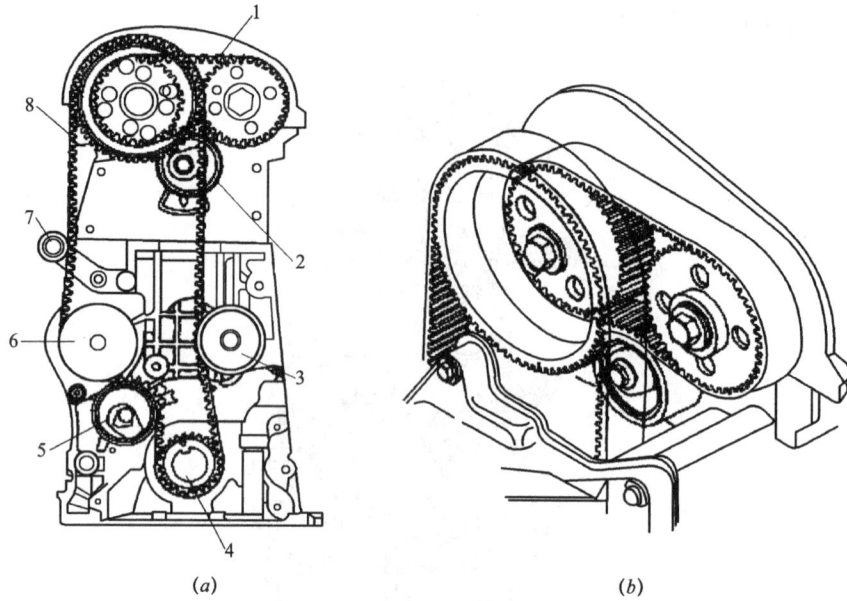

图 2.3.13 双顶置凸轮轴的传动布置图（二）

Figure 2.3.13 Transmission layout of double overhead camshafts (2)

1—连接齿形带（Connecting toothed belt）；2—连接齿形带张紧轮（Connecting tooth belt tensioner）；3—导向轮（guide wheel）；4—曲轴正时齿形带轮（crankshaft timing gear pulley）；5—主齿形带张紧轮（main teeth belt tensioner）；6—水泵齿形带轮（pump teeth belt pulley）；7—导向轮（guide wheel）；8—主齿形带（main toothed belt）

3.1.5 气门间隙（Valve clearance）

通常在发动机冷态装配时，在气门与其传动机构中，留有适当的间隙，以补偿气门受热后的膨胀量，这一间隙通常称为气门间隙。如图 2.3.14 所示。

Generally, when the engine is assembled in cold state, there is an appropriate clearance between the valve and its transmission mechanism to compensate for the expansion of the valve after heating. This clearance is usually called the valve clearance. As shown in Figure 2.3.14.

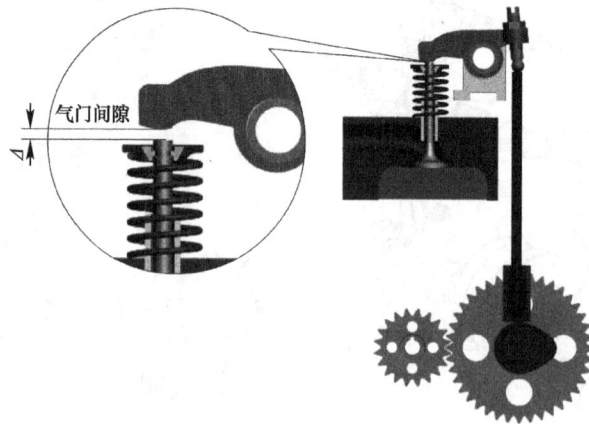

图 2.3.14 气门间隙

Figure 2.3.14 Valve clearance

3.2 气门传动组（Valve transmission group）

气门传动组的主要机件有凸轮轴及其驱动装置，包括挺柱、推杆、摇臂及摇臂轴等。

The main parts of the valve transmission group are camshaft and its driving device, including tappet, push rod, rocker arm and rocker arm shaft, etc.

3.2.1 凸轮轴 (Camshaft)

1. 凸轮轴的作用与材料 (Function and material of camshaft)

凸轮轴是气门传动组中最主要的零件,用来驱动和控制各缸气门的开启和关闭,使其符合发动机的工作顺序、配气相位及气门开度的变化规律等要求。为了满足工作条件的要求,凸轮轴多用优质碳钢或合金钢锻制,也可采用合金铸铁和球墨铸铁铸造。凸轮轴上的轴颈和凸轮工作表面经表面高频淬火(中碳钢)或渗碳淬火(低碳钢)处理后精磨,以改善其耐磨性。

Camshaft is the most important part of the valve transmission group, which is used to drive and control the opening and closing of the valves of each cylinder, so that it meets the requirements of engine work sequence, valve timing and change rule of valve open degree, etc. In order to meet the requirements of working conditions, camshafts are forged with high-quality carbon steel or alloy steel. Alloy cast iron and nodular cast iron can also be used for casting. Precision grinding is used for the journal and working surface of camshaft after surface high frequency quenching (medium carbon steel) or carburizing and quenching (low carbon steel) to improve its wear resistance.

2. 凸轮轴的构造 (Camshaft structure)

凸轮轴主要由凸轮和凸轮轴轴颈等组成,如图 2.3.15 所示。单凸轮轴一般将进、排气凸轮布置在同一根凸轮轴上。四缸发动机凸轮轴同名(同为进气凸轮或同为排气凸轮)凸轮间夹角为 90°,如图 2.3.15 (a) 所示。六缸发动机凸轮轴同名凸轮间夹角为 60°,如图 2.3.15 (b) 所示。双凸轮轴结构中,一根是进气凸轮轴,上面布有各缸的进气凸轮,另一根是排气凸轮轴,上面布有各缸的排气凸轮。

The camshaft is mainly composed of cam and camshaft journal, as shown in Figure 2.3.15. For the single camshaft, intake and exhaust cams are generally arranges on the same camshaft. The angle between cams with the same name (same as intake cam or same as exhaust cam) of four-cylinder engine camshaft is 90 degrees, as shown in Fig. 2.3.15a. The angle between cams with the same name of six-cylinder engine camshafts is 60 degrees, as shown in Fig. 2.3.15b. In the double camshaft structure, one is the intake camshaft, which has the intake cams of each cylinder, and the other is the exhaust camshaft, which has the exhaust cams of each cylinder.

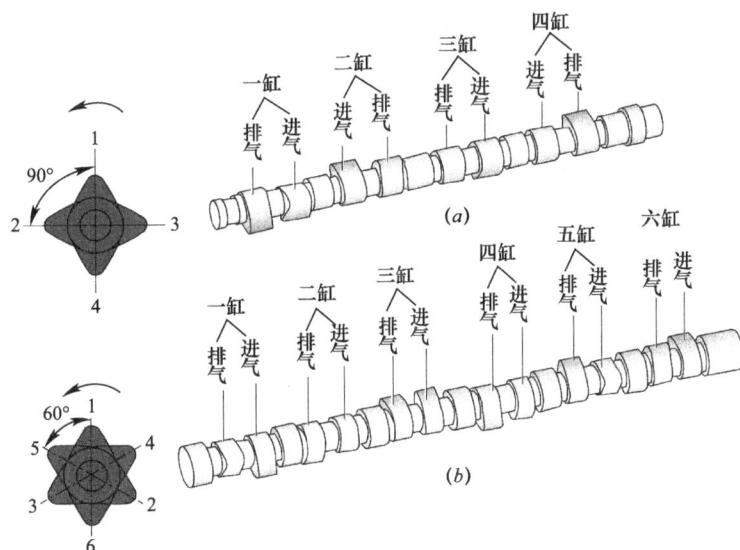

图 2.3.15 凸轮轴结构

Figure 2.3.15 Camshaft Structure

(a) 四缸发动机凸轮轴 (four-cylinder engine camshaft);(b) 六缸发动机凸轮轴 (six-cylinder engine camshaft)

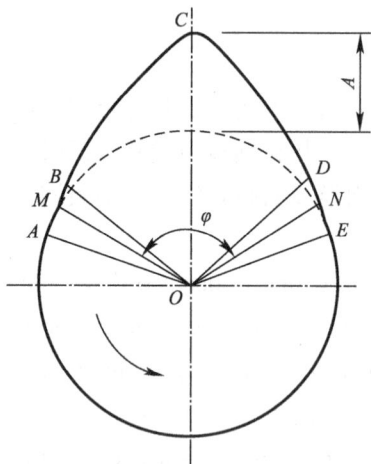

图 2.3.16 凸轮轮廓示意图

Figure 2.3.16 The Diagram of Cam contour

（1）凸轮：凸轮的轮廓应保证气门开启和关闭的持续时间符合配气相位要求，且有合适的升程及其升降过程的运动规律。凸轮的轮廓形状如图 2.3.16 所示，O 为凸轮轴的轴心，圆弧 EA 为凸轮的基圆，圆弧 AB 和 DE 为凸轮的缓冲段，缓冲段中凸轮的升程（升程即轮廓型线上某点较基圆半径凸出的量）变化速度较慢，圆弧 BCD 为凸轮的工作段，此段升程较快，C 点时升程最大（图中 A 值），它决定了气门的最大开度，不同机型凸轮的升程变化规律不同。

（1）Cam：The cam contour should ensure that the duration of valve opening and closing conforms to the requirements of valve timing, and that there is a suitable lift and the law of movement of its lifting and descending process. The cam contour is shown in Figure 2.3.16, O is the axle center of the camshaft, arc EA is the base circle of the cam. Arc AB and DE arcs are the buffer segments of the cam, and the change speed of the cam lift (lift is the amount of protrusion of a point on the contour from the radius of the base circle.) in the buffer segment is slower. The arc BCD is the working segment of the cam, which has the fastest lift and the maximum lift at point C (value A in the figure). It determines the maximum opening of the valve. The change rule of the lift of different cams is different.

（2）凸轮轴轴颈：由于凸轮轴是通过凸轮轴轴颈支撑在凸轮轴轴承孔内的，因此凸轮轴轴颈数目的多少是影响凸轮轴支撑刚度的重要因素。下置式凸轮轴每隔 1～2 个气缸设置一个凸轮轴轴颈。上置式凸轮轴基本上是每隔一个气缸设置一个凸轮轴轴颈。

（2）Camshaft journal：Since the camshaft is supported in the bearing hole of the camshaft through the camshaft journals, the number of camshaft journal is an important factor affecting the support stiffness of the camshaft. The underneath camshaft is provided with a camshaft journal every 1 to 2 cylinders, while the overhead camshaft is basically provided with a camshaft journal every other cylinder.

（3）凸轮轴轴承：凸轮轴轴承一般做成衬套压入整体式的座孔内，最后再加工，与轴颈配合。其材料多与曲轴轴承相同，由低碳钢钢背内浇减摩合金制成，也有的用粉末冶金衬套或铜套。

（3）Camshaft bearings：Camshaft bearings are generally pressed into integral seat holes with the bearing insert. Finally, they are machined and matched with the journal. Most of the materials are the same as crankshaft bearings. They are made of low-carbon steel backing by inner casting anti-friction alloys, and some are made of powder metallurgical inserts or copper inserts.

（4）凸轮轴的轴向限位：为了配气机构的正常工作，防止凸轮轴的轴向窜动，凸轮轴必须有轴向定位装置，凸轮轴的位置不同，其限位方法也不一样。上置式凸轮轴利用凸轮轴轴承盖两侧面代替止推凸缘实现轴向定位。

（4）Axial limited location of Camshaft：In order to work properly and prevent the camshaft from axial movement, the camshaft must have an axial positioning device. The location of camshaft is different, and limited location method is also different. The overhead camshaft uses the two sides of the camshaft bearings' covers to replace the thrust flanges to realize the axial positioning.

3.2.2 挺柱（Tappet）

挺柱的作用是将凸轮工作时产生的推力传给推杆或气门，并承受凸轮轴旋转时所产生的侧向力。一般安装在气缸体或气缸盖镗出的导向孔中，挺柱常用的有普通挺柱和液力挺柱两种。

The function of tappet is to transfer the thrust generated by cam operation to push rod or valve, and to bear the side force generated by camshaft rotation. Tappet is generally installed in the cylinder block or the bored guide hole of the cylinder head. There are two kinds of tappet commonly used: ordinary tappet and hydraulic tappet.

1. 普通挺柱 (Ordinary tappet)

普通挺柱常见的形式有筒形和滚轮式两种（图 2.3.17）。筒形挺柱的下部钻有通孔，便于筒内收集的润滑油流出以对挺柱底面和凸轮加强润滑。底面为凹球形，与推杆下方的凸球形配合。滚轮式挺柱由于滚轮的转动，传力灵活，使滚轮与凸轮间的摩擦阻力小，多用于柴油机中。

For the ordinary tappet, cylindrical and roller types are commonly used, as shown in Fig. 2.3.17. The lower part of the cylindrical tappet is drilled with through holes to facilitate the flow of lubricating oil collected in the cylindrical tappet to enhance the lubrication of the bottom surface of the tappet and the cam. Its bottom surface is a concave sphere, which matches with the convex sphere under the push rod. Because of the rotation of the roller, the transmission of force is flexible, which makes the friction resistance between the roller and the cam small. It is mostly used in diesel engines.

2. 液力挺柱 (Hydraulic tappet)

（1）液力挺柱的组成：液力挺柱由柱塞 2、柱塞套 5、止回阀 3、托架 6、弹簧 4 和挺柱体 1 等零件组成，如图 2.3.18 所示。

Composition of hydraulic tappet: Hydraulic tappet consists of plunger 2, plunger sleeve 5, check valve 3, bracket 6, spring 4 and tappet body 1, as shown in Figure 2.3.18.

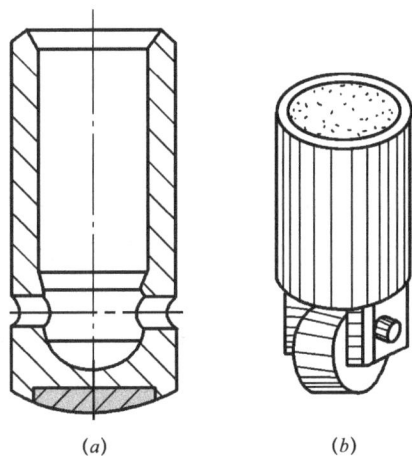

图 2.3.17　挺柱

Figure 2.3.17　Tappet

(a) 筒式 (cylindrical type);

(b) 滚轮式 (roller type)

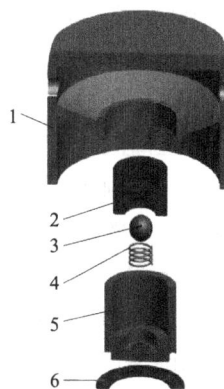

图 2.3.18　液力挺柱的组成

Figure 2.3.18　Composition of hydraulic tappet

1—挺柱体 (tappet body); 2—柱塞 (plunger); 3—止回阀 (check valve);

4—弹簧 (spring); 5—柱塞套 (plunger sleeve); 6—托架 (bracket)

挺柱体的外圆柱面上有一环形油槽，油槽内有一进油孔与低压油腔相通，顶部内侧加工有键形油槽。柱塞套外圆与挺柱体内导向孔配合，内孔则与柱塞配合，两者都有相对运动。柱塞的底部装有一复位弹簧，把止回阀压靠在柱塞的阀座上，止回阀将油缸上部和下部分隔为两个油腔，当止回阀关闭时，上部为低压油腔，下部为高压油腔。当止回阀开启时，则成为一个通腔。复位弹簧还可以使挺柱的顶面和凸轮保持紧密接触，以消除气门间隙。柱塞、柱塞套、止回阀和弹簧装配到一起便构成气门间隙的补偿偶件，液力挺柱装在气缸盖的挺柱孔内，挺柱顶面与凸轮接触，柱塞套底面则与气门杆尾端接触。

There is an annular oil groove on the outer cylindrical surface of the tappet, where an oil inlet hole communicates with the low pressure oil cavity, and a key-shaped oil groove is machined on the inside of the top. The outer circle of the plunger sleeve matches with the guide hole in the tappet body, while the inner hole matches with the plunger, both of which have relative motion. A reset spring is installed at the bottom of the plunger to press the check valve against the valve seat of the plunger. The check valve divides the upper and lower parts of the cylinder into two oil cavities. When the check valve closes, the upper part is a low pressure oil cavity and the lower part is a high pressure oil cavity. When the check valve opens, it becomes a connected cavity. The reset spring can also keep the top of the tappet in close contact with the cam to eliminate valve clearance. Plunger, plunger sleeve, check valve and spring are assembled together to form a compensating coupled parts for valve clearance. The hydraulic tappet is installed in the tappet hole of the cylinder head, the top surface of the tappet contacts the cam, and the bottom surface of the plunger sleeve contacts the end of the valve rod.

（2）液力挺柱工作原理（Working principle of hydraulic tappet）

当凸轮基圆与挺柱接触时，弹簧使挺柱顶面和凸轮保持紧密接触，油缸下端面与气门杆尾部紧密接触，因此没有气门间隙。当挺柱体外圆的环形油槽与缸盖上的斜油孔对齐，来自气缸盖的润滑油从缸盖进油口流入挺柱体内的低压油腔，然后经键形槽进入柱塞上方的低压油腔。这时缸盖主油道与液力挺柱的低压油腔相通。

When the cam base circle contacts the tappet, the spring keeps the top of the tappet in close contact with the cam, and the lower end of the cylinder is in close contact with the end of the valve rod, so there is no valve clearance. When the annular oil groove on the outer circle of the tappet body is aligned with the oblique oil hole on the cylinder head, the lubricating oil from the cylinder head enters the low-pressure oil cavity inside the tappet body from the cylinder head inlet, and then enters the low-pressure oil cavity above the plunger through the key-shaped groove. At this time, the main oil gallery of the cylinder head is connected with the low-pressure oil cavity of the hydraulic tappet.

当凸轮转过基圆凸起与挺柱接触时，凸轮推动挺柱体和柱塞向下移动，高压油腔内润滑油被压缩，油压升高，加之弹簧的作用，使止回阀紧压在柱塞下端的阀座上，这时高压油腔与低压油腔被分开，由于液体的不可压缩性，整个挺柱成为一个刚体，下移并推开气门，气门开启，如图 2.3.19（a）所示。此时，挺柱外圆的环形油槽已离开了气缸盖上的进油位置，从而停止进油。

When the cam rotates the base circle and contacts the tappet, the cam pushes the tappet and plunger downward. The lubricating oil in the high pressure oil cavity is compressed, and the oil pressure is increased. In addition to the effect of the spring, the check valve is pressed tightly on the valve seat at the lower end of the plunger. At this time, the high-pressure oil cavity and the low-pressure oil cavity are separated. Because of the incompressibility of the liquid, the whole tappet becomes a rigid body, which moves down and pushes the valve open, as shown in Figure 2.3.19a. At this time, the annular oil groove of the outer circle of the tappet has left the oil-in position on the cylinder head, thus stopping the oil feeding.

当凸轮重新转到基圆与挺柱接触位置，挺柱体不再受凸轮的推压作用，高压油腔内的压力油和柱塞复位弹簧一起推动柱塞向上运动，使高压油腔内的压力下降，止回阀离开阀座而打开，从低压油腔来的压力油进入高压油腔，使两腔相通并充满油液，保证液力挺柱的顶面仍然和凸轮的基圆接触，从而达到补偿气门间隙的作用，如图 2.3.19（b）所示。

When the cam rotates to the contact position between the base circle and the tappet, the tappet is no longer pushed by the cam. The pressure oil in the high-pressure oil cavity together with the plunger reset spring pushes the plunger upward, which reduces the pressure in the high-pressure oil cavity. The check valve leaves the seat and opens. The pressure oil coming from the low-pressure oil cavity enters the high-pressure oil cavity. The two chambers are connected and filled with oil. The top surface of the hydraulic tappet is still in contact with the base circle of the cam, thus compensating the valve clearance, as shown in Figure 2.3.19b.

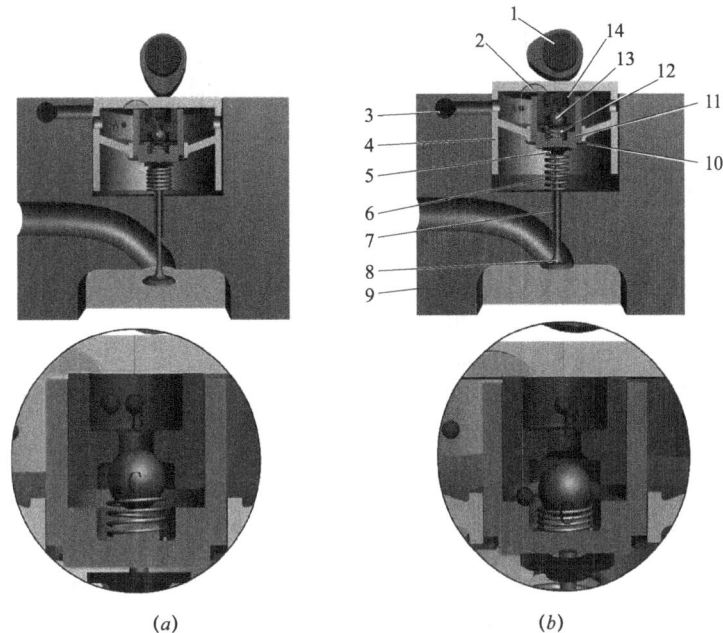

图 2.3.19　液力挺柱工作原理

Figure 2.3.19　Working Principle of Hydraulic Tappet

(a) 气门打开 (Valve-opening)；(b) 气门关闭 (Valve-closing)

1—凸轮轴 (camshaft)；2—键形槽 (key-shaped groove)；3—气缸盖油道 (cylinder head oil gallery)；4—挺柱体 (tappet body)；5—气门弹簧座 (Valve spring seat)；6—气门弹簧 (valve spring)；7—气门导管 (valve guide)；8—气门 (valve)；9—气缸盖 (cylinder head)；10—托架 (bracket)；11—柱塞套 (plunger sleeve)；12—复位弹簧 (reset spring)；13—止回阀 (check valve)；14—柱塞 (plunger)

3.2.3　推杆 (Push rod)

推杆（图2.3.20）的作用是将从凸轮轴经过挺柱传来的推力传给摇臂，它是配气机构中最易弯曲的零件，要求有很高的刚度，在动载荷大的发动机中，推杆应尽量地做得短些。

The function of the push rod is to transfer the thrust from the camshaft through the tappet to the rocker arm. It is the most easily bent part of the valve mechanism, requiring high stiffness. In the engine with large dynamic load, the push rod should be made as short as possible.

对于缸体与缸盖都是铝合金制造的发动机，其推杆最好用硬铝制造。推杆的两端焊接成压配有不同形状的端头，下端头通常是圆球形，以使与挺柱的凹球形支座相适应。上端头一般制成凹球形，以便与摇臂上的气门间隙调整螺钉的球形头部相适应。推杆可以是实心或空心的。

For the engine whose cylinder block and cylinder head are both made of aluminum alloy, the push rod is best made of hard aluminum. The two ends of the push rod are welded and pressed with different shapes, and the lower end is usually spherical to fit the concave spherical support of the tappet. The upper end is usually made into concave spherical head to fit the spherical head of the valve clearance adjustment screw on the rocker arm. Push rods can be solid or hollow.

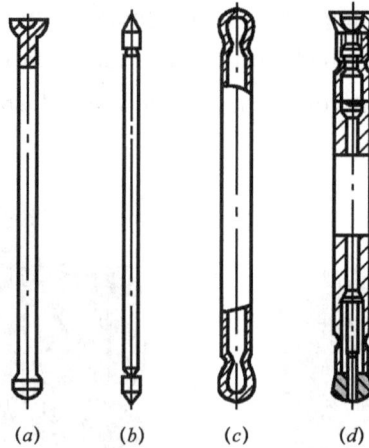

图 2.3.20　推杆

Figure 2.3.20　Push rod

（*a*）钢制实心推杆（solid steel push rod）；（*b*）硬铝棒推杆（hard aluminum push rod）；

（*c*、*d*）钢管制成的推杆（steel pipe push rod）

3.2.4　摇臂（Rocker arm）

摇臂（图 2.3.21）的作用是改变推杆的传力方向，使凸轮产生的推力作用到气门上，使气门下移。

The function of rocker arm is to change the direction of force transmission of push rod, so that the thrust produced by cam acts on the valve and makes the valve move down.

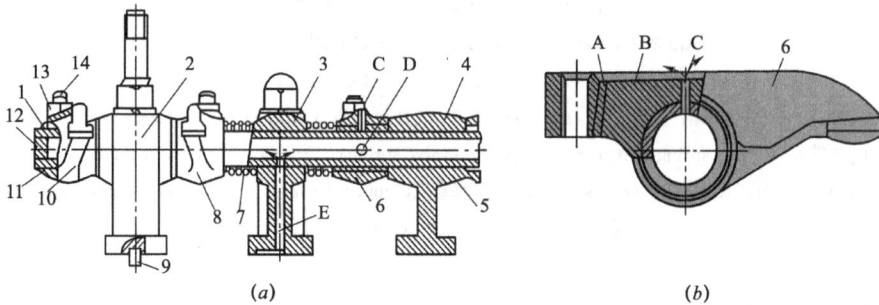

图 2.3.21　摇臂及摇臂组结构示意图

Figure 2.3.21　The diagram of rocker arm and rocker arm group

1—垫圈（gasket）；2、3、4—摇臂轴支座（Rocker shaft support）；5—摇臂轴（rocker shaft）；6、8、10—摇臂（rocker arm）；7—定位弹簧（positioning spring）；9—定位销（locating pin）；11—锁簧（locking spring）；12—堵头（plug）；13—锁紧螺母（lock nut）；14—调节螺钉（adjusting screw）；A、C、D、E—油孔（oil hole）；B—油槽（oil groove）

3.3　气门传动组（Valve transmission group）

如图 2.3.22 所示，气门组的主要机件有气门、气门弹簧、弹簧座、气门座圈、气门导管及锁片等。

As shown in Figure 2.3.22, the main components of the valve group are valves, valve springs, spring seats, valve retainer, valve guide and locking plates, etc.

3.3.1　气门（Valve）

气门由头部 2 和杆部 1 组成（图 2.3.23）。头部用来封闭气缸的进、排气通道；杆部则主要为气门的运动导向。

The valve consists of the head 2 and the stem 1 (Figure 2.3.23). The head is used to seal the inlet and exhaust passages of the cylinder. The rod mainly guides the motion of the valve.

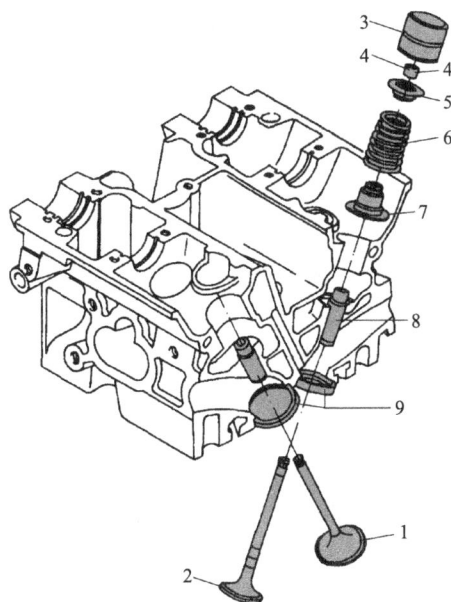

图 2.3.22　气门组结构示意图

Figure 2.3.22　Structural diagram of valve group

1—进气门（inlet valve）；2—排气门（exhaust valve）；3—液力挺柱（hydraulic tappet）；4—气门锁片（valve locking plate）；

5—气门弹簧座（valve spring seat）；6—气门弹簧（valve spring）；7—气门弹簧垫（valve spring cushion）；

8—气门导管（valve guide）；9—进、排气门座圈（intake and exhaust valve retainer）

1. 气门的工作条件与材料（Working conditions and materials of valves）

气门的头部直接与气缸内燃烧的高温气体接触，热负荷大，而散热很困难，因而工作温度较高。气门头部承受落座时受到惯性冲击力，接触气缸内燃烧生成物中的腐蚀介质，润滑困难，因此要求气门必须具有足够的强度、刚度、耐热和耐磨能力。进气门通常用中碳合金钢，如铬钢、镍铬钢、铬钼钢等。

The head of the valve is directly in contact with the burning high temperature gas in the cylinder. The heat load is large and the heat radiation is difficult, so the working temperature is high. The valve head is subjected to inertial impact when it is seated, and it contacts the corro-sive medium in the combustion products in the cylinder. And it is difficult to lubricate. Therefore, the valve must have sufficient strength, stiffness, heat resistance and wear resistance. Inlet valves are usually made of medium carbon alloy steel, such as chromium steel, nickel-chromium steel, chromium-molybdenum steel, etc.

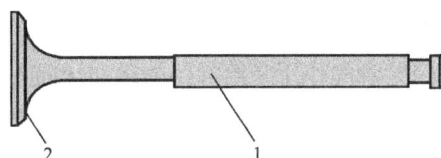

图 2.3.23　气门

Figure 2.3.23　Valves

1—杆部（stem）；2—头部（head）

2. 气门的一般构造（General structure of valves）

气门头部的形状有凸顶、平顶和凹顶，如图 2.3.24 所示。气门头部与气门座接触的工作面，是与杆部同心的锥面，通常将这一锥面与气门顶平面的夹角称为气门锥角（图 2.3.25）。常用的气门锥角为30°和45°。

The shape of the valve head is convex, flat and concave, as shown in Fig. 2.3.24. The working face of the valve head in contact with the valve seat is concentric conical surface with the stem. The angle between the conical surface and the top plane of the valve is usually called the cone angle of the valve (Fig. 2.3.25). The commonly used cone angles of valves are 30 degrees and 45 degrees.

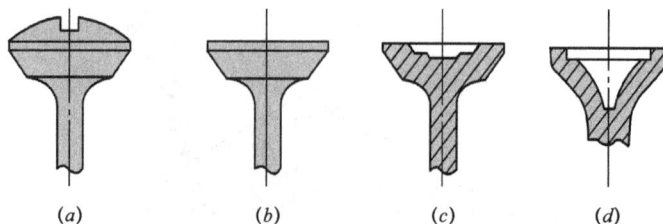

图 2.3.24　气门的顶部形状

Figure 2.3.24　Top shapes of valves

(a) 凸顶 (convex top)；(b) 平顶 (flat top)；(c) 凹顶 (concave top)；(d) 漏斗顶 (funnel top)

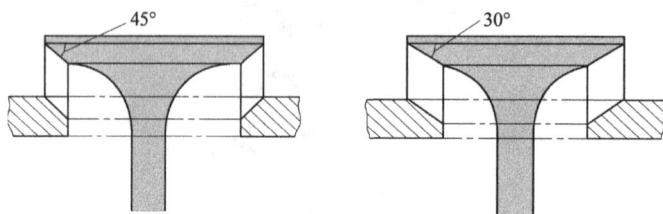

图 2.3.25　气门锥角

Figure 2.3.25　Valve cone angle

3. 气门的杆部 (The stem of the valve)

气门杆部有较高的加工精度和较小的表面粗糙度值，与气门导管保持较小的配合间隙，以减小磨损，并起到良好的导向和散热作用。

The valve stem has higher machining accuracy and smaller surface roughness, and keeps smaller fit clearance with valve guide to reduce wear and play good roles in guiding and heat radiating.

3.3.2　气门导管 (Valve guide)

气门导管的作用是给气门的运动导向，并为气门杆传热。气门导管通常单独制成零件，再压入缸盖（或缸体）的孔中。由于润滑较困难，导管一般用含石墨较多的铸铁或粉末冶金制成，以提高自润滑性能。气门导管的外形如图 2.3.26 所示。

The function of the valve guide is to guide the motion of the valve and to conduct heat for the valve stem. Valve guide is usually made separately and then pressed into holes in the cylinder head (or the cylinder). Because of the difficulty of lubrication, the guides are usually made of cast iron or powder metallurgy containing more graphite to improve self-lubrication performance. The shape of the valve guide is shown in Fig. 2.3.26.

3.3.3　气门座 (Valve seat)

气缸盖的进、排气道与气门锥面相结合的部位称为气门座。气门座的锥角是与气门锥角相适应的，以保证两者紧密贴合，可靠地密封。大多数发动机的气门座是用耐热合金钢或合金铸铁单独制成座圈，然后压入气缸盖中，以提高使用寿命和便于修理更换，如图 2.3.26 所示。

The position where the intake and exhaust passages of the cylinder head are combined with the conical surface of the valve is called the valve seat. The cone angle of the valve seat is compatible with the cone angle of the valve. Most engine valve seats are made of heat-resistant alloy steel or alloy cast iron separately and then pressed into the cylinder head to improve service life and facilitate repair and replacement, as shown in Figure 2.3.26.

3.3.4　气门弹簧 (Valve spring)

气门弹簧的作用是使气门自动回位关闭，并保证气门与气门座的座合压力。另外，还用于吸收气门在开启和关闭过程中各种传动零件所产生的惯性力，以防止各种传动件彼此分离而破坏配气机构正常工作。气门弹簧是圆柱形螺旋弹簧（图 2.3.27），其一端支撑在气缸盖上，而另一端则压靠在气门杆端的弹簧座上，弹簧座用锁片固定在气门杆的末端。

The function of the valve spring is to make the valve return automatically and close, and to ensure the seating force between the valve and the valve seat. In addition, it is also used to absorb the inertia force produced by various transmission parts during the opening and closing process of the valve, so as to prevent various transmission parts from separating from each other and destroying the normal operation of the valve mechanism. Valve spring is a cylindrical helical spring (Figure 2.3.27), one end of which is supported on the cylinder head, while the other end is pressed on the spring seat at the end of the valve stem, which is fixed at the end of the valve stem with locking plates.

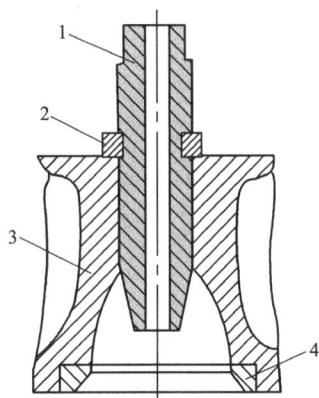

图 2.3.26　气门导管和气门座

Figure 2.3.26　Valve guide and seat

1—气门导管（valve guide）；2—卡环（snap ring）；

3—气缸盖（cylinder head）；4—气门座（valve seat）

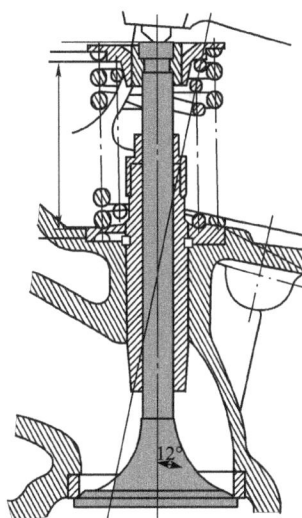

图 2.3.27　双气门弹簧

Figure 2.3.27　Double valve springs

思考与练习

（Reflection and Exercises）

1. 试述配气凸轮各段型线的基本用途。

2. 什么是发动机的充气系数与充填效率？影响发动机充气系数的因素有哪些？如何增大发动机充气系数？

3. 为什么发动机的转矩特性取决于发动机的充气系数特性？

4. 多缸发动机是如何消除进、排气干扰的？

1. Describe the basic use of each section profile of valve cam.

2. What are the charging coefficient and filling efficiency of the engine? What are the factors that affect the charging coefficient of the engine? How to increase the charging coefficient of the engine?

3. Why does the engine's torque characteristic depend on the engine's charging coefficient characteristic?

4. How do multi-cylinder engines eliminate the interference of intake and exhaust?

任务四　汽油机燃料供给系统

Task 4　Fuel Supply System of Gasoline Engines

教学目标

1. 知识目标

（1）了解发动机进气系统；

（2）了解发动机增压技术；

（3）知道汽油的性能及汽油机对混合气的要求；

（4）知道现有汽油机燃油供给系统的结构和原理。

2. 能力目标

（1）具有区分发动机涡轮增压技术和自然吸气发动机的能力；

（2）具有分析电控燃油喷射系统的结构和工作原理的能力；

（3）具有区分各种燃油供给系统的优缺点的能力。

3. 情感和素养目标

（1）培养学生服务意识、质量意识、安全意识；

（2）培养学生一丝不苟的工匠精神。

Teaching objectives

1. Knowledge objectives

（1）Understanding the engine intake system；

（2）Understanding engine turbocharging technology；

（3）Knowing the performance of gasoline and the requirements of gasoline engine for mixture；

（4）Knowing the structure and principle of the fuel supply system of the existing gasoline engines.

2. Ability objectives

（1）The ability to distinguish turbocharging technology engines from natural aspiration engines；

（2）The ability to analyze the structure and working principle of electronic fuel injection system；

（3）The ability to distinguish the advantages and disadvantages of various fuel supply systems.

3. Emotion and quality goals

（1）Cultivate students' service awareness, quality awareness and safety awareness；

（2）Cultivate students' craftsmanship spirit of being meticulous.

4.1　概述（Outline）

4.1.1　汽油及汽油机供油系统（Gasoline and fuel supply system of gasoline engine）

1. 汽油及其使用性能（Gasoline and its Performance）

（1）汽油的组成（Composition of gasoline）

由石油提炼得到的，由多种碳氢化物（如烷烃 C_nH_{2n+2}、环烷烃 C_nH_{2n}、芳香烃 C_nH_{2n-6} 等）混合构成的（含85％的碳和15％的氢），密度较小且易挥发的液态燃料，根据提炼方法的不同可分为直馏型和裂化型两类。

Gasoline can be obtained from petroleum refining, which are liquid fuels of the mixture（85％ carbon and 15％ hydrogen）of various hydrocarbons（such as alkanes C_nH_{2n+2}, cyclane C_nH_{2n}, aromatics C_nH_{2n-6}, etc.）with lower density and volatility. According to different ways of refining, it can be classified into two types：straight-run and cracking.

（2）汽油的使用性能（Performance of gasoline）

1）蒸发性：测定汽油蒸发量 10％、50％、90％时的温度。

2）热值：汽油的热值约为 44000kJ/kg。

3）抗爆性：汽油在压缩过程中避免爆燃的能力。

使用以裂化汽油为主的无铅汽油，且要求汽油机的实际压缩比一般不超过 10。

1）Evaporation：Measure the temperatures with 10％，50％ and 90％ of gasoline evaporation.

2）Calorific value：The calorific value of gasoline is about 44000kJ/kg.

3）Antiknock quality：The ability of gasoline to avoid detonation during compression.

The cracked and unleaded gasoline is mainly used, and the actual compression ratio of gasoline engines is generally no more than 10.

2. 汽油机供油系统（Fuel supply system of gasoline engines）

根据发动机工况需要为发动机配制一定数量与浓度的可燃混合气，并排出废气。电喷发动机供油系统的结构组成如图 2.4.1 所示。

According to the engine working conditions, a certain amount and concentration of combustible mixture is prepared for the engine, and burned gas is discharged. The structure of fuel supply system of EFI engine.

4.1.2　汽油机燃油喷射系统（Fuel injection system of gasoline engine）

1. 喷射系统概述（Overview of injection system）

汽油喷射系统借用喷油器将汽油强制喷入发动机的进气管内（缸外喷射）或汽油机的缸内（缸内喷射），从而与吸进的空气混合成可燃混合气。

The gasoline injection system uses the injector to force the gasoline into the intake ducting (out-of-cylinder injection) of the engine or the cylinder (in-cylinder injection), thus mixing it with the intake air to form a combustible mixture.

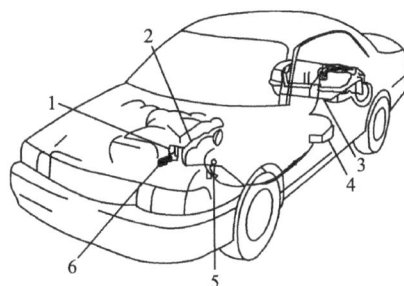

图 2.4.1　汽车的供油系统

Figure 2.4.1　Fuel supply system for automobiles

1—电磁喷油器（electromagnetic injector）；2—进气管（intake ducting）；3—燃油箱及汽油泵（fuel tank and gasoline pump）；4—燃油滤清器（fuel filter）；5—空气滤清器（air filter）；6—油压调节器（oil pressure regulator）

（1）采用喷油器代替化油器（Replacing carburetor with injector）

提高了发动机的充气效率与动力输出（功率与转矩提高 5％～10％），而且也提高了燃油的供油精度，降低了发动机油耗（节油 5％～15％）与排污（减少有毒排放 20％）。

It improves the engine's charging efficiency and power output (power and torque increase by 5％-10％) and also improves the fuel supply accuracy, reduces engine fuel consumption (fuel saving by 5％-15％) and emission (toxic emission reduction by 20％).

（2）采用电控单元控制（Control by electronic control unit）

使混合气浓度和点火提前角都达到最佳的控制状态，不仅改善发动机工况的动态过渡控制（将使汽车加减速更加灵敏），而且还可实现发动机的可变动力控制（如可变压缩比、可变配气相位、可变进气量、可变进气增压、可变进气涡流、可变排量等）以及节能净化控制。

It can make the mixture concentration and spark advance angle reach the optimum control state, and improve the dynamic transition control of engine working conditions (which will make the acceleration and deceleration more sensitive), and realize the variable power control of the engine (such as variable compression ratio, variable valve timing, variable intake volume, variable intake supercharging, variable intake swirl, variable displacement, etc.) as well as energy-saving and purification control.

（3）采用电控燃油喷射系统（Adoption of electronic fuel injection system）

简化供油系统的机械结构，方便汽油机布置，有利于现代汽车发动机的标准化、通用化和系列化。

It simplifies the mechanical structure of the fuel supply system, facilitating the layout of gasoline engines. And it is conducive to the standardization, generalization and serialization of modern automobile engines.

2. 电控汽油喷射系统的结构组成（Structure composition of electronic gasoline injection system）

以空气流量计的形式分类（Classified by the form of air flow meters）：

采用感知板式空气流量计（容积计量）的 K-Jetronic、KE-Jetronic 机械式或机电混合式燃油喷射系统；采用进气管压力计（压力计量）的 D-Jetronic 电控汽油喷油系统；采用翼片式空气流量计（容积计量）或卡门涡式空气流量计（流速计量）的 L-Jetronic 采用热线式或热膜式空气流量计（质量计量）的 Motronic 电控汽油喷油系统等。

K-Jetronic and KE-Jetronic, a mechanical or electromechanical hybrid fuel injection system, which adopts a sensing plate air flow meter (volume metering); D-Jetronic, a electronic gasoline injection system with a intake pressure meter (pressure measurement); L-Jetronic, using a blade air flow meter (volume metering) or Carmen vortex air flow meter (flow velocity metering); Motronic, a electronic control gasoline injection system using hot wire or hot film air flow meter (mass metering), etc.

汽油机电控汽油喷射系统（Electronic gasoline injection system of gasoline engine）：

按喷油器的喷射位置，可分为缸外低压喷射与缸内高压喷射两类（图 2.4.2）。缸外低压喷射是指用喷油器将≤0.4MPa 的低压燃油喷入气缸外的进气管或进气歧管内；缸内高压喷射则是指用喷油器直接将≥3MPa 高压燃喷入气缸内。

According to the injection position of the fuel injector, it can be divided into two categories: the low pressure injection outside the cylinder and the high pressure injection inside the cylinder. The low pressure injection outside the cylinder refers to the injection of low pressure fuel less than or equal to 0.4 MPa into the intake ducting or intake manifold outside the cylinder with an fuel injector, while in-cylinder high pressure injection refers to the injection of high pressure fuel (≥3 MPa) directly into the cylinder with an fuel injector.

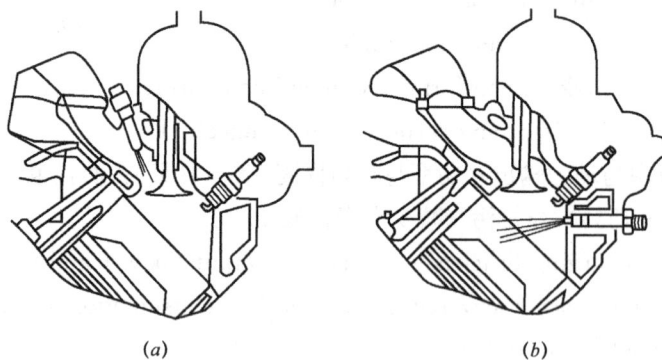

图 2.4.2 汽油喷射的两种基本类型

Figure 2.4.2 Two basic types of gasoline injection

(a) 缸外低压喷射（out-of-cylinder low pressure injection）；(b) 缸内高压喷射（in-cylinder high pressure injection）

喷油器的喷射位置还可分为单点式（SPI）与多点式（MPI）两种（图 2.4.3）。SPI 是将 1～2 个电磁喷油器装于进气总管原化油器的位置。MPI 则是每缸一个喷油器喷射于各缸进气门之前的进气道内。

The injection position of the injector can also be divided into two types: single point injection (SPI) and multiple point injection (MPI). SPI is to install 1 to 2 electromagnetic injectors in the position of intake ducting, where is the position of the former carburetor. MPI is an injector per cylinder injected into the intake port before the intake valves of each cylinder.

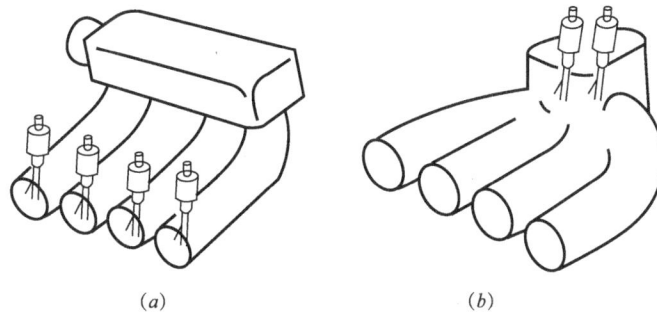

图 2.4.3 汽油喷射的两种形式

Figure 2.4.3 Two forms of gasoline injection

(a) 多点式 MPI (multi-point MPI)；(b) 单点式 SPI (single-point SPI)

其基本特征是 (Its basic characteristics are)：

该系统采用带微处理器（MCU）的电控单元（ECU）实施控制，并实施了氧传感器与爆震传感器的闭环控制。该系统不仅电控喷油与点火，而且还电控其他系统（其控制项目几乎已遍及整个发动机）。例如，电控可变动力控制系统、节能净化系统、备用系统与故障自诊断系统等，如图 2.4.4 所示。

The system is controlled by electronic control unit (ECU) with microprocessor (MCU), and the closed-loop control of the oxygen sensor and the knock sensor is implemented. This system not only electronically controls fuel injection and ignition, but also electronically controls other systems (whose controlling items almost cover the whole engine). For example, electronic variable power control system, energy-saving and purification system, standby system and fault self-diagnosis system, etc.

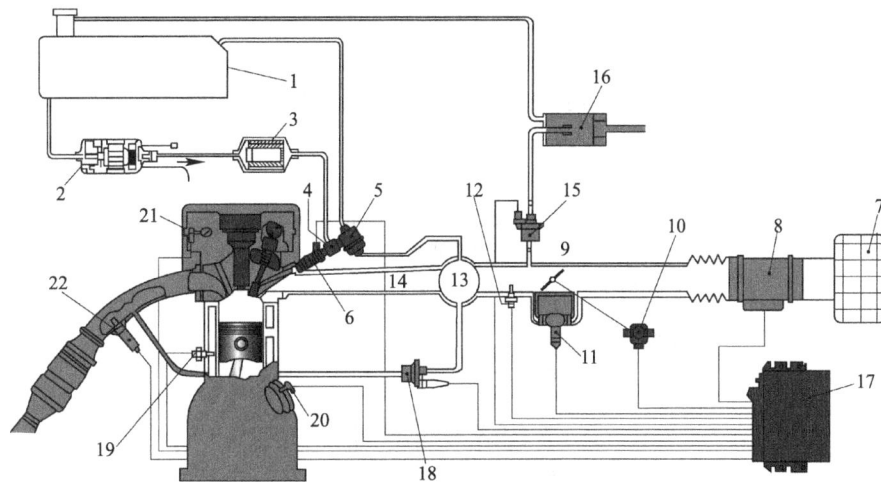

图 2.4.4 电控汽油喷射系统的结构

Figure 2.4.4 Structure of electronic gasoline injection system

1—燃油箱（fuel tank）；2—电动汽油泵（electric gasoline pump）；3—燃油滤清器（fuel filter）；4—燃油分配管（fueldelivery pipe）；5—油压调节器（fuel pressure regulator）；6—电磁喷油器（electromagnetic injector）；7—空气滤清器（air filter）；8—热线式或热膜式空气流量计（hot wire or hot film air flow meter）；9—节气门（throttle valve）；10—节气门位置传感器（throttle position sensor）；11—自动怠速空气阀（automatic idle air valve）；12—进气温度传感器（intake temperature sensor）；13—进气总管（intake ducting）；14—进气歧管（intake manifold）；15—燃油蒸气回收控制阀（fuel vapor recovery control valve）；16—活性炭罐（activated carbon canister）；17—电控单元（ECU）(electronic control unit (ECU))；18—废气再循环阀（exhaust gas recirculation valve）；19—水温传感器（water temperature sensor）；20—转速传感器（speed sensor）；21—凸轮轴位置传感器（camshaft position sensor）；22—氧传感器（oxygen sensor）

电控汽油喷射系统的结构组成包括：供气系统、供油系统、点火系统及电控系统。

Electronic gasoline injection system consists of gas supply system, fuel supply system, ignition system and electronic control system.

（1）供气系统（Gas supply system）

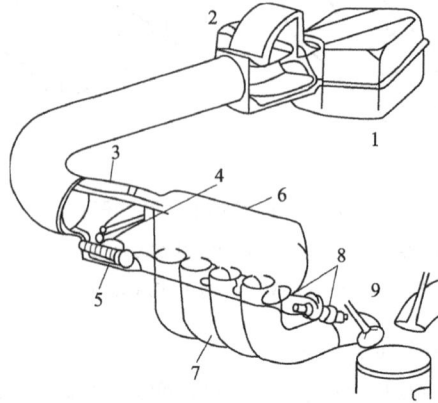

图 2.4.5 供气系统

Figure 2.4.5 Gas suppl system

1—空气滤清器（air filter）；2—空气流量计（air flow meter）；3—节气门体（throttle body）；4—节气门（throttle valve）；5—急速空气阀（idle air valve）；6—进气谐振腔（进气总管）（intake resonator（intakeducting））；7—进气歧管（intake manifold）；8—电磁喷油器（electromagnetic injector）；9—进气门（intake valve）

（2）供油系统（Fuel supply system）

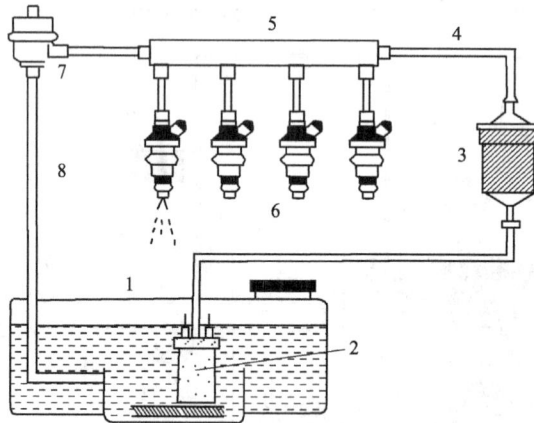

图 2.4.6 供油系统

Figure 2.4.6 Fuel supply system

1—燃油箱（fuel tank）；2—电动汽油泵（electric gasoline pump）；3—燃油滤清器（fuel filter）；4—输油管（fuel delivery pipe）；5—布油管（fuel rail）；6—电磁喷油器（electromagnetic injector）；7—油压调节器（fuel pressure regulator）；8—回油管（fuel return pipe）

不仅电控电磁喷油器，而且还电控电动汽油泵。为改善发动机冷起动性能由各缸电磁喷油器直接完成，取消了冷起动喷嘴。

It controls not only the electromagnetic injector, but also the electric gasoline pump. In order to improve the cold start performance of the engine, the cold start nozzle was cancelled by the electromagnetic injector of each cylinder.

（3）电控点火系统（Electronic ignition system）

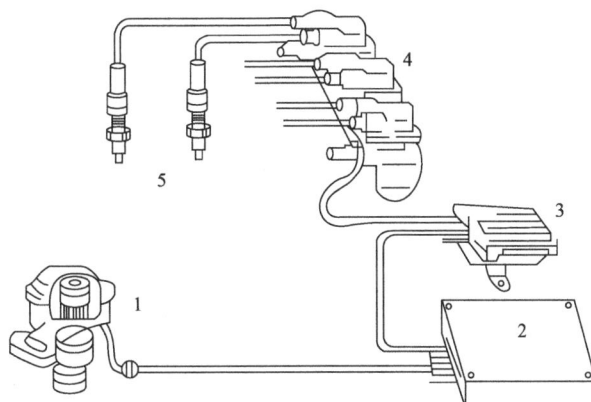

图2.4.7 无分电器的双缸点火系统

Figure 2.4.7 Double-cylinder ignition system without distributor

1—凸轮轴位置传感器（camshaft position sensor）；2—ECU（ECU）；3—点火器（igniter）；

4—点火线圈（ignition coil）；5—火花塞（spark plug）

可分有分电器与无分电器两种。又可分为双缸点火及单缸点火两种。

It can be divided into distributor ones and distributor less ones. If distribution was cancelled, it can also be divided into two types：double-cylinder ignition and single-cylinder ignition.

（4）电控系统（Electronic control system）

电控系统由信号传感器、电控单元（ECU）、电磁执行器三部分组成（图2.4.8）。

信号传感器包括：空气流量计及进气温度、发动机温度、节气门位置、发动机转速及上止点位置、氧传感器、爆震传感器以及蓄电池端电压信号等。

electronic control system consists of three parts：signal sensor, electronic control unit（ECU）and electromagnetic actuator. Signal sensors include：air flow meter, intake temperature, engine temperature, throttle position, engine speed and top dead point position, oxygen sensor, knock sensor and voltage signal of battery, etc.

电磁执行器包括：电磁喷油器、电子点火器、电动汽油泵以及怠速空气阀等。

Electromagnetic actuators include：electromagnetic injector, electronic igniter, electric gasoline pump and idle air valve, etc.

发动机负荷信号（如空气流量计信号及节气门位置信号等）外，发动机转速信号与发动机上止点位置信号也是极其重要的信号。不同发动机所用的曲轴转速传感器与曲轴位置传感器结构可能不同（有磁电式、霍尔式和光电式三类）、数量可能不同（由一个传感器产生或由几个传感器产生），安装位置也可能不同。有的装于曲轴的前端或后端（称为曲轴位置传感器），有的装于凸轮轴的前端或后端（称为凸轮位置传感器），也有的装于分电器内。

Besides engine load signals（such as air flow meter signals and throttle position signals, etc.），engine speed signals and top dead center position signals of the engine are also very important signals. Crankshaft speed sensors and crankshaft position sensors for different engines may be different（there are three types：Electromagnetic type, Hall type and photoelectric type.）in structure, the quantity（produced by one sensor or by several sensors），and the installation location. Some are installed at the front or rear end of the crankshaft（called the crankshaft position sensor），and some are installed at the front or rear end of the camshaft（called the cam position sensor），and some are installed in the distributor.

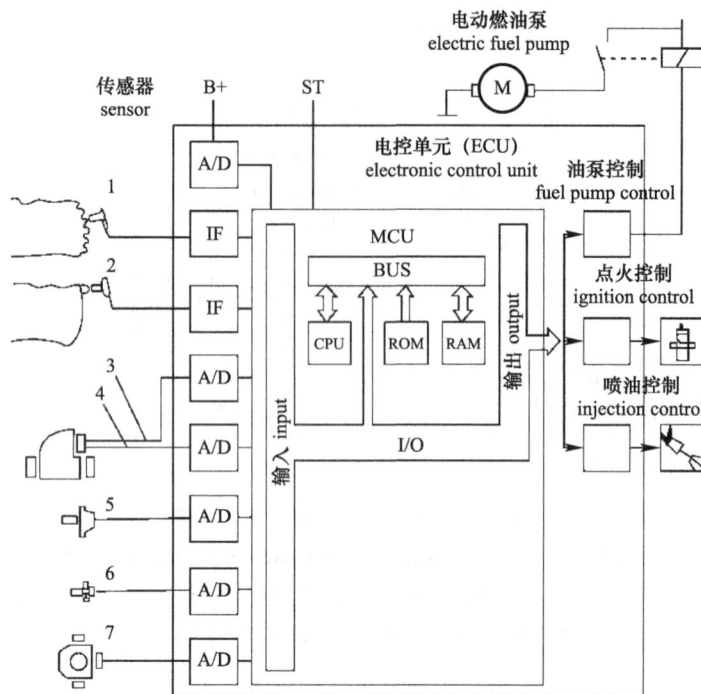

图 2.4.8　电控系统

Figure 2.4.8　Electronic control system

1—曲轴转速传感器（crankshaft speed sensor）；2—曲轴位置传感器（crankshaft position sensor）；3—空气流量传感器
（air flow sensor）；4—进气压力传感器（intake pressure sensor）；5—进气温度传感器（intake temperature sensor）；
6—水温传感器（water temperature sensor）；7—节气门位置传感器（throttle position sensor）

4.2　空气供给系统（Air supply system）

空气供给系统的作用是为发动机可燃混合气的形成提供必要的空气，并计量和控制燃油燃烧时所需要的空气量。空气供给系统如图 2.4.9 所示，空气经空气滤清器、空气流量计、节气门体进入进气总管，再分配到各缸进气歧管。在进气歧管内（或进气门处），空气与喷油器喷出的燃油混合后被吸入气缸内燃烧。

The function of air supply system is to provide necessary air for the formation of engine combustible mixture, and to measure and control the amount of air required for fuel combustion. The air supply system is shown in Fig. 2.4.9. Air enters the intake ducting through the air filter, air flow meter and throttle body. Then it is distributed to the intake manifold of each cylinder. In the intake manifold (or at the intake valve), air is mixed with the fuel sprayed from the injector and then sucked into the cylinder for combustion.

4.2.1　空气滤清器（Air filter）

空气滤清器是用来滤清空气中所含的尘土，以减少气缸、活塞、活塞环等零件的磨损，延长发动机的使用寿命。

Air filter is used to filter the dust contained in the air, so as to reduce the wear of cylinder, piston, piston ring and other parts, and prolong the service life of the engine.

空气滤清器的种类很多，如图 2.4.10 所示为纸质干式空气滤清器，它是通过用树脂处理的纸质滤芯对空气进行过滤。纸质滤芯的寿命取决于纸面大小（通常成波折状以提高过滤面积）及空气本身的清洁程度，一般可连续使用 10000～50000km。纸质滤芯不能清洗，脏污时可用压缩空气吹去灰尘，严重时必须更换。纸质干式滤清器质量轻、结构简单、安装及维护方便、滤清效果好，因此在汽车上得到广泛应用。

There are many kinds of air filters. Figure 2.4.10 shows a paper dry-type air filter. It filters the air through a paper filter element treated with resin. The life of the paper filter element depends on the size of the paper surface (usually in wavy shape to increase the filter area) and the cleanliness of the air itself. Generally, it can be used continuously for 10000-50000 km. Paper filter element cannot be washed. Compressed air can be used to blow away dirt when it is dirty, while it must be replaced in serious condition. Paper dry filter is widely used in automobiles because of its light weight, simple structure, convenient installation and maintenance, and good filtering effect.

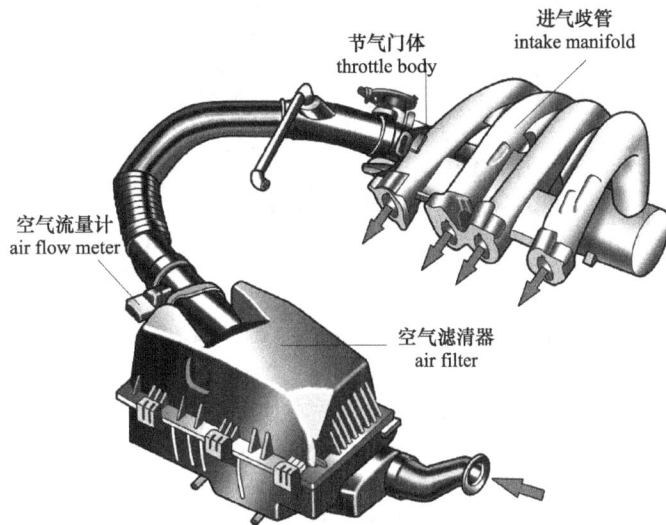

图 2.4.9　空气供给系统

Figure 2.4.9　Air supply system

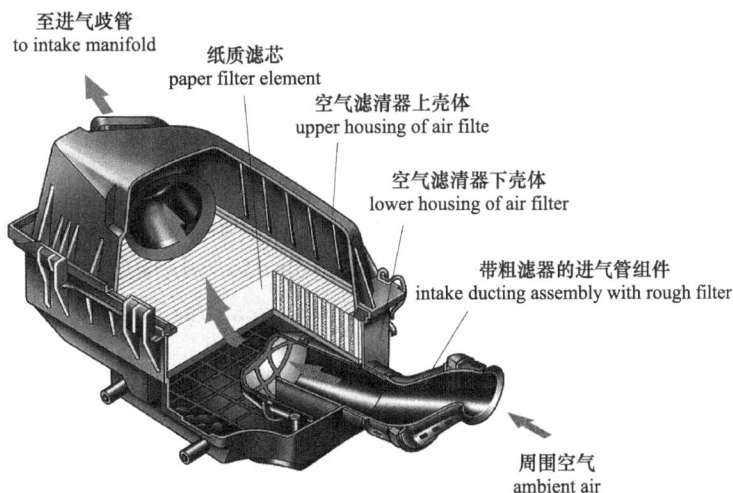

图 2.4.10　纸质干式空气滤清器

Figure 2.4.10　Paper dry-type air filter

4.2.2　节气门体 (Throttle Body)

节气门体 (图 2.4.11) 是调节控制发动机进气的零部件，节气门体主要由节气门、用于检测节气门开闭状态的节气门位置传感器、节气门定位电位计、节气门定位器 (电动机)、节气门电位片和怠速开关等组成。汽车在正常行驶时，空气流量由节气门控制，而节气门则是驾驶人通过加速踏板操纵。

The throttle body (Fig. 2.4.11) is a component that regulates the intake of the engine, which is mainly composed of throttle valve, throttle position sensor used to detect the opening and closing state of the throttle valve，throttle positioning potentiometer，throttle positioner (electric motor)，throttle potential plate and idle switch，etc. When a car is running normally，the air flow is controlled by the throttle，which is operated by the driver through an accelerator pedal.

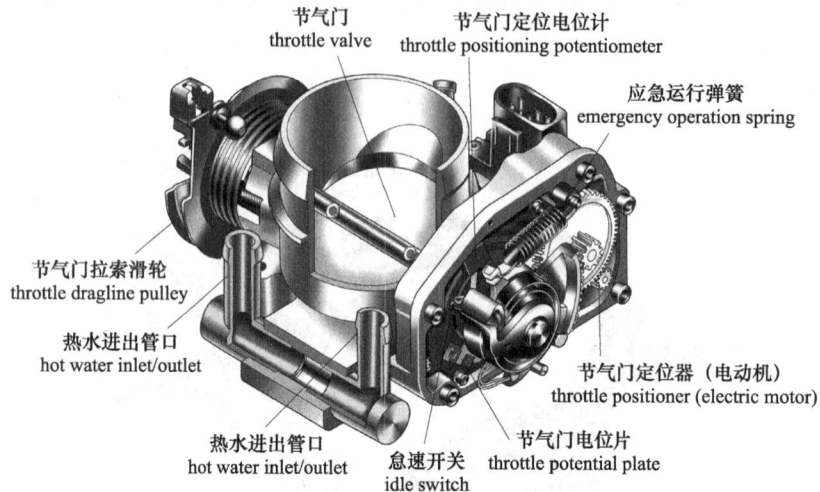

图 2.4.11　节气门体

Figure 2.4.11　Throttle body

4.2.3　进气歧管与稳压箱 (Intake manifold and stable pressure box)

进气歧管的结构如图 2.4.12 所示。进气歧管的功用是将空气或可燃混合气引入气缸，并保证进气充分及各缸进气量均匀一致。进气歧管多用铝合金或铸铁制造，有些也采用复合塑料制作。有些乘用车进气歧管前还设有稳压箱 (也称共鸣腔、谐振腔)，稳压箱的功用是消除进气压力脉动，保证各缸混合气分配均匀。

The structure of the intake manifold is shown in Figure 2.4.12. The function of the intake manifold is to lead air or combustible mixture into the cylinder and ensure that the intake gas is sufficient and the intake volume of each cylinder is uniform. The intake manifold is usually made of aluminum alloy or cast iron，some of which are also made of composite plastics. In some passenger automobiles，there are pressure stabilization boxes (also known as resonant chambers) in front of intake manifolds，whose function is to eliminate the fluctuation of intake pressure and ensure the uniform distribution of mixtures in each cylinder.

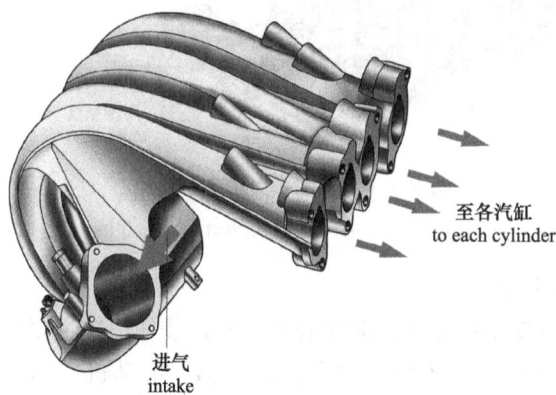

图 2.4.12　进气歧管的结构

Figure 2.4.12　Structure of intake manifold

4.2.4 可变进气系统（Variable intake system）

为提高进气效率，在一些汽油机电控燃油喷射系统中采用了可变进气系统。可变进气系统结构如图 2.4.13 所示，其工作原理如图 2.4.14 所示。

In order to improve the intake efficiency, variable intake system is adopted in some electronic fuel injection systems of gasoline engines. The structure of variable intake system is shown in Fig. 2.4.13, and its working principle is shown in Fig. 2.4.14.

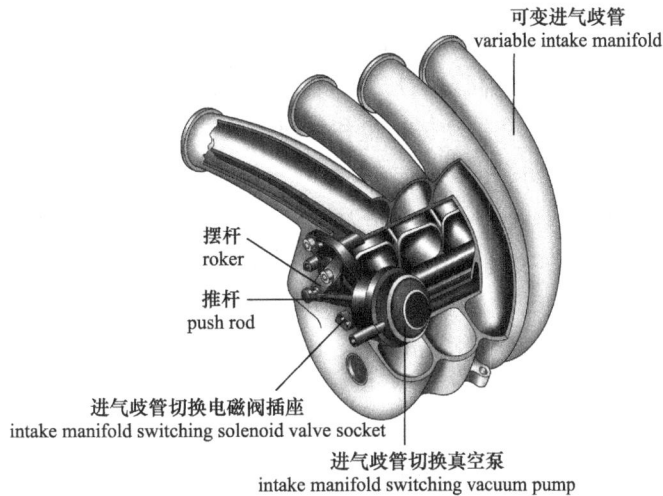

可变进气歧管
variable intake manifold

摆杆
roker

推杆
push rod

进气歧管切换电磁阀插座
intake manifold switching solenoid valve socket

进气歧管切换真空泵
intake manifold switching vacuum pump

图 2.4.13 可变进气系统的结构

Figure 2.4.13 Structure of variable intake system

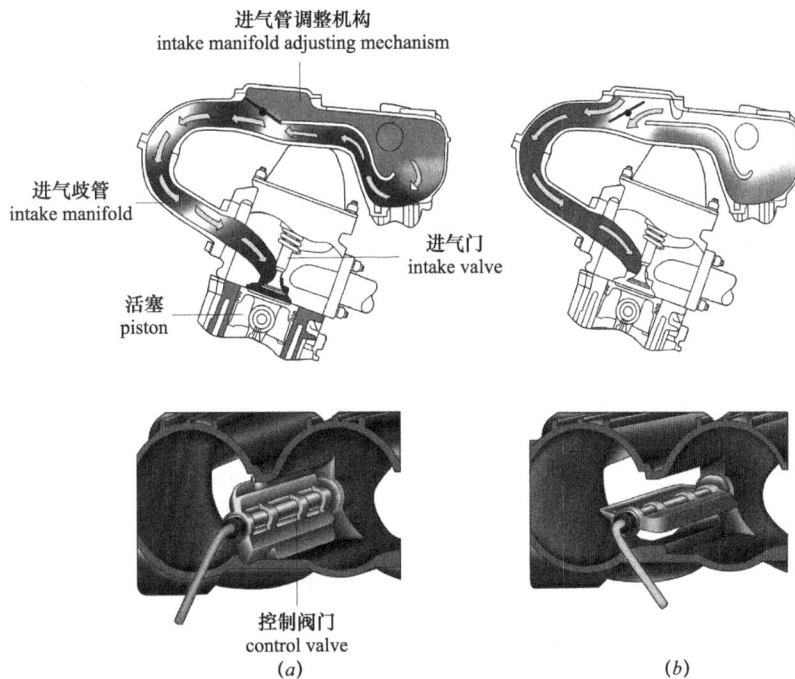

进气管调整机构
intake manifold adjusting mechanism

进气歧管
intake manifold

进气门
intake valve

活塞
piston

控制阀门
control valve
(a)

(b)

图 2.4.14 可变进气系统工作原理

Figure 2.4.14 Working principle of variable intake system

(a) 发动机低转速状态（low speed state of engines）；(b) 发动机高转速状态（high speed state of engines）

发动机在低转速时，进气控制阀门关闭，气流需经过较长的进气歧管进入气缸，这样可利用进气的流动惯性来提高进气效率，使发动机在低转速下获得较大的转矩；而在高转速时，则是通过打开控制阀门来减小进气阻力，气流经过较短的进气歧管进入气缸，从而提高进气效率，可获得较高的最大输出功率。

When the engine runs slowly, the intake control valve closed and the air flow enters the cylinder through a long intake manifold. This can improve the intake efficiency by using the flow inertia of the intake gases, so that the engine can obtain a larger torque at low speed. While at high speed, the intake resistance is reduced by opening the control valve. The air flow enters the cylinder through a shorter intake manifold, thus improving the intake efficiency and obtaining a higher maximum output power.

4.2.5 废气涡轮增压系统 (Exhaust turbocharging system)

废气涡轮增压是指利用发动机排出的高温高压废气能量，驱动涡轮作高速旋转，带动同轴上的压气机，对燃烧所需的空气进行预压缩。这样，在发动机排量和转速不变的情况下，增加了流入发动机的空气量，提高了进气效率，因而可提高发动机的功率。

Exhaust turbocharging refers to the use of high temperature and high pressure exhaust energy from the engine to drive the turbine to rotate at high speed, which drives the compressor on the same shaft, and precompress the air required for combustion. In this way, the amount of air flowing into the engine is increased with the same engine displacement and speed, and the intake efficiency is improved, thus the engine power can be increased.

可调叶片式涡轮增压系统如图 2.4.15 所示，它包括同轴的涡轮与压气机叶轮。涡轮与压气机叶轮上有很多叶片，从气缸排出的废气直接进入涡轮，并推动涡轮旋转，带动压气机叶轮旋转，把吸入的空气增压，送入气缸。由于利用高温废气进行增压，涡轮增压器温度较高，经压缩的空气也温度较高，使进气密度减少，对提高进气效率不利，因此，需要在压缩空气出口到进气歧管之间安装冷却器（中冷器），冷却压缩空气，提高其密度。

The adjustable vane turbocharging system, as shown in Figure 2.4.15, consists of coaxial turbine and compressor impellers. There are many blades on the impellers of turbines and compressors. The exhaust gas discharged from the cylinder enters the turbine directly and drives the turbine to rotate, which drives the impeller of compressors to rotate and pressurizes the inhaled air into the cylinder. Because the high temperature exhaust gas is used to pressurize, the temperature of turbocharger is higher, and the temperature of the compressed air is also higher. It reduces the intake density and it is not conducive to improving the intake efficiency. Therefore, it is necessary to install a cooler (intercooler) between the compressed air outlet and the intake manifold to cool the compressed air and increase its density.

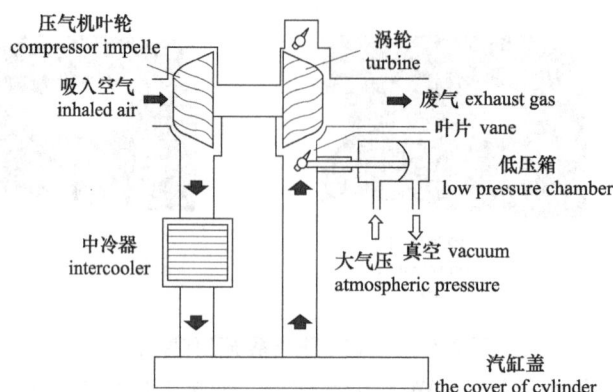

图 2.4.15　可调叶片式涡轮增压系统

Figure 2.4.15　Adjustable vane turbocharger system

可调叶片式涡轮增压系统能够在发动机整个范围内调整进气增压的压力。当发动机转速低时，叶片开度减少，减少废气流通截面，使废气流速增加，提高废气涡轮转速，增加进气压力；当发动机转速高时，叶片开度增大，增加废气流通截面，使废气流速降低，维持废气涡轮转速在正常范围内，保证进气压力的稳定。

The adjustable vane turbocharging system can adjust the intake pressure throughout the engine. When the engine speed is low, the blade opening decreases to reduce exhaust gas flow area, to increase the exhaust gas rate. Then the exhaust gas turbine speed is increased, which increases the intake pressure. While the engine speed is high, the blade opening increases, which brings the increase of the exhaust gas flow area. Then the exhaust gas flow rate decreases, and exhaust gas turbine speed is maintained within the normal range, to ensure the stability of intake pressure.

4.3　燃油供给系统（Fuel supply system）

燃油供给系统的作用是供给发动机燃烧过程所需的燃油。燃油供给系统结构如图 2.4.16 所示，主要由燃油泵、燃油滤清器、油压脉动阻尼器、燃油压力调节器和喷油器等组成。

The function of fuel supply system is to supply fuel for combustion process of engines. The structure of fuel supply system is shown in Fig. 2.4.16. It is mainly composed of fuel pump, fuel filter, fuel pressure pulsation damper, fuel pressure regulator and injector, etc.

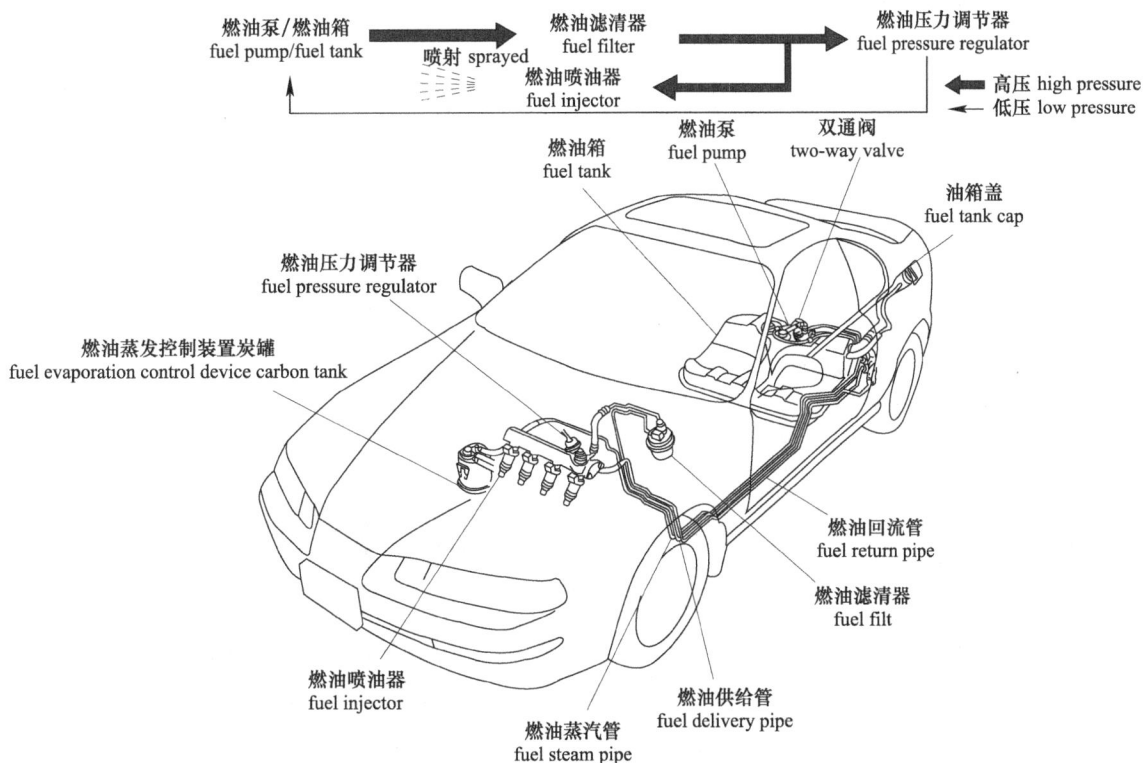

图 2.4.16　燃油供给系统

Figure 2.4.16　Fuel supply system

燃油从燃油箱中被燃油泵吸出，先由燃油滤清器将杂质滤除后再通过输油管送到各个喷油器。喷油器则根据 ECU 发出的指令，将计量后的燃油喷入各进气歧管并与流入发动机内的空气进行混合，形成可燃混合气。发动机在正常工况喷油量只取决于各喷油器通电时间长短。

The fuel is sucked out by the fuel pump from the fuel tank. The impurities are filtered out by the fuel filter. Then the fuel is sent to the each injector through the pipeline. According to the instructions issued by

ECU, the metered fuel is injected into the intake manifolds by the fuel injector and mixed with the air flowing into the engine to form a combustible mixture. The amount of fuel injected into the engine under normal working conditions only depends on the duration of the power supply of each injector.

此外，利用燃油压力调节器可将喷油压力控制在一定的范围内，而将多余的燃油从燃油压力调节器经回油管送回燃油箱。为了消除燃油泵泵油时或喷油器喷油时引起管路中的油压产生微小扰动，在有些发动机的燃油供给系统中还装有油压脉动阻尼器，用于吸收管路中油压波动时的能量，以便抑制管路中油压的脉动，提高系统的喷油精度。

In addition, the fuel injection pressure can be controlled within a certain range by using the fuel pressure regulator, and the extra fuel can be sent back to the fuel tank through the fuel return pipe from the fuel pressure regulator. In order to eliminate the small disturbance of fuel pressure in the pipeline caused by fuel pump or injector injection when they are pumping fuel, some engine fuel supply systems are equipped with fuel pressure pulsation dampers. It is used to absorb the energy of fuel pressure fluctuation in the pipeline, so as to restrain the oil pressure pulsation in the pipeline and improve the injection accuracy of the system.

4.3.1 燃油箱 (Fuel tank)

燃油箱（图 2.4.17）是用来储存燃油的，其容积大小与车型和发动机排量有关，其形状随车型不同而各异，这主要是为了适应在车上的布置安装。

Fuel tank (Fig. 2.4.17) is used to store fuel, whose volume is related to the vehicle type and engine displacement, and shape varies with the vehicle type. This is mainly to adapt to the layout and installation of the vehicle.

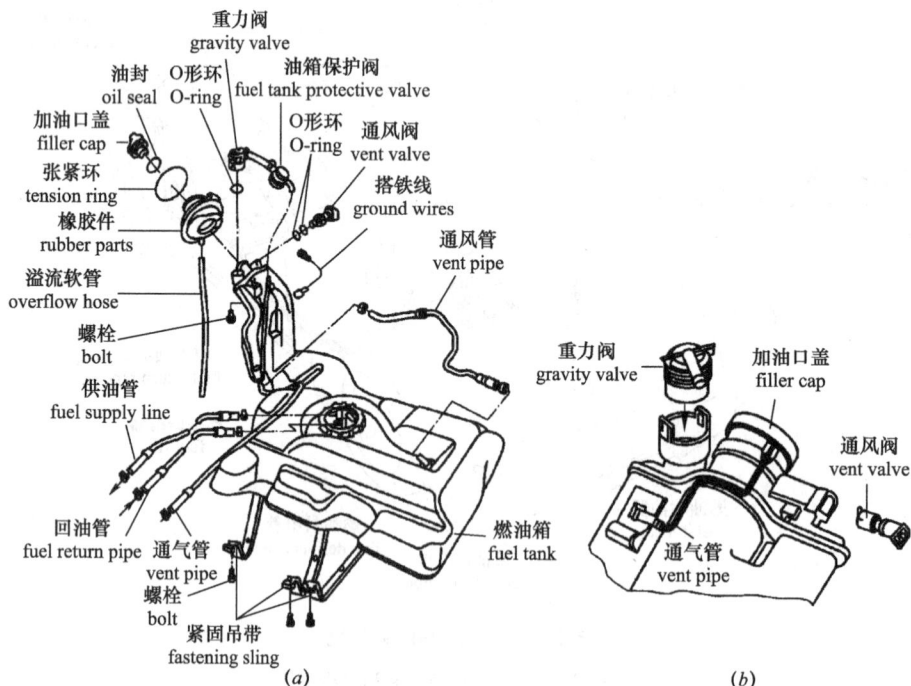

图 2.4.17　带附件的燃油箱
Figure 2.4.17　Fuel tank with accessories

挥发性好的汽油在燃油箱内挥发，直接将挥发的汽油蒸气排到大气中会污染环境，为此设置了燃油箱蒸发排放控制装置（图 2.4.18），将活性炭罐与燃油箱相连接，挥发的汽油蒸气被吸附在活性炭上。发动机工作时，活性炭罐电磁阀通电打开，被吸附在活性炭上的汽油蒸气即可被吸入气缸并燃烧。

The gasoline with good volatility volatilizes in the fuel tank. It will pollute the environment if the volatile gasoline vapor was directly discharged into the atmosphere. For this reason, a fuel tank evaporation emission control device (Figure 2. 4. 18) is set up, which connects the activated carbon tank with the fuel tank, and the volatile gasoline vapor is adsorbed on the activated carbon. When the engine works, the solenoid valve of the activated carbon tank is turned on and the gasoline vapor adsorbed on the activated carbon can be absorbed into the cylinder and burned.

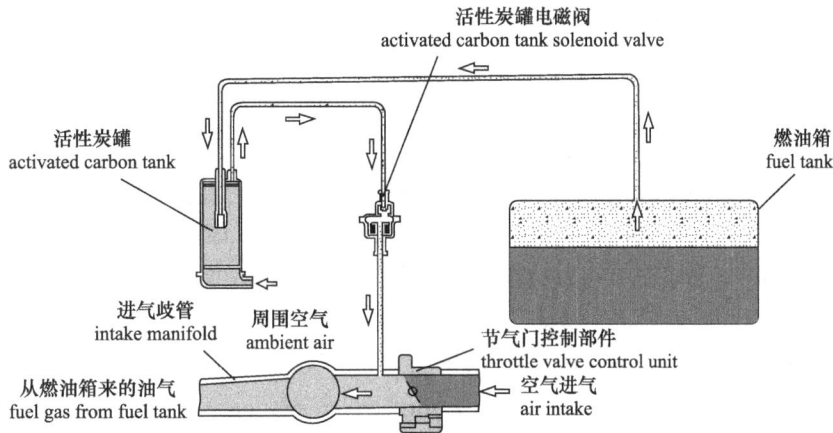

图 2. 4. 18　燃油箱蒸发排放控制装置

Figure 2. 4. 18　Fuel Tank Evaporation Emission Control Devices

4.3.2　电动燃油泵（Electric fuel pump）

电动燃油泵的作用是把燃油从油箱内吸出并通过喷油器供给发动机各气缸。

The function of electric fuel pump is to suck the fuel out of the tank and supply the engine cylinders through the injector.

电控燃油喷射系统中最常用的是内置式燃油泵，即燃油泵安装在燃油箱内。内置式燃油泵不易发生气阻和漏油现象，对泵的自吸性能要求较低，故应用广泛。内置式燃油泵主要有叶片式和滚柱式两种。

The most commonly used fuel pump in electronic fuel injection system is the built-in fuel pump, that is, the fuel pump is installed in the fuel tank. For the built-in fuel pump, it is not easy to cause gas resistance and fuel leakage, and has low self-priming performance requirements, so it is widely used. There are two main types of built-in fuel pump: vane type and roller type.

1. 叶片式电动燃油泵（Vane type electric fuel pump）

叶片式电动燃油泵结构和工作原理如图 2. 4. 19 所示。叶轮是一个圆平板，在平板的圆周上加工有小槽，形成泵油叶片。当叶轮旋转时，圆周上小槽内的燃油随同叶轮一同高速旋转。由于离心力的作用，使出油口处压力增高，而在进油口处产生真空，从而使燃油在进油口处被吸入，在出油口处被排出，这样周而复始地完成燃油的输送。叶片式电动燃油泵运转噪声小，油压脉动小，泵油压力高，叶片磨损小，使用寿命长。

The structure and working principle of vane electric fuel pump are shown in Fig. 2. 4. 19. The impeller is a circular flat plate, with small grooves machined on the circumference of the flat plate to form blades for pumping fuel. When the impeller rotates, the fuel in the grooves on the circumference rotates at high speed together with the impeller. Because of the effect of centrifugal force, the pressure at the outlet rises, and a vacuum is created at the inlet, so that the fuel is sucked in at the inlet and discharged at the outlet, thus completing the fuel transportation cycle after cycle. Blade electric fuel pump has the advantages of low noise, low oil pressure fluctuation, high pump oil pressure, small blade wear and long service life.

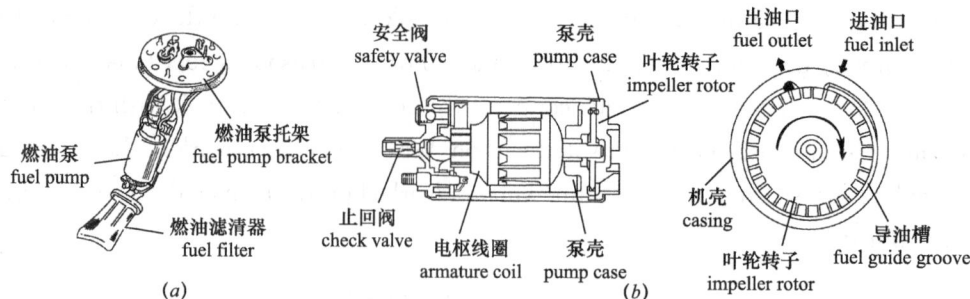

图 2.4.19 叶片式电动燃油泵

Figure 2.4.19 Vane electric fuel pump

（a）燃油泵结构（fuel pump structure）；（b）燃油泵工作原理（working principle of fuel pump）

2. 滚柱式电动燃油泵（Roller type electric fuel pump）

滚柱式电动燃油泵如图 2.4.20 所示。转子偏心地安装在泵体内，滚柱装在转子的凹槽中。在永磁电动机的驱动下，当转子旋转时，滚柱在离心力的作用下紧压在泵体的内表面上，同时在惯性力的作用下，滚柱总是与转子凹槽的一个侧面贴紧，从而形成若干个封闭的工作腔。

Roller type electric fuel pump is shown in Figure 2.4.20. The rotor is eccentrically installed in the pump body and the roller is mounted in the groove of the rotor. Driven by permanent magnet motor, when the rotor rotates, the roller is compressed on the inner surface of the pump body under the action of centrifugal force. At the same time, under the action of inertial force, the roller is always close to one side of the rotor groove, thus forming several closed working chambers.

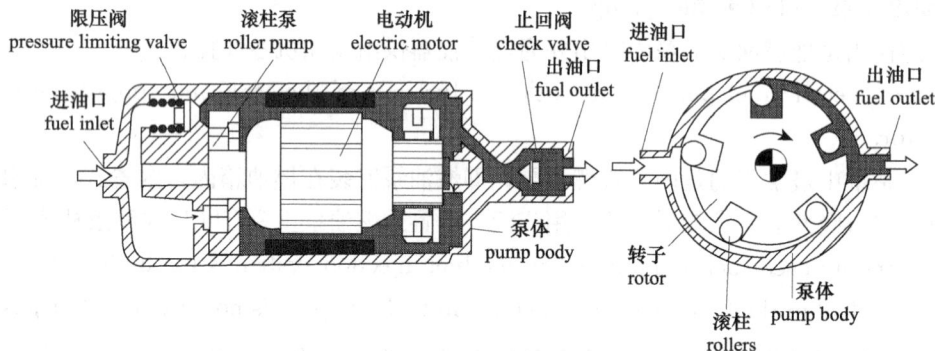

图 2.4.20 滚柱式电动燃油泵

Figure 2.4.20 Roller Electric Fuel Pump

在燃油泵工作过程中，进油口一侧的工作腔容积增大，成为低压吸油腔，燃油经进油口被吸入工作腔内。在出油口一侧的工作腔容积减小，成为高压压油腔，高压燃油从压油腔经出油口流出。油泵转子每转一圈，其排出的燃油就要产生与滚柱数目相同的压力脉动，故在出口处装有油压缓冲器，以减小出口处的油压脉动和运转噪声。

During the working process of the fuel pump, the volume of the working chamber on the fuel inlet side increases and becomes a low pressure suction chamber. The fuel is sucked into the working chamber through the inlet. The volume of the working chamber on the side of the fuel outlet decreases and becomes a high pressure fuel chamber. High pressure fuel flows from the chamber through the fuel outlet. The fuel discharged from the pump rotor will produce the same pressure pulsations as the number of rollers every turn, so the fuel pressure buffer is installed at the outlet to reduce the fuel pressure pulsations and running noise at the outlet.

止回阀的作用主要用于防止燃油倒流，并可保持管路残余压力，以便发动机下次容易起动，并可防止由于温度较高时，油路产生气阻现象。若油泵输出压力超过 400kPa 时，安全阀会自动打开，高压燃油可回至油泵的进油室，并在油泵和电动机内循环，以此可避免由于油路堵塞而引起管路油压过高造成管路破裂或燃油泵损坏等现象。滚柱式电动燃油泵运转时噪声大，油压脉动也大，而且泵体内表面和转子容易磨损。

Check valves are mainly used to prevent fuel back flow and to maintain residual pressure in the pipeline, so that the engine can start easily next time, and to prevent the phenomenon of gas lock in the pipeline due to higher temperature. If the output pressure of the fuel pump exceeds 400 kPa, the safety valve will open automatically, and the high pressure fuel can be returned to the intake chamber of the fuel pump and circulated in the fuel pump and motor, so as to avoid the phenomenon of pipeline break or fuel pump damage caused by the high fuel pressure caused by the blockage of the oil pipeline. Roller type electric fuel pump runs with high noise and oil pressure fluctuation, and the inner surface of pump body and rotor are easy to wear and tear.

4.3.3　燃油滤清器（Fuel filter）

燃油滤清器（图 2.4.21）可清除燃油中的杂质，防止堵塞喷油器等部件，减少运动部件的磨损。

Fuel filter (Fig. 2.4.21) can remove impurities in fuel, prevent blockage of fuel injector and other components, and reduce wear and tear of moving parts.

燃油滤清器与普通的滤清器一样，采用过滤形式，壳体内有一个纸滤芯。滤芯的形式通常有两种，即菊花形和涡卷形。燃油滤清器的滤芯应根据车辆行驶里程、使用的燃油质量情况及时更换，以确保发动机稳定行驶，提高可靠性。

Fuel filters, like ordinary filters, adopt the form of filtration, with a paper filter element in the shell. There are usually two types of filter element, chrysanthemum-shaped and scroll-shaped. The filter element of the fuel filter should be replaced in time according to the mileage of the vehicle and the quality of the fuel used, so as to ensure the stable running of the engine and improve its reliability.

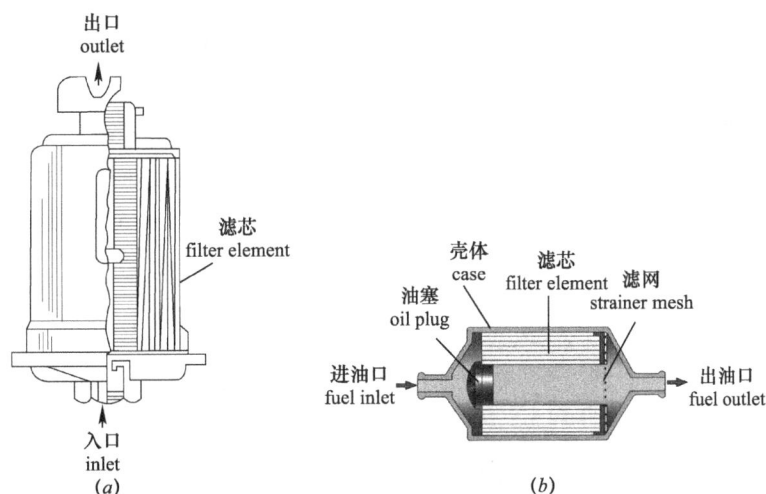

图 2.4.21　燃油滤清器
Figure 2.4.21　Fuel filter
(a) 结构（structure）；(b) 工作原理（working principle）

4.3.4　燃油分配管（Fuel delivery pipe）

燃油分配管（图 2.4.22）的功用是将燃油均匀、等压地输送给各缸喷油器。由于它的容积较大，故有储油蓄压、减缓油压脉动的作用。

The function of the fuel delivery pipe (Fig. 2.4.22) is to deliver fuel uniformly to the cylinder injectors with uniform pressure. Because of its large volume, it has the function of fuel storage and accumulation of pressure and relieving fuel pressure pulsation.

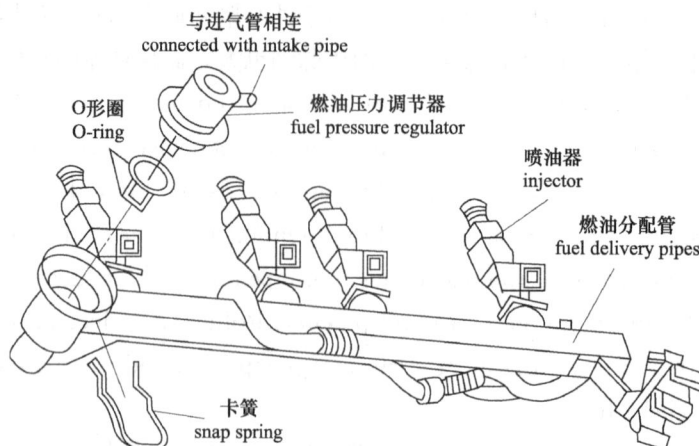

图 2.4.22 燃油分配管

Figure 2.4.22 Fuel delivery pipe

4.3.5 燃油压力调节器 (Fuel pressure regulator)

燃油压力调节器一般安装在燃油分配管上,其作用是根据进气歧管内的绝对压力的变化来调节系统油压(燃油分配管油压),保持喷油器的喷油绝对压力恒定,使喷油器的燃油喷射量只取决于喷油器的开启时间。

The fuel pressure regulator is usually installed on the fuel delivery pipe, whose function is to regulate fuel pressure of the system (fuel pressure of the fuel delivery pipe) according to the change of absolute pressure in the intake manifold, to keep the absolute pressure of fuel injection of the injector constant, so that the amount of fuel injection of the injector only depends on the opening time of the injector.

燃油压力调节器(图 2.4.23)有金属壳体,其内部由橡胶膜片分为弹簧室和燃油室两部分。弹簧室内有一个带预紧力的螺旋弹簧,它作用在膜片上。在膜片上安装一个阀,控制回油。另外,还通过一根真空管与进气歧管相连。

The fuel pressure regulator (Fig. 2.4.23) has a metal shell, whose interior is divided into a spring chamber and a fuel chamber by a rubber diaphragm. There is a coil spring with pre-tightening force in the spring chamber, which acts on the diaphragm. A valve is installed on the diaphragm to control fuel return. In addition, the intake manifold is connected with a vacuum tube.

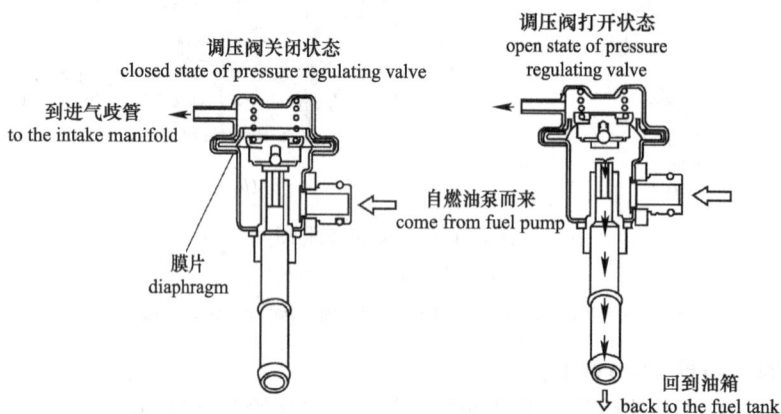

图 2.4.23 燃油压力调节器

Figure 2.4.23 Fuel pressure regulator

当系统油压超过规定值时,燃油压力克服弹簧压力,将膜片向上压,打开阀门,与回油通道接通,燃油流回燃油箱，系统压力降低，系统油压又回到规定值。

When the system fuel pressure exceeds the specified value, the fuel pressure overcomes the spring pressure, which pushes the diaphragm upward and opens the valve, leading to the connection with the fuel return passage. The fuel flows back to the fuel tank, so that the system pressure decreases, and the fuel pressure of the system returns to the specified value again.

如果进气歧管真空度变大，为了维持燃油分配管内部与进气歧管内部的压力差恒定，就必须降低系统油压。把进气歧管真空度引入弹簧室，能够减少膜片上方螺旋弹簧的作用力，进而减少打开阀门的压力，使系统油压下降到规定值。

If the vacuum degree of the intake manifolds increases, in order to maintain the constant pressure difference between the interior of fuel delivery pipe and the interior of intake manifold, the system fuel pressure must be reduced. By leading vacuum degree of intake manifold into the spring chamber, the force of coil spring above diaphragm can be reduced, and then the pressure of opening valve can be reduced, so that the fuel pressure of the system can be reduced to the specified value.

当电动燃油泵停止工作时，在膜片和螺旋弹簧力的作用下使阀门关闭，保持油路中的残余压力。

When the electric fuel pump stops working, the valve is closed under the action of diaphragm and coil spring force to maintain the residual pressure in the oil pipeline.

4.3.6　电磁喷油器（Electromagnetic fuel injector）

电磁喷油器是发动机电控燃油喷射系统的一个重要的执行元件，它接收 ECU 送来的喷油脉冲信号，准确地计量燃油喷射量，同时，将燃油喷射后雾化。

Electromagnetic fuel injector is an important actuating component of electronic fuel injection system of the engine. It receives fuel injection pulse signals from ECU to accurately measure fuel injection volume, and atomizes fuel after injection simultaneously.

轴针式电磁喷油器（图 2.4.24）安装在燃油分配管上，主要由轴针、针阀、衔铁、复位弹簧及电磁线圈等组成。针阀与衔铁制成整体结构，针阀上端安装一复位弹簧。当电磁喷油器停止工作时，弹簧弹力使针阀复位，阀针关闭，轴针压靠在阀座上起到密封作用，防止燃油泄漏。滤网用于过滤燃油中的杂质，O 形密封圈起到密封作用，上部密封圈防止燃油泄漏，下部密封圈防止漏气。

The Axial pin type electromagnetic fuel injector (Fig. 2.4.24) is installed on the fuel delivery pipe, which is mainly composed of Axial pin, needle valve, armature, reset spring and electromagnetic coil, etc. The needle valve and armature are made into an integral structure, and a reset spring is installed at the upper end of the needle valve. When the electromagnetic injector stops working, the spring elasticity makes the needle valve reset and the needle closed. The Axial pin pressing on the valve seat plays a seal role to prevent fuel leakage. The strainer mesh is used to filter impurities in the fuel. O-ring has sealing effect. The upper sealing ring prevents fuel leakage and the lower seal ring prevents gas leakage.

当电磁线圈通电时，电磁吸力使针阀克服复位弹簧的弹力，针阀与轴针上移，阀门打开，燃油便从喷孔喷出。由于燃油压力较高，因此喷出的燃油得到良好雾化。当电磁线圈断电时，电磁吸力消失，针阀与轴针在复位弹簧作用下复位，阀门关闭，喷油停止。

When the electromagnetic coil is electrified, the electromagnetic attractive force makes the needle valve overcome the elastic force of the reset spring, which causes the upward moving of the needle valve and the axial pin. When the valve opens, the fuel is sprayed out from the nozzle. While the power supply of the electromagnetic coil is interrupted, the electromagnetic attractive force disappears and the needle valve and the pin are reset under the action of the reset spring. When the valve closes, the injection stops.

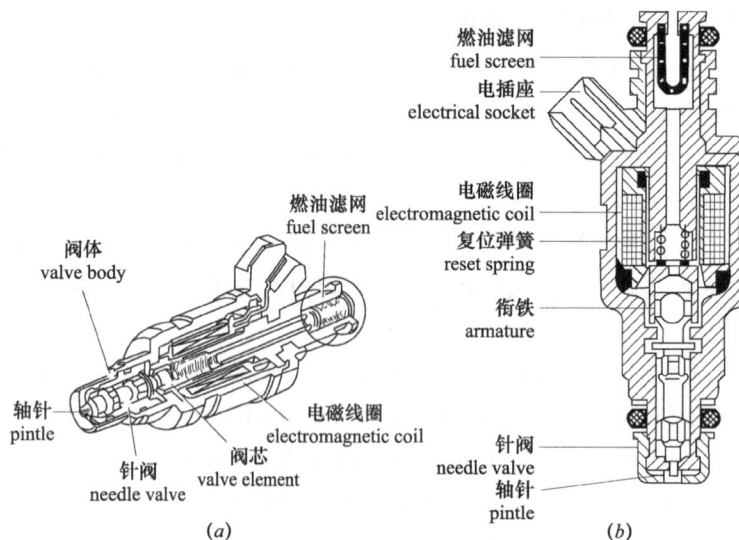

图 2.4.24　轴针式电磁喷油器

Figure 2.4.24　Pintle-type Electromagnetic fuel Injector

(*a*) 结构图（structural diagram）；(*b*) 剖视图（sectional view）

思考与练习

（Reflection and Exercises）

1. 电控系统的基本组成有哪些？

2. 试述电控系统中信号传感器的主要种类。

3. 试述电控系统中电控单元（ECU）的供电电路。

4. 什么是电控系统的故障自诊断系统、备用系统与保险系统？

5. 倘若信号传感器、电控单元及电磁执行器故障，电控系统是怎样处理的？

1. What are the basic components of the electronic control system?

2. Describe the main types of signal sensors in electronic control system.

3. Explain the power supply circuit of the electronic control unit（ECU）in the electronic control system.

4. What are the fault self-diagnosis system，standby system and insurance system of electronic control system?

5. If the signal sensor，electronic control unit and electromagnetic actuator fail，how does the electronic control system deal with it?

任务五　柴油机燃料供给系统

Task 5　Fuel Supply System of Diesel Engines

教学目标

1. 知识目标

（1）了解柴油机供给系统的功用与组成；

（2）知道正确选用柴油的牌号。

2. 能力目标

（1）能叙述电控高压共轨式柴油机燃料供给系统的组成及主要部件的作用；

（2）能正确选用柴油的牌号；

（3）能规范地进行电控高压共轨式柴油机燃料供给系统的维护。

3. 情感和素养目标

（1）培养学生责任感、使命感，树立远大理想；

（2）培养学生家国情怀，良好职业素养、吃苦耐劳的精神。

Teaching objectives

1. Knowledge objectives

（1）Understanding the function and composition of fuel supply system of diesel engines；

（2）Knowing choosing the brand of diesel correctly.

2. Ability objectives

（1）The abilities to describe the composition and the function of the main components of the diesel engine fuel supply system with electronic control，high voltage and common rail；

（2）The ability to choose the brand of diesel correctly；

（3）The maintenance of diesel engine fuel supply system with electronic control，high voltage and common rail can be carried on standardly.

3. Emotion and quality goals

（1）Cultivate students' sense of responsibility and mission，establish great ideals.

（2）Cultivate students' patriotism，professional quality and hard－working spirit.

5.1 概述（Overview）

目前，柴油机不但用于重型载货汽车，而且在轻型载货汽车、皮卡以及少量轿车上运用。

柴油机燃料供给系统的功用是根据柴油机不同工况，定时、适量地以一定的压力将柴油以雾状喷入气缸，使柴油与吸入气缸的新鲜空气形成可燃混合气，并将燃烧后的废气排入大气，本单元主要介绍电控高压共轨式柴油机燃料供给系统。

At present，diesel engines are not only used in heavy-duty trucks，it is also used in light trucks，pick-up trucks and a few cars.

The function of diesel engine fuel supply system is to regularly spray diesel into the cylinder with appropriate amount and certain pressure according to the different working conditions of the diesel engine to form a combustible mixture of diesel fuel and fresh air inhaled into the cylinder，and discharge exhaust gas into the atmosphere. This unit mainly introduces the diesel engine fuel supply system with electronic control，high voltage and common rail.

5.1.1 柴油机电控喷射系统的发展（Development of electronic control injection system of diesel engines）

早在 20 世纪 70 年代，人们就开始研究柴油机电子控制技术来替代机械控制技术。电子控制技术的应用使柴油机在动力性、经济性和排放性能方面都取得了巨大的进步。到目前为止，柴油机电控喷射系统的发展经历了三代。

As early as the 1970s，people began to study the electronic control technology of diesel engines to replace the mechanical control. The application of electronic control technology has made great progress in power，economyand emission performances of diesel engines. So far，the development of electronic control injection system of diesel engines has experienced three generations.

1. 第一代电控柴油喷射系统：位置控制式（The first generation electronic diesel injection system：Position control type）

位置控制式电控柴油喷射系统的主要特点是保留了大部分传统机械柴油机的燃油系统部件，只是使用电子调速器取代了原来的机械调速器，来控制供油齿条或滑套的位置，使得供油量的调节更精确，响应更快。第一代电控柴油喷射系统主要运用带电子调速器的直列泵（图2.5.1）和分配泵（图2.5.2）。

The main characteristic of position control electronic diesel injection system is that it retains most of the fuel system components of traditional mechanical diesel engine，but only the original mechanical governor is replaced with the electronic governor to control the position of fuel supply rack or sliding sleeve，so as to make the adjustment of fuel supply more precise and response faster. The first generation of electronic control diesel injection system mainly uses in-line pumps with electronic governors and distribution pumps.

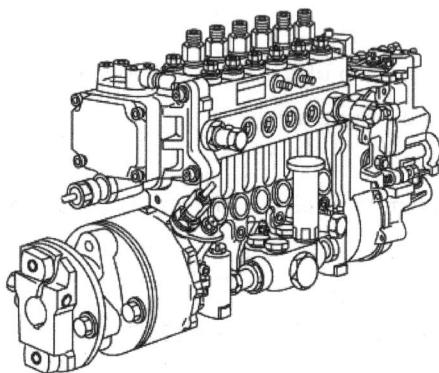

图 2.5.1　直列泵

Figure 2.5.1　In-line Pump

图 2.5.2　分配泵

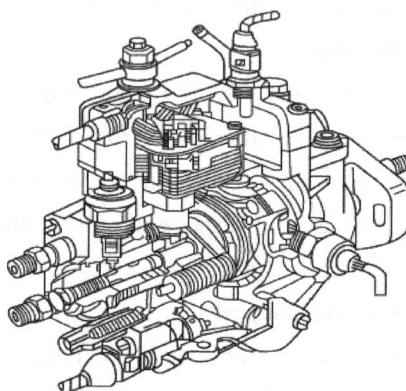

Figure 2.5.2　Distribution Pump

2. 第二代电控柴油喷射系统：时间控制式（Second generation electronic control diesel injection system：Time control type）

时间控制式电控柴油喷射系统的主要特点是其喷油量和喷油定时是由电脑控制的高速电磁阀的开闭时刻所决定。常见的第二代电控柴油喷射系统有电子控制的泵喷嘴和单体泵两种形式（图2.5.3）。

The main characteristic of time-controlled electronic diesel injection system is that the injection quantity and timing are determined by the open and closed time of high-speed solenoid valve controlled by the computer. The common second generation electronic diesel injection system has two forms：electronic pump nozzle and electronic unit pump.

3. 第三代电控柴油喷射系统：时间-压力控制式（高压共轨式）（Third generation electronic diesel injection system：Time-pressure control type (high voltage and common rail)）

电控高压共轨式喷射系统（图2.5.4）属于第三代时间-压力控制方式，包括高速电磁阀控制的喷油器或更为先进的喷油器，部分装备有各缸喷油器共用的共轨管。喷油压力取决于共轨管中的油压，而不取决于受发动机转速高低影响的高压油泵泵油压力，高压油泵仅仅是连续向共轨管供油以维持所需的共轨压力。

Electronic injection system with high-pressure and common rail belongs to the third generation of time-pressure control mode，including the injector controlled by high-speed solenoid valve or more advanced injectors，part of which is equipped with common rail pipe shared by each cylinder injector. The injection pressure depends on the oil pressure in the common rail pipe not on the high-pressure oil pump pressure affected by the engine speed. The high-pressure oil pump only continuously supplies fuel to the common rail pipe to maintain the required common rail pressure.

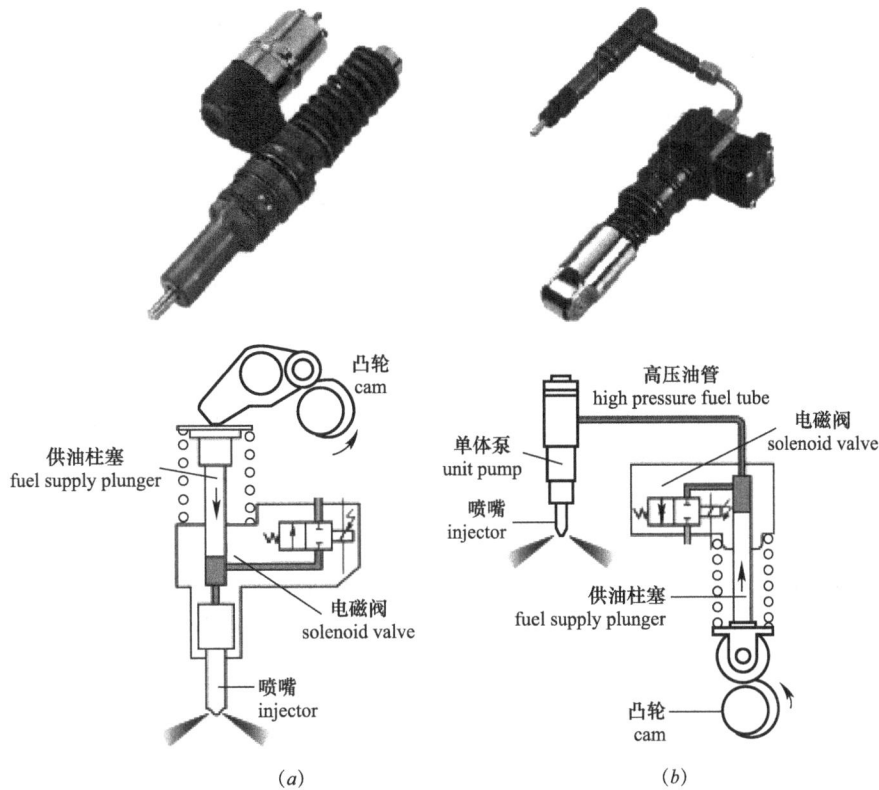

图 2.5.3 泵喷嘴和单体泵控柴油喷射系统

Figure 2.5.3 Electronic control diesel injection system of pump nozzle and unit pump

(a) 泵喷嘴 (pump nozzle); (b) 单体泵 (unit pump)

5.1.2 电控高压共轨式喷射系统的优点 (Advantages of electronic injection system with high pressure and common rail)

与其他喷射系统相比，电控高压共轨式喷射系统具有众多优点，主要包括：

（1）可实现高压喷射，喷油压力可比一般直列泵系统高出一倍，最高达 200MPa；

（2）喷油压力独立于发动机转速，在发动机低速、部分负荷工况下产生高的喷油压力；

（3）可自由选定喷油定时和喷油量，可由单次喷射过程变为多次喷射；

（4）结构简单，可靠性好，适用范围广泛，可在各级各类车辆上应用。

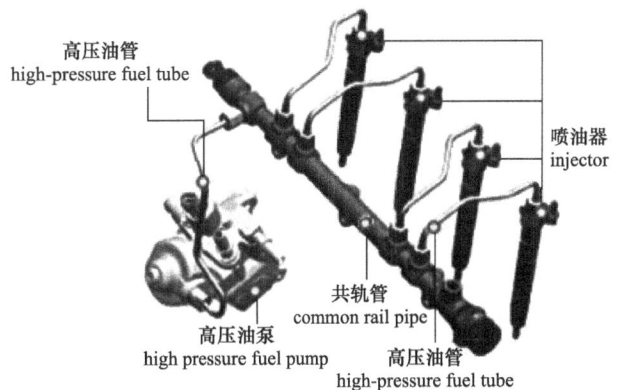

图 2.5.4 电控高压共轨式喷射系统

Figure 2.5.4 Electronic control high pressure common rail injection system

Compared with other injection systems, electronic injection system with high pressure and common rail has many advantages, mainly including：

（1）High pressure injection can be realized, and the injection pressure can be twice as high as that of the general in-line pump system, with a maximum of 200MPa.

（2）The injection pressure is independent of the engine speed, and produces high injection pressure at low speed of the engine and under partial loading conditions.

(3) The injection timing and quantity can be chosen freely, and the single injection process can be changed into multiple injections.

(4) It has simple structure, good reliability and wide application range, which can be used in all kinds of vehicles all levels.

电控高压共轨式喷射系统良好的喷射特性优化了燃烧过程，改进了发动机转矩特性，同时使发动机油耗（与同功率的汽油车相比，油耗可节省25%～30%），颗粒物排放、有害气体排放及噪声等指标都得到明显改善。

The good injection characteristics of the electronic injection system with high pressure and common rail optimize the combustion process and improve the engine torque characteristics. At the same time, the fuel consumption of the engine (compared with the same power gasoline vehicle, the fuel consumption can be saved by 25%-30%) and the emissions of particulate matters and harmful gases, noise and other indicators have been significantly improved.

目前，博世（Bosch）、德尔福（Delphi）、电装（Denso）和西门子（Siemens）等公司都在为汽车工业提供各自的电控高压共轨式喷射系统。

At present, companies such as Bosch, Delphi, Denso and Siemens are providing the automotive industry with their own electronic injection systems of high pressure and common rail.

5.1.3 柴油机燃料（Diesel fuel）

柴油是石油中提炼出来的碳氢化合物。柴油分为轻柴油（180～370℃）和重柴油（350～410℃）两大类。重柴油多用于1000r/min 一下中低速柴油机，汽车用柴油机都是高转速，所以采用轻柴油。

Diesel oil is a hydrocarbon extracted from petroleum, which is divided into two categories: light diesel oil (180-370℃) and heavy diesel oil (350-410℃). Heavy diesel oil is mostly used in low and medium speed diesel engines below 1000r/min. While automobile diesel engines are all high speed, light diesel is used.

柴油燃烧性用十六烷值评定，柴油十六烷值越大，则容易自燃。国家标准定车用柴油的十六烷值不小于45。

The combustibility of diesel oil is evaluated by the cetane value. The higher the cetane value of diesel, the easier it will self-ignite.

国产轻柴油凝点分为10号、5号、0号、—10号、—20号、—35号和—50号等7个牌号，其凝点分别为10℃、5℃、—10℃、—20℃、—35℃和—50℃。

The condensation points of domestic light diesel oil can be divided into seven brands: No. 10, No. 5, No. 0, No. —10, No. —20, No. —35 and No. —50, whose condensation points are 10℃, 5℃, —10℃, —20℃, —35℃ and —50℃, respectively.

柴油使用率越高，如果大量取代汽油，可以降低石油消耗速度。柴油燃烧后的废气与汽油不同，污染物排放低。由于柴油中含有较多杂质，产生较多颗粒物，各汽车公司都在开发降低污染的技术。

The higher the diesel usage rate. If gasoline is replaced by a great amount diesel, the consumption rate of petroleum will decrease. The exhaust gas after diesel combustion is different from that of gasoline, and the emissionof pollutants is low. As diesel contains more impurities and produces more particulate matters, automobile companies are developing technologies to reduce pollution.

5.2 柴油机燃料供给装置（Diesel fuel supply device）

传统柴油喷射系统产生的压力与喷油量跟凸轮与柱塞联系在一起，喷油的压力随着发动机转速与喷油量的增加而增加。这种柴油系统已经无法满足日益严格的排放法规要求和降低油耗的愿望。共轨系统（Common Rail Systems，简称CRS）将燃油在高压下贮存在蓄压器（共轨管）中，从本质上克服了传统柴油机喷射系统的缺陷。电控高压共轨式柴油机燃料供给系统由低压油路部分、高压油路部分和电子控制系统组成（图2.5.5）。

The pressure and fuel injection quantity produced by traditional diesel injection system are connected with cam and plunger, and the injection pressure increases with the increase of engine speed and fuel injection quantity. This diesel system has been unable to meet the increasingly stringent emission regulations and the desire to reduce fuel consumption. Common Rail Systems (CRS for short) stores fuels in the accumulator (common rail pipe) at high pressure, which essentially overcomes the shortcomings of the traditional diesel engine injection system. The electronic fuel supply system of high pressure and common rail of diesel engines consists of low pressure fuel rail, high pressure fuel rail and electronic control system.

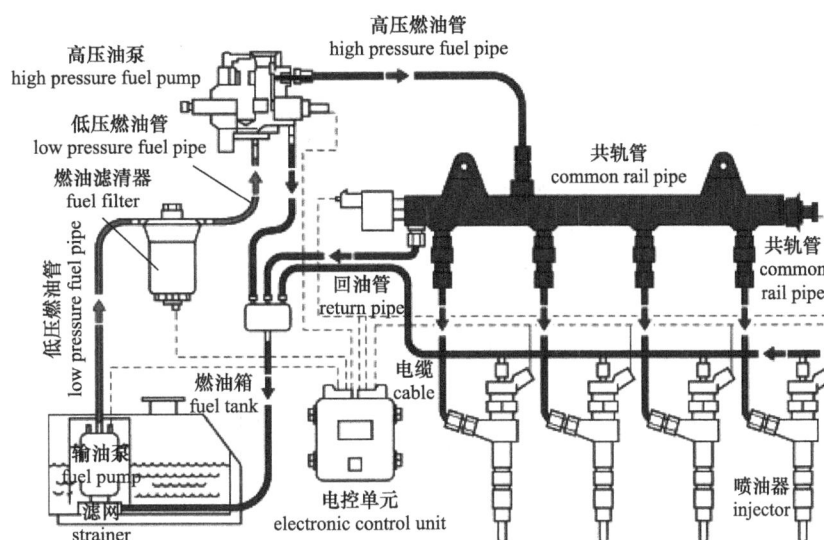

图 2.5.5　高压共轨燃油供给系统

Figure 2.5.5　High pressure common rail fuel supply system

电控高压共轨系统工作时，燃油由电动输油泵从燃油箱中抽出，经过燃油滤清器过滤后进入高压油泵，此时油压较低。在高压油泵内，燃油压力被提升到135MPa或更高，供入共轨管。当输油泵供油量超出高压油泵对共轨管的供油量时，部分燃油会流回燃油箱。共轨管上有共轨压力传感器和压力控制阀，用来调节共轨管内油压至设定值。高压燃油从共轨管流入喷油器后分为两路：一路直接喷入燃烧室，另一路在喷油期间，由喷油器针阀和针阀体的配合表面之间的间隙漏出，流回燃油箱。

When the electronic system of high pressure and common rail works, the fuel is pumped out of the fuel tank by an electric oil transfer pump and filtered through a fuel filter into the high pressure fuel pump. At this time, the fuel pressure is low. In the high pressure fuel pump, fuel pressure is raised to 135MPa or higher, supplied into the common rail pipe. When the fuel supply of the pump exceeds that of the high-pressure pump to the common rail pipe, part of the fuel will flow back to the fuel tank. There are common rail pressure sensors and pressure control valves on the common rail pipe, which are used to adjust the fuel pressure in the common rail pipe to the set value. High-pressure fuel flows into the injector from the common rail pipe and is divided into two routes: one is directly injected into the combustion chamber, the other leaks out from the gap of the mating surface between the needle valve and the needle valve body of the injector during the injection period, and flows back to the fuel tank.

电控高压共轨系统中的喷油器是一种由电磁阀控制的喷油阀，电磁阀的开启和关闭由电控单元控制。电控单元根据发动机的转速和所需喷油量等参数，计算出最佳喷油时间，控制电控喷油器的开启时刻或关闭等，从而精确控制喷油时间。

The injector in the electronic control system of high pressure and common rail is an injection valve controlled by a solenoid valve. The opening and closing of the solenoid valve are controlled by an electronic control unit. The electronic control unit calculates the optimum injection time according to the parameters such as engine speed and fuel injection quantity to control the opening time or closing time of the electronic control injector, etc., so as to precisely control the injection time.

5.2.1 低压油路部分 (Low pressure fuel rail)

低压油路部分包括燃油箱、输油泵、燃油滤清器和低压油管。

The low pressure fuel rail includes fuel tank, fuel pump, fuel filter and low pressure fuel pipe.

1. 输油泵 (Fuel pump)

输油泵的功用是使柴油产生一定的压力，以克服燃油滤清器和管路的阻力，连续向高压油泵输送足够的柴油。目前输油泵常见的有电动输油泵（滚柱泵）和齿轮泵两种。电动输油泵仅用于乘用车或轻型商用车，可装在油箱内或油箱外低压油管上。齿轮式输油泵为机械式，用于乘用车、越野车及各类重型车辆，输油泵与高压油泵组合在一起，或由发动机直接驱动。

The function of fuel pump is to make diesel oil produce certain pressure to overcome the resistance of fuel filter and pipeline and to continuously deliver enough diesel oil to high pressure fuel pump. At present, there are two kinds of fuel transfer pump: electric fuel transfer pump (roller pump) and gear pump. Electric fuel transfer pumps are only used in passenger cars or light commercial vehicles, and can be installed in the fuel tank or low pressure oil pipes outside the fuel tank. Gear fuel supply pumps are mechanical, used in passenger cars, off-road vehicles and various heavy vehicles. The fuel transfer pump is combined with high pressure fuel pumps or driven directly by engines.

（1）电动输油泵（图2.5.6）。电动输油泵内部主要由电动机、滚柱泵和安全阀组成。滚柱泵主要由转子、定子和滚柱组成。转子与定子偏心安装，电动机驱动滚柱泵的转子。当转子转动时，位于转子凹槽内的滚柱在离心力作用下，压靠在定子的内表面上，相邻的两个滚柱间形成一个密封的腔体。在转子旋转过程中，这些腔体的容积不断发生变化，在容积由小变大一侧燃油被吸入，在容积由大变小一侧燃油被压出。发动机起动时，电动输油泵开始运行，不受发动机转速影响。输油泵持续从燃油箱中抽出燃油，经燃油滤清器过滤后送往高压油泵，多余的燃油经溢流阀流回燃油箱。电动输油泵具有安全电路，可防止在停机时向发动机输送燃油。

（1）Electric fuel transfer pump. The interior of an electric oil transfer pump is mainly composed of electric motor, roller pump and safety valve. The roller pump mainly consists of rotor, stator and roller. The rotor and stator are eccentrically installed, and the electric motor drives the rotor of the roller pump. When the rotor rotates, the roller in the groove of the rotor is pressed against the inner surface of the stator under the centrifugal force, and a sealed cavity is formed between the two adjacent rollers. In the process of rotor rotation, the volume of these chambers changes constantly. Fuel is sucked on the side of volume from small to big, and the fuel is squeezed out on the side of volume from big to small. When the engine starts, the electric oil transfer pump starts to run, which is not affected by the engine speed. The fuel transfer pump continuously extracts the fuel from the fuel tank. It is filtered through the fuel filter, and sent to the high pressure fuel pump. The excess fuel flows back to the fuel tank through the overflow valve. The electric oil transfer pump has a safety circuit, which can prevent fuel from being delivered to the engine during shutdown.

（2）齿轮式输油泵。齿轮式输油泵（图2.5.7）内部是一对相互啮合转向相反的齿轮。齿轮式输油泵内的齿轮将齿隙中的燃油从吸油端送往出油端，齿轮间的接触面将吸油端和出油端互相隔绝以防燃油倒流。齿轮式输油泵输油量与发动机转速成正比，输油量的调节借助于吸油端的节流阀或出油端的溢流阀进行调节。

（2）Gear fuel supply pump. The interior of gear pump is a pair of gears which engage with each other and turn to the opposite direction. The gears in the gear pump sends fuel in the backlash from the oil suction end to the oil outlet end, and the contact surface between the gears isolates the oil suction end and the oil outlet end from each other to prevent fuel backflow. The oil delivery capacity of gear pump is proportional to the engine speed, and the adjustment of oil delivery capacity depends on the throttle valve at the oil suction end or the overflow valve at the oil outlet end.

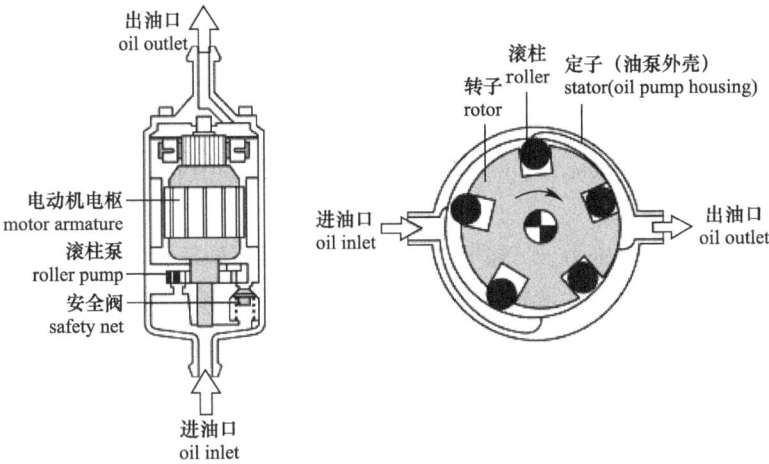

图 2.5.6　输油泵

Figure 2.5.6　Oil transfer pump

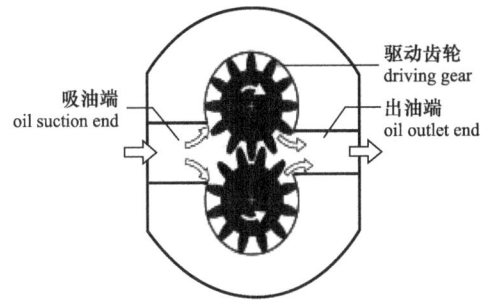

图 2.5.7　齿轮式输油泵

Figure 2.5.7　Gear fuel supply pump

2. 燃油滤清器（Fuel filter）

燃油滤清器（图 2.5.8）装在柴油机供给系的低压油路中，可保持柴油的清洁，以免柴油中含有各种杂质和水进入燃油系统造成腐蚀和损坏。燃油滤清器底部含有放水螺塞，每隔一段时间就须拧开放水螺塞将水放掉。部分车辆装备了自动水位报警装置，当积水过多时，装置的报警灯就会点亮。

It can keep the diesel oil clean to install fuel filter in the low-pressure fuel rail of the diesel engine supply system, so as to avoid the corrosion and damage caused by various impurities and water in the diesel oil entering the fuel system. The bottom of the fuel filter contains a water releasing screw plug, which must be opened at set intervals to release water. Some vehicles are equipped with automatic water level alarm device. When water accumulates too much, the alarm lamp of the device will light up.

5.2.2　高压油路部分（High pressure fuel rail）

高压油路部分主要包括高压油泵、压力控制阀、共轨管、喷油器和高压油管。

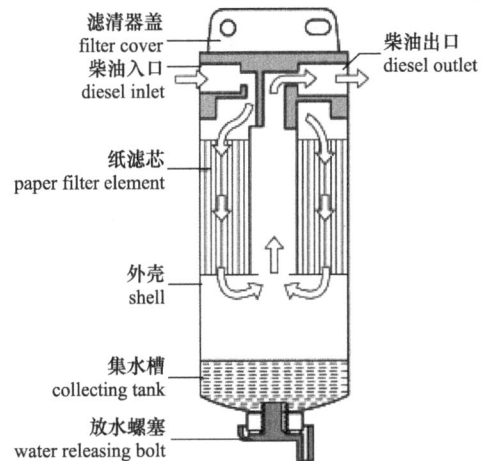

图 2.5.8　燃油滤清器

Figure 2.5.8　Fuel filter

The high-pressure oil pipeline mainly includes high-pressure oil pump, pressure control valve, common rail pipe, injector and high-pressure oil pipe.

1. 高压油泵（High-pressure oil pump）

高压油泵（图 2.5.9）的功用是压缩燃油，并按照发动机性能各方面的要求供应经压缩的燃油。

The function of high-pressure oil pump is to compress fuel and supply compressed fuel according to vari-

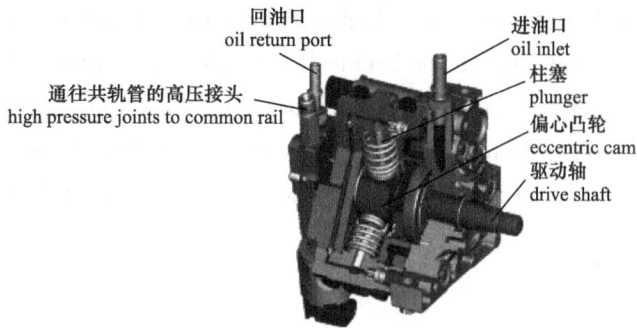

图 2.5.9　高压油泵

Figure 2.5.9　High pressure oil pump

ous requirements of engine performance.

它会不断地将燃油送入共轨管，以保持系统压力。高压泵通常安装在柴油机上，通过联轴器、齿轮、驱动链条或者驱动齿带由发动机驱动。高压油泵可以由低压油路过来的燃油或者发动机主油道过来的机油进行润滑。

It continuously transmits fuel into the common rail pipe to maintain the system pressure. High-pressure pumps are usually mounted on diesel engines and are driven by engines through couplings, gears, drive chains or drive toothed belts. High-pressure oil pump can be lubricated by fuel coming from low-pressure fuel rail or oil coming from main oil gallery of the engine.

部分柴油机利用三缸径向柱塞泵产生高达 135MPa 的压力。三缸径向柱塞泵驱动轴每转 1 圈有 3 个供油行程，驱动峰值扭矩小，受载均匀，可降低运行噪声。在喷油量较小的情况下，为减小功率损耗，将关闭三缸径向柱塞泵中的一个压油单元使供油量减少。

Some diesel engines use a three-cylinder radial piston pump to generate the pressure as high as 135MPa. It has three fuel supply strokes when the driving shaft of three-cylinder radial piston pump turns a circle. The driving peak torque is small and the load is uniform, which can reduce the running noises. In order to reduce power loss, a pressure unit in a three-cylinder radial piston pump will be closed to reduce fuel supply quantity in the case of small injection quantity.

在 2007 年推出的喷油压力高达 200MPa 的高压共轨喷油系统，开始应用双凸起凸轮高压油泵。双凸起凸轮高压油泵只采用了一个柱塞泵油单元，油泵的高压部分被设计成一个紧凑的泵油模块，集成在一个钢壳体中，具有结构紧凑，质量小的优点。双凸起凸轮高压油泵转速高，与高的油泵转速相结合。与传统偏心凸轮泵相比，大大缩减了供油时间，减少了柱塞的泄漏，从而达到最佳液压效率。

In 2007, the high pressure common rail fuel injection system with injection pressure up to 200MPa was introduced, and double cam high pressure oil pump began to be applied. Double cam high-pressure oil pump only uses one plunger pump unit, whose high-pressure part is designed as a compact oil pump module, which is integrated in a steel shell. It has the advantages of compact structure and small mass. Double cam high-pressure oil pump has high speed, which is combined with high pump speed. Compared with the traditional eccentric cam pump, it greatly reduces the oil supply time, reduces the leakage of plunger, and achieves the best hydraulic efficiency.

2. 压力控制阀 (Pressure control valve)

压力控制阀（图 2.5.10）是设定一个正确的、对应于发动机负荷的共轨压力，并且将其保持的装置。压力控制阀是通过一个安装法兰连接到高压油泵或者共轨管上。当共轨压力过大时，压力控制阀打开，一部分燃油经回油管路流回燃油箱；当共轨压力过小时，压力控制阀关闭。

Pressure control valve is a device that sets and maintains the correct common rail pressure corresponding to engine load. The pressure control valve is connected to the high pressure oil pump or common rail pipe through a mounting flange. When the common rail pressure is too high, the pressure control valve is opened and part of the fuel flows back to the fuel tank through the return pipe. When the common rail pressure is too small, the pressure control valve is closed.

压力控制阀未通电时，来自于共轨管或者高压油泵泵出的燃油压力，作用于球阀。由于未通电的电磁铁不产生作用力，当燃油压力超过弹簧弹力时，球阀打开泄压，直至燃油压力与弹簧弹力平衡。若需要增大燃油压力，电控单元向压力控制阀通电，由电磁铁产生的力与弹簧的弹力一起作用于球阀，球阀被关闭，直到燃油压力与弹簧弹力和电磁铁的合力平衡。接着，球阀保持部分开启，维持较高的燃油压力。

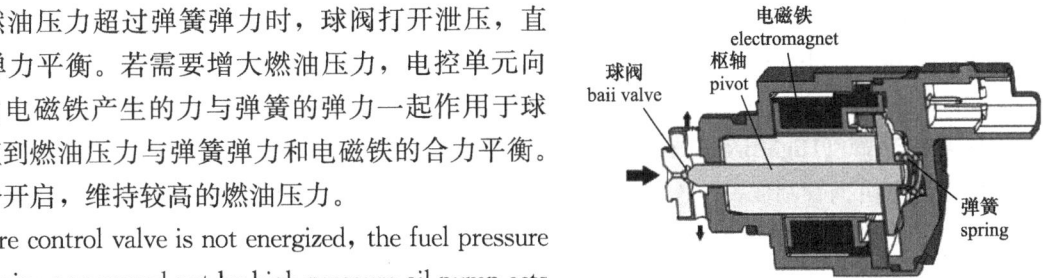

图 2.5.10　压力控制阀
Figure 2.5.10　Pressure control valve

When the pressure control valve is not energized, the fuel pressure from the common rail pipe or pumped out by high pressure oil pump acts on the ball valve. Because the electromagnet which is not energized does not produce acting force, when the fuel pressure exceeds the spring elastic force, the ball valve is opened to relieve pressure until the fuel pressure is balanced with the spring elastic force. If the fuel pressure needs to be increased, the electronic control unit energizes the pressure control valve. The force produced by the electromagnet acts on the ball valve together with the spring elastic force, and the ball valve is closed until the fuel pressure is balanced with the the combined force between spring elastic force and the the electromagnet force. Then, the ball valve keeps part open to maintain high fuel pressure.

3. 共轨管 （Common rail pipe）

共轨管（图 2.5.11）用于存贮高压燃油，高压油泵供油和喷油器喷油造成的压力波动可在共轨管中得到抑制，保持喷油器的喷油压力恒定。

Common rail pipe is used to store high-pressure fuel. The pressure fluctuation caused by high-pressure pump fuel supply and fuel injection of injector can be suppressed in the common rail tube to keep injection pressure of injector constant.

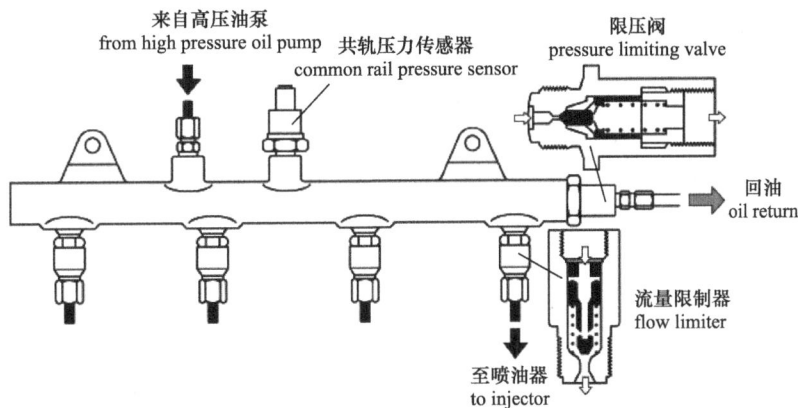

图 2.5.11　共轨管
Figure 2.5.11　Common rail pipe

共轨管上安装有共轨压力传感器、限压阀和流量限制器。共轨压力传感器向电控单元提供共轨管内的实时压力信号，作为共轨压力闭环控制的输入信号。限压阀是一个机械阀，当压力超过一定限值时即开启，以保证共轨管在出现压力异常时，将压力迅速释放从而确保系统安全。流量限制器的作用是阻止在非正常情况下喷油器常开导致的持续喷油，一旦输出的油量超过规定的水平，流量限制器就关闭通往喷油器的油路。

The common rail pressure sensor, pressure limiting valve and flow limiter are installed on the common rail pipe. The common rail pressure sensor provides real-time pressure signals in common rail tube to the electronic control unit as input signals of closed-loop control of the common rail pressure. The pressure limiting valve is a mechanical valve, which is opened when the pressure exceeds a certain limit to ensure that the common rail pipe releases the pressure rapidly in case of abnormal pressure, so as to ensure the safety of the system. The function of the flow limiter is to prevent the continuous fuel injection caused by the normal open of the injector under abnormal conditions. Once the output quantity of the fuel exceeds the required level, the flow limiter closes the fuel rail to the injector.

4. 高压油管（High-pressure fuel pipe）

高压油管由钢管制成，是连接共轨管和电控喷油器的通道。它应有足够的燃油流量，以减小燃油流动时的压降，并使高压管路系统中的压力波动较小，而且使启动时共轨油压能很快建立。各高压油管应尽可能短，以使从共轨管到喷油器的压力损失最小。各缸高压油管的长度应尽量相等，以使柴油机每个喷油器有相同的喷油压力，从而减少发动机各缸喷油量的偏差。

The high pressure oil pipe is made of a steel pipe, which is the channel connecting common rail pipe and electronic control injector. It should have enough fuel flow to reduce the pressure drop during the flowing of fuel, and make the pressure fluctuation in the high-pressure pipeline system smaller, and make the common rail oil pressure can be established quickly when it is started. The high pressure fuel pipe should be as short as possible to minimize the pressure loss from the common rail pipe to the injector. The length of each cylinder high-pressure fuel pipe should be as equal as possible so that each injector of the diesel engine has the same injection pressure, thus reducing the deviation of the injection quantity of each cylinder of the engine.

共轨管与各缸喷油器之间的不同间距是通过各缸高压油管的弯曲程度不同进行长度补偿。

The different spacing between common rail pipe and each cylinder injector is compensated by the different bending degree of high pressure fuel pipe of each cylinder.

5.2.3 喷油器（Injector）

喷油器（图 2.5.12）是电控高压共轨系统中最关键和最复杂的部件之一。喷油器根据电控单元发出的电信号控制电磁阀的开启和关闭，将共轨管中的燃油以最佳的喷油时刻、喷油量和喷油率喷入柴油机的燃烧室内。这种喷油器称为电磁阀式喷油器。

The injector is the most critical and complex component in the electronic high pressure common rail system. The injector controls the opening and closing of the solenoid valve according to the electric signals from the electronic control unit, and injects the fuel in the common rail pipe into the combustion chamber of the diesel engine with the optimum injection time, quantity and rate. This injector is called solenoid valve injector.

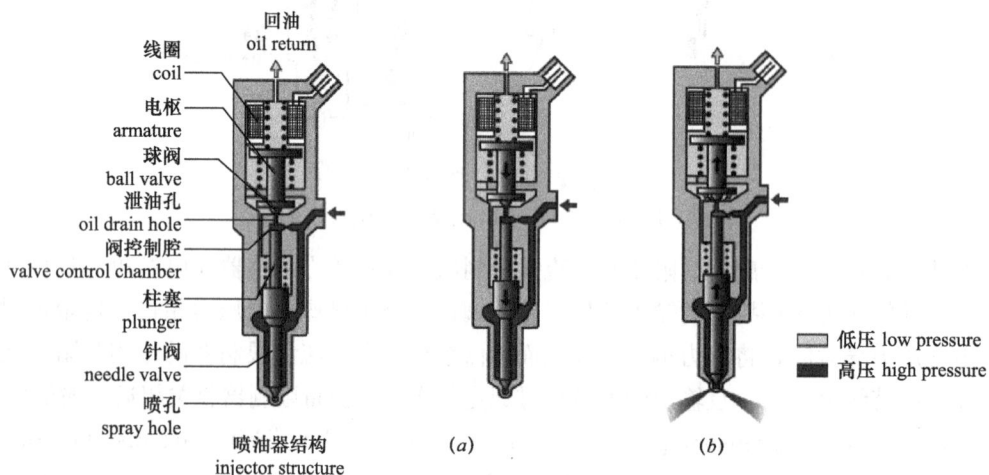

图 2.5.12 喷油器

Figure 2.5.12 Injector

（a）喷油器关闭（injector closing）；（b）喷油器开启（fuel injector opening）

当喷油器电磁阀未被触发时，小弹簧将电枢的球阀压向泄油孔，泄油孔被关闭，在阀控制腔内形成共轨高压。同样，在喷油器内也形成共轨高压。共轨高压对柱塞断面向下的压力和喷嘴弹簧向下的压力之和，大于高压燃油作用在针阀锥面上的开启力，使针阀压紧在其阀座上，喷油器保持关闭状态。

When the solenoid valve of the injector is not triggered, the small spring presses the ball valve of the armature against the oil drain hole, and the oil drain hole is closed, forming common rail high pressure in the valve control chamber. Similarly, common rail high pressure is formed in the injector as well. The sum of the downward pressure of common rail high pressure on plunger section and the downward pressure of nozzle spring is larger than the opening force of high pressure fuel on needle valve conical surface, which makes needle valve press on its seat and the injector keep closed.

当电磁阀被触发时，电枢向上移动，将泄油孔打开，燃油从阀控制腔流到上方的空腔中，从空腔通过回油管返回燃油箱。此时，阀控制腔内压力降低，减小了作用在柱塞断面上的力，高压燃油作用在针阀锥面上的开启力使针阀上移，喷油器开始喷油。

When the solenoid valve is triggered, the armature moves upward to peon the drain hole, and the fuel flows from the valve control chamber to the upper cavity, and returns to the fuel tank through the return pipe from the cavity. At this time, the pressure in the valve control chamber decreases, which reduces the force acting on the plunger section. The opening force of the high-pressure fuel acting on the conical surface of the needle valve makes the needle valve move upward and the injector begins to inject fuel.

思考与练习

(Reflection and Exercises)

1. 简述柴油机供给系统的作用及组成。
2. 简述柴油供给系统的工作原理。
3. 简述喷油器的作用、类型及其工作原理。
4. 简述高压共轨电控柴油机喷射系统的构成及原理。

1. Describe the Function and Composition of Diesel Engine Fuel Supply System.

2. Describe the working principle of diesel engine fuel supply system.

3. Describe the function, type and working principle of injectors.

4. Describe the composition and principle of electronic high pressure common rail fuel injection system of diesel engine.

任务六 冷却系统

Task 6 Cooling System

教学目标

1. 知识目标

(1) 了解强制循环水冷系统的结构；

(2) 了解冷却液的成分；

(3) 掌握强制循环水冷系统的各部件工作原理。

2. 能力目标

(1) 具有分析发动机冷却系统的各部件安装位置及冷却液的流经路线的能力；

（2）具有区分大小循环的能力。

3. 情感和素养目标

（1）培养学生良好的心理素质、善于发现困难的意识；

（2）培养学生爱岗敬业的意识、不断专研探究的工匠品质。

Teaching objectives

1. Knowledge objectives

（1）Understanding the structure of the forced circulation water cooling system；

（2）Understanding the composition of the coolant；

（3）Mastering the working principle of the components of the forced circulation water cooling system.

2. Ability objectives

（1）The ability to analyze the installation position of the components of the engine cooling system and the flow path of the coolant.

（2）The ability to distinguish between large and small cycles.

3. Emotion and quality goals

（1）Cultivate students′ psychological quality and the awareness to overcome difficulties.

（2）Cultivate students′ awareness of being dedicated to their jobs and craftsmanship spirit of striving for exploration.

6.1 概述（Overview）

6.1.1 冷却系统的作用（Function of cooling system）

当发动机运转时，燃料的燃烧和运动件间的摩擦都将产生大量的热量，发动机温度随之升高。冷却系统为强制性地将零件所吸收到的热量及时散去的系统，起到保持发动机温度在一定工作范围，确保发动机的正常运转，如图 2.6.1 所示。

When the engine runs, the combustion of fuel and friction between moving parts will generate a lot of heat，and the engine temperature will rise accordingly. Cooling system is a system that forces the heat absorbed by the parts to be dissipated in time to keep the engine temperature within a certain working range and ensure the normal operation of the engine.

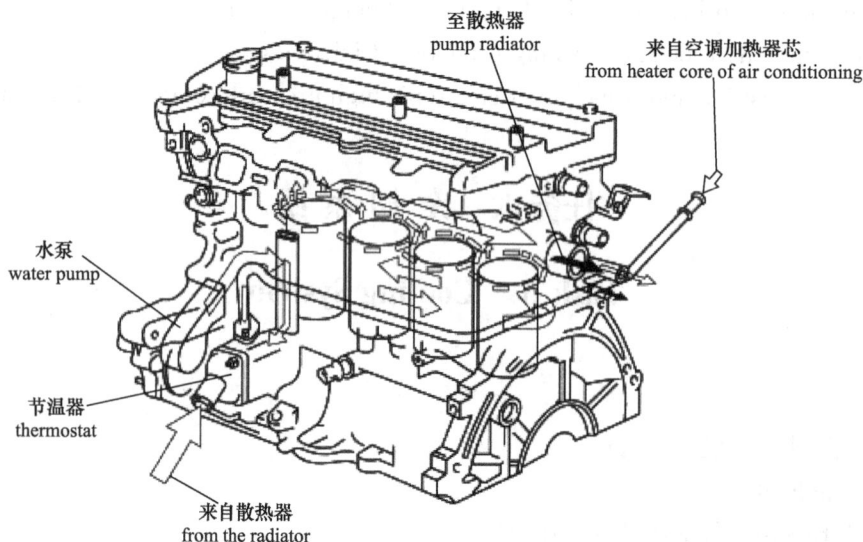

图 2.6.1　冷却系统

Figure 2.6.1　Cooling system

6.1.2 冷却液（Coolant）

冷却液又称防冻液、抗冻液等，由水、防冻剂和添加剂三部分组成，按防冻剂成分不同可分为酒精型、甘油型和乙二醇型等类型。目前国内外发动机所使用的和市场上所出售的冷却液几乎都是乙二醇型冷却液，推荐使用乙二醇含量在50%～70%的冷却液。通常根据汽车行驶里程或时间长短来定期更换发动机的冷却液。冷却液除散热外还有以下作用：

Coolant, also known as antifreeze liquid and anti-freezing liquid, etc., consists of water, antifreeze agent and additive. According to the composition of antifreeze agent, it can be divided into alcohol type, glycerol type and ethylene glycol type. At present, almost all the coolants used in engines at home and abroad and sold in the market are ethylene glycol type coolants. Coolants containing more than 50% ethylene glycol and less than 70% ethylene glycol are recommended. Generally, the engine coolant is replaced regularly according to the mileage of the vehicle or the duration. Coolant has the following functions besides heat dissipation:

1. 冬季防冻功能（Antifreezing function in winter）

为了防止汽车在冬季停车后，冷却液结冰而造成水箱、发动机缸体胀裂，要求冷却液的冰点应低于该地区最低温度10℃左右，以备天气突变。

In order to prevent the water tank and engine block from cracking due to the freezing of the coolant after the car stops in winter, it is required that the freezing point of the coolant should be lower than the minimum temperature in the area of about 10 degrees Celsius in case of a sudden change of weather.

2. 防腐蚀功能（Anticorrosion function）

冷却系统中散热器、水泵、缸体及缸盖、分水管等部件是由钢、铸铁、黄铜、紫铜、铝、焊锡等金属组成，由于不同金属的电极电位不同，在电解质的作用下容易发生电化学腐蚀；同时冷却液中的二元醇类物质分解后形成的酸性产物、燃料燃烧后形成的酸性废气也可能渗透到冷却系统中，促进冷却系统腐蚀。因此冷却液中都加入一定量的防腐蚀添加剂，防止冷却系统产生腐蚀。

Radiator, water pump, cylinder block, cylinder head and distributed water pipe and other parts in cooling system are composed of steel, cast iron, brass, red copper, aluminium, soldering tin and other metals. Due to the different electrode potentials of different metals, electrochemical corrosion is prone to occur under the action of electrolytes. Moreover, the acidic products formed by the decomposition of dihydric alcohols in the coolant and the acid exhaust gas formed by the combustion of fuel may also permeate into the cooling system to promote the corrosion of the cooling system. Therefore, a certain amount of anti-corrosion additives are added to the coolant to prevent the corrosion of the cooling system.

3. 防水垢功能（Anti-scale function）

冷却液在循环中应尽可能多地减少水垢的产生，以免堵塞循环管道，影响冷却系统的散热功能。

Coolant in the circulation should be as much as possible to reduce the generation of water scale, so as to avoid blocking the circulating pipeline, affecting the heat dissipation function of the cooling system.

4. 防开锅功能（Anti-boiling function）

符合国家标准的冷却液，沸点通常都是超过105℃，因此冷却液能耐受更高的温度而不沸腾（开锅），在一定程度上满足了高负荷发动机的散热冷却需要。

The boiling point of the coolant which meets national standards is usually more than 105℃. Therefore, the coolant can withstand higher temperature without boiling, and to some extent meets the requirements of heat dissipation and cooling of the high-load engine.

6.2 水冷却系统（Water-cooling system）

一般发动机的冷却系统组成大体相同，由水泵、水套、散热器、节温器和冷却风扇等组成。为保证发动机正常工作，冷却液必须按照规定的路径流动，如图 2.6.2 所示。

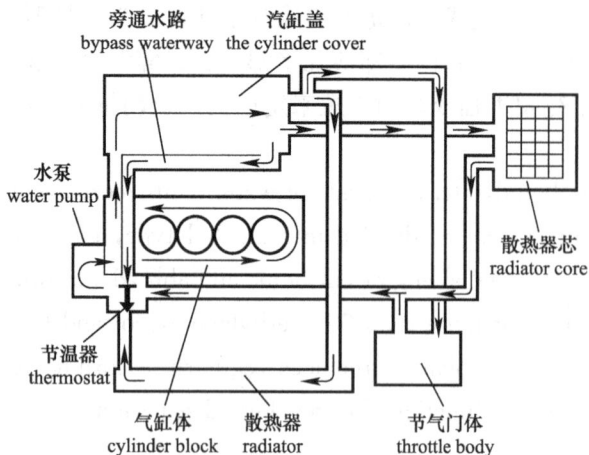

图 2.6.2　水冷却系统组成

Figure 2.6.2　Composition of water cooling system

The composition of the engine cooling systems are generally the same, which is composed of water pump, water jacket, radiator, thermostat and cooling fans, etc. In order to ensure the normal operation of the engine, the coolant must flow along the prescribed path.

在冷却系统中，其实有两个散热循环：一个是冷却发动机的主循环，另一个是车内取暖循环。这两个循环都以发动机为中心，使用的是同一冷却液。

In the cooling system, there are actually two cooling circulations: one is the main cycle of cooling the engine, the other is the heating cycle inside the car. Both cycles are engine-centered and use the same coolant.

主循环中包括了两种工作循环，即"冷车循环"和"正常循环"。冷车着车后，发动机在渐渐升温，冷却液的温度还无法打开系统中的节温器，冷却液只是经过水泵在发动机内进行"冷车循环"即小循环。目的是使发动机尽快地达到正常工作温度。随着发动机的温度升高，冷却液温度升到了节温器的开启温度，冷却循环开始了"正常循环"，即大循环。这时候的冷却液从发动机出来，经过车前端的散热器，散热后，再经水泵进入发动机。

The main cycle includes two kinds of working cycles, namely "cold car cycle" and "normal cycle". After the cold car starts, the engine is gradually warming up. The temperature of the coolant can not open the thermostat of the system. Coolant is only circulated through the water pump in the engine, that is, the small cycle, whose aim is to make the engine work at normal temperature as soon as possible. As the engine temperature rises, the coolant temperature rises to the opening temperature of the thermostat, and the cooling cycle begins a "normal cycle", that is, a large cycle. At this time, the coolant comes out of the engine, passing through the radiator at the front end of the car. After heat dissipation, it enters the engine via the water pump.

车内取暖循环同样是一个发动机的冷却循环。冷却液经过车内的采暖装置，将冷却液的热量送入车内，然后回到发动机。有一点不同的是：取暖循环不受节温器的控制，只要打开暖气，循环就开始进行，不管冷却液是冷的、还是热的。

The heating cycle inside the car is also a cooling cycle of the engine. The coolant passes through the heating device in the car, feeds the heat of the coolant into the car, and then returns to the engine. There is one difference that the heating cycle is not controlled by the thermostat. As long as the heater is turned on, the cycle begins, whether the coolant is cold or hot.

冷却系统的主要部件有节温器、散热器、风扇和水泵等。

The main components of cooling system are thermostat, radiator, fan and water pump, etc.

6.2.1　节温器（Thermostat）

节温器安装在水泵的进水口或气缸盖的出水口处，节温器能根据发动机负荷大小和水温的高低自动改变冷却液循环流动的路径及流量，达到调节冷却系统的冷却强度，以保证发动机工作正常温度的目的。

The thermostat is installed at the inlet of the water pump or the outlet of the cylinder head, which can automatically change the circulation path and flow quantity of the coolant according to the load of the engine and water temperature, so as to adjust the cooling intensity of the cooling system to ensure the normal operating temperature of the engine.

1. 传统节温器 (Traditional thermostat)

传统节温器（图 2.6.3）有蜡式和膨胀式两种，目前多数发动机采用蜡式节温器。节温器上一般标有阀门开启温度。节温器附近的冷却液温度在 82℃左右时阀门开始打开。如果冷却系统工作正常，发动机冷却液的温度就应该在节温器的开启温度和全开温度之间变化。

There are two kinds of traditional thermostats: wax-type thermostat and expansion type thermostat. At present, most engines use wax type thermostat. The temperature of valve-opening is generally marked on the thermostat. The valve is opened when the coolant temperature near the thermostat is about 82℃. If the cooling system works properly, the temperature of the engine coolant should vary between the opening temperature of the thermostat and the full opening temperature.

将节温器浸入水中，慢慢将水加热，检查阀门开启温度，阀门的开启温度应为 80～84℃，阀门升程在 95℃时应不小于 10mm，如图 2.6.4 所示。当节温器处于较低温度（低于 77℃）时，阀门应该完全关闭。

Immerse the thermostat in water, slowly heat the water, check the opening temperature of the valve. The opening temperature of the valve should be 80～84℃, and the lift of the valve should be at least 10 mm or more at 95℃, as shown in Figure 2.6.4. When the thermostat is at a lower temperature (below 77℃), the valve should be completely closed.

图 2.6.3 传统节温器

Figure 2.6.3 Traditional thermostat

图 2.6.4 节温器的检查

Figure 2.6.4 Inspection of thermostat

2. 电子节温器 (Electronic thermostat)

当发动机部分负荷时，较高的发动机温度能降低燃油消耗、降低有害物质排放；发动机全负荷时，较低的发动机温度能使进气加热作用较小，提高发动机性能、增加动力输出。因此发动机的负荷与发动机的冷却强度是相对的。

When the engine is partially loaded, higher engine temperature can reduce fuel consumption and emissionsof harmful substances. While the engine is fully loaded, the lower engine temperature can make less effect on the intake heating, improve the engine performance and increase the power output. Therefore, the load of the engine is relative to the cooling intensity of the engine.

电子节温器（图 2.6.5）除了具备传统节温器的功能外还能根据发动机负荷的变化为发动机设定一个适宜的工作温度。

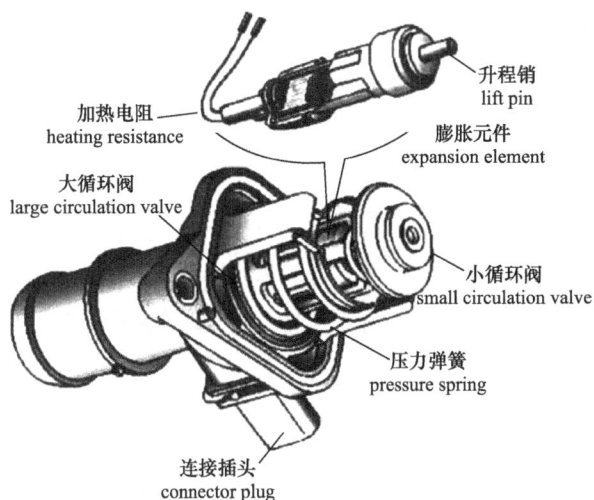

图 2.6.5 电子节温器

Figure 2.6.5 Electronic Thermostat

Electronic thermostat not only has functions of traditional thermostat，but also can set a suitable working temperature for engine according to the change of engine load.

(1) 冷却液小循环路径（Small circulation path of coolant）

冷却液经过发动机缸盖，小循环阀门打开，冷却液流经小阀门后被水泵直接抽吸回去，形成小循环（图 2.6.6）。

The coolant passes through the engine cylinder head，and the small circulation valve is opened. After the coolant flows through the small valve，it is directly sucked back by the water pump to form a small circulation.

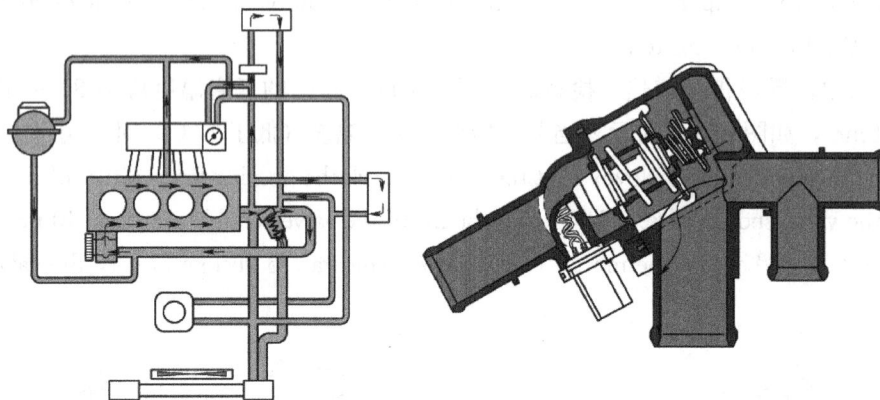

图 2.6.6　小循环路径

Figure 2.6.6　Small circulation paths

(2) 冷却液大循环路径（Large circulation path of coolant）

发动机全负荷运转时，冷却系统需具备较高的冷却强度。发动机控制单元根据相应的传感器信号进行计算后输出电信号给电子节温器，溶解石蜡体。大循环阀门打开（图 2.6.7），同时关闭小循环通道，切断小循环，使冷却液温度保持在 85～95℃ 之间。石蜡的加热程度由发动机控制单元输出的脉冲信号脉宽决定。

When the engine runs with full load，the cooling system should have higher cooling intensity. The engine control unit calculates according to the corresponding sensor signal and then outputs the electric signal to the electronic thermostat to dissolve the paraffin body. When the large circulation valve is opened and the small circulation channel is closed，and the small circulation is cut off，the coolant temperature can be kept between 85 and 95 degrees Celsius. The degree of paraffin heating is determined by the pulse width of the output signal from the engine control unit.

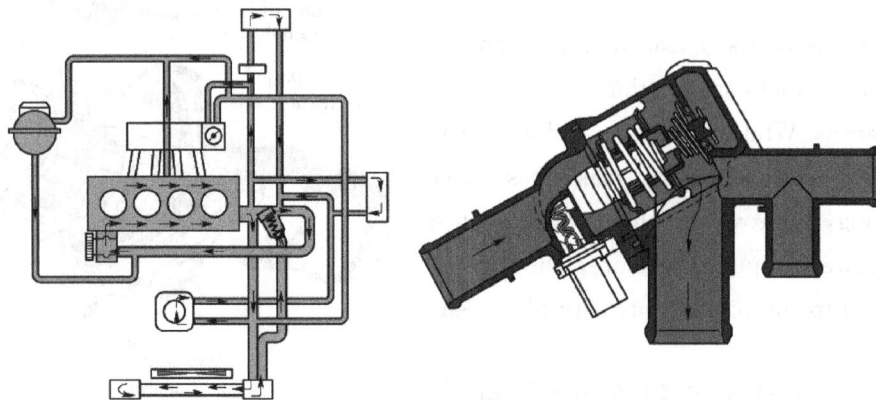

图 2.6.7　大循环路径

Figure 2.6.7　Large circulation paths

6.2.2 散热器（Radiator）

散热器（图2.6.8）由上储水室、下储水室、散热器芯和散热器盖等组成。冷却液在散热器芯内流动，空气在散热器芯外通过。热的冷却液由于向空气散热而变冷，冷空气则因为吸收冷却液散出的热量而升温，所以散热器是一个热交换器。

The radiator is composed of upper water storage chamber, lower water storage chamber, radiator core and radiatorcap, etc. The coolant flows inside the radiator core, while air passes through outside the radiator core. The hot coolant becomes cold by dissipating heat into the air, while the cold air is heated by absorbing the heat of the coolant, so the radiator is a heat exchanger.

汽车散热器的材质主要有两种：铝质和铜制。前者用于一般乘用车，后者用于大型商用车。

There are two main materials of automobile radiators: aluminium and copper. The former is used for general passenger cars, while the latter is used for large commercial vehicles.

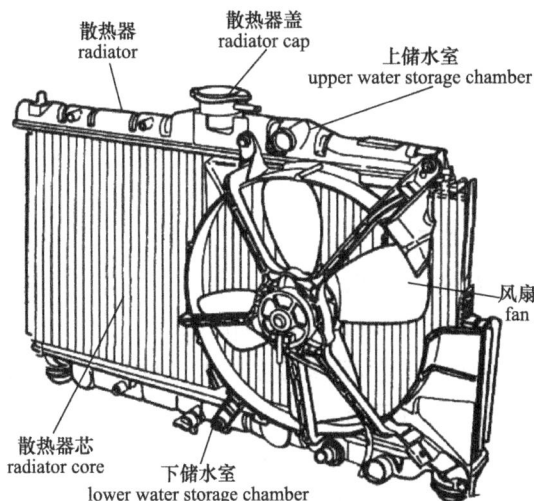

图2.6.8 散热器组成示意图

Figure 2.6.8 Composition diagram of radiator

6.2.3 水泵（Water pump）

水泵通过叶轮的旋转对冷却液加压，使冷却液循环流动，保证发动机工作温度。当冷却液进入到水泵转子工作室后，冷却液在转子的带动下一起转动，由于离心力的作用，冷却液被甩到转子的边缘，随后由于冷却液分子间的推动作用使冷却液向出水口流出而进入发动机缸体水套，与此同时，在转子的中部形成吸力将冷却液吸入，随后又被甩到转子叶片边缘。冷却液便在水泵的作用下不停地循环流动（图2.6.9）。

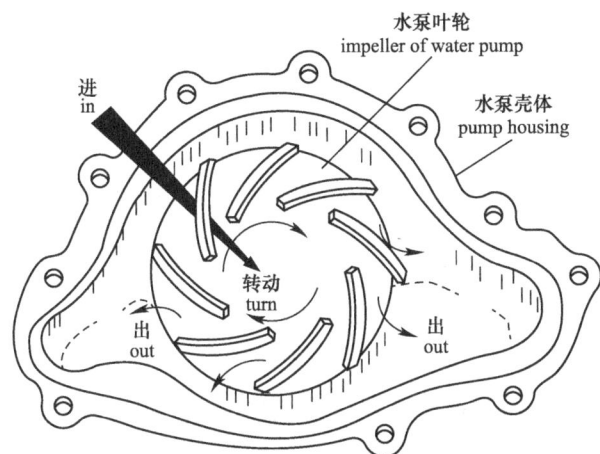

图2.6.9 离心式水泵工作原理

Figure 2.6.9 Working principle of centrifugal water pump

The pump pressurizes the coolant through the rotation of the impeller, which makes the coolant circulate and ensures the working temperature of the engine. When the coolant enters the pump rotor chamber, the coolant rotates together driven by the rotor. Because of centrifugal force, the coolant is thrown to the edge of the rotor, and then the coolant flows out to the outlet and enters the water jacket of the engine block due to the driving effect of the coolant molecules. Meanwhile, a suction force is formed in the middle of the rotor to suck the coolant, which is then thrown to the edge of the rotor blade. The coolant circulates continuously under the action of the water pump.

思考与练习

(Reflection and Exercises)

1. 简述冷却系统的作用、组成以及工作原理。
2. 简述电子节温器的工作原理。

3. 简述大循环与小循环的区别。

1. Describe the function, composition and working principle of cooling system.

2. Describe the working principle of electronic thermostat.

3. Describe the differences between large circulation and small circulation.

任务七 润滑系统

Task 7 Lubrication System

教学目标

1. 知识目标

(1) 知道润滑系统的作用；

(2) 知道润滑系统的主要结构和工作原理。

2. 能力目标

(1) 具有区分不同种机油的能力；

(2) 能根据不同车型选择机油的能力。

3. 情感和素养目标

(1) 培养学生高压自我调节意识，面对困难敢于挑战的人格品质；

(2) 培养学生能遵纪守法，吃苦耐劳的精神。

Teaching objectives

1. Knowledge objectives

(1) Knowing the functions of lubrication system；

(2) Knowing the main structure and working principle of lubrication system.

2. Ability objectives

(1) The ability to distinguish different kinds of engine oil；

(2) The ability to select engine oil according to different types of vehicles.

3. Emotion and quality goals

(1) Cultivate students' self-adjusting consciousness under high pressure and the personality quality to dare to challenge when facing difficulties；

(2) Cultivate students' awareness to observe laws and disciplines and hard-working spirit.

7.1 概述 （Overview）

7.1.1 润滑系统的作用 （The functions of lubrication system）

发动机工作时，发动机的润滑是由润滑系统来实现的，润滑系统连续不断地将润滑油输送到各摩擦表面，并在摩擦表面形成一层薄的油膜，以减小摩擦阻力、降低功率损耗、减轻机件磨损，润滑系统有润滑、清洁、冷却、密封和防蚀五大作用。

When the engine runs, the lubrication of the engine is realized by the lubrication system. The lubrication system continuously transfers the lubricant to the friction surfaces and forms a thin oil film on the friction surfaces to reduce the friction resistance, power loss and wear of the engine parts. The lubrication system has five functions: lubrication, cleaning, cooling, sealing and corrosion prevention.

7.1.2 发动机的润滑方式 （Lubrication mode of engines）

发动机工作时，由于各运动零件的工作条件不同，因而所要求的润滑强度和方式也不同。零件表面的润滑，按其供油方式可分为压力润滑和飞溅润滑。此外还有润滑脂润滑。现代汽车发动机一般采用复合式润滑方式。

When the engine works, because the working conditions of the moving parts are different, the required lubrication strength and mode are also different. The lubrication of part surface can be divided into pressure lubrication and splash lubrication according to the way of oil supply. In addition, there is grease lubrication. Compound lubrication is adopted in modern automobile engines.

7.1.3 润滑系统组成 (Composition of lubrication system)

汽车发动机润滑系统的组成及油路布置大致相似，只是由于润滑系统的工作条件和具体结构的不同而稍有差别。发动机润滑系统的组成，如图2.7.1所示。

The composition and oil path arrangement of the lubrication system of automobile engines are similar, but they are slightly different because of the different working conditions and specific structures of the lubrication system. The consists of engine lubrication system, as shown in Figure 2.7.1.

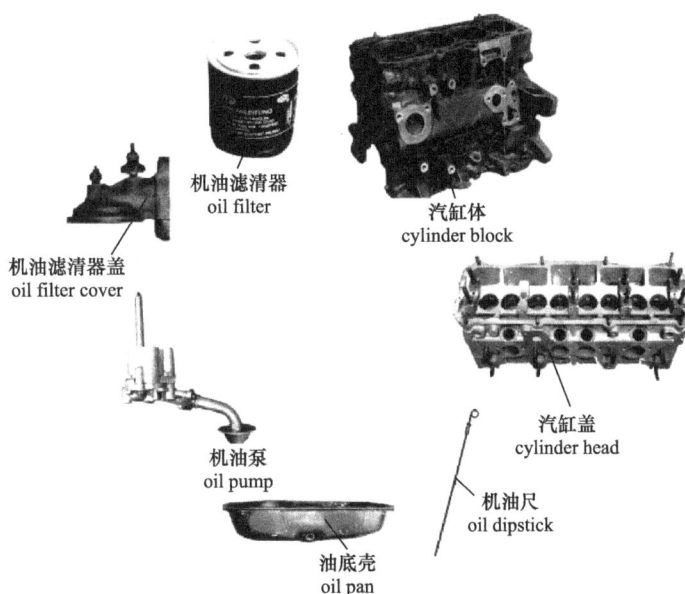

图2.7.1 润滑系统的组成
Figure 2.7.1 Composition of lubrication system

7.1.4 润滑系统油路 (Oil path of lubrication system)

汽油机与柴油机润滑油路略有不同，分别如图2.7.2和图2.7.3所示。

The lubricating oil path of gasoline engine is slightly different from that of diesel engine, as shown in Figs. 2.7.2 and Figs. 2.7.3 respectively.

7.2 润滑系统构造 (Lubrication system structure)

现代汽车发动机润滑系统的组成及油路布置方案大致相似，只是由于润滑系统的工作条件和具体结构的不同而稍有差别。润滑系统一般由油底壳、机油泵、机油滤清器、主油道、限压阀、旁通阀、传感器和机油压力报警指示灯等组成。

The composition and arrangement of lubrication system of modern automobile engine are similar, but slightly different because of the different working conditions and specific structures of lubrication system. Lubrication system is generally composed of oil pan, oil pump, oil filter, main oilgallery, pressure limiting valve, bypass valve, sensors and oil pressure alarm indicator light, etc.

机油必须按照规定的流经路径流动，如图2.7.4所示。

Oil must flow along the prescribed flow path, as shown in Figure 2.7.4.

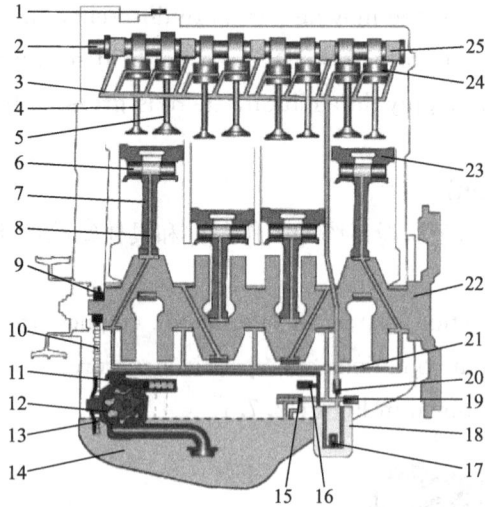

图 2.7.2　润滑系统的组成

Figure 2.7.2　Composition of lubrication system

1—加机油盖：oil filler cap；2—凸轮轴：camshaft；3—缸盖主油道：main oil gallery of cylinder head；4—进气门：intake valve；5—排气门：exhaust valve；6—活塞销：piston pin；7—连杆：connecting rod；8—连杆油道：connecting rod oil channnel；9—曲轴链轮：crankshaft sprocket；10—链条：chain；11—溢流阀：relief valve；12—机油泵：oil pump；13—机油泵链轮：oil pump sprocket；14—油底壳：oil pan；15—限压阀：pressure limiting valve；16—油压开关：oil pressure switch；17—旁通阀：bypass valve；18—机油滤清器：oil filter；19—油压开关：oil pressure switch；20—止回阀：check valve；21—气缸主油道：cylinder main oil gallery；22—曲轴：crankshaft；23—活塞：piston；24—液力挺柱：hydraulic tappet；25—凸轮轴支撑轴颈：camshaft journal

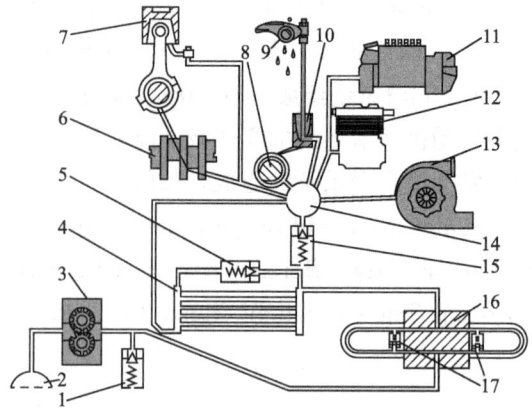

图 2.7.3　柴油机润滑系统油路示意图

Figure 2.7.3　Oil circuit diagram of diesel engine lubrication system

1—机油限压阀：oil pressure limiting valve；2—集滤器：suction filter；3—机油泵：oil pump；4—机油冷却器：oil cooler；5—机油冷却器限压阀：oil cooler pressure limiting valve；6—曲轴：crankshaft；7—连杆小头：connecting rod small end；8—凸轮轴：camshaft；9—摇臂轴：rocker arm shaft；10—挺柱：tappet；11—喷油泵：fuel injection pump；12—空气压缩机：air compressor；13—增压器：turbocharger；14—主油道：main oil way；15—限压阀：pressure limiting valve；16—机油滤清器：oil filter；17—滤清器旁通阀：filter bypass valve.

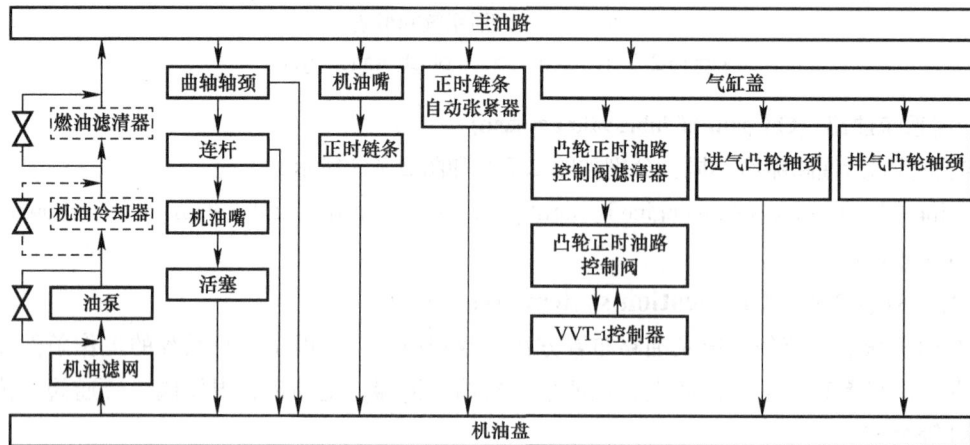

图 2.7.4　润滑系统机油流经路径

Figure 2.7.4　Oil path of lubrication system

注：主油路：main oil gallery；燃油滤清器：fuel filter；机油冷却器：oil cooler；油泵：oil pump；机油滤网：oil filter screen；曲轴轴颈：crankshaft journal；连杆：connecting rod；机油嘴：oil nozzle；活塞：piston；正时链条：timing chain；正时链条自动张紧器：timing chain automatic tensioner；气缸盖：cylinder head；凸轮正时油路控制阀滤清器：cam timing oil circuit control valve filter；凸轮正时油路控制阀：cam timing oil circuit control valve；VVT-i控制器：VVT-i controller；进气凸轮轴颈：intake cam journal；排气凸轮轴颈：exhaust cam journal.

7.2.1 机油泵 (Oil pump)

机油泵的作用是将一定压力和足够数量的润滑油压送到各摩擦表面，并保证润滑油在系统内的正常循环流动。发动机润滑系统中广泛采用的是转子式机油泵和齿轮式机油泵两种。

The function of the oil pump is to send lubricating oil with a certain pressure and sufficient amount to the friction surfaces, and to ensure the normal circulation of lubricating oil in the system. Rotor-type oil pump and gear-type oil pump are widely used in engine lubrication system.

1. 转子式机油泵 (Rotor-type oil pump)

转子式机油泵（图 2.7.5）由壳体、内转子、外转子和泵盖等组成。

Rotor oil pump is composed of shell, inner rotor, outer rotor and pump cover, etc.

转子齿形齿廓设计使得转子转到任何角度时，内、外转子每个齿的齿形廓线上总能互相成点接触。这样内、外转子间形成 4 个工作腔，随着转子的转动，这 4 个工作腔的容积是不断变化的。在进油道的一侧空腔，由于转子脱开啮合，容积逐渐增大，产生真空形成吸油腔，机油被吸入。转子继续旋转，机油被带到出油道的一侧，随着转子啮合，使这一空腔容积减小，油压升高，机油从齿间挤出并经出油道压送出去。这样，随着转子的不断旋转，机油就不断地被吸入和压出。

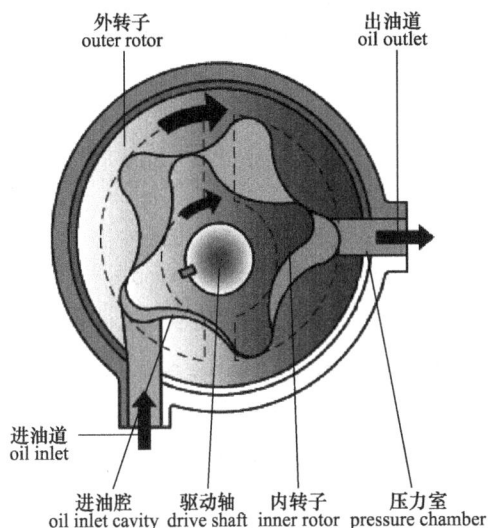

图 2.7.5 转子机油泵结构图
Figure 2.7.5 Structure Diagram of Rotor Oil Pump

The tooth profile of the rotor is designed so that when the rotor rotates to any angle, the tooth profile of each tooth of the inner and outer rotor can always have point contact with each other. In this way, four working chambers are formed between the inner and outer rotors. With the rotation of the rotor, the volumes of these four working chambers are constantly changing. On one side of the oil inlet, the volume of the cavity increases gradually due to the disengagement of the rotors, resulting in a vacuum to form an oil-suction chamber, where the oil is sucked into. As the rotor continues to rotate, the oil is brought to the side of the oil outlet. With the engagement of the rotors, the volume of the cavity decreases and the oil pressure increases. The oil is extruded through the spaces between the teeth and pressed out through the oil outlet. In this way, with the continuous rotation of the rotor, the oil is constantly sucked in and pressed out.

转子式机油泵结构紧凑，外形尺寸小，质量轻，吸油真空度较大，泵油量大，供油均匀度好，成本低，在中、小型发动机上应用广泛。

Rotor oil pump has compact structure, small size, light weight, large oil suction vacuum, large pump oil quantity, good uniformity of oil supply, low cost, and is widely used in small and medium-size engines.

2. 齿轮式机油泵 (Gear type oil pump)

齿轮式机油泵（图 2.7.6）结构，由主动轴、主动齿轮、从动轴、从动齿轮、壳体等组成。

The structure of gear type oil pump is composed of driving shaft, driving gear, driven shaft, driven gear and shell, etc.

齿轮式机油泵结构简单，机械加工方便，工作可靠，使用寿命长，应用较广泛。

Gear oil pump has simple structure, convenient mechanical processing, reliable operation, long service life and wide application.

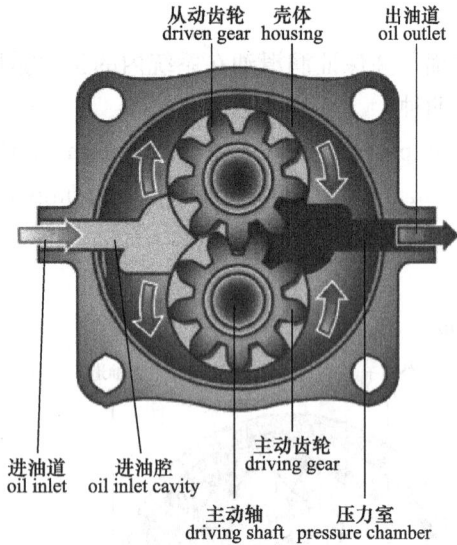

图 2.7.6 齿轮式机油泵
Figure 2.7.6 Gear oil pump

7.2.2 机油滤清器 (Oil filter)

发动机工作时,金属磨屑和大气中的尘埃以及燃料燃烧不完全所产生的炭粒会渗入机油中,机油本身也因受热氧化而产生胶状沉淀物,机油中含有这些杂质。如果把这样的脏机油直接送到运动零件表面,机油中的机械杂质就会成为磨料,加速零件的磨损,并且引起油道堵塞及活塞环、气门等零件胶结。因此必须在润滑系统中设有机油滤清器,使循环流动的机油在送往运动零件表面之前得到净化处理、保证摩擦表面的良好润滑,延长其使用寿命。

When the engine works, metal abrasive dust, dust in the atmosphere and carbon granules produced by incomplete combustion of fuel will penetrate into the oil. The oil itself also produces gelatinous precipitates due to thermal oxidation. The oil contains these impurities. If such dirty oil is sent directly to the surface of the moving parts, the mechanical impurities in the oil will become abrasives, which accelerates the wear of the parts, and cause the blockage of the oil passages and the cementation of the piston rings, valves and other parts. Therefore, an oil filter must be installed in the lubrication system to purify the circulating oil before it is sent to the surface of moving parts, to ensure good lubrication of the friction surface, and to prolong its service life.

1. 集滤器 (Suction filter)

集滤器(图 2.7.7)是具有金属网的滤清器,集滤器安装于机油泵进油管上,其作用是防止较大的机械杂质进入机油泵。浮式集滤器飘浮于机油表面吸油,能吸入油面上较清洁的机油,但油面上的泡沫易被吸入,使机油压力降低,润滑欠可靠,因此目前应用不广泛。固定式集滤器淹没在油面之下,吸入的机油清洁度较差,但可防止泡沫吸入,润滑可靠,结构简单,逐步取代浮式集滤器。

The suction filter (Figure 2.7.7) is a filter with metal mesh, which is installed on the oil inlet pipe of the oil pump, whose function is to prevent the larger mechanical impurities from entering the oil pump. Floating filter is floating on the surface of the oil to suck oil, which can suck the cleaner oil on the oil surface. The foams on the oil surface is easy to be inhaled, so that the oil pressure is reduced and the lubrication is not reliable, so it is not widely used at present. The fixed type suction filter is submerged under the oil surface, so the oil cleanliness is poor. It can prevent foam inhalation. Due to the reliable lubrication and simple structure, it gradually replaces the floating filter.

2. 机油滤清器 (Oil filter)

机油在发动机工作过程中经常会受到灰尘、积炭和机械磨损的铜、铁屑等其他杂质的污染。因此必须在机油进入主油道之前采用机油滤清器对其进行过滤,使之保持清洁,以减少机件的磨损,延长机件和润滑油的使用寿命,目前中小型发动机普遍使用旋装式一次性机油滤清器。机油滤清器(图 2.7.8)主要由外壳、纸质滤芯、螺纹盖板和旁通阀等组成。

Oil is often polluted by the impurities such as dust, carbon deposit and copper and iron filings from mechanical wear and others during engine operation. Therefore, the oil filter must be used to filter the oil before it enters the main oil gallery to keep it clean so as to reduce the wear and tear of the parts and prolong the service life of the parts and lubrication oil. At present, spin-on disposable oil filter is widely used in small and medium engines. Oil filter (Figure 2.7.8) is mainly composed of casing, paper filter element, screw cover plate and bypass valve, etc.

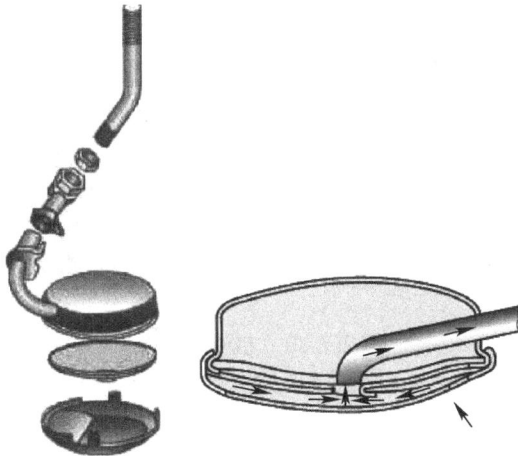

图 2.7.7　集滤器示意图
Figure 2.7.7　Diagram of suction filter

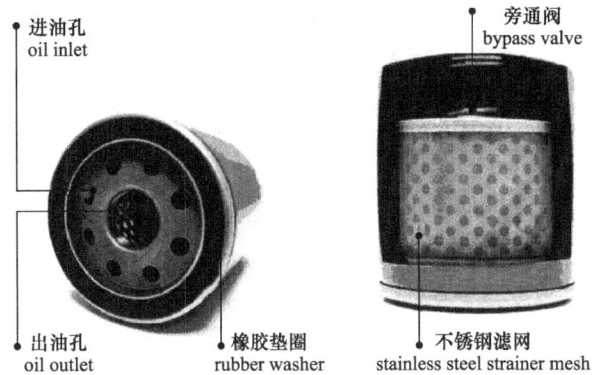

图 2.7.8　机油滤清器
Figure 2.7.8　Oil filter

（标注：进油孔 oil inlet；出油孔 oil outlet；橡胶垫圈 rubber washer；旁通阀 bypass valve；不锈钢滤网 stainless steel strainer mesh）

发动机工作时，机油以一定压力输送到滤清器的进油口（螺纹盖板的多个冲孔），进入滤清器的滤芯表面，经滤芯过滤后进入中心管，再从出油口（即中心螺纹孔）流进发动机的主油道进行润滑。机油滤清器必须定期更换，一般在更换机油时一起更换。

When the engine works, the oil is transported to the oil inlet of the filter (multiple punched holes of the screw blind flange) at a certain pressure and enters the surface of the filter core. After filtered by the filter core, the oil enters the central pipe, and then flows into the main oil passage of the engine from the oil outlet (i. e. the central threaded hole) for lubrication. Oil filters must be replaced regularly. Generally, they should be replaced together when oil is replaced.

7.2.3　机油散热器和冷却器（Oil radiator and cooler）

1. 机油散热器（Oil radiator）

机油散热器（图 2.7.9）由散热管、限压阀、开关、进出水管等组成，其结构与冷却系统散热器相似。

Oil radiator (Figure 2.7.9) is composed of radiating pipes, pressure limiting valve, switch, inlet and outlet pipes, etc. , whose structure is similar to that of cooling system radiator.

机油散热器一般安装在冷却系统散热器的前面，与主油道并联。机油泵工作时，将一部分机油供给主油道，另一部分机油经过限压阀、机油散热器开关进入机油散热器内，经过冷却后流回油底壳，如此不断循环流动。

Oil radiator is usually installed in front of cooling system radiator and connected in parallel with main oil gallery. When the oil pump works, part of the oil is supplied to the main oil passage. The other part of the oil passes through the pressure limiting valve and oil radiator switch into the oil radiator. After cooled, it flows back to the oil pan, so it circulates continuously.

2. 机油冷却器（Oil cooler）

一般来说热负荷不大的发动机没有机油冷却器，但对于高性能、高输出功率的发动机来说确实必不可少。风冷式机油冷却器一般安装在保险杠内等隐蔽的地方，利用流动的空气对机油进行冷却，如图 2.7.10 所示。

Generally speaking, engines with low heat load do not have oil coolers, but they are essential for engines with high performance and high output power. Air-cooling oil coolers are usually installed in hidden places such as bumpers, which use flowing air to cool the oil, as shown in Figure 2.7.10.

图 2.7.9　机油散热器

Figure 2.7.9　Oil radiator

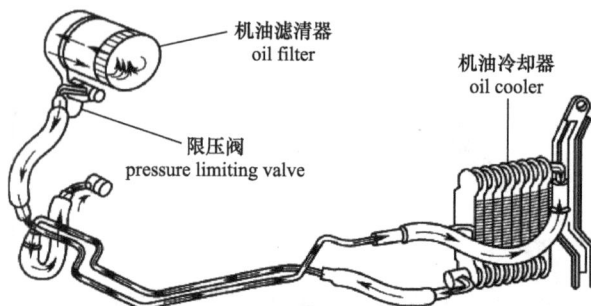

图 2.7.10　机油冷却器

Figure 2.7.10　Oil cooler

水冷式机油冷却器是指在润滑系统中设置的水冷式散热元件，因体积小和温度稳定等优点而被广泛使用。水冷式冷却器安装在机油滤清器的上方，从机油泵出来进入机油滤清器的机油在进行过滤的同时即冷却，然后流到发动机的主油道再流至运动零件。

Water-cooling oil cooler is a kind of water-cooling heat dissipation element in lubrication system. It is widely used because of its small size and stable temperature. The water-cooling cooler is installed on the top of the oil filter. The oil that comes out of the oil pump and enters the oil filter, which is filtered and cooled at the same time, and then flows to the main oil passage of the engine and then to the moving parts.

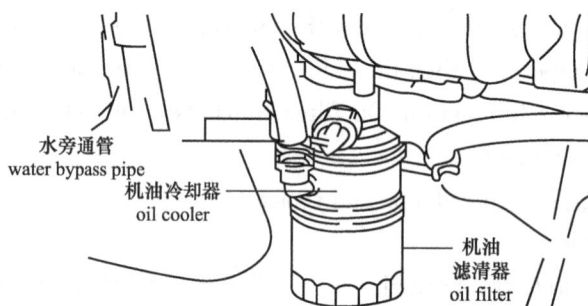

图 2.7.11　机油冷却器的安装位置

Figure 2.7.11　Installation location of oil cooler

思考与练习

(Reflection and Exercises)

1. 润滑系统一般由哪些零部件组成？
2. 简述润滑系统的功用及基本组成。
3. 发动机中哪些部件采用压力润滑？哪些部件采用飞溅润滑？
4. 齿轮式和转子式机油泵结构与工作原理各有什么特点？

1. Which parts do lubrication systems usually consist of?

2. Describe the function and basic composition of lubrication system.

3. Which parts of the engine adopt pressure lubrication? Which parts are lubricated by splash lubrication?

4. What are the characteristics of the structure and working principle of gear-type and rotor-type oil pumps respectively?

任务八　汽油机点火系统

Task 8　Ignition System of Gasoline Engines

教学目标

1. 知识目标

（1）掌握起动系的组成；

（2）掌握起动机的工作原理。

2. 能力目标

（1）具有识别不同类型的起动机的能力；

（2）具有区分不同点火系统的能力。

3. 情感和素养目标

（1）激发学生的学习工作热情，树立远大理想目标的意识；

（2）培养学生爱岗敬业的情怀、契合自身发展选择合适岗位的意识。

Teaching objectives

1. Knowledge objectives

（1）Master the composition of starting system；

（2）Master the working principle of starter.

2. Ability objectives

（1）The ability to identify different types of engines；

（2）The ability to distinguish different ignition systems.

3. Emotion and quality goals

（1）Stimulate students' enthusiasm to study and work, and cultivate the consciousness of establishing great ideals；

（2）Cultivate students' feelings of being dedicated to their jobs and the awareness of choosing appropriate positions in line with their own development.

8.1　概述（Overview）

点火系统是汽油发动机重要的组成部分，点火系统的性能良好与否对发动机的功率、油耗和排气污染等影响很大。能够在火花塞两电极间产生电火花的全部设备称为发动机"点火系统"。

汽车发动机点火系统的组成　The Composition of Ignition System in Vehicle Engine

Ignition system is an important part of gasoline engine. The performance of ignition system has a great influence on engine power, fuel consumption and exhaust pollution, etc. All the equipment that can produce sparks between the two electrodes of spark plug are called engine ignition system.

汽油机在压缩接近上止点时，可燃混合气是由火花塞点燃的，从而燃烧对外作功，为此，汽油机的燃烧室中都装有火花塞。点火系统的功用就是按照气缸的工作顺序定时地在火花塞两电极间产生足够能量的电火花。

When the gasoline engine is compressed near the top dead center, the combustible mixture is ignited by the spark plug, thus combustion does work to the the external. Therefore, spark plugs are installed in the combustion chamber of the gasoline engine. The function of the ignition system is to generate enough energy sparks between the two electrodes of the spark plug regularly according to the working sequence of the cylinder.

按照点火线圈的控制方法，可将点火系统分为传统点火系统（触点式点火系统）和电子点火系统。当前

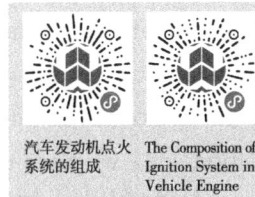

大多数轿车都采用电子点火系统。电子点火系统又分为普通电子点火系统（无触点式点火系统）和微机控制的点火系统。微机控制的点火系统按照有无分电器又分为有分电器的微机控制点火系统和无分电器的微机控制点火系统。

According to the control method of ignition coil, the ignition system can be divided into traditional ignition system (contact-type ignition system) and electronic ignition system. At present, most cars adopt electronic ignition system. Electronic ignition system is divided into ordinary electronic ignition system (non-contact ignition system) and microcomputer controlled ignition system. According to whether there are distributors or not, the microcomputer controlled ignition system can be divided into the microcomputer controlled ignition system with distributors and the microcomputer controlled ignition system without distributors.

8.2 传统点火系统 (Traditional ignition system)

传统点火系统（图2.8.1）主要由点火线圈、分电器、点火开关、高压线、火花塞和电源（发电机与蓄电池）等组成，目前已经很少使用。

The traditional ignition system is mainly composed of ignition coil, distributor, ignition switch, high voltage wire, spark plug and power supply (generator and battery), etc., which is seldom used at present.

电源是蓄电池，其电压为12V或24V，由点火线圈和断电器共同产生高压10000V以上。分初级回路和次级回路。点火线圈实际上是一个变压器，主要由初级绕组、次级绕组和铁芯组成。断电器是一个凸轮操纵的开关。断电器凸轮由发动机配气凸轮驱动，并以同样的转速旋转，即曲轴齿轮每转两圈，凸轮轴转一圈，为了保证曲轴转两圈各缸轮流点火一次，断电器凸轮的凸棱数一般等于发动机的气缸数，断电器的触点与点火线圈的初级绕组串联，用来切断或接通初级绕组的电路。

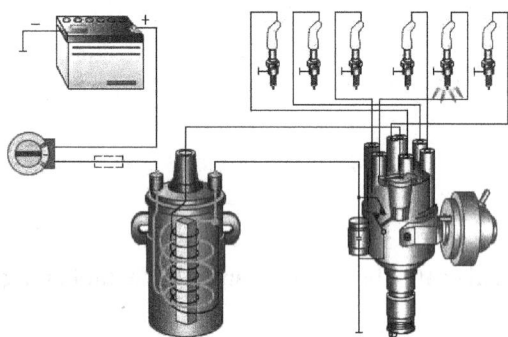

图2.8.1 传统点火系统

Figure 2.8.1 Traditional ignition system

The power supply is a battery with a voltage of 12V or 24V. The ignition coil and the circuit breaker together produce a high voltage of more than 10000V. It is divided into primary circuit and secondary circuit. The ignition coil is actually a voltage transformer, which is mainly consists of primary winding, secondary winding and iron core. The breaker is a switch operated by a cam. The breaker cam is driven by the engine valve cam and rotates at the same speed, that is, the crankshaft gear rotates twice and the camshaft rotates once. In order to ensure that each cylinder of crankshaft is ignited once during the crankshaft rotating twice, the number of convex edges of the breaker cam is generally equal to the number of cylinders of the engine. The contacts of the breaker are connected in series with the primary winding of the ignition coil, which is used to cut off or connect the circuit of the primary winding.

触点闭合时，初级电路通电，初级电流从蓄电池的正极经点火开关、点火线圈的初级绕组、断电器触点臂、触点，搭铁流回蓄电池的负极，为低压电路。触点断开时，在初级绕组通电时，其周围产生磁场，并由于铁芯的作用而加强。当断电器凸轮顶开触点时，初级电路被切断，初级电路迅速下降到零，铁芯中的磁通随之迅速衰减以至消失，因而在匝数多、导线细的次级绕组中感应出很高的电压，使火花塞两极之间的间隙被击穿，产生火花。

When the contacts are closed, the primary circuit is electrified, and the primary current from the positive electrode of the battery passes through the ignition switch, the primary winding of the ignition coil, the contact arm, contacts of the breaker and Grounding to the negative electrode of the battery, which is a low voltage circuit. When the contacts are disconnected，and the primary winding is energized，a magnetic field is generated around it，which is strengthened by the role of the iron core. When the breaker cam pushes against and opens the contact point，the primary circuit is cut off. The primary circuit drops rapidly to zero，and the magnetic flux in the iron core decreases rapidly to disappear. As a result，a high voltage is induced in the secondary windings with many turns and thin wires，which breaks down the gap between the two poles of spark plug and generates sparks.

初级绕组中电流下降的速度愈大，铁芯中磁通的变化就愈大，次级绕组中的感应电压也就愈高。初级电路为低压电路，次级电路为高压电路。

The faster the current drops in the primary winding，then the greater the flux changes in the iron core and the higher the induced voltage in the secondary winding. The primary circuit is a low voltage circuit and the secondary circuit is a high voltage circuit.

在断电器触点分开瞬间，次级电路中分火头恰好与侧电极对准，次级电流从点火线圈的次级绕组，经蓄电池正极、蓄电池、搭铁、火花塞侧电极、火花塞中心电极、高压导线、配电器流回次级绕组。

At the moment when the contacts of the breaker are separated，the rotor is aligned with the lateral electrode in the secondary circuit. The secondary current flows from the secondary winding of the ignition coil through the positive electrode of the battery，the storage battery，the ground，the side electrode of the spark plug，the central electrode of the spark plug，the high voltage wire and the distributor to the secondary winding.

8.3　电子点火系统（Electronic ignition system）

传统点火系工作时，断电器触点分开瞬间，会在触点处产生火花，烧损触点。当火花塞积炭时，易漏电，次级电压上不去，不能可靠地点火，产生高速缺火现象。半导体点火系统克服了这些缺点，具有较强的跳火能力，使点火可靠。

When the traditional ignition system works，when the contacts of the breaker are separated，sparks will be generated at the contacts and the contacts will be burned. When spark plug carbon deposits，it is easy to leak electricity. The secondary voltage cannot go up，and cannot reliably ignite，resulting in high-speed misfiring. Semiconductor ignition system overcomes these shortcomings，which has strong sparkover ability and makes ignition reliable.

主要由点火信号发生器、电子点火模块、点火线圈、分电器、高压线和火花塞等组成，如图2.8.2所示。

It is mainly composed of ignition signal generator，electronic ignition module，ignition coil，distributor，high voltage wire and spark plug，etc.，as shown in the figure.

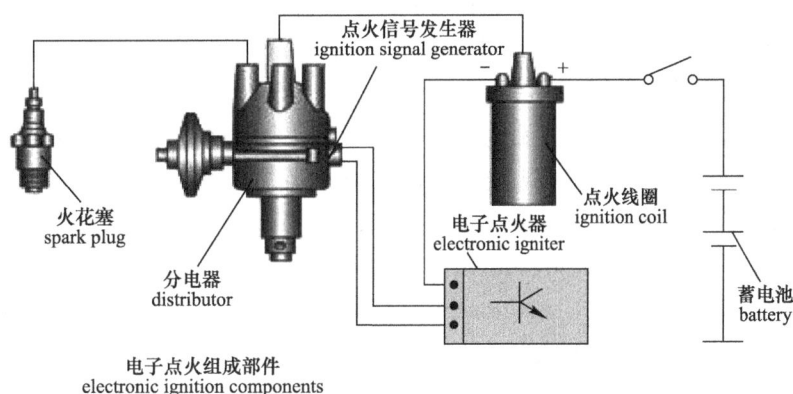

图2.8.2　电子点火系统

Figure 2.8.2　Electronic ignition system

所有类型的点火系统都必须具有的主要部件是点火线圈和火花塞。

The main components required for all types of ignition systems are ignition coils and spark plugs.

1. 点火线圈（Ignition coils）

点火线圈是利用电磁互感原理将蓄电池或发电机所供给的12V或24V的低压直流电转变为15～20kV的高压直流电。

点火线圈分为开磁路和闭磁路两种线圈。闭磁路点火线圈的优点是：漏磁少，能量损失小，体积小。因此，电子点火系普遍采用闭磁路点火线圈。

The ignition coil uses the principle of electromagnetic mutual inductance to convert the 12V or 24V low voltage direct current supplied by storage battery or generator into 15～20kV high voltage direct current.

The ignition coil is divided into two types: open magnetic circuit coil and closed magnetic circuit coil. The advantages of closed magnetic circuit ignition coil are less magnetic leakage, less energy loss and small volume. Therefore, closed magnetic circuit ignition coil is widely used in electronic ignition systems.

2. 火花塞（Spark plugs）

火花塞（spark plugs），俗称火嘴，它的作用是把高压导线送来的脉冲高压电放电，击穿火花塞两电极间空气，产生电火花以此引燃气缸内的混合气体。

Spark plugs, commonly known as nozzles, are used to discharge pulse high-voltage electricity from high-voltage conductors to break through the air between the two electrodes of the spark plugs, and generate sparks to ignite mixed gases in the cylinder.

主要类型：按照热值高低来分，有冷型和热型；按照电极材料来分，有镍合金、银合金和铂合金等；如果更专业一下，火花塞的类型大体上有如下几种：准型火花塞、缘体突出型火花塞、电极型火花塞、座型火花塞、极型火花塞、面跳火型火花塞等。

Main types: according to heat value, there are cold and hot types; according to electrode materials, there are nickel, silver and platinum alloys, etc. In a more professional way, the types of spark plugs are generally as follows: standard spark plug, insulator-protruding spark plug, electrode type spark plug, seat spark plug, side electrode spark plug, surface sparkover spark plug, etc.

此外，为了抑制汽车点火系统对无线电的干扰，又生产了电阻型和屏蔽型火花塞。电阻型火花塞是在火花塞内装有5～10Ω的陶瓷电阻器，屏蔽型火花塞是利用金属壳体把整个火花塞屏蔽密封起来。屏蔽型火花塞不仅可以防止无线电干扰，还可用于防水、防爆的场合。

In addition, in order to restrain the interference by automobile ignition system on the radio, resistor and shielding spark plugs are produced. Resistor spark plug contains a ceramic resistor with 5-10Ω in the spark plug. While the shielding spark plug uses a metal shell to shield and seal the whole spark plug. Shielding spark plug can not only prevent radio interference, but also be used in waterproof and explosion-proof occasions.

通常情况下，普通铜芯火花塞的使用寿命为30000km，而贵金属材质火花塞（铂金、铱金）的使用寿命为60000～90000km，不同车型汽车厂商所规定的保养周期不完全相同，具体更换周期以汽车厂商要求为准。

Usually, the service life of common copper core spark plug is 30,000 kilometers, while that of precious metal spark plug (platinum, iridium) is 60,000-90,000 kilometers. The maintenance period stipulated by automobile manufacturers of different models is not exactly the same. The specific replacement cycle is based on the requirements of automobile manufacturers.

8.4 微机控制的点火系统（Microcomputer controlled ignition system）

有分电器的微机控制点火系统由电源、点火开关、控制单元（ECU）、点火模块、点火线圈、分电器、火花塞、高压线和各种传感器等组成。

The microcomputer controlled ignition system with distributor consists of power supply，ignition switch，control unit（ECU），ignition module，ignition coil，distributor，spark plug，high voltage wire and various sensors，etc.

无分电器的微机控制点火系统由电源、点火开关、控制单元（ECU）、点火模块、点火线圈、火花塞、高压线和各种传感器等组成。目前，有的无分电器点火系统还将点火线圈直接装在火花塞上方，取消了高压线。

The computer controlled ignition system without distributor consists of power supply，ignition switch，control unit（ECU），ignition module，ignition coil，spark plug，high voltage wire and various sensors，etc. At present，for some distributorless ignition systems，the ignition coil is directly installed above the spark plug，eliminating the high-voltage wire.

思考与练习

（Reflection and Exercises）

1. 点火系统是由哪几部分组成?

2. 点火系统分哪几种?

3. 点火系统是如何工作的?

1. What are the components of the ignition system?

2. What kinds of ignition systems are there?

3. How does the ignition system work?

任务九 起 动 系 统

Task 9　Starting System

教学目标

1. 知识目标

（1）掌握起动系的组成；

（2）掌握起动机的工作原理。

2. 能力目标

（1）能识别不同类型的起动机；

（2）培养职业素养能力。

3. 情感和素养目标

（1）培养学生安全操作意识；

（2）培养学生的系统性思维意识、团队协作的精神品质。

Teaching objectives

1. Knowledge objectives

（1）Mastering the composition of starting system；

（2）Mastering the working principle of starter.

2. Ability objectives

（1）To identify different types of engine；

（2）To cultivate the ability of professional qualities.

3. Emotion and quality goals

(1) Cultivate students' awareness to operate safely;

(2) Cultivate students' consciousness of systematic thinking and spirit of teamwork.

发动机不能自行由静止转入工作状态，必须用外力转动曲轴，直到曲轴达到发动机开始燃烧所必需的转速，保证混合气的形成、压缩和点火能够顺利进行。发动机由静止转入工作状态的全过程，称发动机的启动。完成发动机启动过程所需的一系列装置称发动机起动系统。起动系统是通过电磁感应原理，把电能转变成机械能。不同车型需要不同型号的起动机以满足自动要求。分为行星齿轮型起动机和直接传动型起动机。起动机按照工作原理分为直流电起动机、汽油起动机、压缩空气起动机等。内燃机上大都采用的是直流电起动机，其特点是结构紧凑、操作简单且便于维护。汽油起动机是一种带有离合器与变速机构的小型汽油机，功率大且受气温影响较小，可起动大型内燃机，并适用于高寒地带。压缩空气起动机分为两类，一种是将压缩空气按照工作顺序打入气缸，一种是使用气动马达驱动飞轮。压缩空气起动机的用途接近于汽油起动机，通常用于大型内燃机的起动，如图 2.9.1 所示。

Because the engine can not transfer from static state into working state by itself, the crankshaft must be rotated by external force until the crankshaft reaches the speed necessary for the engine to start combustion, so as to ensure the mixture formation, and compression and ignition can proceed smoothly. The whole process of engine from static to working state is called engine start-up. A series of devices needed to complete the engine start-up process are called engine starting system. The starting system converts electrical energy into mechanical energy through electromagnetic induction principle. Different automobile models need different types of engines to meet the automatic requirements. It is divided into planetary gear type and direct drive type. Starters are divided into DC electric starters, gasoline starters and compressed air starters according to their working principles. DC electric starter is widely used in internal combustion engines, which is characterized by compact structure, simple operation and easy maintenance. Gasoline starter is a small gasoline engine with clutch and transmission mechanism, which has high power and is less affected by temperature. It can start a large internal combustion engine and is suitable for high and cold area. Compressed air starters can be divided into two categories: one is to put compressed air into the cylinder according to the working principle and the other is to use air motor to drive the flywheel. The use of compressed air starter is similar to that of gasoline starter, which is usually used to start large internal combustion engines.

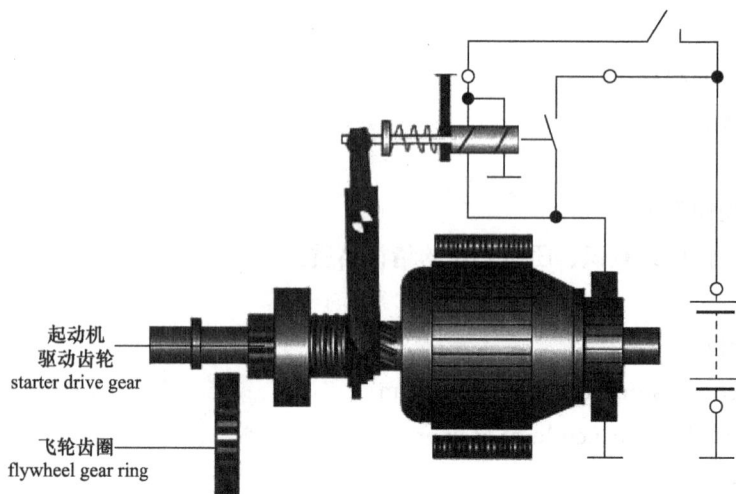

起动机
驱动齿轮
starter drive gear

飞轮齿圈
flywheel gear ring

图 2.9.1 起动系统

Figure 2.9.1 Starting system

9.1 起动机结构（Starter structure）

电动机启动装置一般由直流电动机、操纵机构和离合机构三大部分组成，如图 2.9.2 所示。汽车发动机普遍采用串激直流电动机作为启动电机，因为这种电动机在低速时转矩很大，随转速的升高，其转矩逐渐减小，这一特性非常适合发动机启动的要求。

Motor starting device is generally composed of three parts: DC motor, control mechanism and clutch mechanism. Series-excitation DC motor is widely used as starter motor in automobile engines, because the motor has a large torque at low speed, and its torque decreases gradually with the increase of speed, which is very suitable for the requirements of engine starting.

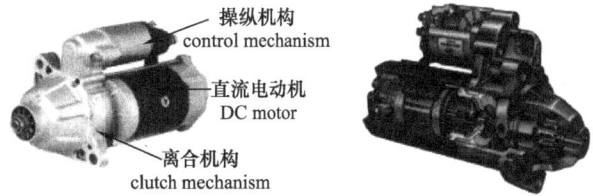

图 2.9.2 起动机
Figure 2.9.2 The starter motor

汽车发动机常用的启动方式有电动机启动和手摇启动两种。手摇启动结构简单，但加重了驾驶人员的劳动强度，而且操作不便，故很少采用。目前绝大多数汽车发动机都采用电动机启动。

Motor starting and hand starting are two common starting modes of automobile engines. Hand starting is simple in structure, but it aggravates the labor intensity of drivers and is inconvenient to operate, so it is seldom used. At present, most automobile engines are started by electric motors.

汽油机所用启动电机的功率一般在 1.5kW 以下，电压为 12V。柴油机启动功率较大（可达 5kW 或更大），为使电枢电流不致过大，其电压一般采用 24V。

The starter motor power of gasoline engine is generally less than 1.5kW and the voltage is 12V. The starting power of diesel engine is larger (up to 5kW or larger). In order to keep the armature current from being too large, the voltage of diesel engine is usually 24V.

9.1.1 直流电动机（Direct-current motor）

电动机（图 2.9.3）由磁场（定子）、电枢（转子）和整流子组成，为了增大扭矩采用多极磁场，常见有 4 个磁场。当电流通过电枢线圈时，整个线圈会受到一个转矩而转动。由于直流电动机通电后会产生一种反电动势，并与发动机转速成正比，与扭矩成反比，因此能满足发动机起动时的要求。起动机起动电流很大，因此，操作时启动时间一定要短。

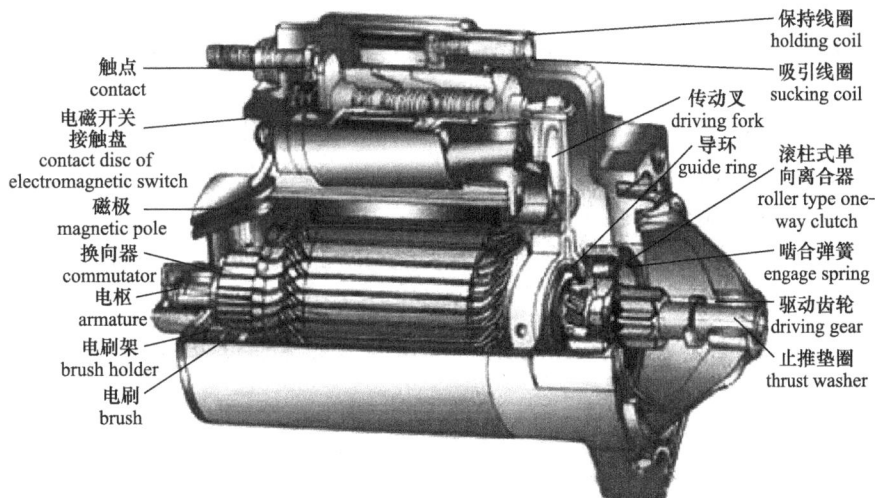

图 2.9.3 直流电动机
Figure 2.9.3 The starter motor

The motor consists of magnetic field (stator), armature (rotor) and commutator. In order to increase the torque, a multi-pole magnetic field is used. There are four common magnetic fields. When the current passes through the armature coil, the whole coil is rotated by a torque. Because DC motor will produce a kind of counter electromotive force when it is electrified, it is proportional to the engine speed and inversely proportional to the torque. Therefore, it can meet the requirements of engine starting. The starting current of the starter is very large, so the starting time must be short during operation.

9.1.2　起动机操纵机构 (Starter control mechanism)

汽车上使用的启动电机按其操纵方式的不同，有直接操纵式和电磁操纵式两种。前者是由驾驶员通过启动踏板和杠杆机构直接操纵启动开关，并使传动齿轮副进入啮合；后者则是由驾驶员通过启动开关操纵继电器，而由继电器操纵启动电机电磁开关和齿轮副，或通过启动开关直接操纵启动电机电磁开关和齿轮副。直接操纵式启动电机结构简单、使用可靠，但操作不便，目前已很少采用。电磁操纵式启动电机宜于远距离操纵，布置灵活，使用方便。目前汽车汽油发动机、柴油发动机几乎都采用电磁操纵式启动电机。电磁操纵式启动电机使用时，常通过启动继电器接通或切断启动电机电磁开关的电路，控制启动电机的工作，以保护启动开关。

Starter motors used in automobiles can be divided into two types, direct control and electromagnetic control, according to their different operating modes. The former is that the driver directly operates the start switch through the start pedal and lever mechanism, and makes the drive gear pair engaged. While in the latter case, the driver controls the relay through the start switch, then the relay controls the electromagnetic switch and gear pair of the starter motor, or directly controls the electromagnetic switch and gear pair of the starter motor through the start switch. Direct-operated start motor is simple in structure and reliable in use, but it is inconvenient in operation, so it is seldom used at present. Electromagnetic-operated starter motor is suitable for long-distance operation, flexible layout and convenient use. At present, almost all automobile gasoline engines and diesel engines adopt electromagnetic-operated starter motors. When using the electromagnetic-operated starter motor, the starting relay is often used to switch on or cut off the circuit of the electromagnetic switch of the starter motor to control the work of the starter motor to protect the start switch.

9.1.3　离合机构 (Clutch mechanism)

起动机应该只在起动时才与发动机曲轴相联，而当发动机开始工作之后，起动机应立即与曲轴分离。否则，随着发动机转速的升高，将使起动机大大超速，产生很大的离心力，而使起动机损坏（起动机电枢绕组松弛，甚至飞散）。

The starter should be connected to the crankshaft of the engine only when it is started. When the engine starts to work, the starter motor should be separated from the crankshaft immediately. Otherwise, with the increase of engine speed, the starter motor will be greatly overspeed, resulting in a great centrifugal force to damage the starter motor (starter armature winding is relaxed, or even flies away).

因此，起动机中装有离合机构。在起动时，它保证起动机的动力能够通过飞轮传递给曲轴；起动完毕，发动机开始工作时，立即切断动力传递路线，使发动机不可能反过来通过飞轮驱动起动机以高速旋转。滚柱式离合机构是常用的离合机构。

Therefore, the starter is equipped with a clutch mechanism. When starting, it guarantees that the power of the starter can be transmitted to the crankshaft through the flywheel. When the engine starts to work, it cuts off the power transmission line immediately so that the engine can not drive the starter to rotate at high speed through the flywheel in turn. Roller clutch mechanism is a common clutch mechanism.

滚柱式离合机构由开有楔形缺口的外座圈、内座圈、滚柱以及连同弹簧一起装在外座圈孔中的柱塞组成。作为内座圈毂的套筒和起动机轴用花键连接。固定在外座圈上的齿轮随电枢轴一起转动，驱动飞轮齿圈而使曲轴旋转。

The roller clutch mechanism consists of an outer race with a wedge-shaped notch, an inner race, a roller and a plunger installed in the hole of the outer race together with a spring. The sleeve as the inner race hub is in splined connection with the starter shaft. The gear fixed on the outer race rotates with the armature shaft, driving the flywheel gear ring to rotate the crankshaft.

当电枢连同内座圈依箭头所示方向旋转时（图2.9.4），滚柱借摩擦力和弹簧推力而楔紧在内外座圈之间的楔形槽的窄端。于是起动机轴上的转矩便可通过楔紧的滚子传到外座圈，因此固定在外座圈上的齿轮随电枢轴一同旋转，驱动飞轮齿圈而使曲轴旋转。

When the armature and the inner race rotate in the direction indicated by the arrow(Figure 2.9.4), the roller is wedged tightly into the narrow end of the wedge groove between the inner and outer races by means of friction and spring thrust. Therefore, the torque on the starter shaft can be transmitted to the outer race through wedged rollers, so the gears fixed on the outer race rotate with the armature shaft, driving the flywheel gear ring to rotate the crankshaft.

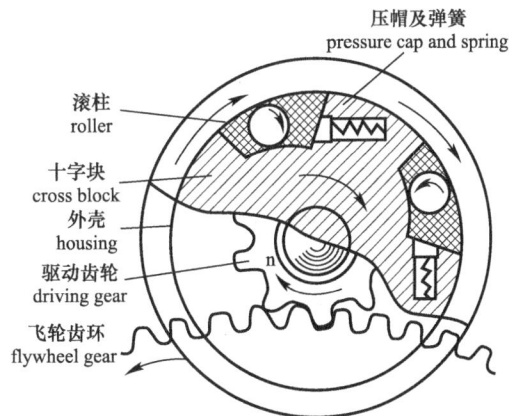

图2.9.4　起动机滚柱式单向离合器工作原理图

Figure 2.9.4　Working principle diagram of roller-type one-way clutch of starter

当发动机开始工作，曲轴转速升高以后，即有飞轮齿圈带动起动机齿轮高速旋转的趋势。此时虽然齿轮的旋转方向不变，但已由主动轮变成了从动轮。于是，滚柱在摩擦力的作用下克服弹簧张力而向楔形槽较宽的一端滚动，从而，高速旋转的小齿轮与电枢轴脱开，防止了起动机超速的危险。

When the engine starts to work and the crankshaft speed increases, there is a trend that the flywheel gear ring drives the starter gear to rotate at high speed. At this time, although the rotation direction of the gear remains unchanged, it has changed from the driving gear to the driven gear. And then under the action of the friction, the roller overcomes the spring tension and rolls towards the wide end of the wedge groove. Thus, the pinion with high speed rotation is separated from the armature shaft, which prevents the danger of starter overspeed.

9.1.4　减速机构（Reducing mechanism）

减速齿轮机构的驱动齿轮与发动机飞轮接合而启动发动机，采用单向驱动方式。当电动机上的小齿轮的转速高于发动机飞轮齿圈的速度时，电动机带动发动机转，当发动机的转速高于电动机时，它们之间的动力传递关系自动解除。

The driving gear of the gear reducing mechanism engages the flywheel of the engine to start the engine, and adopts the one-way driving mode. When the speed of pinion in the motor is higher than that of the fly-wheelgear ring, the motor drives the engine to rotate. When the speed of the engine is higher than that of the motor, the power transfer relationship between them is automatically relieved.

减速起动机主要由电磁啮合开关、减速齿轮、电动机、起动齿轮（小齿轮）及单向啮合器等部分组成。

The decelerating starter is mainly composed of electromagnetic meshing switch, reducing gear, electric motor, starting gear (pinion) and one-way meshing device, etc.

9.2　起动机分类 (Classification of starters)

9.2.1　减速起动机 (Deceleratings starter)

在起动机的电枢轴与驱动齿轮之间装有齿轮减速器的起动机，称为减速起动机。

A starter equipped with a gear reducer between the armature shaft of the starter and the driving gear is called a decelerating starter.

串励式直流电动机的功率与电动机的转矩和转速成正比。可见，当提高发动机转速的同时降低其转矩时，可以保持起动机功率不变。因此，当采用高速、低扭矩的串励式直流电动机作为起动机时，在功率相同的情况下，可以使起动机的体积和重量大大减小。但是，起动机的转矩过低，不能满足起动发动机的要求。为此，在起动机中采用高速、低转矩的直流电动机时，在电动机的电枢轴和驱动齿轮之间安装齿轮减速器，可以降低电动机转速的同时提高其转矩。

The power of series excitation DC motor is proportional to the torque and the speed of the motor. It shows that when the engine speed is increased while the torque is reduced, the power of the starter can be maintained unchanged. Therefore, when high-speed, low-torque and series-excitation DC motor is used as starter, the volume and weight of starter can be greatly reduced under the same power. However, the torque of the starter is too low to meet the requirements to start engine. For this reason, when high-speed and low-torque DC motor is used in starter, gear reducer is installed between armature shaft and driving gear, which can reduce the speed of motor and increase its torque.

减速起动机的齿轮减速器有外啮合式、内啮合式和行星齿轮式等三种不同形式，如图 2.9.5 所示。

The gear reducer of decelerating starter has three different forms: external engagement type, internal engagement type and planetary gear type.

外啮合式减速起动机，其减速机构在电枢轴和起动机驱动齿轮之间利用惰轮作中间传动，且电磁开关铁心与驱动齿轮同轴心，直接推动驱动齿轮进入啮合，无需拨叉。因此，起动机的外形与普通的起动机有较大的差别。外啮合式减速机构的传动中心距较大，因此受到起动机构的限制，其减速比不能太大，一般不大于5，多用于小功率的起动机上。

External engagement decelerating starter, whose reducing mechanism uses idle wheel as intermediate transmission between armature shaft and starter driving gear, and the iron core of electromagnetic switch and the driving gear are coaxial, which directly drives the driving gear into meshing without fork shifting. Therefore, the shape of the starter is quite different from that of the ordinary starter. The transmission center distance of external meshing reducing mechanism is large, so it is limited by the starting mechanism. Its reduction ratio can not be too large, which is generally less than 5, which is mostly used in low power starter.

内啮合式减速起动机，其减速机构传动中心距小，可有较大的减速比，故适用于较大功率的起动机。但内啮合式减速起动机构噪声较大，驱动齿轮仍需拨叉拨动进行啮合，因此起动机的外形和普通起动机相似。

Internal meshing decelerating starter has small transmission center distance and large reduction ratio, so it is suitable for high power starter. However, the internal meshing decelerating starting mechanism has large noises, and the driving gear still needs to shift fork to engage, so the shape of the starter is similar to that of the ordinary starter.

行星齿轮式减速起动机减速机构结构紧凑，传动比大、效率高。由于输出轴与电枢轴同轴线、同旋向，电枢轴无径向载荷，振动小，因而整体尺寸小。

The reducing mechanism of planetary gear decelerating starter has compact structure，high reduction ratio and high efficiency. Because the output axis and armature axis are coaxial and have same rotation direction，and armature axis has no radial load and small vibration，so the overall size is small.

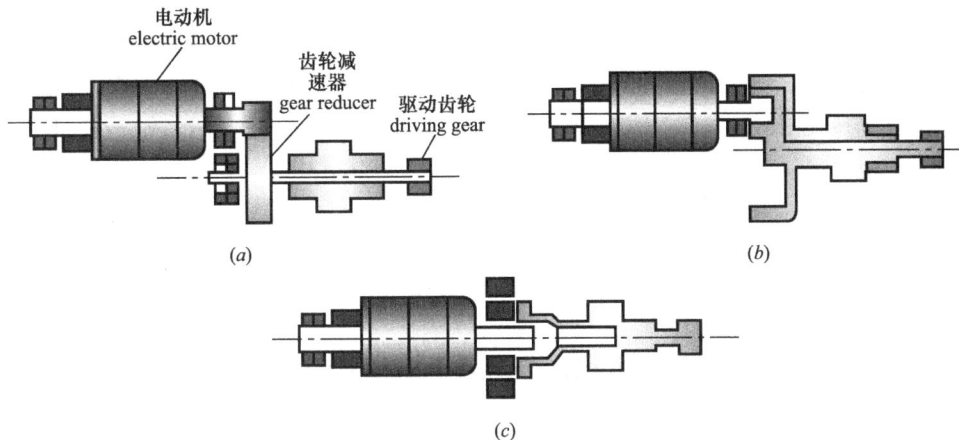

图 2.9.5　减速起动机的三种形式

Figure 2.9.5　Three forms of decelerating starter

(a) 外啮合式（external meshing type）；(b) 内啮合式（internal meshing type）；(c) 行星齿轮式（planetary gear type）

9.2.2　永磁起动机（Permanent magnet starter）

以永磁材料作为磁极的起动机，称为永磁起动机。它取消了传统起动机中的励磁绕组和磁极铁心，使起动机的结构简化，体积和质量大大减小，可靠性提高，并节省了金属材料。

The starter motor with permanent magnet material as magnetic pole is called permanent magnet starter. It eliminates the excitation winding and pole core in the traditional starter，which simplifies the structure of the starter，and greatly reduces the volume and mass. It improves the reliability，and saves metal materials as well.

9.2.3　永磁减速起动机（Permanent magnet decelerating starter）

采用高速、低转矩的永磁电动机，并在驱动齿轮与电枢轴之间安装齿轮减速器的起动机，称为永磁减速起动机。永磁减速起动机的体积和质量可以进一步减小，目前已得到广泛应用。

The starter adopting permanent magnet motor of high speed and low torque，and gear reducer installed between drive gear and armature shaft is called permanent magnet decelerating starter. The volume and mass of permanent magnet decelerating starter can be further reduced，and it has been widely used.

9.3　起动机工作原理（Working principle of starter）

起动时，接通起动开关，起动机电路通电，电磁开关中的吸引线圈和保持线圈同时通电，产生很强的磁力，吸引铁芯左移，并带动驱动杠杆绕其销轴转动，使齿轮移出与飞轮齿圈啮合。与此同时，由于吸引线圈的电流通过电动机的绕组，电枢开始转动，齿轮在旋转中移出，减小冲击。

When starting，the starting switch is turned on，and the starter circuit is energized. The sucking coil of the relay and the holding coil are energized，which gener-

汽车起动系统的工作原理　Working Principle of Automobile Starting System

115

ates a strong magnetic force and attracts the iron core to move left, and drives the driving lever to rotate around its pin axis, so that the gear moves out to mesh with the flywheel gear ring.

At the same time, because the current of the sucking coil passes through the motor winding, the armature begins to rotate, and the gear moves out during rotation to reduce the impact.

如果齿轮与飞轮齿端相对，不能马上啮合，此时弹簧压缩，当齿轮转过一个角度后，齿轮与飞轮迅速啮合。当铁芯移动到使短路开关闭合的位置时，短路线路接通，吸引线圈被短路，失去作用，保持线圈所产生的磁力足以维持铁芯处于开关吸合的位置。

If the gear is opposite to the flywheel gear end, it can not mesh immediately. At this moment, the spring is compressed. When the gear rotates an angle, the gear and the flywheel mesh rapidly. When the iron core moves to the position where the short-circuit switch is closed, the short circuit is connected, and the sucking coil is shorted, thus losing its function. The magnetic force generated by the holding coil is sufficient to maintain the iron core in the position where the switch is closed.

思考与练习

(Reflection and Exercises)

1. 起动系统由哪些部分组成？
2. 起动机的工作原理是什么？
3. 起动机有哪些分类？

1. What parts does the starting system consist of?
2. What are the working principle of starter?
3. What are the classifications of starters?

项目三　汽车底盘
Item 3　Automobile Chassis

任务一　汽车底盘概述
Task 1　Overview

教学目标

1. 知识目标

了解汽车底盘的总体结构。

2. 能力目标

（1）理解各个系统的作用；

（2）掌握系统的安装位置。

3. 情感和素养目标

（1）培养学生的团结合作、善于人际交往沟通的意识；

（2）培养学生责任感、使命感，树立远大理想，弘扬爱国精神。

Teaching objectives

1. Knowledge objectives

Understanding the general structure of automobile chassis.

2. Ability objectives

（1）Understanding the role of each system；

（2）Mastering the installation position of the system.

3. Emotion and quality goals

（1）Cultivate students' awareness of being united and cooperative and being good at interpersonal communication；

（2）Cultivate students' sense of responsibility and mission, establish great ideals and promote patriotism.

汽车底盘由传动系、行驶系、转向系和制动系四部分组成（图3.1.1）。底盘作用是支承、安装汽车发动机及其各部件、总成，成形汽车的整体造型，并接受发动机的动力，使汽车产生运动，保证正常行驶。

The automobile chassis is composed of four parts: transmission system, driving system, steering system and braking system. The functionof chassis is to support and install the automobile engine and its components and assemblies, to form the overall shape of the automobile, and to accept the power of the engine, so that the automobile can generate movement and ensure normal driving.

其中传动系统的作用是将发动机输出的动力传给驱动车轮；行驶系的作用是将传动系统传来的转扭力转化为汽车行驶的驱动力，并将汽车构成一个整体，支撑汽车的总重量，承受、传递各种力和力矩，减小振动、缓和冲击，保证汽车的平稳行驶；转向系的作用是保证汽车能够按驾驶员选定的方向行驶；制动系作用是行驶的汽车减速或者停车并保证汽车靠地驻停。

The function of the transmission system is to transfer the output power from the engine to the driving wheel. The function of the driving system is to convert the torque transmitted by the transmission system into the driving force of the vehicle, and make the vehicle as a whole, supporting the total weight of the vehicle, bearing and transmitting various forces and moments, reducing vibrations and easing impacts to ensure the smooth running of automobiles. The role of steering system is to ensure that the automobile can run in the direction chosen by the driver; the role of braking system is to slow down or stop the car and ensure that the car is parked.

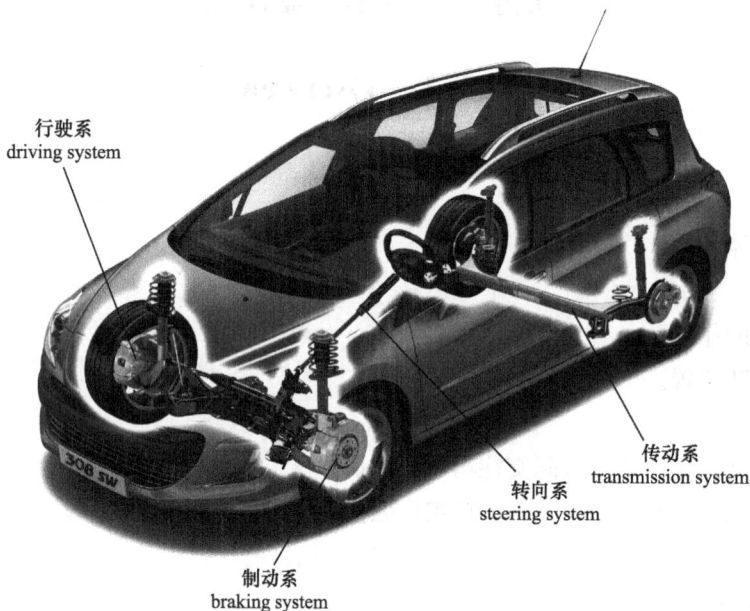

图 3.1.1　汽车底盘

Figure 3.1.1　The automobile chassis

任务二　传 动 系 统

Task 2　Transmission System

教学目标

1. 知识目标

（1）了解传动系统的结构；

（2）了解离合器的基本工作原理；

（3）了解变速器的结构与作用。

2. 能力目标

（1）会分辨不同的自动变速器优点；

（2）能解释变速器结构和工作原理。

3. 情感和素养目标

（1）培养学生良好的职业道德和注重产品的品质意识；

（2）培养学生吃苦耐劳，精益求精的思想意识。

Teaching objectives

1. Knowledge objectives

（1）Understanding the structure of the transmission system；

（2）Understanding the basic working principle of clutch；

（3）Understanding the structure and function of transmission.

2. Ability objectives

（1）To distinguish the advantages of different automatic transmissions；

（2）To explain the structure and working principle of transmission.

3. Emotion and quality goals

（1）Cultivate students' professional ethics and awareness of paying attention to the quality of products；

（2）Cultivate students' ideological consciousness of being hard-working and striving for excellence.

2.1　概述（Overview）

2.1.1　传动系统的组成和作用（Composition and function of transmission system）

传动系统是将发动机输出的动力传给驱动车轮。一般由离合器、变速器、万向装置、传动轴、驱动轴、差速器等组成。

The transmission system transmits the output power from the engine to the driving wheel. Generally，it consists of clutch，transmission，universal device，transmission shaft，drive shaft and differential，etc.

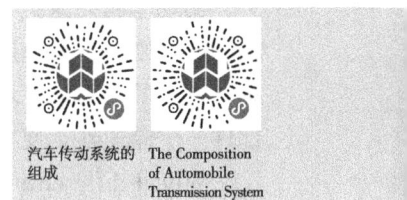

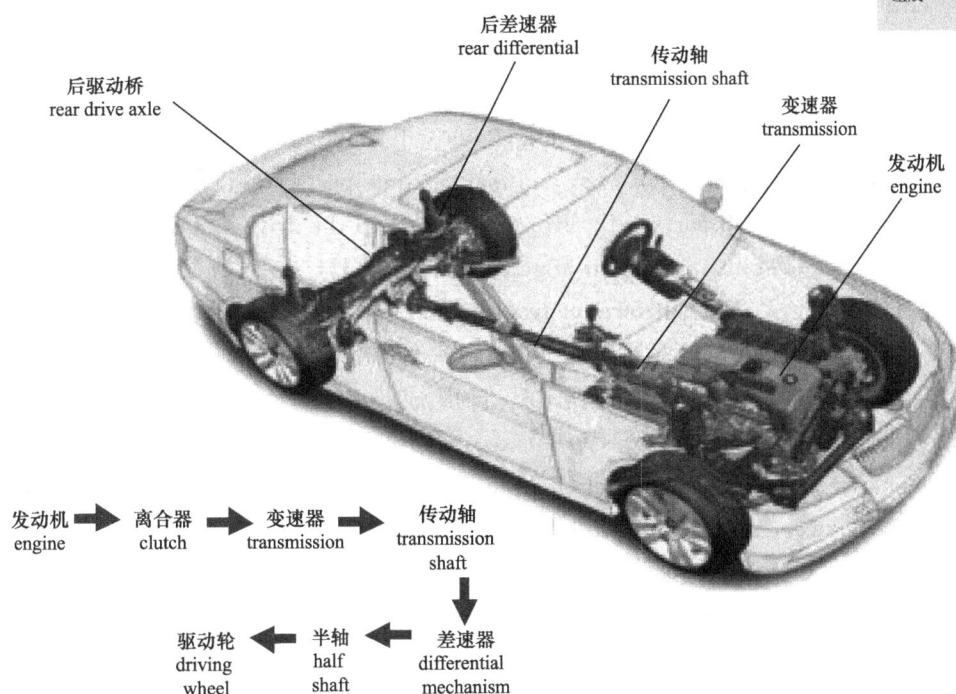

汽车传动系统的组成　The Composition of Automobile Transmission System

图 3.2.1　汽车动力传递流程示意图

Figure 3.2.1　Diagram of automobile power transfer process

其为了满足汽车行驶的各种需求，汽车传动系应具有以下功用：

In order to meet the various requirements of automobile driving, the automobile transmission system should have the following functions：

减速增扭、减扭增速，起到变速的功用。汽车的使用条件，诸如汽车的实际装载量、道路坡度、路面状况，以及道路宽度和曲率、交通情况所允许的车速等，都在很大范围内不断变化。

It should have the effects of reducing speed with generating large torque, and reducing torque with generating large speed, which plays the role of varying speed. The service conditions of automobiles, such as the actual weight of load of automobiles, road grade, road surface conditions, road width and curvature, allowed speed of traffic conditions, etc. , are constantly changing in a large range.

实现汽车倒车。车辆在某些情况下需要倒车行驶，而发动机的旋转方向是固定的，因此需要传动系将发动机的输出后的动力进行方向改变，实现倒车的需求。

Backing a car is realizable. Automobiles need to reverse in some cases, but the engine rotation direction is fixed, so the transmission system needs to change the direction of the output power of the engine to achieve the demand of reverse.

实现动力中断。在一些特定情况下（如怠速驻车、发动机启动等），需要传动系将发动机的动力和驱动进行切断和连接。

Power interruption is realizable. In some specific cases (such as idle parking, engine start, etc.), the transmission system is needed to cut off and connect the power and drive of the engine.

实现车轮差速。当汽车转弯行驶时，左右车轮在同一时间内滚过的距离不同，如果两侧驱动轮仅用刚性轴驱动，则二者角速度必然相同，因而在汽车转弯时必然产生车轮相对于地面滑动的现象。这将使转向困难，汽车的动力消耗增加，传动系内某些零件和轮胎加速磨损。所以，需要在驱动桥内装置具有差速作用的部件——差速器，使左右两驱动轮可以以不同的角速度旋转。

Wheel differential is realizable. When a car is turning, the distance between the left and right wheels is different during the same period. If the driving wheels on both sides are driven only by a rigid axle, the angular velocity of the two wheels will be the same. Therefore, the phenomenon of wheel sliding relative to the ground will inevitably occur when the car is turning. This will make steering difficult, increasing the power consumption of the car, and accelerate the wear and tear of some parts and tires in the transmission system. Therefore, it is necessary to install parts with differential effect in the drive axle, differential, so that the left and right driving wheels can rotate at different angular speeds.

2.1.2　传动系的布置形式 (Layout form of transmission system)

发动机前置、前轮驱动（FF型），是将发动机布置在汽车前部，并运用传动系将发动机动力传递给前轮驱动。一般由离合器、变速器、减速器、差速器、驱动轴组成。

Front engine and front-wheel drive (FF type) is to arrange the engine in the front of the automobile, and transfer the engine power to the front-wheel drive by the transmission system. Generally, it consists of clutch, transmission, reducer, differential and drive shaft, etc.

发动机前置、后轮驱动（FR型），是将发动机布置在汽车前部，并运用传动系将发动机动力传递给后轮驱动。一般由离合器、变速器、传动轴、减速器、差速器、驱动轴组成。

Front engine and rear-wheel drive (FR) is to arrange the engine in the front of the car and transfer the engine power to the rear wheel drive by the transmission system. Generally, it consists of clutch, transmission, transmission shaft, reducer, differential and drive shaft.

发动机中置，后轮驱动（MR型），是将发动机布置在汽车中部，并运用传动系将发动机动力传递给后轮驱动。一般由离合器、变速器、传动轴、减速器、差速器、驱动轴组成。

Middle-engine and rear-wheel drive (MR) is to arrange the engine in the middle of the car and transfer the engine power to the rear wheel drive by the transmission system. Generally, it consists of clutch, transmission, transmission shaft, reducer, differential and drive shaft.

发动机后置，后轮驱动（RR 型），是将发动机布置在汽车后部，并运用传动系将发动机动力传递给后轮驱动。一般由离合器、变速器、减速器、差速器、驱动轴组成。

Rear-engine and rear-wheel drive (RR) is to arrange the engine in the rear of the car and transfer the engine power to the rear wheel drive by the transmission system to. Generally, it consists of clutch, transmission, reducer, differential and drive shaft.

四轮驱动（4WD 型），一般是将发动机布置在汽车前部或后部，并运用传动系将发动机动力传递给四个轮驱动。一般由离合器、变速器、中央差速器、传动轴、减速器、差速器、驱动轴组成。

For four-wheel drive (4WD), the engine is generally arranged in the front or rear of the automobile and the power of the engine are transmitted to four wheels by the transmission system. Generally, it consists of clutch, transmission, central differential, transmission shaft, reducer, differential and drive shaft.

2.2 离合器 (Clutch)

离合器的安装位置：离合器安装在发动机与变速器之间，用来切断或传递前后两者之间动力联系。

Mounting position of clutch: the clutch is installed between the engine and the transmission, which is used to cut off or transfer the power connection between the former and the latter.

离合器的作用：1. 传递扭矩，将发动机扭矩通过离合器传递给变速器。2. 保证车辆平稳起步，汽车由静止到行驶的过程中，汽车速度由零逐渐增大，可通过离合器控制逐渐结合来逐步控制车速的平稳递增。3. 切断动力传递，当离合器完全分离时，可切断发动机和变速器的扭矩传递。4. 防止动力传递过载，可控制发动机和传动系做功时急剧降低转速，避免对传动系造成超过其承载能力的载荷，而使机件损坏。

The function of clutch: 1. Transfer the torque. Transfer the engine torque to the transmission through the clutch. 2. Ensure the automobile starts smoothly. During the process from static state to driving state, the vehicle speed increases gradually from zero, and the steady increase of the vehicle speed can be controlled gradually through the gradual combination of clutch control. 3. Cut off transmission of power. When the clutch is completely separated, the torque transmission between the engine and the transmission can be cut off. 4. Prevent overload of power transmission. The speeds can be reduced sharply when the engine and transmission system work, so as to avoid the load exceeding its load carrying capacity of the transmission system and the damage of the parts.

离合器的构成：飞轮、离合器盖、从动轴、从动盘、压盘、膜片弹簧、分离拨叉、分离轴承、离合器踏板。

Composition of clutch: flywheel, clutch cover, driven shaft, driven disc, pressure plate, diaphragm spring, release shifting fork, release bearing, clutch pedal.

离合器的工作原理：当离合器盖未安装到飞轮上时，膜片弹簧不受力而处于自由状态，此时离合器盖与飞轮之间有一距离。当离合器盖通过螺栓固定在飞轮上时，离合器盖靠向飞轮，消除距离，后钢丝支承环压紧膜片，使之发生弹性变形（锥角变小），此时膜片弹簧外端对压盘产生压紧力，使离合器处于接合状态。当踩下离合器踏板时，分离轴承左移推动膜片弹簧，使膜片弹簧被压在前支承环上，其径向截面以支承环为支点转动（膜片弹簧呈反锥形），外圆周向后翘起，通过分离钩拉动压盘后移，使离合器分离。

The working principle of the clutch: When the clutch cover is not installed on the flywheel, the diaphragm spring is in a free state without force, and there is a distance between the clutch cover and the flywheel. When the clutch cover is fixed on the flywheel by bolts, the clutch cover is close to the flywheel, eliminating the distance, and then the diaphragm is compressed by the steel wire supporting ring, which causes the elastic deformation (the cone angle becomes smaller). At this time, the outer end of the diaphragm spring produces a pressing force on the pressure plate, which makes the clutch in the engaged state. When the clutch pedal is depressed, the release bearing moves left to push the diaphragm spring, so that the diaphragm spring is pressed on the front supporting ring, whose radial cross section rotates with the supporting ring as the fulcrum (the diaphragm spring is anti-conical), the outer circumference is raised backward, and the pressure plate is pulled back by the disengaging hook to separate the clutch.

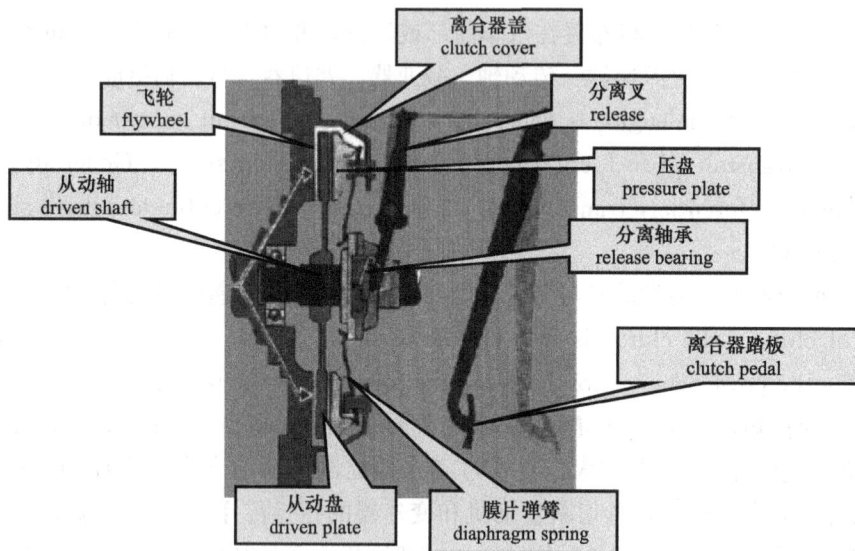

图 3.2.2　离合器结构

Figure 3.2.2　Clutch struction

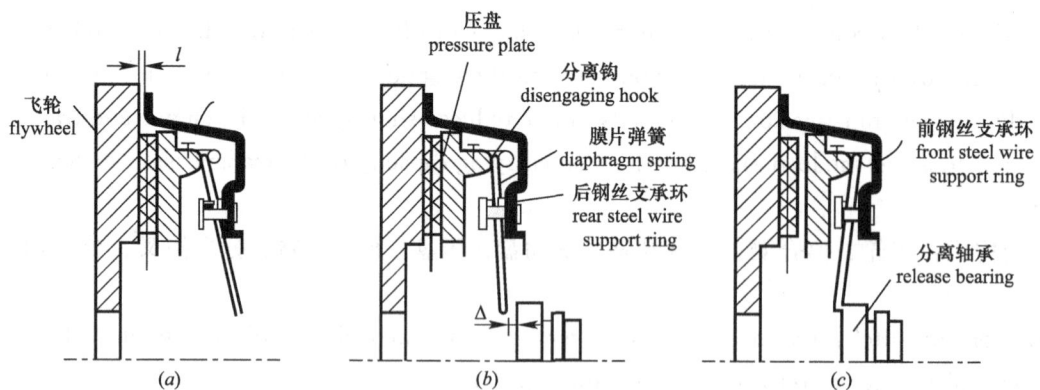

图 3.2.3　离合器的工作原理

Figure 3.2.3　Working principle of clutch

(a) 安装前位置 (pre-installation position)；(b) 安装后 (接合) 位置 (post-installation (engaged) position)；(c) 分离位置 (separation position)

2.3　变速机构 (Speed change mechanism)

2.3.1　变速机构的作用 (The function of speed change mechanism)

汽车变速器都需具备以下作用：

Automobile transmission should have the following functions:

实现变速变矩，通过改变传动比扩大或减小驱动轮扭矩和转速，以适应汽车在不同工况下所需要的牵引力，并尽可能的降低油耗。

It can achieve the variable speed and torque. By changing the transmission ratio to enlarge or reduce the driving wheel torque and speed, in order to adapt to the traction required by the car under different conditions, and as far as possible to reduce fuel consumption.

实现倒车，发动机的做功方向是不可改变，为了实现车辆反向行驶，可通过变速器的倒挡实现。

It can reverse. The working direction of the engine is unchangeable. In order to realize the reverse driving of the vehicle, the reverse gear of transmission can be used.

实现中断动力传动，在发动机启动、急速、汽车滑行和停车时都需要中断发动机的动力传动，因此变速器中需设有空挡，达到动力传动的中断。

It can achieve interruption of power transmission. It is necessary to interrupt the power transmission of the engine when the engine is starting, idling, coasting and parking. Therefore, there is a neutral in the transmission, which can achieve the interruption of power transmission.

2.3.2　变速器的种类（Types of transmission）

变速器按传动比的级数可分为有级式、无级式和综合式。按操纵方式可分为手动变速器、自动变速器和手动自动一体变速器。

According to the stage number of transmission ratio, it can be divided into three types: stage, stageless and comprehensive. According to the mode of operation, it can be divided into manual transmission, automatic transmission and manual automatic integrated transmission.

2.3.3　手动变速器（Manual transmission）

1. 齿轮传动的原理（The principle of gear transmission）

普通齿轮变速器是利用不同齿数的齿轮啮合传动来实现转矩和转速的改变。齿轮传动的基本原理如图 3.2.4 所示，一对齿数不同的齿轮啮合传动时可以实现变速，而且两齿轮的转速比与其齿数成反比。设主动齿轮转速为 n_1，齿数为 z_1，从动齿轮转速为 n_2，齿数为 z_2。主动齿轮（即输入轴）转速与从动齿轮（即输出轴）转速之比值称为传动比，用字母 i_{12} 表示。即由 1 传到 2 的传动比：

Common gear transmission uses gear meshing transmission with different number of teeth to realize the change of torque and speed. The basic principle of gear transmission is shown in Fig. 3.2.4. When a pair of gears with different number of teeth is engaged, the speed can be changed, and the speed ratio of the two gears is inversely proportional to the number of teeth. Suppose the speed of driving gear is n_1, and the number of teeth is z_1. While the speed of driven gear is n_2, and the number of teeth is z_2. The ratio of the speed of the driving gear (i. e. the input shaft) to that of the driven gear (i. e. the output shaft) is called the transmission ratio, which is denoted by the letter i_{12}. That is, the transmission ratio from 1 to 2:

$$i_{12}=n_1/n_2=z_2/z_1$$

当小齿轮为主动齿轮，带动大齿轮转动时，输出转速降低，即 $n_2<n_1$，称为减速传动，此时传动比 $i>1$；大齿轮驱动小齿轮时，输出转速升高，即 $n_2>n_1$，称为增速传动，此时传动比 $i<1$，如图 3.2.4 所示。这就是齿轮传动的变速原理。汽车变速器就是根据这一原理利用若干大小不同的齿轮副传动而实现变速的。

When the pinion is the driving gear and drives the big gear to rotate, the output speed decreases, i. e. $n_2<n_1$, which is called deceleration drive. At this time, the transmission ratio i is greater than 1. When the big gear drives the pinion, the output speed increases, i. e. $n_2>n_1$, which is called speed-increasing transmission. At this time, the transmission ratio is less than 1, as shown in Fig. 3.2.4. This is the principle of gear transmission. According to this principle, the transmission of automobile is realized by using several gear pairs of different sizes.

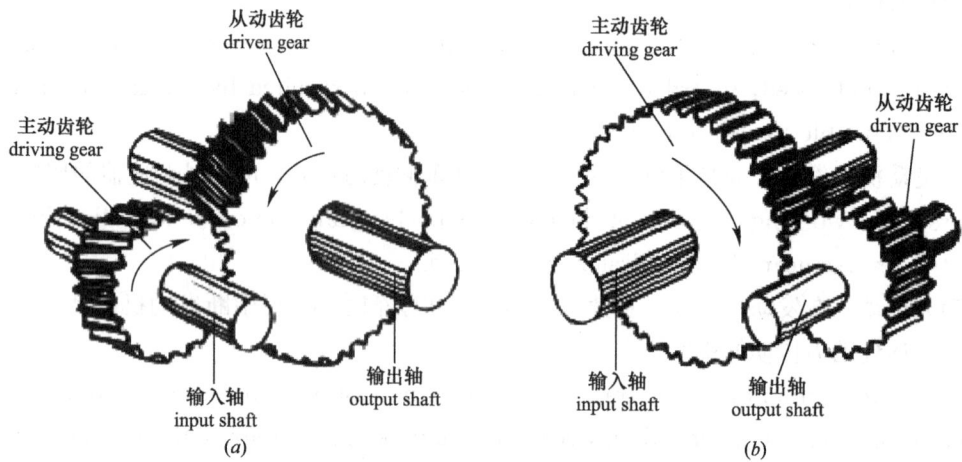

图 3.2.4 传动齿比

Figure 3.2.4 Gear ratio

(a) 减速传动 (deceleration transmission); (b) 增速传动 (speed-increasing transmission)

2. 手动变速器的结构 (Structure of manual transmission)

手动变速器按照传动齿轮传动轴的数目可以分为：两轴式和三轴式变速器。

Manual transmission can be divided into two-axis transmission and three-axis transmission according to the number of gearing shaft.

(1) 传动机构 (Transmission mechanism)

手动变速器包括变速传动机构和操纵机构两大部分。变速传动机构的主要作用是改变转矩和转速的数值和方向；操纵机构的作用是实现变速器传动比的变换—换挡。普通轿车一般采用横向布置二轴式手动变速器（图 3.2.5）。

Manual transmission consists of transmission mechanism and control mechanism. The main function of the transmission mechanism is to change the numerical values and directions of the torque and speed, and the function of the control mechanism is to change the transmission ratio of the transmission - shift. Two-axle manual transmission with transverse arrangement is commonly used in ordinary cars (Fig. 3.2.5).

这变速器的变速传动机构由输入轴和输出轴平行布置，输入轴同时是离合器的从动轴，输出轴是主减速的主动锥齿轮轴。该变速器具有 5 个前进挡和一个倒挡，采用锁环式惯性同步器执行换挡。

This transmission mechanism of the transmission is arranged parallel by the input shaft and the output shafts. The input shaft is the driven shaft of the clutch at the same time, and the output shaft is the driving bevel gear shaft which is mainly responsible for deceleration. This transmission has five forward gears and one reverse gear, and the lock-ring inertial synchronizer is used to perform shift.

变速器的输入轴前端通过轴承支撑在发动机曲轴后端的中心孔内。输入轴上有一至五挡主动齿轮和倒挡齿。输出轴由一至五挡从动齿轮、一二挡同步器、三四挡同步器和五挡同步器。

The front end of the input shaft of the transmission is supported in the central hole of the rear end of the engine crankshaft through bearings. There are first- fifth drive gears and reverse gear on the input shaft. The output shaft consists of first-fifth driven gears, first and second synchronizer, third and fourth synchronizer and fifth synchronizer.

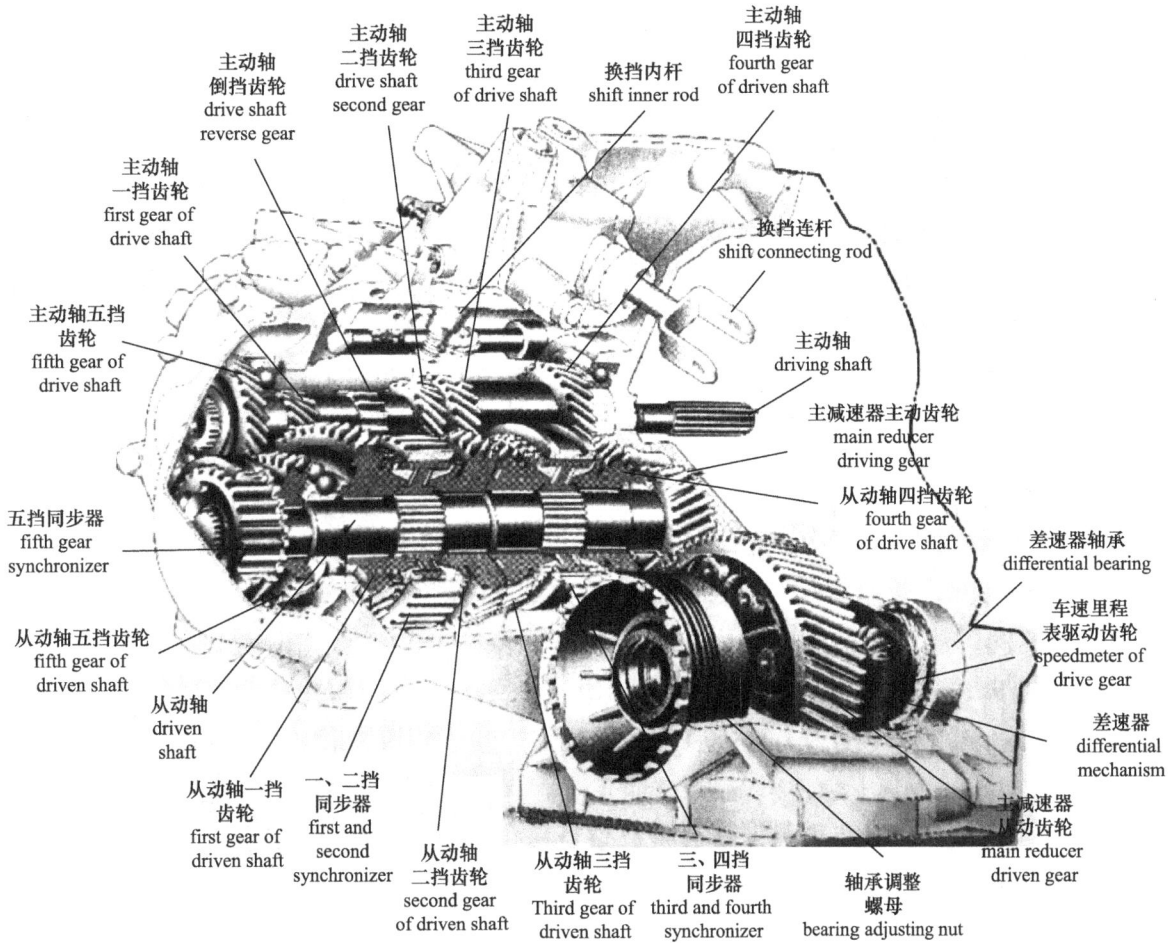

图 3.2.5　二轴式手动变速器

Figure 3.2.5　Two-axis manual transmission

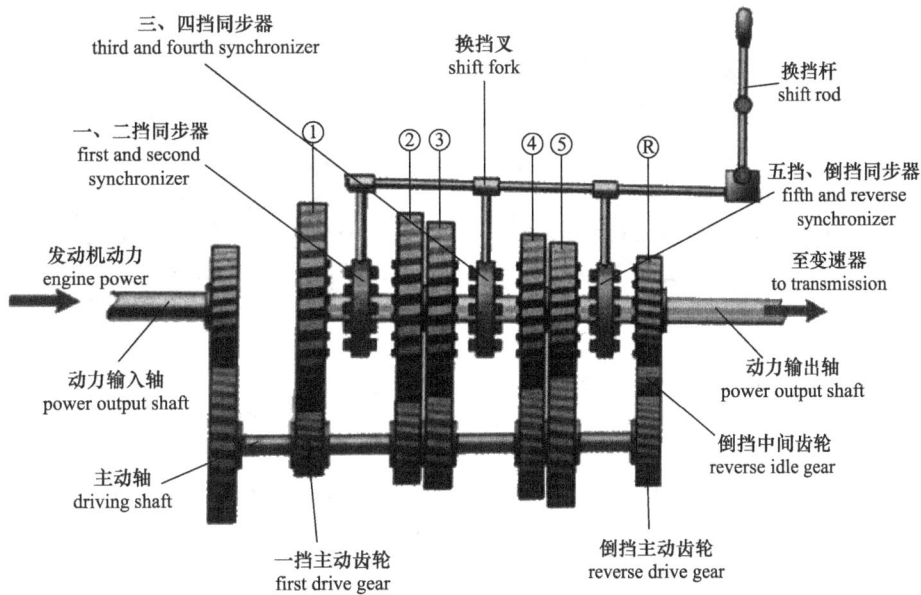

图 3.2.6　二轴式手动变速器主要元件

Figure 3.2.6　Main components of dual-axis manual transmission

锁环式同步器（图 3.2.7）的花键毂用内花键套装在轴的外花键上，用垫圈、卡环轴向定位。三个滑块分别装在花键毂上三个均布的轴向槽内，沿槽可以轴向移动。花键毂两端与齿轮之间各有一个青铜制成的锁环（即同步环）。锁环有内锥面，与接合齿圈外锥面相配合，组成锥面摩擦副。通过这对锥面摩擦副的摩擦，可使转速不等的两齿轮在接合之前迅速达到同步。

The spline hub of the lock ring synchronizer (as shown in Figure 3.2.7) is fitted with an internal spline on the outer spline of the shaft and positioned axially with washer and clasp ring. The three sliders are respectively installed into three uniformly distributed axial grooves on the spline hub, and can move along the groove axially. There is a bronze lock ring (synchronous ring) between the two ends of the spline hub and the gear respectively. The lock ring has an inner conical surface, which engages the outer conical surface of the meshing gear ring to form a conical friction pair. Through the friction of the pair of conical friction pairs, the two gears with different rotational speeds can quickly achieve synchronization before engaging.

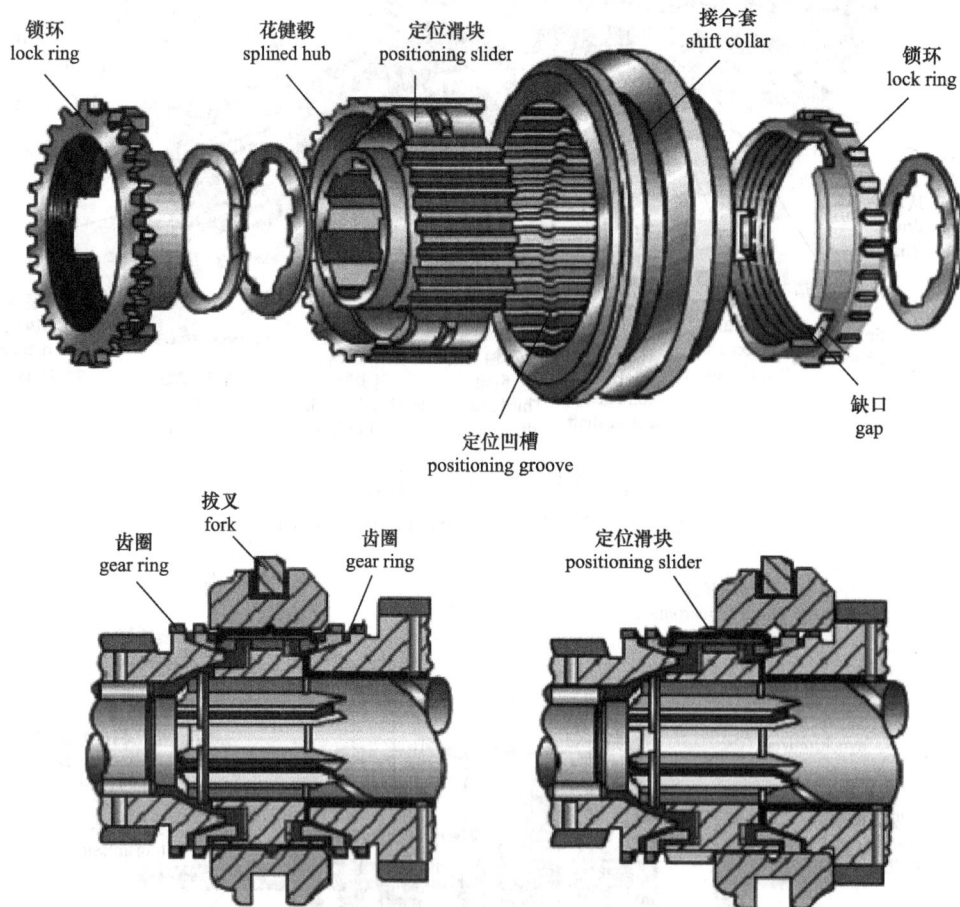

图 3.2.7　锁环式同步器

Figure 3.2.7　Lock ring synchronizer

在换挡的时候，同步锁环内锥面与待接合齿轮齿圈外锥面接触，在摩擦力矩的作用下齿轮转速迅速降低（或升高）到与同步锁环转速相等，两者同步旋转，齿轮相对于同步锁环的转速为零，因而惯性力矩也同时消失，这时在作用力的推动下，接合套不受阻碍地与同步锁环齿圈接合，并进一步与待接合齿轮的齿圈接合而完成换挡过程。如图 3.2.8 所示。

When shifting, the inner conical surface of synchronous lock ring engages the outer conical surface of gear ring to be engaged. Under the action of friction moment, the speed of gear reduces (or increases) rapidly to the same speed as that of synchronous lock ring. Both of them rotate synchronously, and the speed of gear relative to synchronous lock ring is zero, so the inertia moment also disappears at the same time. At this time, driven by the acting force, the shift collar engages the gear ring of synchronous lock ring. And it further engages the gear ring to be engaged to complete the shift process. As shown in the Figure 3.2.8.

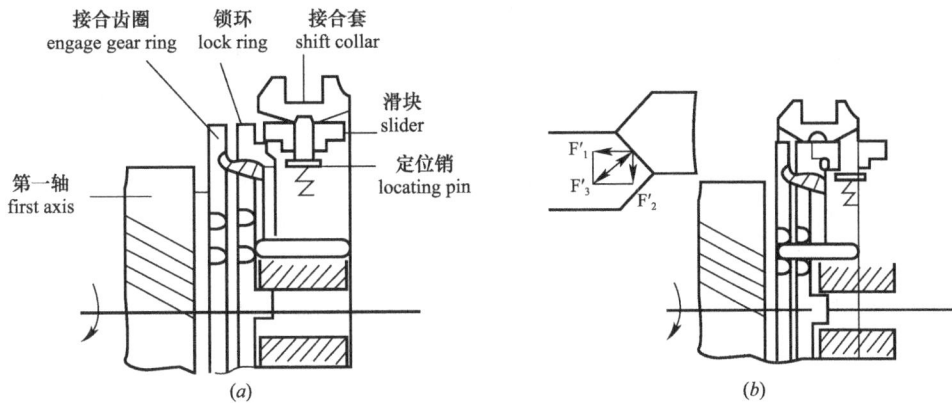

图 3.2.8　锁环式同步器原理

Figure 3.2.8　Principle of lock ring synchronizer

(*a*) 接合之前 (before engagement)；(*b*) 接合之后 (after engagement)

（2）操纵机构 (Control mechanism)

变速器操纵机构按照变速操纵杆（变速杆）位置的不同，可分为直接操纵式和远距离操纵式。发动机前置后轮驱动的车辆多采用直接操纵；发动机前置前轮驱动的汽车上多采用远距离操纵式，其结构如图 3.2.9 所示。

According to the different position of the transmission lever (gear shifting lever), the transmission control mechanism can be divided into direct control and long-distance control. Vehicles of front engine and rear-wheel drive (FR) mostly adopt direct control, while those of front engine and front-wheel drive (FF) mostly adopt long-distance control, whose structure is shown in the Figure 3.2.9.

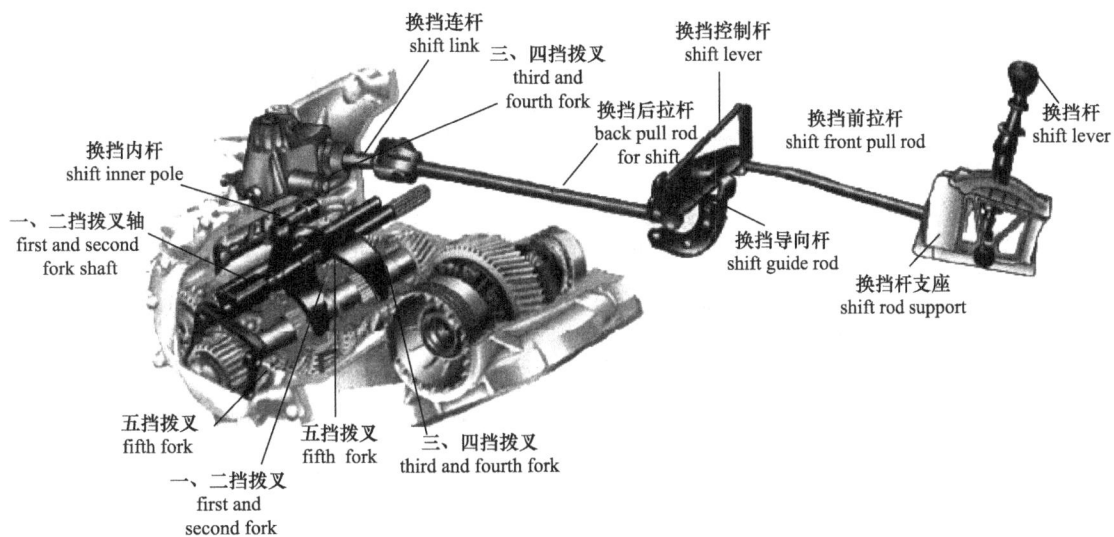

图 3.2.9　操纵机构

Figure 3.2.9　Control mechanism

为了保证变速器的可靠工作，变速器操纵机构应能满足以下要求：

127

In order to ensure the reliable operation of the transmission，the transmission control mechanism should meet the following requirements：

挂挡后应保证结合套与结合齿圈的全部套合（或滑动齿轮换挡时，全齿长都进入啮合）。在振动等条件影响下，操纵机构应保证变速器不自行挂挡或自行脱挡。为此在操纵机构中设有自锁装置。

After shifting，it should be ensured that the shift collar is fully engaged with the gear ring (or when sliding gear to shift，the full tooth length is meshed). Under the influence of vibration and other conditions，the control mechanism should ensure that the transmission does not shift or out of gear spontaneously. For this reason，a self-locking device is installed in the control mechanism.

为了防止同时挂上两个挡而使变速器卡死或损坏，在操纵机构中设有互锁装置。

In order to prevent the transmission from being stuck or damaged by hanging two gears at the same time，an interlocking device is installed in the control mechanism.

为了防止在汽车前进时误挂倒挡，导致零件损坏，在操纵机构中设有倒挡锁装置。

In order to prevent the parts from being damaged caused by selecting reverse gear in error when the car is moving forward，a reverse lock device is installed in the control mechanism.

（3）传动路线（Transmission line）

二轴五挡变速器动力传递路线，见表 3.2.1。

Power Transfer Route of Two-Axis，Five-Gear Transmission，in Table 3.2.1.

传动路线

表 3.2.1

Transmission line

Table 3.2.1

挡位 gear position	动力传递路线 power transmission route
一挡 first gear	变速器操纵杆从空挡向左、向前移动，实现： 动力→主动轴→主动轴→挡齿轮→从动轴→挡齿轮→从动轴一、二挡同步器→从动轴→动力输出 the transmission control lever moves from neutral to left and forward to realize： power→driving shaft→driving shaft→gear→driven shaft→gear→first and second synchronizer of driven shaft→driven shaft→power output
二挡 the second gear	变速器操纵杆从空挡向左、向后移动，实现： 动力→主动轴→主动轴二挡齿轮→从动轴二挡齿轮→从动轴一、二挡同步器→从动轴→动力输出 the transmission lever moves from neutral to left and backward to realize： power→driving shaft→drive shaft second gear→second gear of driven shaft→first and second synchronizer of driven shaft→driven shaft→power output
三挡 the third gear	变速器操纵杆从空挡向前移动，实现： 动力→主动轴→主动轴三挡齿轮→从动轴三挡齿轮→从动轴三、四挡同步器→从动轴→动力输出 the transmission lever moves forward from neutral to achieve： power→driving shaft→third gear of drive shaft→third gear of driven shaft→third and fourth gear synchronizer of driven shaft→driven shaft→power output
四挡 fourth	变速器操纵杆从空挡向后移动，实现： 动力→主动轴→主动轴四挡齿轮→从动轴四挡齿轮→从动轴三、四挡同步器→从动轴→动力输出 the transmission lever moves backward from neutral to achieve： power→driving shaft→fourth gear of driving shaft→fourth gear of driven shaft→third and fourth gear synchronizer of driven shaft→driven shaft→power output
五挡 fifth	变速器操纵杆从空挡向右、向前移动，实现： 动力→主动轴→主动轴五挡齿轮→从动轴五挡齿轮→从动轴五挡同步器→从动轴→动力输出 the transmission lever moves from neutral to right and forward to realize： power→driving shaft→fifth gear of driven shaft→fifth gear of driven shaft→fifth synchronizer of driven shaft→driven shaft→power output

挡位 gear position	动力传递路线 power transmission route
倒挡 side gear	变速器操纵杆从空挡向左、向前移动，实现： 动力→主动轴→主动轴倒挡齿轮→倒挡惰轮→倒挡从动齿轮（一、二挡同步器）→从动轴→动力反向输出 the transmission control lever moves from neutral to left and forward to realize: power→driving shaft→driving shaft side gear→reverse idle wheel→reverse driven gear (first and second synchronizer)→driven shaft→power reverse output

2.3.4　自动变速器（Automatic transmission）

自动变速箱是相对于手动变速箱而出现的一种能够自动根据汽车车速和发动机转速来进行自动换挡操纵的变速装置。目前汽车自动变速箱常见的有四种型式，分别是液力自动变速箱（AT）、无级自动变速箱（CVT）、电控机械自动变速箱（AMT）和双离合自动变速箱。

Automatic transmission is a kind of transmission device which can automatically shift gears according to vehicle speed and engine speed compared with manual transmission. At present, there are four common types of automobile automatic transmission, namely, hydraulic automatic transmission (AT), continuously variable transmission (CVT), electronical control mechanical automatic transmission (AMT) and double clutch automatic transmission.

液力自动变速箱（AT）由以下元件组成：①液力变矩器作用起步离合器，在一定范围内增强输入轴扭矩。总成的变矩器跨接离合器在特定操作状况下，直接连接泵轮与涡轮，防止扭矩器流量损失；②行星轮变速器后接于变矩器，转变扭矩和转速，倒挡时改变行驶方向；③控制器用液力和电力进行控制，通过自行操作增高或降低挡位。如图3.2.10所示。

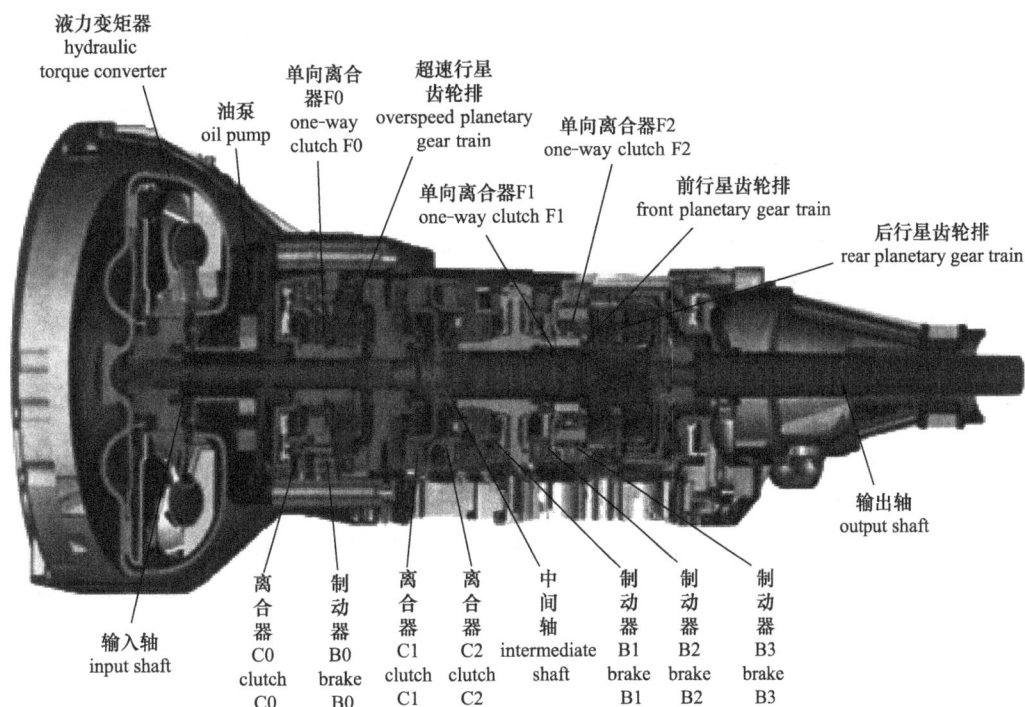

图3.2.10　液力自动变速器

Figure 3.2.10　Hydraulic automatic transmission

The hydraulic automatic transmission (AT) consists of the following components: ① the hydraulic torque converter acts on the starting clutch to enhance the input shaft torque within the range of variable torque. The torque converter assembly is cross-connected with the clutch, under specific operating conditions, which directly connects the pump wheel and the turbine to prevent the flow loss of the torque converter. ② Thenthe planetary gear transmission is connected with the torque converter to change the torque and speed, and change the direction of driving when reversing. ③ The controller is controlled by hydraulic and electric power to increase or decrease gear by self-operation (Figure 3.2.10).

无级自动变速箱（CVT）由以下元件组成：①起步离合器，起步离合器的主要作用是使汽车以足够大的牵引力平顺地起步，提高驾驶舒适性，必要时切断动力传输。目前用于汽车起步的装置主要有三种：湿式离合器、电磁离合器和液力变矩器；②行星齿轮机构，CVT 的行星齿轮机构用以实现前进挡和倒挡之间的切换操作，采用双行星齿轮机构，行星架上固定有内、外行星齿轮，其中，外行星齿轮和齿圈啮合，内行星齿轮和太阳轮啮合。前进挡时，太阳轮主动旋转，行星架随太阳轮同速旋转，即整体同步旋转；倒挡时，太阳轮主动旋转而齿圈不动，此时行星架与太阳轮反向旋转；③无级变速机构，无级变速机构由金属传动带、主动轮组、从动轮组组成。其中，主动轮组和从动轮组都由可动锥盘和固定锥盘组成。如图 3.2.11 所示。

Continuously variable transmission (CVT) consists of the following components: ① Start clutch. The main function of start clutch is to make the car start smoothly with enough traction, improve driving comfort and cut off power transmission when necessary. At present, there are mainly three kinds of devices used for automobile starting: wet clutch, electromagnetic clutch and hydraulic torque converter. ② Planetary gear mechanism. The planetary gear mechanism of CVT is used to realize the switching operation between forward gear and reverse gear. Double planetary gear mechanism is adopted. There are internal and external planetary gears fixed on the planetary carrier. Among them, the outer planetary gear engages the gear ring, and the inner planetary gear engages sun gears. When the forward gear is engaged, the sun gear rotates actively, and the planetary carrier rotates at the same speed with the sun wheel, that is, the whole body rotates synchronously. When reversing, the sun gear rotates actively and the gear ring does not move. At this time, the planetary carrier rotates inversely with the sun gear. ③ Stepless variable speed mechanism, which consists of metal transmission belt, driving wheel group and driven wheel group. Among them, the driving wheel group and the driven wheel group are both composed of movable cone disc and fixed cone disc (Figure 3.2.11).

电控机械自动变速箱（AMT）由以下元件组成：①被控对象包括发动机、离合器和变速器；②履行机构包含步进电机、电磁阀（普通电磁阀和高速电磁阀）及液压缸（离合器动作缸和选、换挡油缸）等；③传感器包含速度传感器（发动机转速传感器、输进轴转速传感器、车速传感器）、油门开度传感器和挡位传感器等；④电控单元（ECU）包括 CPU、ROM 和 I/O 接口等。AMT 的执行机构由选、换挡执行机构、离合器执行机构和油门执行机构等组成。油门执行机构一般采用步进电机或磁电式电机驱动油门。选、换挡和离合器执行机构有气动式和液动式两种，现在更常用的是液压操纵系统。

The AMT consists of the following components: ①The controlled objects includes engine, clutch and transmission; ②The actuators include stepping motors, solenoid valves (ordinary solenoid valves and high-speed solenoid valves) and hydraulic cylinders (clutch action cylinders and selection, shift cylinders), etc. ③The sensor includes speed sensor (engine speed sensor, input shaft speed sensor, vehicle speed sensor), throttle open degree sensor and gear sensor, etc. ④Electronic control unit (ECU) includes CPU, ROM and I/O interfaces, etc. The actuator of AMT is composed of selecting and shifting actuator, clutch actuator and throttle actuator, etc. The throttle actuator usually uses stepping motor or magnetoelectric motor to drive the throttle. Selecting, shifting and clutch actuator are pneumatic and hydraulic. Hydraulic control system is more commonly used nowadays.

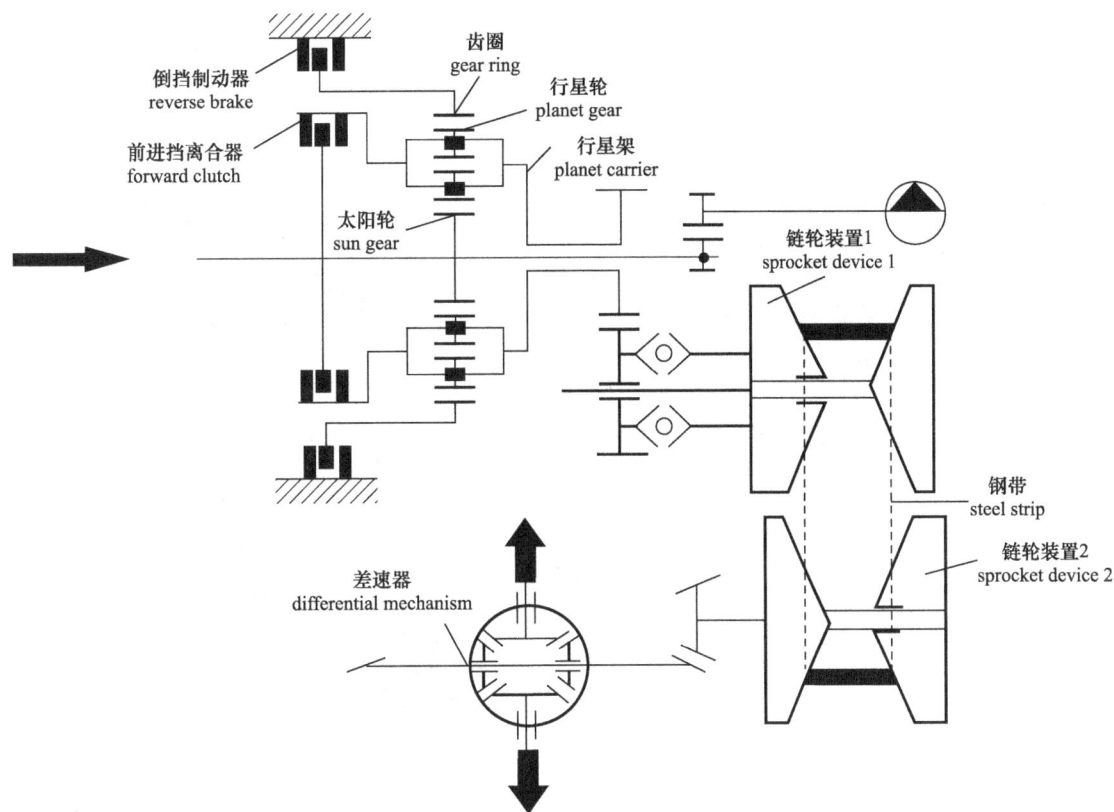

图 3.2.11　无级变速器

Figure 3.2.11　*Continuously variable transmission*

双离合自动变速箱基于手动变速箱基础之上。而与手动变速箱所不同的是，DCT 中的两离合器与两根输入轴相连，换挡和离合操作都是通过一集成电子和液压元件的机械电子模块来实现。而不再通过离合器踏板操作。就像 tiptronic 液力自动变速器一样，驾驶员可以手动换挡或将变速杆处于全自动 D 挡（舒适型，在发动机低速运行时换挡）或 S 挡（任务型，在发动机高速运行时换挡）模式。此种模式下的换挡通常由挡位和离合执行器实现。两离合器各自与不同的输入轴相连。如果离合器 1 通过实心轴与挡位 1、3、5 相连，那么离合器 2 则通过空心轴与挡位 2、4、6 和倒挡相连。通俗的说，这种变速箱形式就有两个离合器，一个控制 1、3、5 挡，一个控制 2、4、6 挡。使用一挡的时候二挡已经准备好了，所以换挡时间大大缩短，没有延时。如图 3.2.12 所示。

Double clutch automatic transmission is based on manual transmission. Unlike manual gearbox, two pairs of clutches in DCT are connected with two input shafts. Shifting and clutch operation are realized by a mechanical and electronic module which integrates electronic and hydraulic components, not by operating the clutch pedal any longer. Just like tiptronic hydraulic automatic transmission, drivers can shift gears manually or put the transmission lever in full-automatic D gear (for comfortable type, shift is operated at low speed of the engine) or S-gear (for task type, shift is operated at high speed of the engine) mode. In this mode shift is usually achieved by gears and clutch actuators. The two pairs of clutches are respectively connected with different input axes. If clutch 1 is connected to gears 1, 3 and 5 through solid axis, then clutch 2 is connected to gear 2, 4, 6 and reverse through hollow axis. Generally speaking, there are two clutches in this type of transmission, one controlling gear 1, 3, 5 and the other controlling gear 2, 4 and 6. The second gear is ready when using the first gear, so the shift time is greatly shortened and there is no delay (Figure 3.2.12).

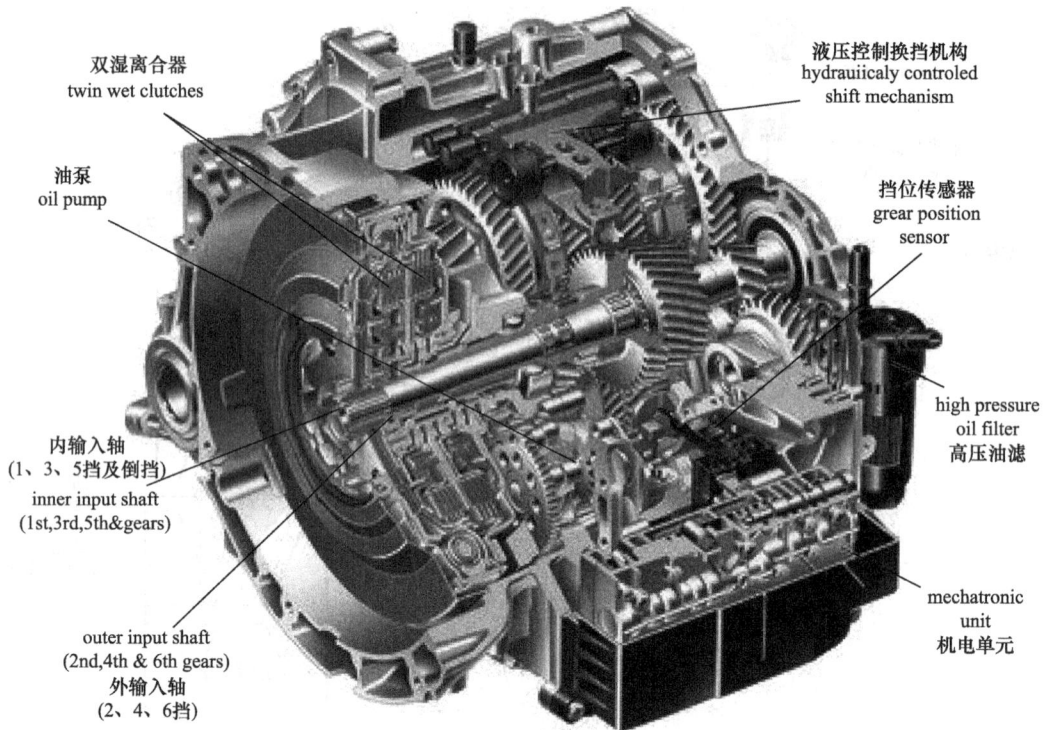

图 3.2.12 双离合变速器

Figure 3.2.12 Dual Clutch Transmission

2.4 万向传动装置（Universal drive）

万向传动装置是用来在工作过程中相对位置不断改变的两根轴间传递动力的装置。其作用是连接不在同一直线上的变速器输出轴和主减速器输入轴，并保证在两轴之间的夹角和距离经常变化的情况下，仍能可靠地传递动力。它主要由万向节、传动轴和中间支承组成。安装时必须使传动轴两端的万向节叉处于同一平面。

Universal drive is used to transfer power between two shafts whose relative position is constantly changing in the working process, whose function is to connect the output shaft of the transmission and the input shaft of the main reducer, which are not on the same line, and to ensure that the power can be reliably transmitted even when the angle and distance between the two axes are constantly changing. It mainly consists of universal joint, transmission shaft and intermediate support. The universal joint fork at both ends of the transmission shaft must be in the same plane when it is installed.

按万向节在扭转方向上是否有明显的弹性可分为刚性万向节和挠性万向节。刚性万向节又可分为不等速万向节（常用的为十字轴式）、准等速万向节（如双联式万向节）和等速万向节（如球笼式万向节）三种。

According to whether the universal joint has obvious elasticity in the torsional direction, it can be divided into rigid universal joint and flexible universal joint.

Rigid universal joints can also be divided into three types: unconstant velocity universal joint (commonly used as cross-axis type), near constant velocity universal joint (such as double cardan joint) and constant speed universal joints (such as double offset universal joint).

万向节所连接的输出轴和输入轴以始终相等的瞬时角速度传递运动的万向节。它又分为：

The universal join, which connected the output shaft and input shaft transferring motion at same instantaneous angular velocity can be further divided into:

1. 球叉式等速万向节。由有滚道的球叉和钢球组成的万向节。而其中的圆弧槽滚道型球叉式万向节是指球叉上的钢球滚道为圆弧型的万向节。其结构特点是在球叉的主动叉和从动叉上做有圆弧凹槽，两者装合后形成四个钢球滚道，滚道内共容纳 4 个钢球。定心钢球装在主、从动叉中心的球形凹槽内。直槽滚道型球叉式万向节是指球叉上的钢球滚道为直槽滚道型的万向节。它的结构特点是在两个球叉上做有直槽，各直槽与轴的中心线相倾斜，且倾斜的角度相同并彼此对称。于两个球叉之间的滚道内装有 4 个钢球。

1. Bendix weiss constant velocity universal joint, which consists of ball fork with raceway and steel ball. The arc groove raceway Bendix-weise joint refers to the universal joint, in which the steel ball raceway on the ball fork is arc. The joint structure is characterized by circular grooves on the driving fork and the driven fork of the ball fork. After the engaging of the two, four ball raceways are formed, and a total of four balls are contained in the raceways. The centering steel ball is installed in a spherical groove in the center of the driving and driven forks. For the straight groove raceway Bendix weiss joint, its steel ball raceway on the ball fork is straight groove. Its structure is characterized by making straight grooves on two ball forks. Each straight grooves are inclined to the center line of its axis, and the inclined angles are the same and symmetrical to each other. There are four steel balls in the raceway between the two forks.

2. 球笼式等速万向节。根据万向节轴向能否运动，又可区分为轴向不能伸缩型（固定型）球笼式万向节和可伸缩型球笼式万向节。结构上固定型球笼式万向节的星形套的内表面以内花键与传动轴连接，它的外表面制有 6 个弧形凹槽作为钢球的内滚道，外滚道做在球形壳的内表面上。星形套与球形壳装合后形成的 6 个滚道内各装 1 个钢球，并由保持架（球笼）使 6 个钢球处于同一平面内。动力由传动轴经钢球、球形壳传出（图 3.2.13）。可伸缩型球笼式万向节的结构特点是于筒形壳的内壁和星形套的外部做有圆柱形直槽，在两者装合后所形成的滚道内装有钢球。钢球同时也装在保持架的孔内。星形套内孔做有花键用来与输入轴连接。这一结构允许星形套与形壳相对在轴向方向移动。

2. Birfield ball-joint. According to whether the universal joint can move axially, it can be divided into two types: axial non-retractable (fixed) Birfield ball-joint and retractable Birfield ball-joint. Structurally, the inner surface of the star sleeve of the fixed Birfield ball-joint is connected with the transmission shaft by an internal spline. Its outer surface is made of six arc grooves as the inner raceway of the steel ball, and the outer raceway is made on the inner surface of the spherical shell. The six raceways are formed by the star sleeve and the spherical shell. Each raceway contains a steel ball, and the six steel balls are placed in the same plane by the cage. The power is transmitted from the transmission shaft through the steel ball and spherical shell (Fig. 3.2.13). Thestructural characteristics of the retractable Birfield ball-joint are that the inner wall of the cylindrical shell and the outer part of the star sleeve are made of cylindrical straight grooves, and steel balls are installed in the raceway formed by the combination of the two. The steel ball is also mounted in the hole of the cage. The inner hole of the star sleeve is splined to connect with the input shaft. This structure allows the star sleeve to move in the axial direction relative to the cylindrical shell.

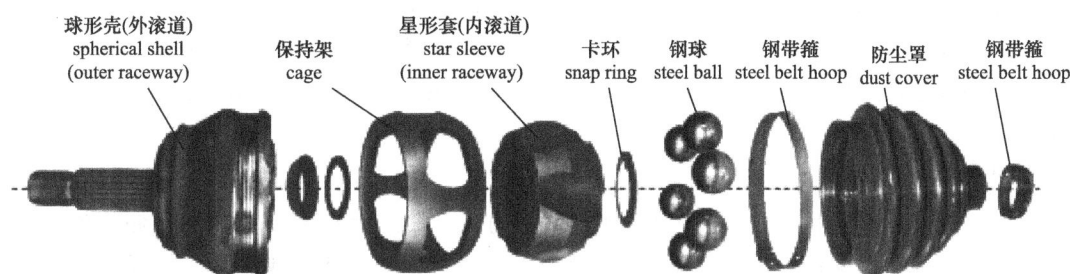

图 3.2.13　球笼式等速万向节

Figure 3.2.13　Birfield ball-joint

万向节连接的两轴夹角大于 0 时，输出轴和输入轴之间以变化的瞬时角速度比传递运动，但万向节的平均角速度是相等的。

When the angle between the two axes of the universal joint is greater than zero, the motion between the output axle and the input axle is transmitted by variable instantaneous angular velocity ratio, but the mean angular velocity of the universal joint is equal.

3. 十字轴式刚性万向节由万向节叉、十字轴、滚针轴承、油封、套筒、轴承盖等件组成。工作原理为：转动叉中之一则经过十字轴带动另一个叉转动，同时又可以绕十字轴中心在任意方向摆动。转动过程中滚针轴承中的滚针可自转，以便减轻摩擦。与输入动力连接的轴称为输入轴（又称主动轴），经万向节输出的轴称为输出轴（又称从动轴）。在输入、输出轴之间有夹角的条件下工作，两轴的角速度不等，并因此会导致输出轴及与之相连的传动部件产生扭转振动和影响这些部件的寿命。如图 3.2.14 所示。

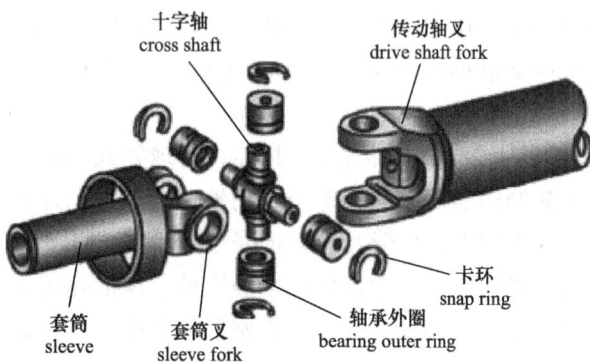

图 3.2.14　十字轴式刚性万向节

Figure 3.2.14　The cross-axis universal joint

3. The cross-axis universal joint is composed of universal joint fork, cross shaft, needle bearing, oil seal, sleeve and bearing cover, etc. The working principle is that one of the rotating forks rotates through the cross axis to drive another fork, and at the same time it can swing in any direction around the center of the cross axis. In the process of rotation, the needles in needle bearing can rotate to reduce friction. The shaft connected with the input power is called the input shaft (also known as the active shaft), and the shaft output through the universal joint is called the output shaft (also known as the driven shaft). When the input and output shafts are angled, the angular velocities of the two shafts are different, which will cause torsional vibration of the output shafts and the transmission components connected with them and affect the service life of these components(Figure 3.2.14).

三枢轴球面滚轮式等速万向节又称为自由三枢轴万向节，其结构如图 3.2.15 所示。由 3 个位于同一平面内互成 120°的枢轴构成，它们的轴线交于输入轴上一点，并且垂直于驱动轴。3 个外表面为球面，滚子轴承分别活套在各枢轴上，一个漏斗形轴，在其筒形部分加工出 3 个槽形轨道。3 个槽形轨道在筒形圆周上是均匀分布的，轨道配合面为部分同柱面，3 个滚子轴承分别装入各槽形轨道，可沿轨道滑动。

Three-pivot spherical roller type constant speed universal joint is also called free three-pivot universal joint. Its structure is shown in the figure. It consists of three pivots in the same plane with 120 degrees each other. Their axes intersect at a point on the input axis and are perpendicular to the driving axis. Three outer surfaces are spherical. Roller bearings are looped on each pivot. and one funnel-shaped shaft. There is a funnel-shaped shaft, in whose cylindrical part, three groove-shaped tracks are machined. The three grooved tracks are evenly distributed around the cylindrical circle, and the track mating surface is partially the same cylindrical surface. The three roller bearings are respectively located into each grooved track and can slide along the track(Figure 3.2.15).

2.5　驱动桥（Driving axle）

主减速器的存在有两个作用，第一是改变动力传输的方向，第二是作为变速器的延伸为各个挡位提供一个共同的传动比。变速器的输出是一个绕纵轴转动的力矩，而车轮必须绕车辆的横轴转动，这就需要有一个装置来改变动力的传输方向。之所以叫主减速器，就是因为不管变速器在什么挡位上，这个装置的传动比都是总传动比的一个因子。有了这个传动比，可以有效地降低对变速器的减速能力的要求，这样设计的好处是可以有效减小变速器的尺寸，使车辆的总布置更加合理。如图3.2.16所示。

The main reducer has two functions. The first is to change the direction of power transmission. The second is to provide a common transmission ratio for each gear as an extension of the transmission. The output of the transmission is a moment rotating around the longitudinal axis, while the wheel must rotate around the transverse axis of the vehicle, which requires a device to change the direction of power transmission. The reason why it is called the main reducer is that the transmission ratio of this device is a factor of the total transmission ratio regardless of the gear position of the transmission. With this transmission ratio, it can effectively reduce the requirement for the decelerability of the transmission. The advantage of this design is that it can effectively reduce the size of the transmission and make the overall layout of the vehicle more reasonable (Figure 3.2.16).

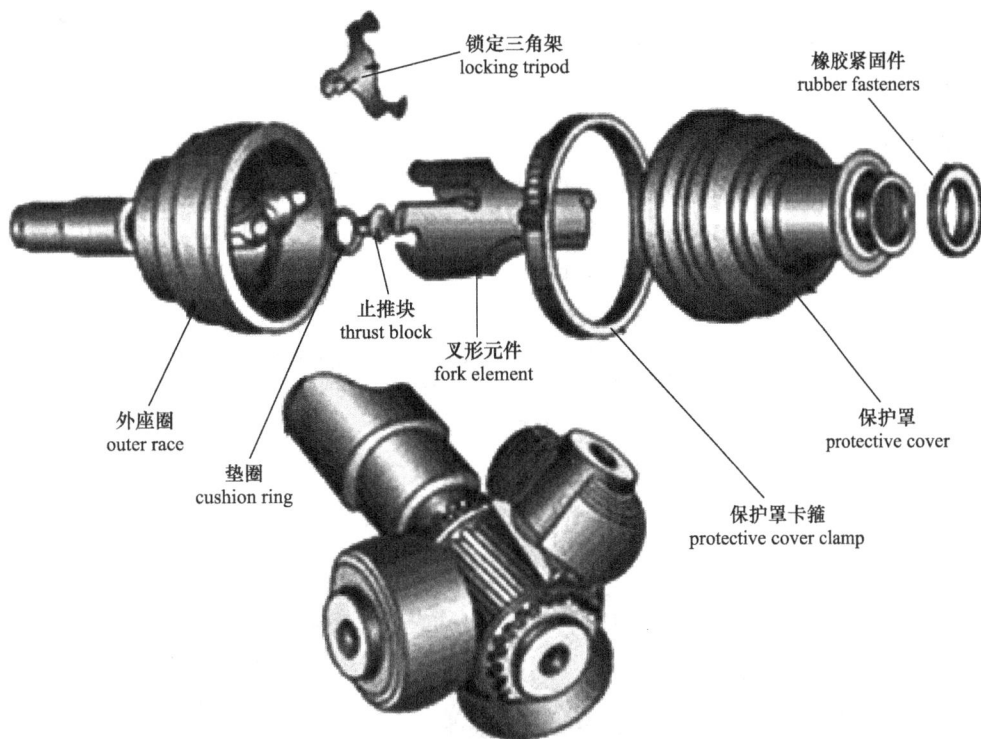

图3.2.15　三枢轴球面滚轮式等速万向节

Figure 3.2.15　Three pivot spherical roller type constant speed universal joint

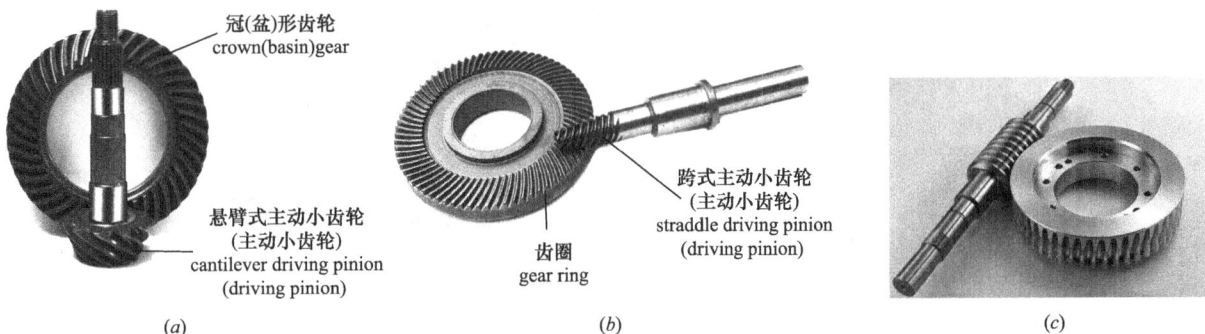

图3.2.16　主减速器形式

Figure 3.2.16　Main reducer form

（a）圆锥齿轮式（bevel gear type）；（b）准双曲面齿轮式（hypoid gear type）；（c）圆柱齿轮式（cylindrical gear type）

汽车主减速器最主要的作用，就是减速增扭。我们知道发动机的输出功率是一定的，根据功率的计算公式 $W = M \times v$（功率＝扭矩×速度），当通过主减速器将传动速度降下来以后，能获得比较高的输出扭矩，从而得到较大的驱动力。此外，汽车主减速器还有改变动力输出方向、实现左右车轮差速或中后桥的差速功能，如图 3.2.17 所示。

The main function of automobile main reducer is to reduce speed and increase torsion. It is known that that the output power of the engine is certain. According to the formula $W = M \times v$（power＝torque×speed），when the transmission speed is reduced through the main reducer, a higher output torque can be obtained and a larger driving force can be obtained as well. In addition, the automobile main reducer also has the functions of changing the power output direction, realizing the differential speed between the left and right wheels or the middle and rear axles as shown in Figure 3.2.17.

差速器的工作原理如图 3.2.18 所示。两齿条 a、b 和行星齿轮啮合，且两齿条质量相等，当向上拉起行星齿轮时，两齿条一起被拉起；当 a 齿条受到阻力时，向上拉起行星齿轮必导致齿条 b 向上移动。齿条 a、b 相当于差速器中的半轴齿轮。

The working principle of the differential is shown in Figure 3.2.18 Two racks a and b engage a planetary gear, and the mass of the two racks is equal. When the planetary gear is pulled up, the two racks are pulled together. When the rack is dragged, pulling upward the planetary gear will cause rack b to move upward. Racks and b are equivalents to half-axle gears in differential.

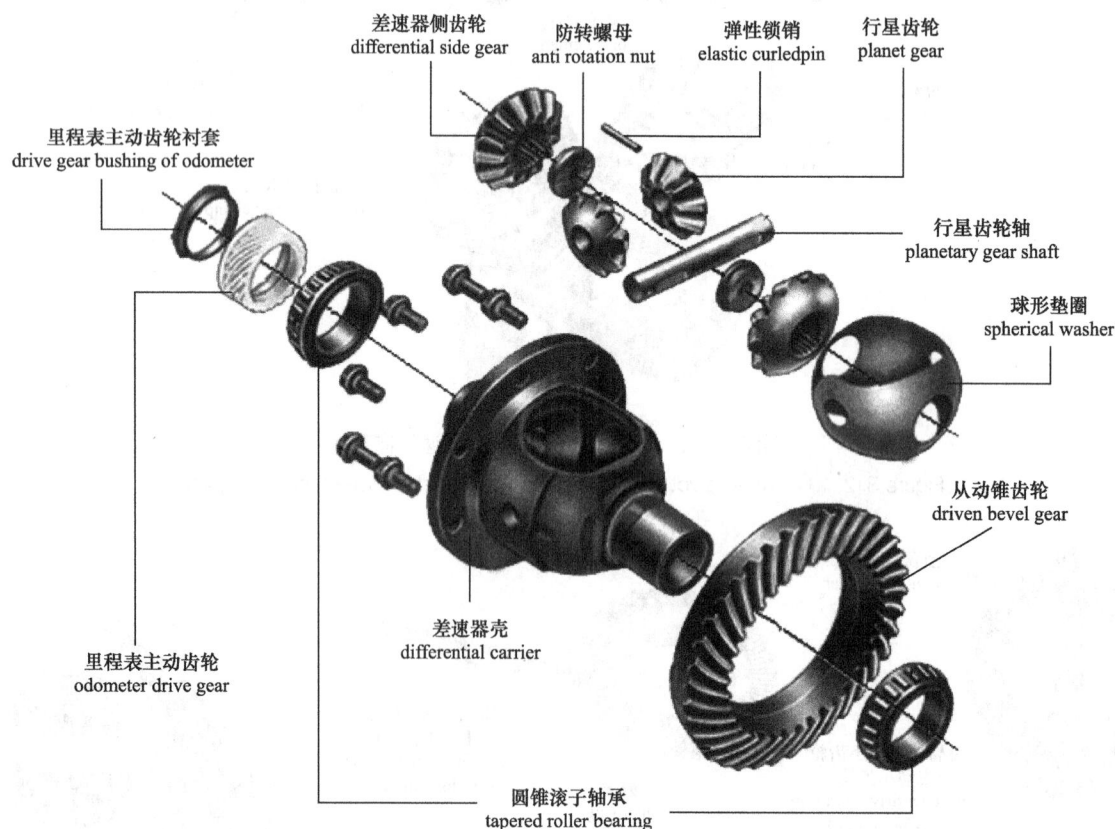

图 3.2.17　主减速器和差速器

Figure 3.2.17　Main reducer and differential

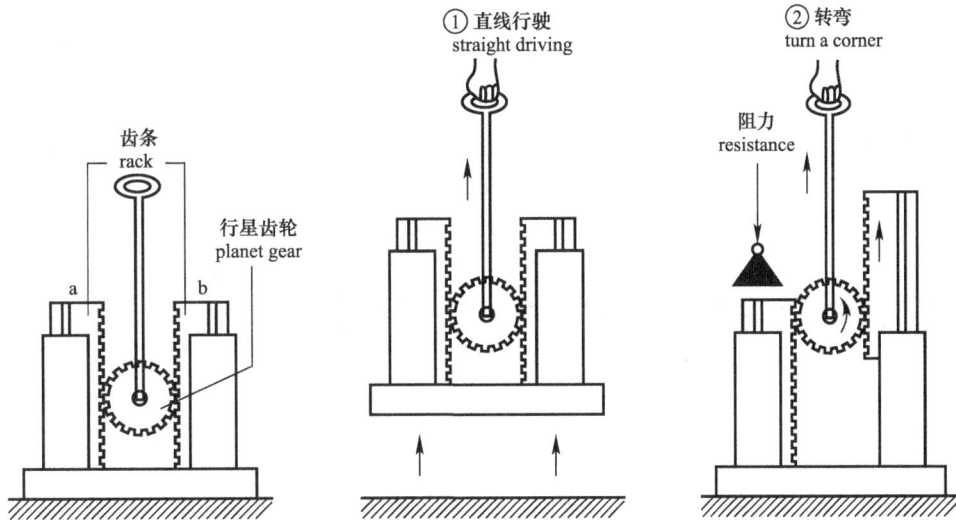

图 3. 2. 18　差速器的工作原理 1

Figure 3. 2. 18　Working principle 1 of differential

当车辆直线行驶时，左右两个轮受到的阻力一样，行星齿轮不自转，把动力传递到两个半轴上，这时左右车轮转速一样（相当于刚性连接），如图 3. 2. 19 所示。当车辆转弯时，左右车轮受到的阻力不一样，行星齿轮绕着半轴转动并同时自转，从而吸收阻力差，使车轮能够与不同速度旋转，保证汽车顺利过弯。

When the vehicle runs in a straight line, the resistances of the left and right wheels are the same. The planetary gear does not rotate on its own axis and transfers power to the two half axles. At this time, the speed of the left and right wheels is the same (equivalent to the rigid connection), as shown in the Fig. 3. 2. 19. When the vehicle turns, the resistances of the left and right wheels are different. The planetary gears rotate around the half axle and rotate on its own axis at the same time, so as to absorb the resistance difference, so that the wheels can rotate with different speeds to ensure the smooth turning of the vehicle.

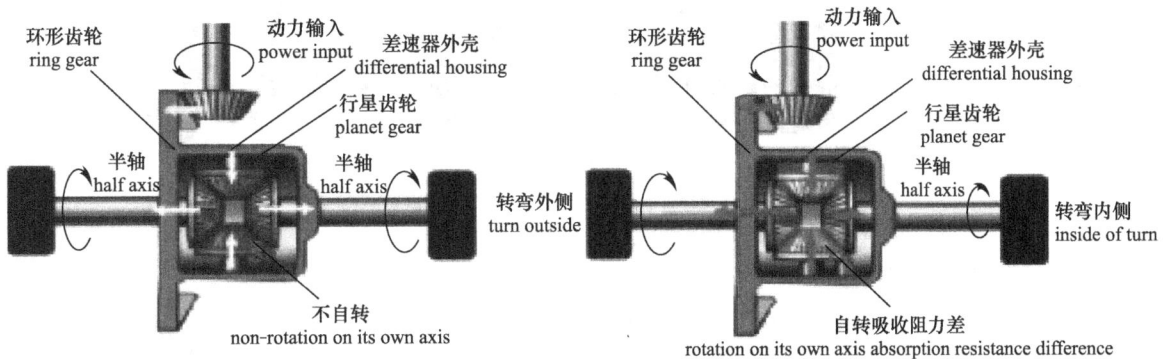

图 3. 2. 19　差速器的工作原理 2

Figure 3. 2. 19　Working principle 2 of differential

半轴是在差速器与驱动轮之间传递动力的实心轴，用于将差速器半轴齿轮的输出转矩传到驱动轮或轮间减速器上，半轴实物与结构如图 3. 2. 20 所示。其内端用花键与差速器的半轴齿轮连接，而外端用凸缘与驱动轮的轮毂相连，半轴齿轴的轴颈支承于差速器壳两侧轴颈的孔内，而差速器壳又以其两侧轴颈借助轴承直接支承在主减速器壳上。

The half-axis is a solid shaft which transfers power between the differential and the driving wheel. It is used to transfer the output torque of the differential half axle gear to the driving wheel or the inter-wheel reducer. The material object and structure of the half-axis are shown in the Fig. 3. 2. 20. The inner end is in splined connection with the half-axle gear of the differential, while the outer end is connected with the hub of the driving wheel by the flange. The Journal of the semi-axle gear shaft is supported in the holes of the journals on both sides of the differential housing, and the differential housing is directly supported on the main reducer housing by means of bearings on both sides of the journal.

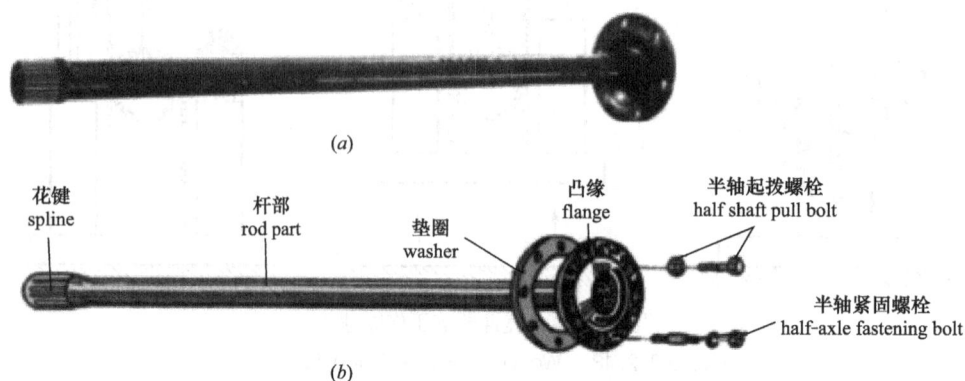

花键
spline

杆部
rod part

垫圈
washer

凸缘
flange

半轴起拨螺栓
half shaft pull bolt

半轴紧固螺栓
half-axle fastening bolt

图 3. 2. 20 半轴

Figure 3. 2. 20 Half axis

(a) 实物 (material object); (b) 结构 (structure)

驱动桥壳的作用是：支承并保护主减速器、差速器和半轴等，使左右驱动车轮的轴向相对位置固定，同从动桥一起支承车架及其上的各总成质量；汽车行驶时，承受由车轮传来的路面反作用力和力矩，并经悬架传给车架。桥壳实物与结构如图 3.2.21 所示。

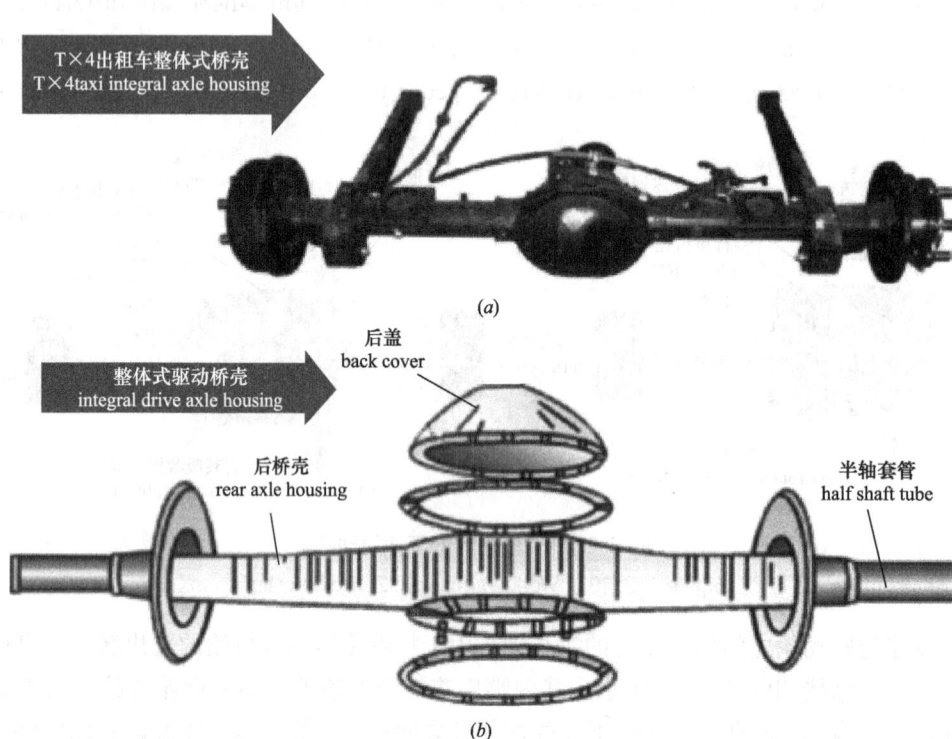

T×4出租车整体式桥壳
T×4taxi integral axle housing

整体式驱动桥壳
integral drive axle housing

后盖
back cover

后桥壳
rear axle housing

半轴套管
half shaft tube

图 3. 2. 21 驱动桥壳

Figure 3. 2. 21 Drive axle housing

(a) 实物 (material object); (b) 结构 (structure)

The function of the driving axle housing is to support and protect the main reducer, differential and half axle, etc., so as to fix the relative position of the left and right driving wheels and support the frame and its assembly mass together with the driven axle. When a car is running, it bears the road reaction force and moment from the wheels and passes it to the frame through the suspension. The material object and structure of the axle housing are shown in the Fig. 3. 2. 21.

思考与练习

（Reflection and Exercises）

1. 变速器的功用有哪些？

2. 万向传动装置的种类有哪些？

3. 自动变速器的种类有哪些？它们的优点分别是什么？

1. What are the functions of the transmission?

2. What kinds of universal transmission are there?

3. What are the types of automatic transmission? What are their advantages respectively?

任务三　行　驶　系　统

Task 3　Driving System

教学目标

1. 知识目标

（1）知道悬架的分类及差异；

（2）了解车桥、车轮、悬架的基本结构和原理。

2. 能力目标

（1）能区分轿车常用的车桥、车轮和悬架；

（2）能说常用的车桥、车轮和悬架类型。

3. 情感和素养目标

（1）培养学生服务意识的品质，质量意识、安全意识。

（2）培养学生一丝不苟的工匠精神。

Teaching objectives

1. Knowledge objectives

（1）Knowing the classification and difference of suspension；

（2）Understanding the basic structure and principle of axle, wheel and suspension.

2. Ability objectives

（1）To distinguish the axles, wheels and suspensions commonly used in cars；

（2）Knowing commonly used types of axles, wheels and suspensions.

3. Emotion and quality goals

（1）Cultivate students' service awareness, quality awareness and safety awareness；

（2）Cultivate students' craftsmanship spirit of being meticulous.

汽车行驶系的功用是接受发动机传动系传来的转矩，并通过驱动轮与路面间附着作用，产生路面对汽车的牵引力以保证整车正常行驶；传递并承受路面作用于车轮上的各向反力及其形成的力矩，缓和各种冲击和振动，

保证汽车平顺行驶，并且与汽车转向很好地配合工作，实现汽车行驶方向的正确控制，以保证汽车操纵稳定性。

The function of automobile driving system is to accept the torque from engine transmission system and produce traction force formed by road surface and acting on the automobile, which ensure the normal running of the vehicle. It transmits and bear the reaction force and the moment formed by road surface and acting on the wheel, and ease all kinds of impact and vibration, to ensure the smooth running of the vehicle. It should cooperate well with the steering of the vehicle to achieve the correct control of the direction of vehicle running to ensure vehicle handling stability.

3.1 车桥（Axle）

车桥位于悬架与车轮之间，其两端安装车轮，通过悬架与车架（或车身）相连，其功用是传递车架（或车身）与车轮之间各种载荷。按悬架结构不同，车桥分为整体式和断开式。整体式车桥与非独立悬架配用；断开式车桥与独立悬架配用。按车桥上车轮的作用不同，车桥分为转向桥、驱动桥、转向驱动桥和支持桥。

The axle is located between the suspension and the wheel. Wheels are installed at both ends of the axle. The axle is connected with the frame (or body) through the suspension. Its function is to transfer various loads between the frame (or body) and the wheel. According to the different suspension structure, axle can be divided into integral and disconnected modes. Integral axle matches with the independent suspension, and disconnected axle matches with the independent suspension. According to the different roles of the wheels on the axle, the axle is divided into steering axle, driving axle, steering drive axle and supporting axle.

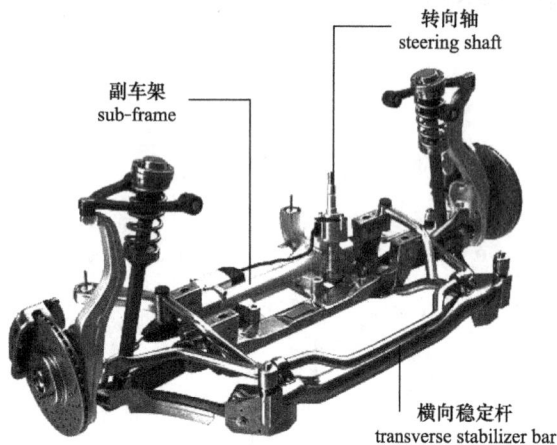

图 3.3.1　前桥

Figure 3.3.1　Front axle

1. 转向桥通常位于汽车前部，故也称为前桥。转向桥的作用是支承部分重量，安装前轮及制动器（前），连接车架，承受车架与车轮之间的作用力及其产生的弯矩和转矩，同时还要使前轮偏转以实现转向。转向桥基本结构由前轴（副车架）、转向节、主销、轮毂等部分组成（图3.3.1）。

1. The steering axle is usually located in the front of the car, so it is also called the front axle. The role of the steering bridge is to support part of the weight, installing the front wheel and brake (front), connecting the frame, bearing the force between the frame and the wheels and its bending moment and torque, and also make the front wheel deflect to achieve steering. The basic structure of the steering axle is composed of front axle (sub-frame), steering knuckle, master pin and hub, etc(Figure 3.3.1).

2. 驱动桥处于动力传动系的末端，其基本功能是：①将万向传动装置传来的发动机转矩通过主减速器、差速器、半轴等传到驱动车轮，实现降速增大转矩；②通过主减速器圆锥齿轮副改变转矩的传递方向；③通过差速器实现两侧车轮差速作用，保证内、外侧车轮以不同转速转向；④通过桥壳体和车轮实现承载及传力矩作用（图3.3.2）。

2. The driving axle is at the end of the transmission system, and its basic functions are: ①The engine torque from the universal transmission device is transmitted to the driving wheel through the main reducer, differential, half-axle and so on, so as to reduce the speed and increase the torque; ②To change the transmission direction of the torque through the bevel gear pair of the main reducer; ③The differential effect of the

wheels on both sides is realized by the differential, which ensures that the inner and outer wheels steer at different speeds; ④The axle housing and wheels are used to carry load and transfer moment(Figure 3.3.2).

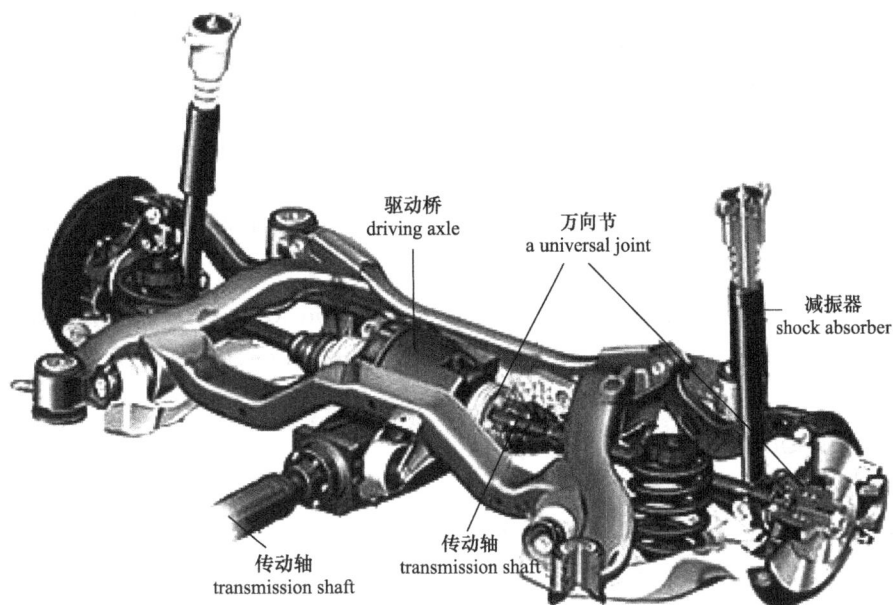

图 3.3.2 驱动桥

Figure 3.3.2 Driving axle

3. 转向驱动桥一般由主减速器、差速器、半轴和桥壳组成。现在普通轿车普遍采用的是断开式、独立悬架转向驱动桥。车桥上端通过左、右悬架与承载式车身相连接，下端通过左、右下摆臂与固定在车身上的副车架相连接。悬架车轮轴承壳与下摆臂之间通过可移动球形接头连接，从而使前轮固定，并通过下摆臂上的长孔可调整车轮外倾角，为了减小车辆转向时的车身倾斜，在副车架与下摆臂之间还装有横向稳定器（图3.3.3）。

3. Steering driving axle is generally composed of main reducer, differential, half axle and axle housing. At present, disconnected and independent suspension steering drive axle is widely used in ordinary cars. The upper end of the axle is connected with the load-bearing body by left and right suspensions, and the lower end is connected with the sub-frame fixed on the body by left and right lower swing arms. The front wheel is fixed by a movable spherical joint between the suspension wheel bearing shell and the lower swing arm, and the wheel camber angle can be adjusted by a long hole in the lower swing arm. In order to reduce the body tilt during steering, a roll stabilizer is installed between the sub-frame and the lower swing arm(Figure 3.3.3).

图 3.3.3 转向驱动桥

Figure 3.3.3 Steering drive axle

3.2 悬架 (Suspension)

悬架是车架（或车身）与车桥（或车轮）之间一切传力连接装置的总称。

Suspension is the general name of all power transmission junction device between frame (or body) and axle (or wheel).

1. 悬架的功能 (Suspension function)

悬架具有以下的功能：

（1）连接车架（或车身）和车轮，把路面作用到车轮的各种力传给车架（或车身）。

（2）缓和冲击、衰减振动，使乘坐舒适，具有良好的平顺性。

（3）利用悬架的某些传力构件使车轮按一定轨迹相对于车架或车身跳动，即起导向作用。

（4）保证汽车具有良好的操纵稳定性。

The suspension has the following functions：

（1）It connects the frame (or body) with the wheel, and transfers the various forces acting on the wheel from the road surface to the frame (or body).

（2）It mitigates the impact and attenuates the vibration to make the ride comfortable and have good smooth running.

（3）It uses some force transmission components of suspension to make the wheels jump relative to the frame or body according to a certain trajectory, that is to say, to play a guiding role.

（4）It ensures that the vehicle has good handling stability.

2. 悬架的分类（Classification of suspensions）

汽车悬架可分为两大类：非独立悬架和独立悬架

Automobile suspensions can be divided into two categories：non-independent suspensions and independent suspensions.

非独立悬架的结构特点是两侧车轮由一根整体式车桥相连，车轮连同车桥一起通过弹性悬架悬挂在车架或车身的下面。非独立悬架具有结构简单、成本低、强度高、保养容易、行车中前轮定位变化小的优点，但由于其舒适性及操纵稳定性都较差，在现代轿车中基本上已不再使用，多用在货车和大客车上。

The structural characteristics of the non-independent suspension are that the wheels on both sides are connected by an integral axle, and the wheels are suspended under the frame or body through the elastic suspension together with the axle. Non-independent suspension has the advantages of simple structure, low cost, high strength, easy maintenance and small change of front wheel alignment while driving. However, due to its poor comfort and handling stability, it is no longer used in modern cars, and is mostly used in trucks and buses.

独立悬架的每一侧车轮都是单独地通过弹性悬架悬挂在车架或车身下面的。其优点是：质量轻，减少了车身受到的冲击，并提高了车轮的地面附着力；可用刚度小的较软弹簧，改善汽车的舒适性；可以使发动机位置降低，汽车重心也得到降低，从而提高汽车的行驶稳定性；左右车轮单独跳动，互不相干，能减小车身的倾斜和震动。不过，独立悬架存在着结构复杂、成本高、维修不便的缺点。现代轿车大都是采用独立式悬架，按其结构形式的不同，独立悬架又可分为横臂式、纵臂式、多连杆式、烛式以及麦弗逊式悬架等。

Independent suspension is that wheels on each side are suspended separately under the frame or body through elastic suspension. It has advantages of light weight, less impact on the body, and it improves the adhesion between ground and wheels. Soft springs with small stiffness can be used to improve the comfort of the car. It can make the position of the engine and the center of gravity of the car lower, so as to improve the driving stability of the vehicle. The left and right wheels hop alone and are not related to each other, which can reduce the tilt and vibration of the automobile body. However, the independent suspension has the disadvantages of complex structure, high cost and inconvenient maintenance. Modern vehicles mostly adopt independent suspension. According to their different structure forms, independent suspensions can be divided into cross arm type, longitudinal arm type, multi-link type, candle type and Macpherson suspension, etc.

3. 悬架的结构（Suspension structure）

弹性元件是指钢板弹簧、螺旋弹簧、扭杆弹簧、油气弹簧和空气弹簧等，如图 3.3.4 所示。弹性元件用来承受并传递垂直载荷，缓和汽车在不同路面上行驶所引起的冲击。

Elastic elements refer to leaf springs, coil springs, torsion bar springs, hydro-pneumatic springs and air springs, etc., as shown in Figure 3.3.4 Elastic elements are used to withstand and transmit vertical loads to mitigate the impacts caused by vehicle driving on different road surfaces.

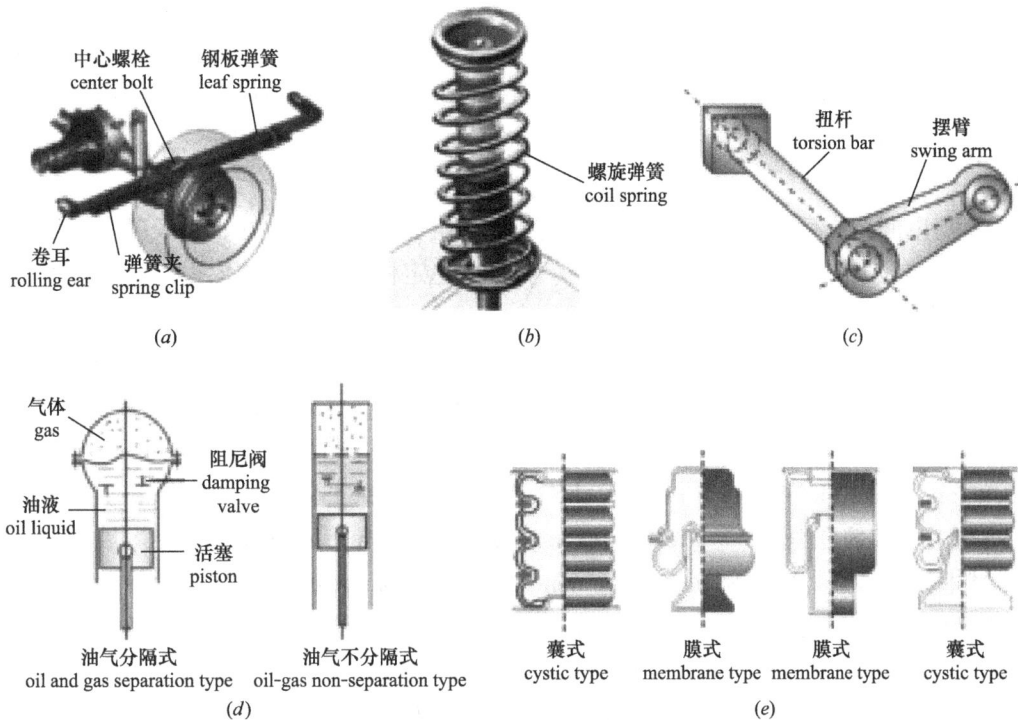

图 3.3.4　弹性元件

Figure 3.3.4　Elastic element

(a) 钢板弹簧 (leaf spring); (b) 螺旋弹簧 (coil spring); (c) 扭杆弹簧 (torsion bar spring);

(d) 油气弹簧 (hydro pneumatic spring); (e) 空气弹簧 (air spring)

减振器在汽车中的作用是迅速衰减由车轮通过悬架弹簧传给车身的冲击和振动，提高汽车行驶的平顺性。减振器在汽车悬架中与弹性元件并联安装。

The role of shock absorber in automobiles is to rapidly attenuate the impact and vibration transmitted by wheels through suspension springs, and to improve the ride comfort of automobiles. The shock absorber is mounted in parallel with the elastic element in the automobile suspension.

减震器的基本原理：当车架与车桥作往复的相对运动而使活塞在缸筒内往复移动时，减振器壳体内的油液便反复地从内腔通过一些窄小的孔隙流入另一内腔，此时孔壁与油液间的摩擦及液体分子内的摩擦便形成对振动的阻尼力，使车身和车架的振动能量转化为热能被油液和减振器壳体所吸收，然后扩散到大气中。减振器阻尼力的大小随车架与车桥（或车轮）间相对速度的变化而增减，并且与油液的黏度有关。如图 3.3.5 所示。

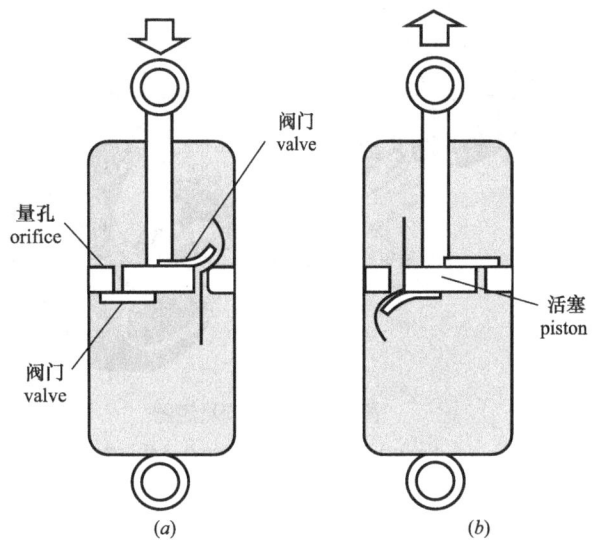

图 3.3.5　减震器的基本原理

Figure 3.3.5　Basic principle of shock absorber

(a) 压缩行程 (compression stroke);

(b) 伸张行程 (stretching stroke)

The basic principle of shock absorber: When the piston moves back and forth in cylinder cylinder due to the relative motion between the frame and the axle, the oil liquid in the shock absorber shell flows into another chamber repeatedly through some narrow holes. At this time, the friction between the holes walls and the oil and the friction between the liquid molecules form the damping force to the vibration, which converts the vibration energy of the body and the frame into heat energy. It is absorbed by oil and shock absorber shell and then diffused into the atmosphere. Damping force magnitude of shock absorber increases and decreases with the change of relative velocity between frame and axle (or wheel), and it is related to oil viscosity. As shown in Figure 3.3.5.

横向稳定器利用扭杆弹簧原理，将左右车轮通过横向稳定杆连接起来。在车身倾斜时，稳定杆两边的纵向部分向不同方向偏转，于是横向稳定杆便被扭转。弹性的稳定杆产生的扭转内力矩就阻碍了悬架弹簧的变形，从而减少车身的横向倾斜。如图 3.3.6 所示。

The transverse stabilizer uses the torsion bar spring principle to connect the left and right wheels through the transverse stabilizer bar. When the body tilts, the longitudinal parts of the stabilizer bar deflect in different directions, and the stabilizer bar is twisted. The internal torque produced by the elastic stabilizer bar hinders the suspension. Spring deformation reduces the lateral tilt of the body. As shown in Figure 3.3.6.

3.2.1 非独立悬架的分类 (Classification of non-independent suspensions)

1. 扭力梁式非独立悬架 (Torsion beam type non-independent suspension)

钢板弹簧被用做非独立悬架的弹性元件，由于它兼起导向机构的作用，使得悬架系统大为简化。这种悬架广泛用于货车的前、后悬架中。它中部用 U 型螺栓将钢板弹簧固定在车桥上。悬架前端为固定铰链，也叫"死吊耳"。它由钢板弹簧销钉将钢板弹簧前端卷耳部与钢板弹簧前支架连接在一起，前端卷耳孔中为减少磨损装有衬套。后端卷耳通过钢板弹簧吊耳销与后端吊耳与吊耳架相连，后端可以自由摆动，形成活动吊耳。当车架受到冲击弹簧变形时，两卷耳之间的距离有变化的可能（图 3.3.7）。

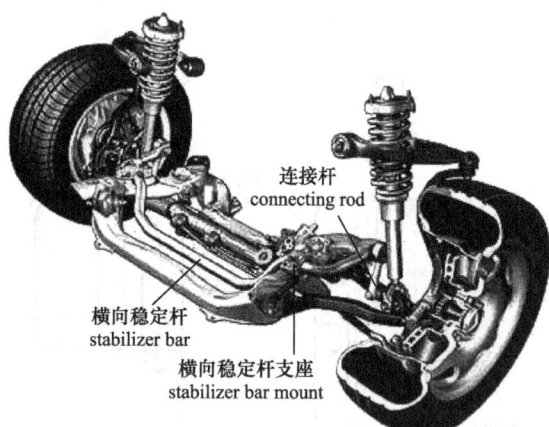

图 3.3.6 横向稳定器
Figure 3.3.6 Transverse stabilizer

图 3.3.7 扭力梁式非独立悬架
Figure 3.3.7 Torsion beam type non-independent suspension

Leaf spring is used as an elastic element of non-independent suspension. Because it acts as a guide mechanism as well, the suspension system is greatly simplified. This kind of suspension is widely used in front and rear suspensions of trucks. In the middle, the leaf spring is fixed on the axle with U-bolts. The front end of the suspension is the fixed hinge, also known as 'dead lifting ear'. The front end rolling ear of the leaf spring is connected with the front bracket of the leaf spring by the leaf spring pin, and a bushing is installed in the front end ear coil hole to reduce friction loss. The rear end rolling ear is connected with the lifting ear frame by the leaf spring lifting ear pin and the rear lifting ear. The rear end can swing freely to form a movable lifting ear. When the frame is impacted and the spring deforms, the distance between the two ears may change(Fig. 3. 3. 7).

2. 整体桥式非独立悬架（Integral axle non-independent suspension）

整体桥就是车桥不能断开，同一车桥上的两个车轮没有相对运动。整体桥悬挂的历史几乎伴随汽车的诞生就开始了，发展到如今，它的结构并没有太大的变化。对于驱动桥来说，主要还是由差速器壳体、桥管、半轴、轴承等部分组成，而对于非驱动桥的整体桥来说，其结构更为简单，且现在多为货车采用（图 3. 3. 8）。

The integral axle is that the axle can not be disconnected and the two wheels on the same bridge have no relative motion. The history of integral axle suspension almost began with the birth of automobiles, and its structure has not changed much until now. For the driving axle, it is mainly composed of differential case, axle tube, half axle and bearings, etc. For the whole axle of non-drive axle, its structure is simpler, and now it is mostly used by trucks(Fig. 3. 3. 8).

3. 扭力梁式非独立悬架（Torsion beam type non-independent suspension）

扭力梁式半独立悬架，是汽车后悬挂装置类型的一种，是在扭力梁式非独立悬架上增加一个平衡杆来使车轮产生倾斜，保持车辆的平稳。采取这种悬挂系统的汽车一般平稳性和舒适性较差，但由于其构造较简单、承载力大，该悬挂多用于载重汽车、普通客车和一些其他特种车辆上（图 3. 3. 9）。

Torsion beam semi-independent suspension is a type of vehicle rear suspension device. It adds a balancing pole to the torsion beam non-independent suspension to tilt the wheel and keep the vehicle stable. The vehicle with this suspension system is generally less stable and comfortable. But because of its simple structure and large bearing capacity, the suspension is mostly used in trucks, ordinary buses and some other special vehicles.

图 3. 3. 8 整体桥
Figure 3. 3. 8 Integral axle

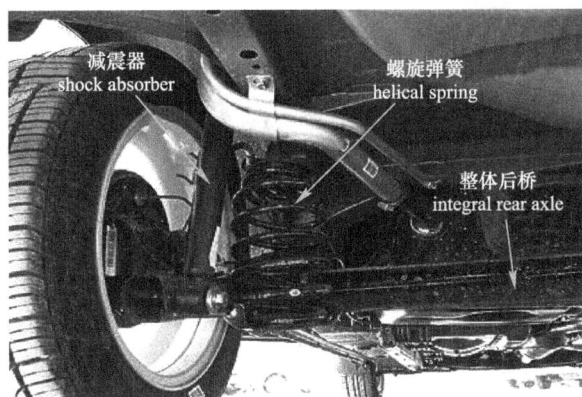

图 3. 3. 9 扭力梁式非独立悬架
Figure 3. 3. 9 Torsional beam non-independent suspension

3. 2. 2 独立悬架的分类（Classification of independent suspensions）

1. 麦弗逊式独立悬架（MacPherson independent suspension）

弗逊式悬架是目前应用比较普遍的悬架结构形式。麦弗逊式悬架中筒式减振器为滑动立柱，横摆臂的内端通过铰链与车身相连，外端通过球铰链与转向节相连（图 3. 3. 10）。

MacPherson suspension is a widely used suspension structure at present. The cylindrical shock absorber of the MacPherson suspension is a sliding column. The inner end of the swing arm is connected to the body by hinges, and the outer end is connected to the steering knuckle by spherical hinges(Fig. 3. 3. 10).

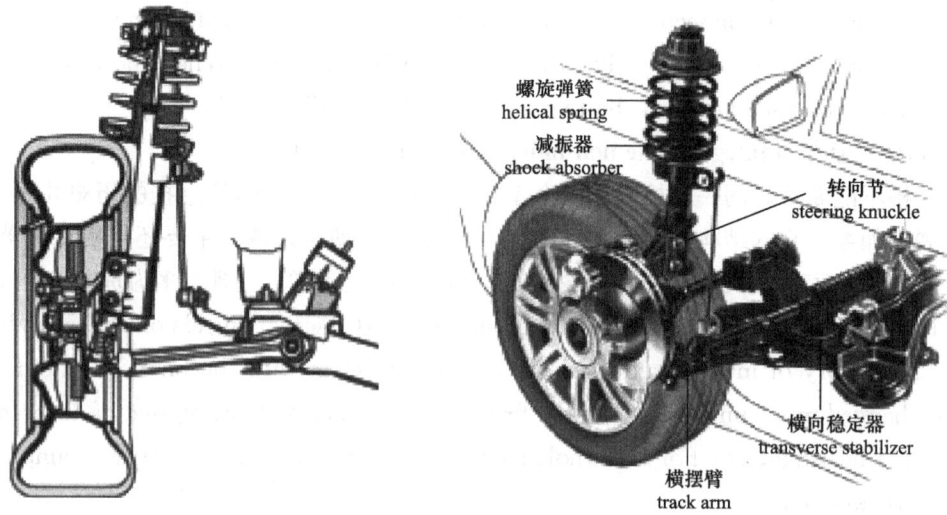

图 3.3.10　麦弗逊式独立悬架

Figure 3.3.10　MacPherson independent suspension

2. 双叉臂式独立悬架（Double-fork-arm independent suspension）

双叉臂式独立悬架，又称双A臂式独立悬挂，采用上下不等长叉臂（上短下长），不仅让车轮在上下运动时能自动改变外倾角并且减小轮距变化减小轮胎磨损，并且能自适应路面，轮胎接地面积大、贴地性好。双叉臂式悬挂运动性出色，为法拉利、玛莎拉蒂等超级跑车所运用（图3.3.11）。

图 3.3.11　双叉臂式独立悬架

Figure 3.3.11　Double-arm independent suspension

Double-fork-arm independent suspension, also known as double-A-arm independent suspension, uses up-down unequal-length fork arm (upper is short and lower is long), so that wheels can automatically change the camber angle and reduce the change of wheelbase and tire wear. It can also adapt to road surface by itself, and has large tire grounding area and good adhesion to the ground. Double-fork-arm suspension has excellent motility, which is used by supercars such as Ferrari and Maserati, etc(Fig. 3.3.11).

双叉臂式独立悬架拥有横向刚度大、抗侧倾性能优异、抓地性能好等优点，但占用空间较大，成本较高、悬架定位参数设定复杂。

Dual-fork-arm independent suspension has the advantages of large transverse stiffness, excellent anti-roll performance and good grip performance, but it takes up more space, and has higher costs, and complex setting of suspension positioning parameters.

3. 多连杆式独立悬架（Multi-link independent suspension）

独立悬架中多采用螺旋弹簧，因而对于侧向力、垂直力以及纵向力需增设导向装置，即采用杆件来承受和传递这些力，因而一些汽车上为减轻车重和简化结构采用多连杆式悬架（图3.3.12）。

Coil springs are often used in independent suspensions. Therefore, a guide device is needed for lateral force, vertical force and longitudinal force. Rods are used to bear and transmit these forces. Therefore, multi-link suspensions are used in some automobiles to reduce vehicle weight and simplify the structure(Fig. 3.3.12).

以常见的五连杆式后悬架为例，五根连杆：主控制臂、前置定位臂、后置定位臂、上臂和下臂分别对各个方向的作用力进行抵消。

Taking the common five-connecting rod rear suspension as an example, five connecting rods are the main control arm, the front positioning arm, the rear positioning arm, the upper arm and the lower arm, which counteract the forces in each direction respectively.

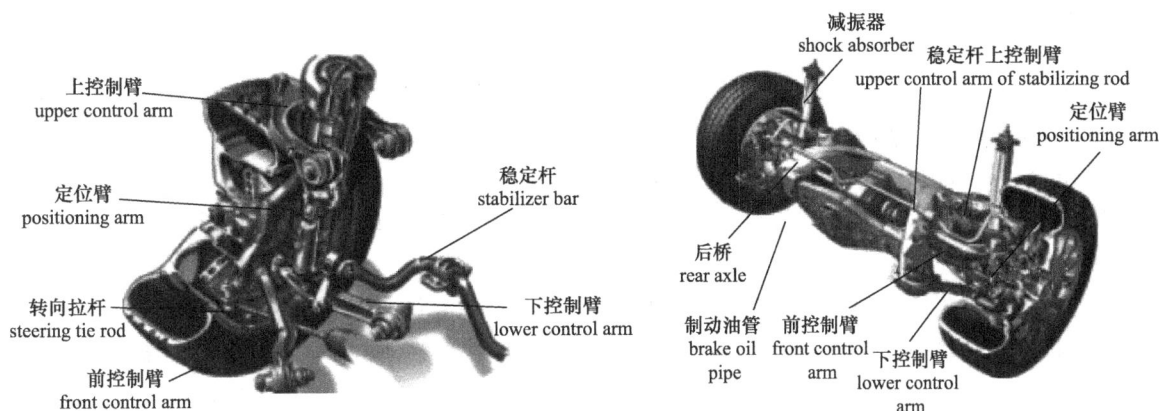

图 3.3.12　多连杆式独立悬架

Figure 3.3.12　Multi-link independent suspension

思考与练习

(Reflection and Exercises)

1. 车桥是如何进行分类的? 有哪些类型?

2. 215/60R17 95V 这个轮胎标注代表了哪些参数?

3. 独立悬架的分类有哪些?

1. How are the axles classified and what types are there?

2. 215/60R17 95V, which parameters does the tire marking represent?

3. What are the classifications of independent suspensions?

任务四　转向系统

Task 4　Steering System

教学目标

1. 知识目标

(1) 了解转向系的功用、类型;

(2) 了解转向的分类。

2. 能力目标

(1) 会分辨各类助力转向系;

(2) 认识转向系的各个部件。

3. 情感和素养目标

(1) 培养学生良好的心理素质、善于发现困难的意识。

(2) 培养学生爱岗敬业的意识、不断专研探究的工匠品质。

Teaching objectives

1. Knowledge objectives

（1）Understanding the functions and types of steering system；

（2）Understanding the classification of steering.

2. Ability objectives

（1）To distinguish all kinds of power steering systems；

（2）Knowing the components of steering system.

3. Emotion and quality goals

（1）Cultivate students' psychological quality and the awareness to overcome difficulties；

（2）Cultivate students' awareness of being dedicated to their jobs and craftsmanship spirit of striving for exploration.

车在行驶过程中，需按驾驶员的意志经常改变其行驶方向，即所谓汽车转向。就轮式汽车而言，实现汽车转向的方法是，驾驶员通过一套专设的机构，使汽车转向桥（一般是前桥）上的车轮（转向轮）相对于汽车纵轴线偏转一定角度。在汽车直线行驶时，往往转向轮也会受到路面侧向干扰力的作用，自动偏转而改变行驶方向。此时，驾驶员也可以利用这套机构使转向轮向相反方向偏转，从而使汽车恢复原来的行驶方向。

汽车转向系统的组成 The Composition of Vehicle Steering System

这一套用来改变或恢复汽车行驶方向的专设机构，即称为汽车转向系统。因此，汽车转向系的功用是：保证汽车能按驾驶员的意志而进行转向行驶。

In the course of driving, it is often required to change the direction of driving according to the driver's purpose, that is, automobile steering. For wheeled vehicles, the way to realize vehicle steering is that the driver deflects the wheels (steering wheels) on the steering axle (usually the front axle) at a certain angle relative to the longitudinal axis of the vehicle through a set of special mechanisms. During the straight driving, the steering wheel is often affected by the side interference force of the road surface, and automatically deflects to change the driving direction. At this time, the driver can also use this mechanism to deflect the steering wheel in the opposite direction, so that the vehicle can resume its original direction. This set of special mechanism used to change or restore the direction of the vehicle is called automobile steering system. Therefore, the function of automobile steering system is to ensure that the automobile can steer according to the driver's purpose.

转向系统主要由主要由转向操纵机构、转向器和转向传动机构三大部分组成。

The steering system is mainly composed of steering control mechanism, steering device and steering transmission mechanism.

4.1 转向器（Steering gear）

汽车转向器又名转向机、方向机，它是汽车转向系中最重要的部件。它的作用是：增大转向盘传到转向传动机构的力和改变力的传递方向。常用的有齿轮齿条式、蜗杆曲柄销式和循环球式。

Automobile steering gear, also known as automobile steering device and automobile redirector, is the most important part of automobile steering system. Its function is to increase the force transmitted from the steering wheel to the steering transmission mechanism and change the direction of force transmission. The gear rack type, worm crank pin type and recirculating ball type are commonly used.

（1）蜗杆曲柄销式转向器：它是以蜗杆为主动件，曲柄销为从动件的转向器。蜗杆具有梯形螺纹，手指状的锥形指销用轴承支承在曲柄上，曲柄与转向摇臂轴制成一体。转向时，通过转向盘转动蜗杆、嵌于蜗杆螺旋槽中的锥形指销一边自转，一边绕转向摇臂轴做圆弧运动，从而带动曲柄和转向垂臂摆动，再通过转向传动机构使转向轮偏转。这种转向器通常用于转向力较大的载货汽车上（图3.4.1）。

（1）Worm crank pin type steering device is a steering gear with worm as driving part and crank pin as the driven one. The worm has trapezoidal threads. The fingerlike tapered finger pin is supported on the crank by bearings. The crank is made with the steering rocker shaft into a whole part. When steering, the worm is rotated by the steering wheel, the tapered finger pin embedded in the worm spiral groove rotates on its own axis while doing arc motion around the axis of steering rocker shaft, thus driving the crank and the steering vertical arm to swing, and then the steering wheel is deflected by the steering transmission mechanism. Thus, the crank and the steering plumbing arm are driven to swing, and then the steering wheel is deflected by the steering transmission mechanism. This kind of steering gear is usually used in trucks with large steering force(Figure 3. 4. 1).

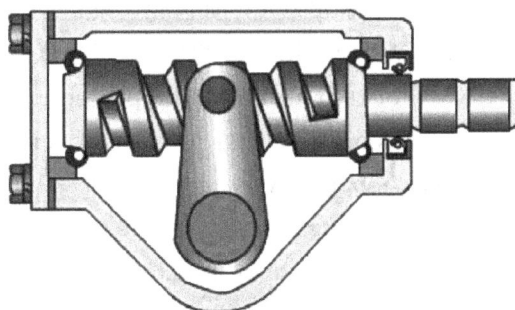

图 3.4.1 蜗杆曲柄销式转向器

Figure 3. 4. 1 Worm crank pin steering gear

（2）齿轮齿条转向器：它是一种最常见的转向器。其基本结构是一对相互啮合的小齿轮和齿条。转向轴带动小齿轮旋转时，齿条便做直线运动。有时，靠齿条来直接带动横拉杆，就可使转向轮转向。所以，这是一种最简单的转向器。它的优点是结构简单，成本低廉，转向灵敏，体积小，可以直接带动横拉杆。在汽车上得到广泛应用（图 3.4.2）。

（2）Gear-rack steering gear is the most common steering gear. Its basic structure is a pair of pinion and rack engaging with each other. When the steering shaft drives the pinion to rotate, the rack moves in a straight line. Sometimes the steering wheel can be steered by directly driving the tie rod by the rack, so it is the simplest steering gear. Its advantages are simple structure, low cost, sensitive steering, small size, and can directly drive the tie rod, which is widely used in automobiles (Figure 3. 4. 2).

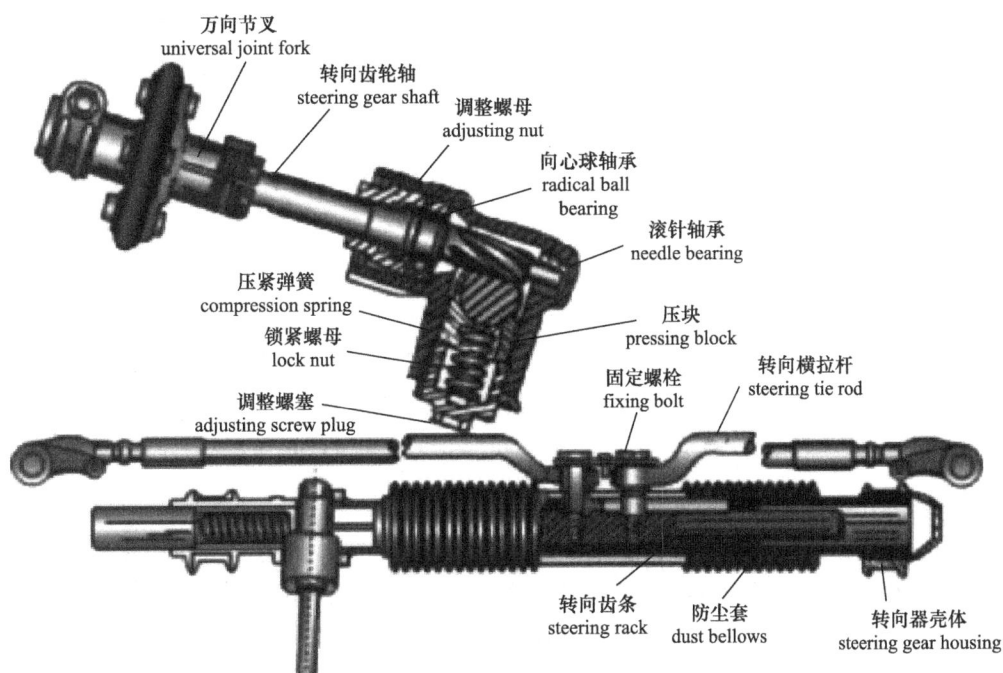

万向节叉 universal joint fork
转向齿轮轴 steering gear shaft
调整螺母 adjusting nut
向心球轴承 radical ball bearing
滚针轴承 needle bearing
压紧弹簧 compression spring
压块 pressing block
锁紧螺母 lock nut
固定螺栓 fixing bolt
转向横拉杆 steering tie rod
调整螺塞 adjusting screw plug
转向齿条 steering rack
防尘套 dust bellows
转向器壳体 steering gear housing

图 3.4.2 齿轮齿条转向器

Figure 3. 4. 2 Gear-rack steering gear

（3）循环球式转向器：循环球助力转向系统主要结构由两大部分组成：机械部分与液压部分。机械部分由壳体、侧盖、上盖、下盖、循环球螺杆、齿条螺母、转阀阀芯、扇齿轴组成。其中有两对传动副：一对是螺杆、螺母，另一对是齿条、齿扇或扇齿轴。在螺杆和齿条螺母之间装有可循环滚动的钢球，使滑动摩擦变为滚动摩擦，从而提高了传动效率。这种转向器的优点是，操纵轻便，磨损小，寿命长。缺点是结构复杂，成本较高，转向灵敏度不如齿轮齿条式。随着动力转向的应用与加工技术的不断提高，循环球式转向器近年来已经得到广泛使用于重型汽车与工程车上（图3.4.3）。

(3) For recirculating ball type steering gear, its main structure of the circulating ball power steering system consists of two parts: mechanical part and hydraulic part. The mechanical part is composed of housing, side cover, upper cover, lower cover, circulating ball screw, rack nut, rotary valve spool and gear sector shaft, etc. Among them, there are two pairs of transmission pairs: one pair is screw, nut, and the other pair is rack, gear sector or gear sector shaft. A recirculating rolling steel ball is installed between the screw and the rack nut to change the sliding friction into rolling friction, thus improving the transmission efficiency. The advantages of this kind of steering gear are easy operation, small wear and tear, and long service life. The disadvantage is that the complex structure and high cost, and the steering sensitivity is not as good as the rack-and-pinion type. With the application of power steering and the continuous improvement of processing technology, recirculating ball steering has been widely used in heavy trucks and engineering vehicles in recent years(Figure 3.4.3).

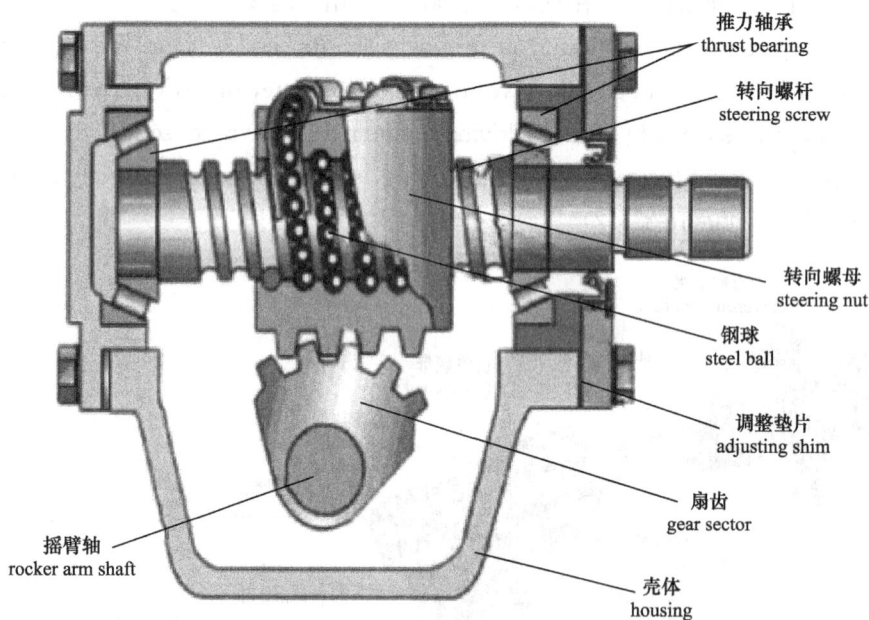

图3.4.3　循环球式转向器

Figure 3.4.3　Recirculating ball steering gear

4.2　转向操纵机构 (Steering control mechanism)

转向操纵机构的作用是产生转动转向器所必需的操纵力，并具有一定的调节性和安全性。转向操纵机构要将驾驶员操纵转向盘的力传给转向器，同时为了驾驶员的舒适驾驶，还要求转向操纵机构能进行调节，以满足不一样驾驶员的需求；为了防止车辆撞击后对驾驶员的损伤，还要求转向操纵机构具有一定的安全保护装置。转向操纵机构一般由转向盘、转向轴、转向管柱、万向节和转向传动轴组成（图3.4.4）。

The role of steering control mechanism is to produce the necessary steering force for rotating steering gear, and it has certain adjustability and safety. The steering mechanism should transfer the driver's steering wheel force to the steering gear. At the same time, for the driver's comfortable driving, the steering mechanism should be adjusted to meet the needs of different drivers. In order to prevent the driver from being injured after the vehicle collision, the steering control mechanism is also required to have a certain safety protection device. Steering control mechanism generally consists of steering wheel, steering shaft, steering column, universal joint and steering transmission shaft (Figure 3.4.4).

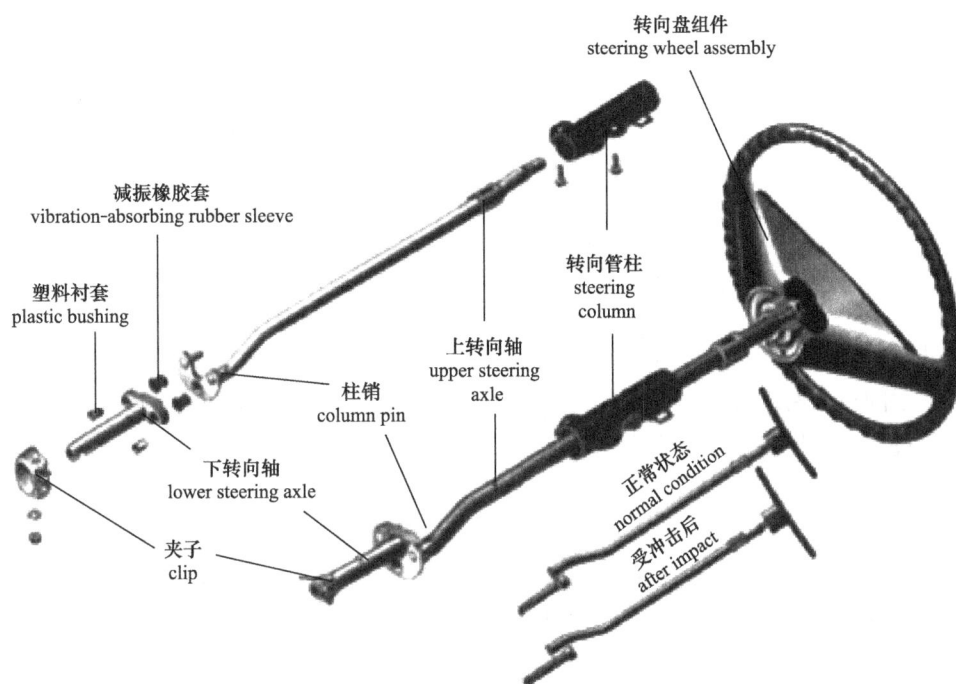

图 3.4.4 转向操纵机构

Figure 3.4.4 Steering control mechanism

4.3 转向传动机构 (Steering transmission mechanism)

转向传动机构的功用是将转向器输出的力和运动传给转向轮，使两侧转向轮偏转以实现汽车转向，并保证左右转向轮的偏转角按一定关系变化。现代普通轿车前桥普遍采用独立悬架，转向桥是断开式的，因此转向传动机构也呈断开状态。同时，与独立悬架配用的多数是齿轮齿条式转向器，转向器布置在车身上，转向横拉杆通过球头销与齿条及转向节臂相连。

The function of steering transmission mechanism is to transfer the output force and motion of the steering gear to the steering wheel, to deflect the steering wheels on both sides so as to realize the steering of the vehicle, and to ensure that the deflection angle of the left and right steering wheels changes in a certain relationship. Independent suspension is widely used in the front axle of modern ordinary vehicles, and the steering axle is disconnected, so the steering transmission mechanism is also disconnected. At the same time, most of the independent suspensions are equipped with rack-and-pinion steering gear. The steering gear is arranged on the body, and the steering tie rod is connected with the rack and the steering knuckle arm through the ball head pin.

转向传动机构的功用是：将转向器输出的力和运动传到转向桥两侧的转向节，使两侧转向轮偏转，且使两转向轮偏转角按一定关系变化，以保证汽车转向时车轮与地面的相对滑动尽可能小（图 3.4.5）。

The function of steering transmission mechanism is to transfer the output force and motion of the steering gear to the steering knuckles on both sides of the steering axle, to deflect the steering wheels on both sides, and to change the deflection angle of the two steering wheels according to a certain relationship, so as to ensure that the relative slip between the wheels and the ground is as small as possible when the vehicle steers (Figure 3.4.5).

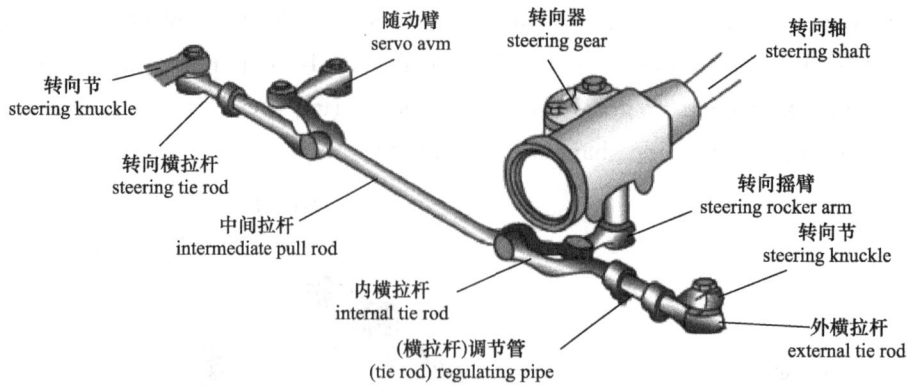

图 3.4.5　转向传动机

Figure 3.4.5　Steering transmission mechanism

转向器带动转向摇臂沿圆弧（左右往复）摆动，使中间拉杆也左右移动。随动臂与车架铰接，便于转向传动机构的支撑。中间拉杆两端分别与两根横拉杆相连。当中间拉杆左右移动时，两根横拉杆跟着移动，而横拉杆与转向节通过球头铰连接，这样就带动转向节使车轮偏转。每个横拉杆上均带有调节管，可用于调整横拉杆的有效长度。

The steering gear drives the steering rocker arm to swing along the arc (left and right reciprocating), so that the middle tie rod moves left and right. The servo arm is hinged with the frame to facilitate the support of the steering transmission mechanism. The two ends of the middle tie rod are respectively connected with two tie rods. When the middle tie rod moves left and right, the tie rods follow, and the tie rod is connected with the steering knuckle through the ball head hinge, thus driving the steering knuckle to deflect the wheel. Each tie rod is equipped with a regulating tube, which can be used to adjust the effective length of the tie rod.

转向传动机构由连杆机构和转向节等组成，以将转向器提供的转向意志体现在车轮的偏转上。

The steering transmission mechanism is composed of connecting rod mechanism and steering knuckle, so that the steering purpose provided by the steering gear is reflected in the wheel deflection.

齿轮齿条式转向器传动机构比较简单，直接将转向横拉杆与转向节臂连接。转向横拉杆的安装方式主要有两种：外接托架式与转向齿条直连接式。

The transmission mechanism of rack-and-pinion steering gear is relatively simple, which directly connects the steering tie rod with the steering knuckle arm. There are two main installation methods of steering tie rod: external bracket type and steering rack direct connection type.

转向横拉杆的作用：转向横拉杆将转向摇臂传来的力和运动传给转向梯形臂（或转向节臂）。由于它所受的力既有拉力，也有压力，因此转向横拉杆都是采用优质特种钢材制造的，以保证工作可靠。在转向轮偏转或因悬架弹性变形而相对于车架跳动时，转向横拉杆与转向摇臂及转向节臂的相对运动都是空间运动，为了不发生运动干涉，上述三者间都采用球头销连接（图 3.4.6）。

The function of steering drag link is transferring the force and motion from the steering rocker arm to the steering trapezoidal arm (or steering knuckle arm). Because it is subjected to both tension and pressure, steering drag links are made of high quality special steel to ensure reliable operation. When the steering wheel is deflected or jumps relative to the frame due to the elastic deformation of the suspension, the relative motion of the steering drag link with the steering rocker arm and the steering knuckle arm is space motion. In order to avoidmotion interference, the ball head pins are used among the aforementioned three parties (Figure 3.4.6).

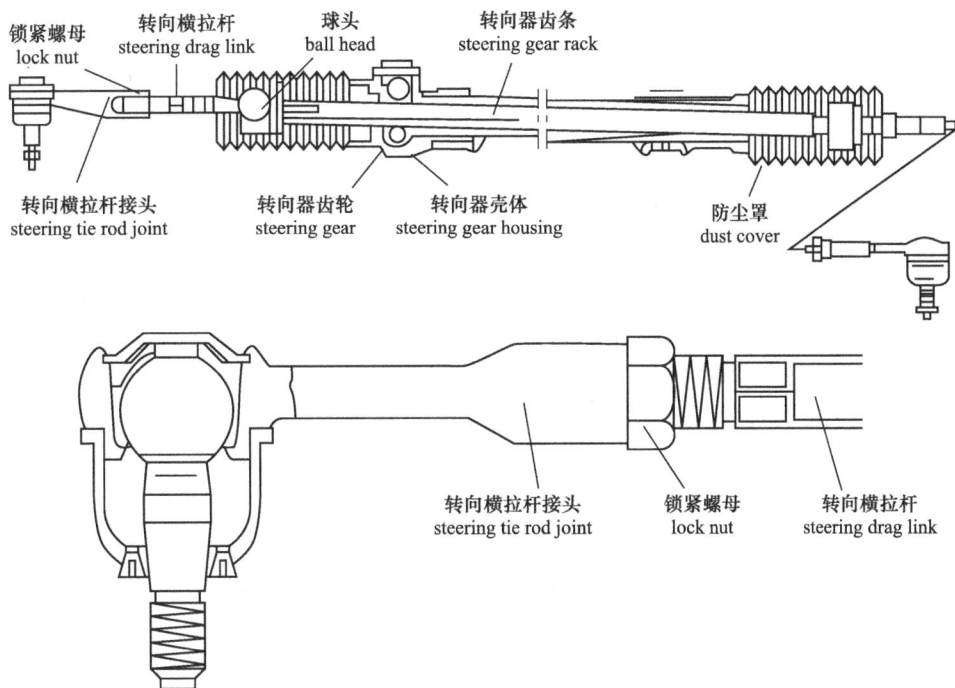

图 3.4.6　转向横拉杆

Figure 3.4.6　Steering drag link

4.4　动力转向器（**Power steering gear**）

1. 液压式转向助力系统（**Hydraulic steering power system**）

液压式转向助力系统一般由液压泵、油罐、管路等零件组成，由于工作压力大、部件结构简单紧凑、反应迅速、能缓和冲击，所以在目前汽车上得到了广泛的应用（图3.4.7）。

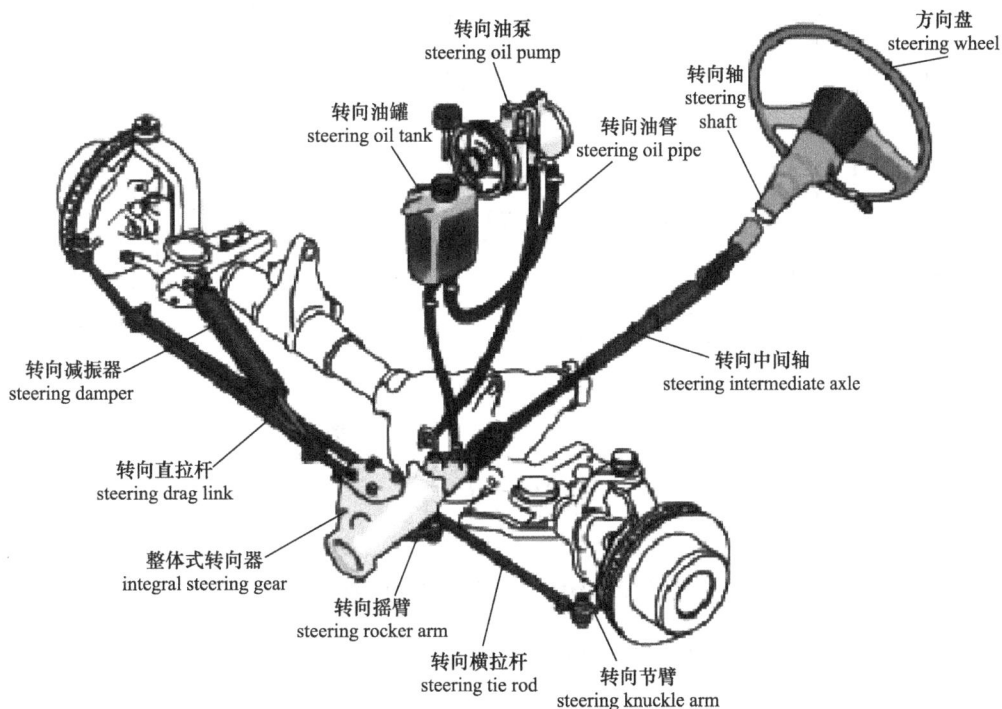

图 3.4.7　液压式转向助力系统

Figure 3.4.7　Hydraulic steering power system

Hydraulic steering power system is generally composed of hydraulic pump，oil tank，pipeline and other parts. Because of its high working pressure，simple and compact structure，rapid response and impact mitigation，it has been widely used in automobiles(Figure 3.4.7).

2. 电动式转向助力系统 （Electric power steering system）

电动转向助力系统是用一部直流电机代替传统的液压压力缸，用蓄电池和电动机提供动力的系统。微电脑控制的转向助力系统相比传统液压转向助力系统不仅具有部件少、体积小、质量轻的特点，并且具有最优化的转向作用力和转向回正特性，提高了汽车的转向能力和转向响应特性，增加了汽车低速时的机动性以及调整行驶时的稳定性，是未来转向助力系统的发展方向（图3.4.8）。

Electric power steering system is a system that uses a DC motor to replace the traditional hydraulic pressure cylinder and uses batteries and electric motors to provide power. Compared with the traditional hydraulic steering power system, the steering power system controlled by micro-computer has the characteristics of less components, smaller volume and lighter weight，and has the optimized steering force and steering return characteristics. It improves the steering ability and steering response characteristics of the vehicle, increasing the mobility of the vehicle at low speed and adjusts the stability of the driving, which is the development trend of the future steering power system(Figure 3.4.8).

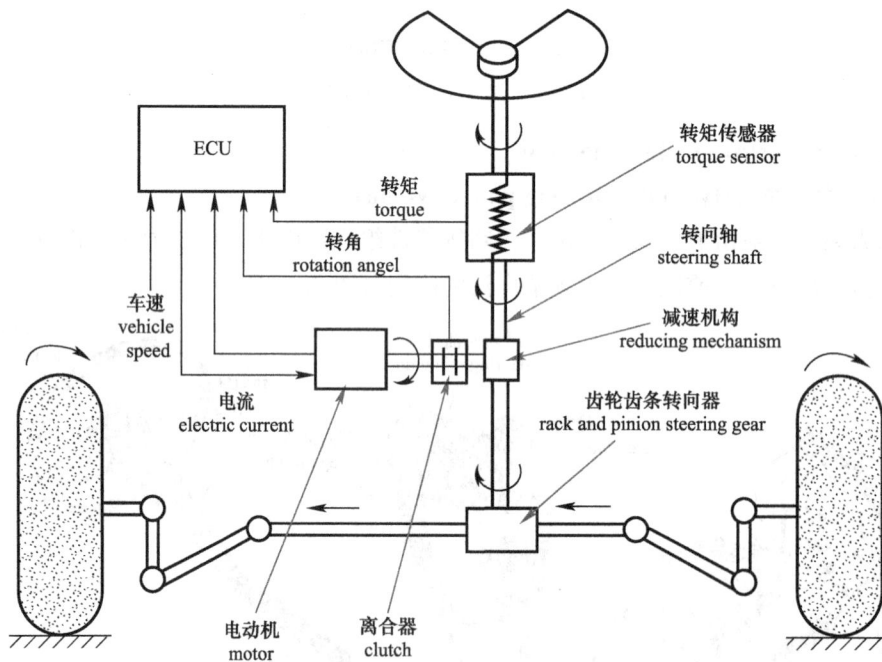

图3.4.8 电动式转向助力系统

Figure 3.4.8 Electric power steering system

思考与练习

（Reflection and Exercises）

1. 助力转向的分类有哪些？并讲解各自的优点。

2. 转向机的分类有哪些？

3. 学习并讲解电助力转向的工作原理。

1. What are the classification of power steering and their respective advantages?

2. What is the classification of steering gear?

3. Learning and explaining the working principle of electric power steering.

任务五　制 动 系 统

Task 5　Brake System

教学目标

1. 知识目标

（1）了解制动系的功用和基本组成；

（2）了解液压式制动系的基本组成和原理。

2. 能力目标

能讲解制动系的结构和原理。

3. 情感和素养目标

（1）激发学生的学习工作热情，树立远大理想目标的意识；

（2）培养学生爱岗敬业的情怀，契合自身发展，选择合适岗位的意识。

Teaching objectives

1. Knowledge objectives

（1）Understanding the functions and basic composition of the brake system；

（2）Understanding the basic composition and principle of hydraulic brake system.

2. Ability objectives

Explaining the structure and principle of brake system.

3. Emotion and quality goals

（1）Stimulate students' enthusiasm to study and work，and cultivate the consciousness of establishing great ideals；

（2）Cultivate students' feelings of being dedicated to their jobs and the awareness of choosing appropriate positions in line with their own development.

5.1　概述（Overview）

1. 制动器的作用（The functions of brakes）

① 行驶中的车辆按照驾驶员意愿进行减速或停车。

② 保持车辆能在不同道路实现稳定驻车。

③ 车辆可靠稳定的下坡行驶。

① It can decelerate or park of moving automobiles according to the driver's purpose.

② Keep the vehicle stable and park on different roads.

③ The vehicle can run downhill reliably and steadily.

2. 制动系统的组成（Composition of brake system）

制动器主要由制动器、驻车制动装置、制动传动装置、制动防抱死系统组成。

The brake is mainly composed of arrester, parking brake device, brake transmission device and anti-lock brake system.

3. 制动系的工作原理（Working principle of brake system）

制动系统的一般工作原理是：利用与车身（或车架）相连的非旋转元件和与车轮（或传动轴）相连的旋转元件之间的相互摩擦来阻止车轮的转动或转动（图 3.5.1）。

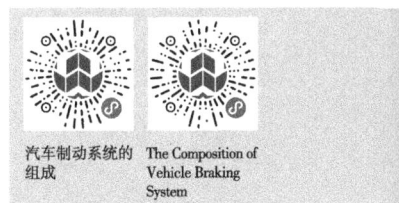

The general working principle of the brake system is to prevent the wheel from turning or turning trend by using the friction between the non-rotating elements connected with the body (or frame) and the rotating elements connected with the wheel (or transmission shaft)(Figure 3.5.1).

① 制动系不工作时（When brake system is not working）

蹄鼓间有间隙，车轮和制动鼓可自由旋转。

There is a gap between brake shoe and brake drum. Wheels and brake drums can rotate freely.

② 制动时（When braking）

要汽车减速，脚踏下制动器踏板通过推杆和主缸，使主缸油液在一定压力下流入轮缸，并通过两轮缸活塞推动使制动蹄绕支承销转动，上端向两边分开而以其摩擦片压紧在制动鼓的内圆面上。不转的制动蹄对旋转制动鼓产生摩擦力矩，从而产生制动力。

To decelerate the vehicle, stamping down the brake pedal makes oil fluid of the master cylinder flow into the wheel cylinder under a certain pressure through the push rod and the master cylinder. The pistons of two wheel cylinders push the brake shoe to rotate around the rest pin. The upper end is separated in both sides and its friction plate is pressed on the inner surface of the brake drum. The non-rotating brake shoe generates friction moment to the rotating brake drum, which generates brake force.

③ 解除制动（Release brake）

当放开制动踏板时回位即将制动蹄拉回原位，制动力消失。制动主缸的作用是将自外界输入的机械能转换成液压能，从而液压能通过管路再输给制动轮缸。

When the brake pedal is released and returns, the brake shoe will be pulled back to its original position and the brake force disappear. The function of the main brake cylinder is to convert the mechanical energy from outside into hydraulic energy, so that the hydraulic energy can be transferred to the brake cylinder through pipelines.

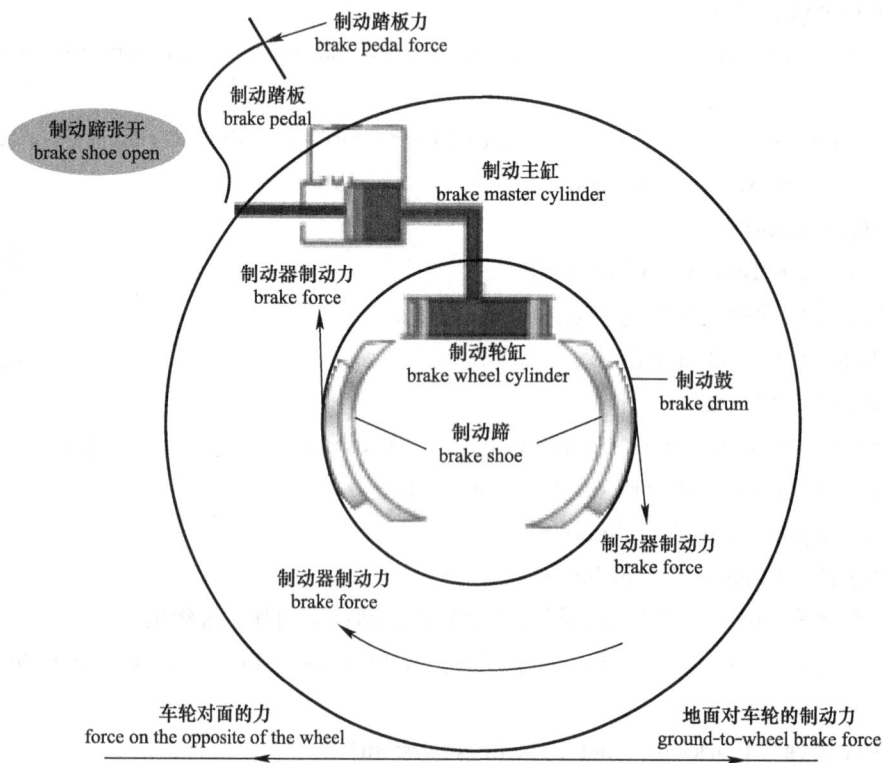

图 3.5.1 制动系统工作原理

Figure 3.5.1 Working principle of brake system

5.2 制动器 (Brake)

按照结构的不同制动器可以分为鼓式制动器和盘式制动器。鼓式制动器是利用制动传动机构使制动蹄将制动摩擦片压紧在制动鼓内侧，从而产生制动力，根据需要使车轮减速或在最短的距离内停车，以确保行车安全，并保障汽车停放可靠不能自动滑移。盘式制动器摩擦副中的旋转元件是以端面工作的金属圆盘，称为制动盘。摩擦元件从两侧夹紧制动盘而产生制动。固定元件则有多种结构形式，大体上可将盘式制动器分为钳盘式和全盘式两类。

According to the different structure, brakes can be divided into drum brake and disc brake. Drum brake uses brake transmission mechanism to make brake shoe press brake friction plate on the inside of brake drum to produce braking force. The wheel can be decelerated or parked in the shortest distance according to the need, so as to ensure the safety of driving and the reliability of automobile parking without automatic sliding. The rotating element in the friction pair of disc brake is a metal disc working on the end face, which is called the brake disc. The friction element clamps the brake disc from both sides to generate brake. Fixing elements have many kinds of structural forms, which generally can be divided into two types: caliper disc brakes and full disc brakes.

5.2.1 鼓式制动器 (Drum brake)

轿车后轮鼓式制动器主要由制动底板、制动分泵、制动蹄及制动鼓等组成。鼓式制动器的结构原理：两制动蹄下端插在制动底板下端的相应槽内，上端靠在制动分泵的活塞上，然后用上、下拉力弹簧拉紧。制动蹄通过限位弹簧和限位螺钉使其靠在制动底板上。制动蹄外表面上铆有摩擦片。制动时，驾驶员踩下制动踏板，制动液进入制动分泵，迫使制动分泵内的两个活塞向外移动，推动制动蹄克服上、下拉力弹簧的拉力使其向外张开，压在旋转的制动鼓内缘，使制动鼓和车轮减速到停止运转。解除制动时，驾驶员松开制动踏板，在上、下拉力弹簧的作用下，制动蹄离开制动鼓回到原位，制动鼓又可以自由转动。

The rear wheel drum brake of car is mainly composed of brake bottom plate, brake wheel cylinder, brake shoe and brake drum, etc. The structural principle of drum brake is that the lower end of two brake shoes is inserted in the corresponding groove at the lower end of the brake bottom plate. The upper end leans on the piston of the brake wheel cylinder, and then tensioned by the upper and lower tension springs. The brake shoe is rested on the brake bottom plate by the limit spring and the limit screw. Friction discs are riveted on the outer surface of the brake shoe. When braking, the driver stamps down the brake pedal and the brake fluid enters the brake wheel cylinder, forcing the two pistons in the brake wheel cylinder to move outward, pushing the brake shoe to overcome the pulling force of the upper and lower tension springs to open outwards, pressing on the inner edge of the rotating brake drum, and slowing down the brake drum and wheels to stop running. When the brake is released, the driver releases the brake pedal, and under the action of the upper and lower tension springs, the brake shoe leaves the brake drum and returns to its original position, and the brake drum can rotate freely again.

制动蹄和制动鼓间的间隙可以通过装在推杆右端槽内的调整楔进行自动调整。调整楔的下端与固定在制动蹄上的调整弹簧相连。如果制动蹄和制动鼓间的间隙大，制动过程中，调整弹簧拉动调整楔下移，调整楔上宽下窄，这样使拉杆向外移动一点，而使制动蹄和制动鼓的间隙保持在标准值范围内（图 3.5.2）。

The clearance between the brake shoe and the brake drum can be automatically adjusted by the adjusting wedge installed in the right groove of the push rod. The lower end of the adjusting wedge is connected with the adjusting spring fixed on the brake shoe. If the gap between the brake shoe and the brake drum is large, in the braking process, adjusting spring pulls adjusting wedge downward. The adjusting wedge is wide at the top and narrow at the bottom, which makes the pull rod move outward a little, so that the gap between the brake shoe and the brake drum remains within the standard value range(Figure 3.5.2).

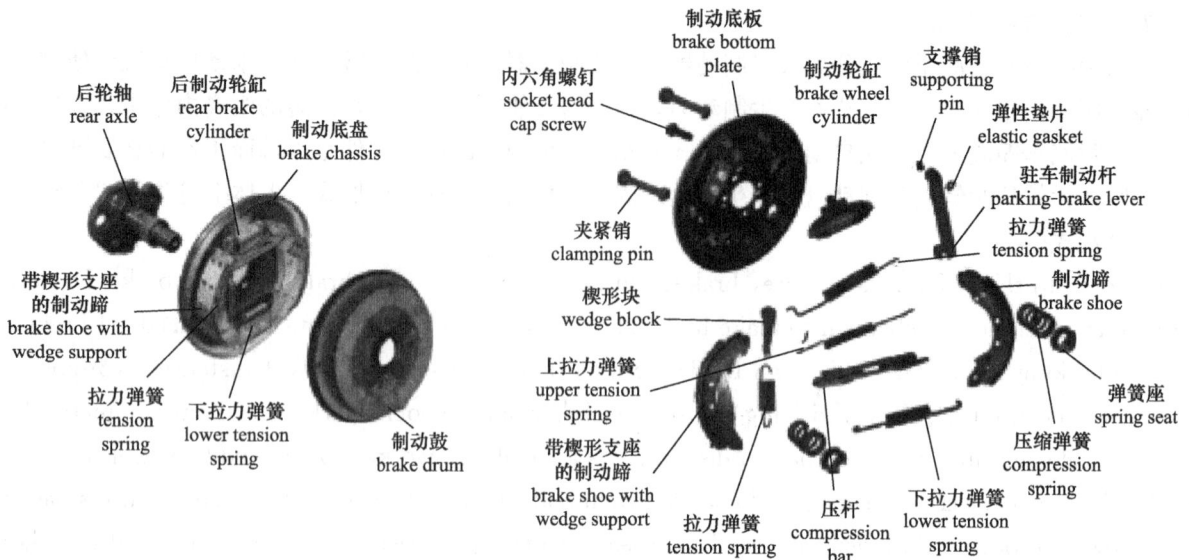

图 3.5.2　鼓式制动器

Figure 3.5.2　Drum brake

5.2.2　盘式制动器（Disc brake）

目前汽车上采用的盘式制动器主要有两种：一种是固定钳盘式制动器；另一种是浮动钳盘式制动器。捷达轿车采用的是浮动钳盘式制动器。

At present，there are two main disc brakes used in automobiles：one is fixed caliper disc brake and the other is floating caliper disc brake. Jetta car uses floating caliper disc brake.

固定钳盘式制动器，制动盘 1 固定在轮毂上，制动钳 5 固定在车桥上，既不能旋转也不能沿制动盘轴向移动。制动钳内装有两个制动轮缸活塞 2，分别压住制动盘两侧的制动块 3。当驾驶员踩下制动踏板使汽车制动时，来自制动主缸的制动液被压入制动轮缸，制动轮缸的液压上升，两轮缸活塞在液压作用下移向制动盘，将制动块压靠到制动盘上，制动块夹紧制动盘，产生阻止车轮转动的摩擦力矩，实现制动（图 3.5.3）。

For the fixed caliper disc brake, brake disc 1 is fixed on the hub, and brake caliper 5 is fixed on the axle, which can neither rotate nor move along the axle of the brake disc. Brake calipers are equipped with two brake wheel cylinder pistons 2, which respectively press the brake block 3 on both sides of the brake disc. When the driver stamps down the brake pedal to stop the vehicle, the brake fluid from the main brake cylinder is pressed into the brake wheel cylinder. The hydraulic pressure of the brake wheel cylinder rises. The piston of the two wheel cylinders moves to the brake disc under the action of hydraulic pressure，then the brake block is pressed on the brake disc，and the brake block clamps the brake disc to produce the friction moment that prevents the wheel from turning to achieve brake(Figure 3.5.3).

浮钳盘式制动器的制动钳是浮动的，可以相对于制动盘轴向移动。制动钳 1 一般设计成可以相对于制动盘 4 轴向移动。在制动盘的内侧设有液压油缸 9，外侧的固定制动块 5 附装在钳体上。制动时，制动液被压入油缸中，在液压作用下活塞向左移动，推动活动制动块也向左移动并压靠到制动盘上，于是制动盘给活塞一个向右的反作用力，使活塞连同制动钳体整体沿导向销 2 向右移动，直到制动盘左侧的固定制动块 5 也压到制动盘上。这时两侧制动块都压在制动盘上，制动块夹紧制动盘，产生阻止车轮转动的摩擦力矩，实现制动（图 3.5.4）。

The brake caliper of the floating caliper disc brake is floating and can move axially relative to the brake disc. Brake caliper 1 is generally designed to move axially relative to the brake disc 4. The inner side of the brake disc is provided with a hydraulic cylinder 9, and the outer fixed brake block 5 is attached to the caliper body. When braking, the brake fluid is pressed into the cylinder. The piston moves to the left under the action of hydraulic pressure, pushing the movable brake block to the left and pressing it against the brake disc, so the brake disc gives the piston a reaction force to the right, so that the piston and the brake caliper body move to the right along the guide pin 2 as a whole, until the fixed brake block 5 on the left side of the brake disc is also pressed on the brake disc. At this time, both sides of the brake block are pressed on the brake disc, and the brake block clamps the brake disc to produce friction moment that prevents the wheel from turning, thus realizing braking(Figure 3.5.4).

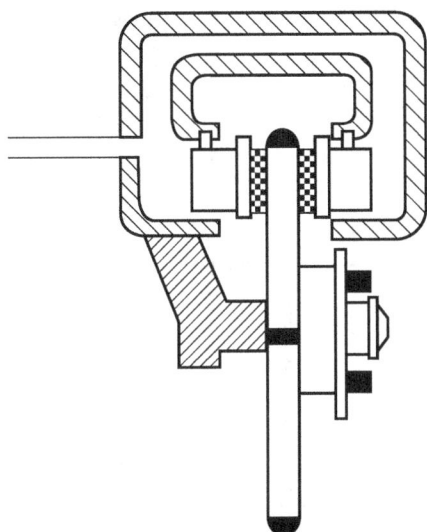

图 3.5.3 固定钳盘式制动器
Figure 3.5.3 Fixed caliper disc brake

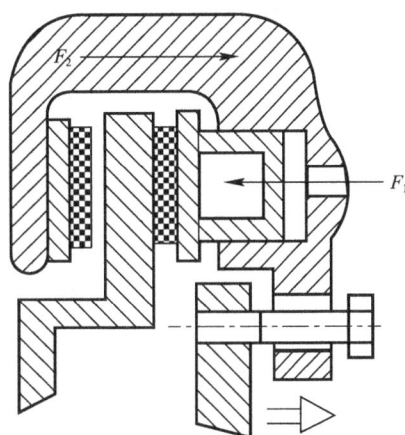

图 3.5.4 浮动钳盘式制动器
Figure 3.5.4 Floating caliper disc brake

5.3 制动传动装置 (Brake transmission device)

目前，轿车的行车制动系统都采用了液压传动装置，主要由制动主缸、液压管路、后轮鼓式制动器中的制动轮缸、前轮钳盘式制动器中的液压缸等组成。主缸与轮缸间的连接油管除用金属管（铜管）外，还采用特制的橡胶制动软管。各液压元件之间及各段油管之间还有各种管接头。制动前，液压系统中充满专门配制的制动液（图 3.5.5）。

At present, hydraulic transmission device is used in car braking system, which mainly consists of brake-master cylinder, hydraulic pipeline, brake wheel cylinder in rear wheel drum brake and hydraulic cylinder in front wheel caliper disc brake. The connecting oil pipe between the main cylinder and the wheel cylinder is made of special rubber brake hose besides metal pipe (copper pipe). There are also various pipe joints between the hydraulic components and each section of the oil pipe. Before braking, the hydraulic system is filled with specially prepared brake fluid(Figure 3.5.5).

液压传动装置的工作原理：踩下制动踏板，制动主缸将制动液压入制动轮缸和制动钳，并将制动块推向制动鼓和制动盘。在制动器间隙消失并开始产生制动力矩时，液压与踏板力方能继续增长直到完全制动。此过程中，在液压作用下，由于油管的弹性膨胀变形和摩擦元件的弹性压缩变形，踏板和轮缸活塞都可以继续移动一段距离。放开踏板，制动蹄和轮缸活塞在回位弹簧作用下回位，将制动液压回制动主缸。

The working principle of the hydraulic transmission device is that when the brake pedal is stamped down, the brake master cylinder presses the brake fluid into the brake wheel cylinder and the brake caliper, and pushes the brake block to the brake drum and the brake disc. When the brake clearance disappears and the braking moment is generated, the hydraulic pressure and pedal force can continue to increase until complete brake. In this process, under the action of hydraulic pressure, the pedal and the cylinder piston can continue to move for a certain distance because of the elastic expansion deformation of the oil pipe and the elastic compression deformation of the friction elements. When the pedal is released, brake shoe and cylinder piston return under the action of return spring to press brake fluid back to the brake master cylinder.

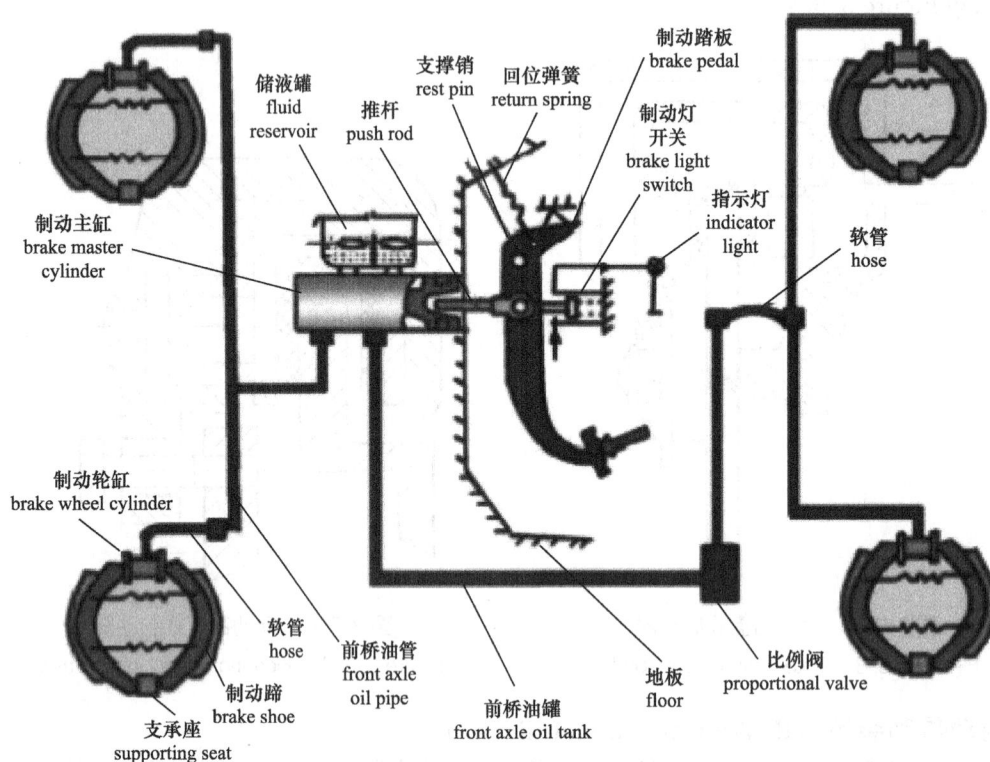

图 3.5.5 制动传动装置

Figure 3.5.5 Brake transmission drive

1. 制动轮缸（制动分泵）（Brake wheel cylinder）

制动轮缸又称制动分泵，装在制动器中，是车轮制动力的来源，其功用是：将液体压力转变为使制动蹄张开的机械推力。在车辆的行驶过程中，制动轮缸时常出现漏油、锈死等故障，导致制动力下降甚至丧失，这时应及时对制动轮缸进行检修。出现这种情况时，一般更换轮缸修理包即可恢复制动性能（图 3.5.6）。

Brake wheel cylinder, also known as brakesub-pump, is installed in the brake, which is the source of wheel braking force. Its function is to change the liquid pressure into the mechanical thrust to make the brake shoes open. In the course of vehicle running, oil leakage and rust often occur in the brake cylinder, which leads to the decrease or even loss of braking force. At this time, the brake cylinder should be repaired in time. When this happens, the braking performance can be restored by replacing the cylinder repair kit(Figure 3.5.6).

2. 制动管路（Brake lines）

制动管路和制动软管必须能承受高压，而且必须有良好的耐热性，能在严酷的环境下工作。制动管路的尺寸、材料、接头形式和安装位置不能随意变更，否则会造成严重的安全隐患。制动管路一般由镀锌或镀铜的双壁钢管制成，接头多用钢或黄铜制成，制动软管一般由合成橡胶浸渍过的多层纤维制成。

Brake pipes and hoses must be able to withstand high pressure, and they must have good heat resistance and work in harsh environments. The size, material, joint form and installation position of brake pipeline can not be changed at will, otherwise serious potential safety hazard will be caused. Brake pipes are usually made of galvanized or copper-plated double-walled steel pipes. Joints are usually made of steel or brass. Brake hoses are generally made of multi-layer fibers impregnated with synthetic rubber.

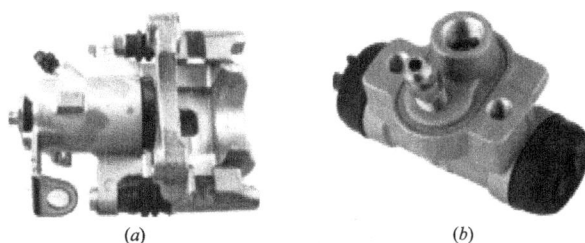

图 3.5.6　制动轮缸
Figure 3.5.6　Brake wheel cylinder
(a) 盘式制动器 (disc brake)；(b) 鼓式制动器 (drum brake)

5.4　驻车制动 (Parking brake)

驻车制动，一般叫做手刹，它的作用就是在停车时，给汽车一个阻力，使汽车不溜车。驻车制动，也就是手刹或者自动挡中的停车挡，锁住传动轴或者后轮。驻车制动比行车制动的力小很多很多，仅仅是在坡路停车不溜车就可以了。

Parking brake, commonly known as hand brake, its role is to prevent the vehicle from sliding by providing the resistance. Parking brake, which is the hand brake or the parking gear in automatic transmission, locks the transmission shaft or rear wheels. The parking brake is much less powerful than the driving brake, just stoping on the slope without skipping.

驻车制动按驱动形式分为：机械式、电子式和气压式三种。其中，机械式驻车系统广泛应用在低端车型上，电子式驻车系统普遍用于高端轿车上，气压式驻车系统用于货车上居多。

Parking brake can be divided into mechanical, electronic and pneumatic types according to the driving form. Among them, mechanical parking system is widely used in low-end vehicles, while electronic parking system is widely used in high-end cars, and pneumatic parking system is mostly used in trucks.

机械式驻车制动器俗称手制动器，主要用来保证汽车停止后的可靠停放。它由驻车制动操纵手柄、驻车制动拉索、调节压板、调整螺母等组成。当实施驻车制动时，驾驶员将手制动操纵杆向上拉起，通过拉杆、调节压板将驻车制动拉索拉紧。驻车制动拉索的端头套在后制动器拉臂下端的沟槽内，以使左、右制动蹄内外张开，压紧制动鼓内表面，实现驻车制动。驻车制动器是通过在后轮制动器的基础上，另加装一套手动机械操纵机构来实现的。由于和后轮制动器合用一套制动器，所以其结构简单，质量较轻（图 3.5.7）。

Mechanical parking brake, commonly known as hand brake, is mainly used to ensure the reliable parking of automobiles after stopping. It consists of parking brake control handle, parking brake cable, adjustingplaten, adjusting nut and so on. When parking brake is operated, the driver pulls up the hand brake lever, and tightens the parking brake cable by pull rod and adjusting platen. The end of the parking brake cable is in the groove of the lower end of the rear brake arm, so that the left and right brake shoes are opened inside and outside, and the inner surface of the brake drum is pressed to realize parking brake. Parking brake is realized by installing a set of manual mechanical control mechanism on the basis of rear wheel brake. Because a set of brake is shared with the rear wheel brake, the structure of the brake is simple and the weight is light (Figure 3.5.7).

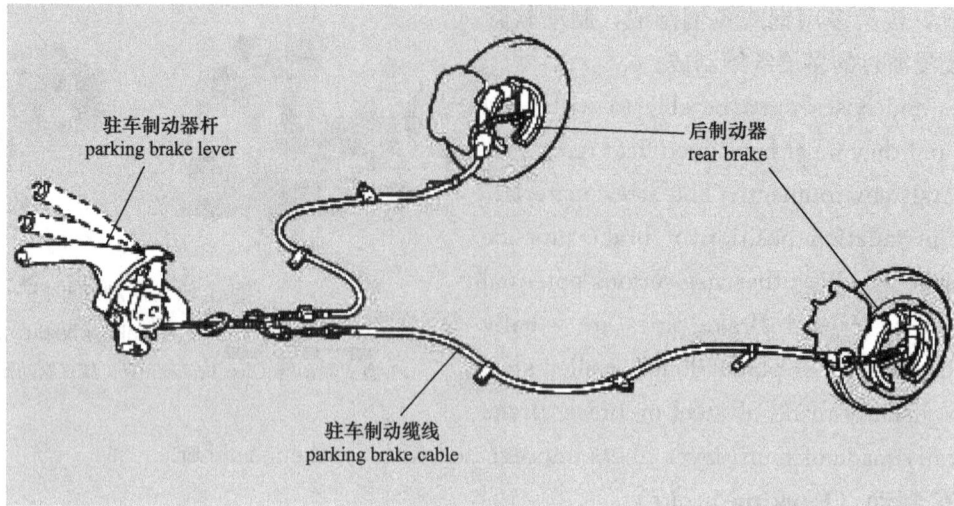

图 3.5.7　驻车制动

Figure 3.5.7　Parking brake

5.5　制动防抱死系统（Anti-lock braking system）

5.5.1　防抱死系统的组成（Composition of Anti-lock Braking System）

汽车防抱死系统（ABS）是一种安全控制制动系，目前已成为汽车的标准配置。ABS 系统既有普通制动功用，也有防止车轮抱死的作用。ABS 系统由：轮速传感器、制动压力调节器、电子控制单元和 ABS 指示灯等组成（图 3.5.8）。

Automobile anti-lock braking system（ABS）is a safety control braking system，which has become the standard equipment of automobiles. ABS system not only has general function of braking，but also prevents the wheels from being locked up. ABS system consists of wheel speed sensor，brake pressure regulator，electronic control unit and ABS indicator lamp（Figure 3.5.8）.

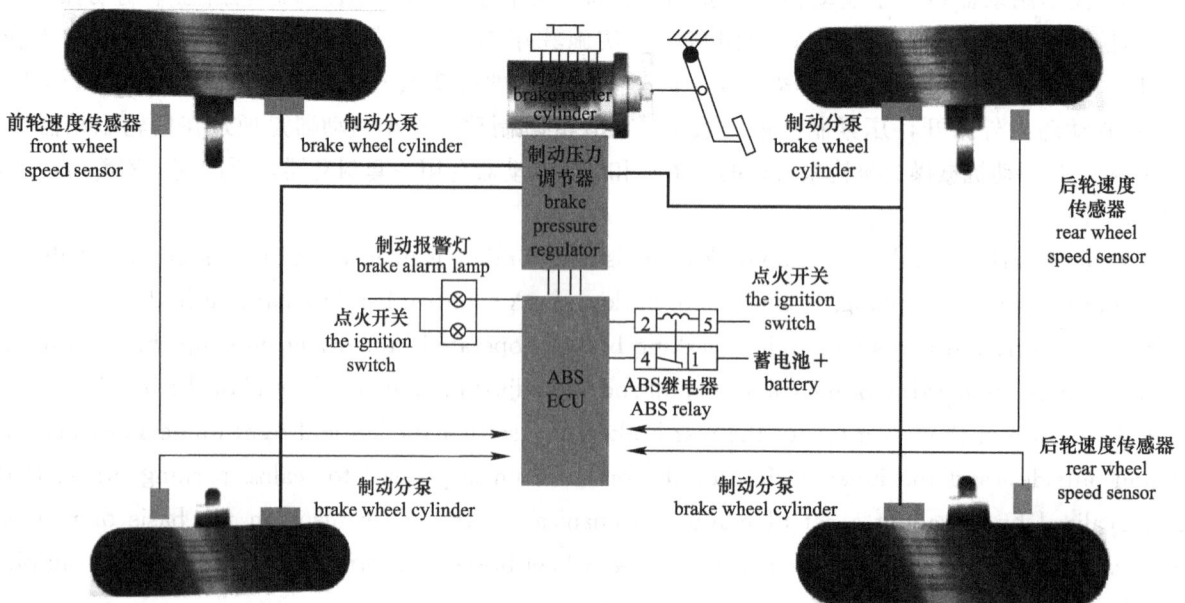

图 3.5.8　汽车防抱死系统

Figure 3.5.8　Automobile anti-lock braking system

5.5.2 ABS 系统工作原理（Working principle of ABS system）

在装配了防抱死系统的汽车上，高速行驶时在驾驶员因误操作的情况下仍能防止汽车产生侧滑和跑偏。当踩下刹车时，由于车轮的高速转动很容易在结合部分产生锁死点，而防抱死制动系统在 ABS 阀体中安装了一个气囊，当人本能地在汽车晃动过程中急踩刹车时，ABS 就会由传感器通知启动并对刹车油施加压力，充斥到 ABS 的阀体气囊中，而此时气囊利用充气后的中间空气隔层将压力驳回，让车轮避过锁死点。即使当车轮再次到达下一个锁死点时，刹车油的压力仍能使得气囊重复产生作用，且每秒钟的作用次数达到 9～31 次，相当于驾驶员不停地刹车、放松，也就是我们俗称的"点刹"（图 3.5.9）。

On a vehicle equipped with anti-lock braking system, the sideslip and off-tracking of the vehicle can be prevented even when the driver misoperates at high speed. When the brake is pressed, due to the high speed rotation of the wheels, the locking dead point can easily occur in the joint part. The ABS valve body is equipped with an air bag. When a person instinctively slams on the brake during the shaking of the car, the ABS will be activated by the sensor notification and exert pressure on the brake fluid, filling the valve body airbag of the ABS. At this time, the air bag uses the air buffer after inflating to reject the pressure, so that the wheel can avoid the lock dead point. Even when the wheel reaches the next lock point again, the pressure of the brake oil can make the airbag work repeatedly, and the number of action per second reaches 9 to 31, which is equivalent to the driver braking and relaxing constantly, which is commonly known as "point brake" (Figure 3.5.9).

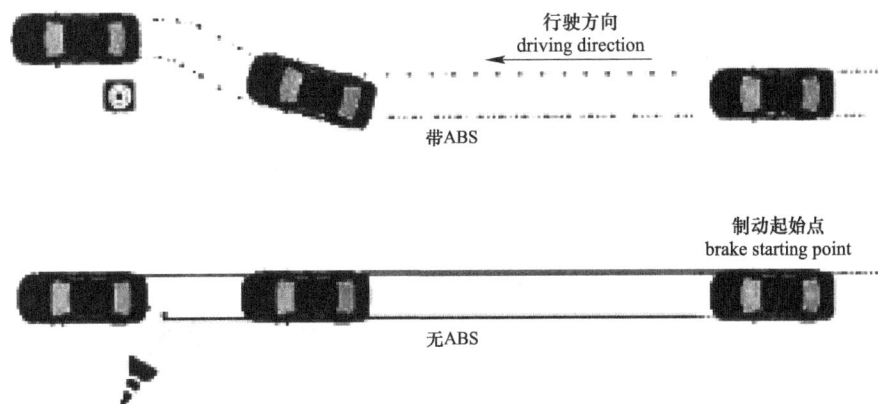

图 3.5.9 有无 ABS 系统的制动对比

Figure 3.5.9 Braking comparison between ABS system and non-ABS system

ABS 系统在每个车轮内侧的一个固定装置上安装有轮速传感器，轮速传感器内包含了大量可供产生磁力线的电磁线圈，车轮转动时带动车轮轮辋上的齿圈转动，这时所产生的磁力线被齿圈切割使传感器内的电磁线圈感应出交变电流，传输给 ABS 控制单元，控制单元将固有的车轮滑移率与轮速传感器传来的车轮转速进行对比，依照对比数据 ABS 控制单元对制动压力调节器进行控制，达到制动轮缸实现增压、保压、减压三个过程的迅速循环，使制动盘（制动鼓）达到每秒钟 9～31 次的点刹制动效果（图 3.5.10～图 3.5.12）。

The ABS system is equipped with a wheel speed sensor on a fixed device on the inside of each wheel. The wheel speed sensor contains a large number of electromagnetic coils which can generate magnetic lines of force. When the wheel rotates, it drives the gear ring on the rim of the wheel to rotate. At this time, the generated magnetic lines of force are cut by the gear ring, which causes the electromagnetic coil in the sensor to induce alternating current and transmit it to the ABS control unit, which compares the inherent wheel slip ratio with the wheel speed transmitted by the wheel speed sensor, and controls the brake pressure regulator according to the comparative data to achieve the rapid cycle of three processes of pressurization, pressure maintaining and decompression of the brake wheel cylinder, and the brake disc (brake drum) can achieve the point braking effect of 9 to 31 times per second(Figure 3.5.10~Figure 3.5.12).

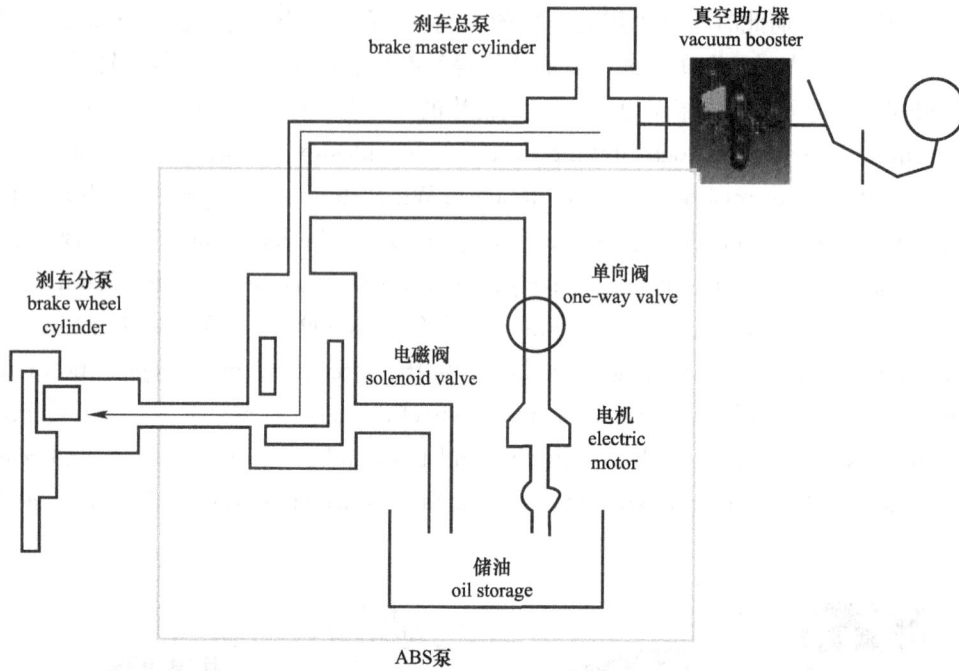

图 3.5.10　ABS 增压状态

Figure 3.5.10　ABS pressurization state

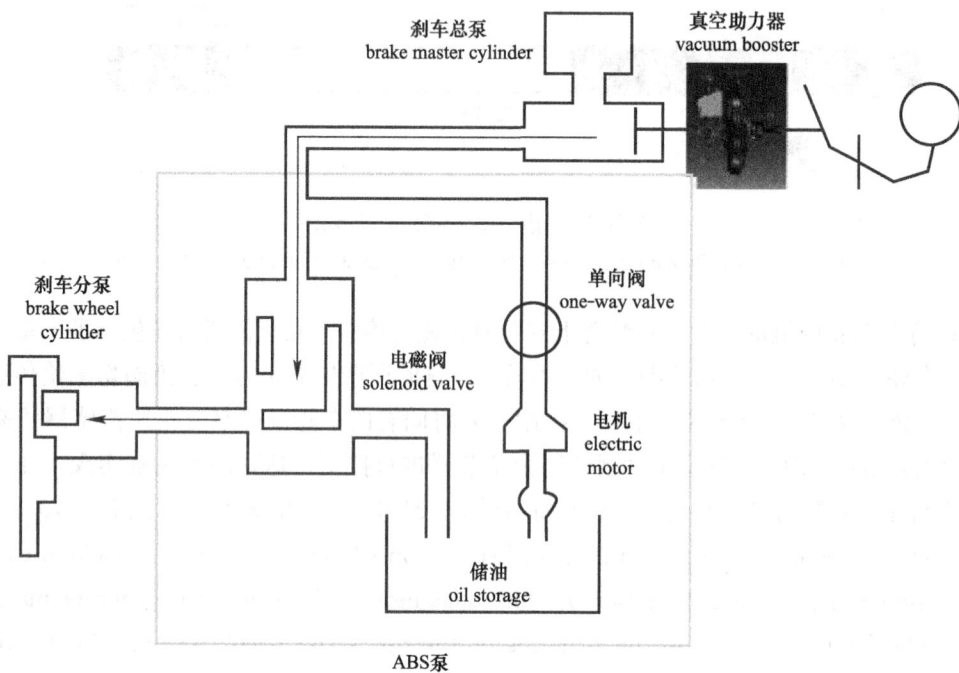

图 3.5.11　ABS 保压状态

Figure 3.5.11　ABS pressure maintaining state

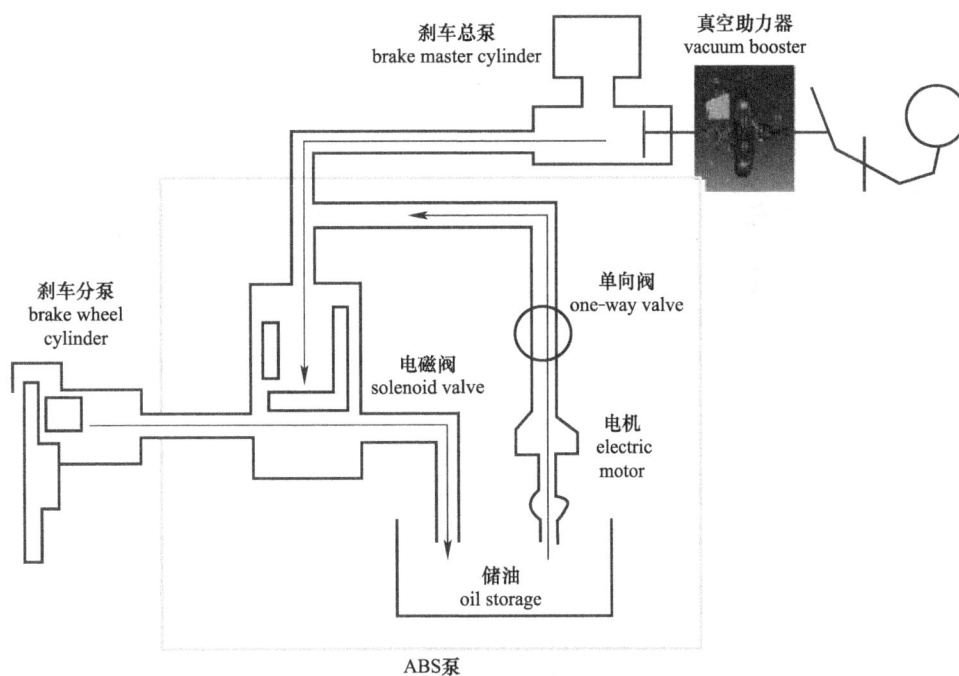

图 3.5.12　ABS 减压状态

Figure 3.5.12　ABS decompression state

思考与练习

（Reflection and Exercises）

1. 制动系的组成有哪些?

2. 盘式制动器分为哪两种? 写出它们的区别和特点。

3. 依据图 3.5.11、图 3.5.12 写出 ABS 的工作原理。

1. What are the components of the brake system?

2. What are the two types of disc brakes? Write out their differences and characteristics.

3. Write out the working principle of ABS according to Figure 3.5.11、Figure 3.5.12.

项目四 汽车车身
Item 4 Automobile Body

任务一 汽车车身概述

Task 1 Overview

教学目标

1. 知识目标

（1）了解汽车的车身壳体；

（2）了解汽车车身主要附件及内饰。

2. 能力目标

能识别车身壳体不同材质。

3. 情感和素养目标

培养学生服务意识的品质，质量意识、安全意识。

Teaching objectives

1. Knowledge objectives

（1）Understanding the automobile body shell；

（2）Understanding the main accessories and interiors of automobile body.

2. Ability objectives

It can identify the different materials of the body shell.

3. Emotion and quality goals

Cultivate students′ service awareness, quality awareness, and safety awareness.

汽车车身壳体造型设计中不乏中国传统文化元素，设计师们通过抽象、概括、简化、提炼、变形等手法将我国的传统文化元素融入到汽车车身等造型设计中，制造出能真正代表中国文化特色的汽车。

There are many traditional Chinese cultural elements in the modeling design of automobile body shells. Designers integrate Chinese traditional cultural elements into the automobile bodies and other modeling design by means of abstraction, generalization, simplification, refinement, deformation and other techniques to create cars that can truly represent Chinese cultural characteristics.

红旗 HQE 车型外观设计凸显前脸格栅设计，并创造性地融入了传统建筑文化元素"九梁十八柱"，18根金属柱两两一组，竖直排列，整齐而有序，代表着一种威严和秩序感。前车灯的设计延续了老红旗车的圆灯和筒状翼子板造型，尾灯则对老红旗的立式宫灯进行创新；旗杆和后视镜分别以飘扬的火焰和红旗为创意元素进行美化；车轮毂的造型源自于光芒四射的红太阳。总之，这款全手工精心制造的座驾，无论是整体外观还是局部细节的设计，处处都体现了中国的文化特色。

The exterior design of Hongqi HQE highlights the front face grille design, and creatively integrates the traditional architectural culture elements "nine beams and eighteen columns", of which the 18 metal columns are arranged in pairs, vertically, neatly and orderly, representing a sense of majesty and order. The design of the front light is the design of the round lamp and tubular fender of the old one, and the taillight is innovated from the vertical lamp of the old one. Taking fluttering flame and red flag as creative elements, the flagpole and rear-view mirror are beautified with these two elements respectively while the modeling of the car rim is derived from the radiant sun. In short, this handmade elaborate car, whether from the overall appearance or local details of the design, all reflects the Chinese cultural characteristics everywhere.

车身是驾驶员工作的场所，也是装载乘客和货物的场所。典型的货车车身包括驾驶室、车厢等部件。乘用车通常应用承载式车身，由纵梁立柱等组成。如图 4.1.1 所示。

The automobile body is the place where the driver works and also the place where passengers and goods are loaded. Typical truck body includes cab, carriage and other components. Passenger automobiles usually use load-bearing body, which is composed of longitudinal beams and columns, etc. ,as shown in Figure 4.1.1.

1.1　汽车车身的功用(Function of automobile body)

①为驾驶员、乘客（或货物）提供舒适安全的乘坐或位置的空间和环境；②有效地引导周围气流，以减少空气阻力，降低油耗，提高行驶稳定性，改善发动机的冷却条件；③使外形美观，增加艺术性和美感。

①It provides comfortable and safe space and environment for drivers, passengers (or cargo) to ride or locate;②It effectively guides the surrounding air flow to reduce air resistance, reduce fuel consumption, improve driving stability and improve engine cooling conditions;③It makes the appearance beautiful, increasing artistry and aesthetic feeling.

1.2　汽车车身的分类(Classification of automobile body)

1. 车身结构按照受力形式可分为非承载式、半承载式和承载式三种。

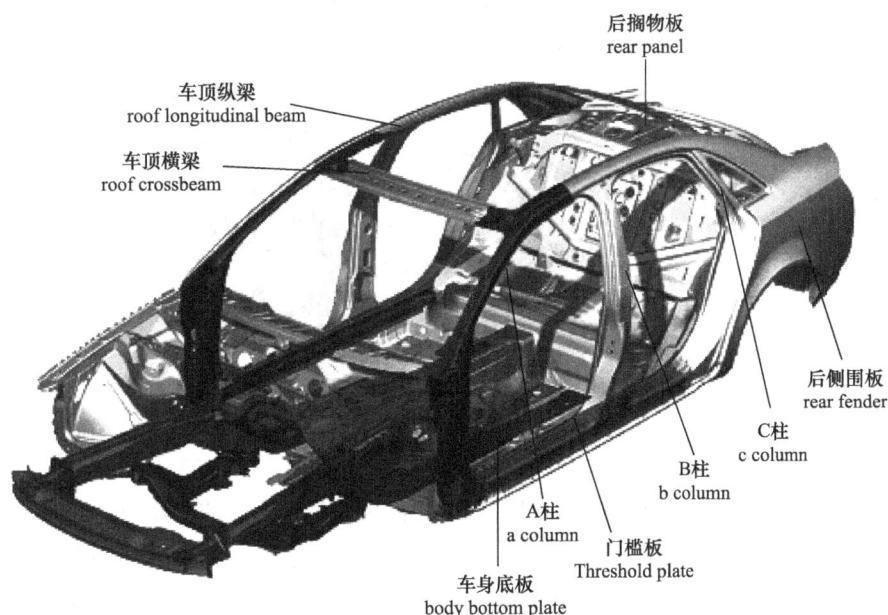

图 4.1.1　汽车车身
Figure 4.1.1　Automobile body

The body structure can be divided into three types：non-load-bearing type，semi-load-bearing type and load bearing type.

（1）非承载式车身（Non-load-bearing body）

车身以弹性元件与车架相连，车身仅承受自重和货物及乘客的质量引起的载荷以及行驶时的空气阻力和惯性力，其他的载荷则由车架承受。非承载式车身广泛用于客车及货车，有些高级轿车也采用这种形式的车身（图4.1.2）。

The body is connected with the frame by elastic elements. The body only bears the load caused by the dead weight and the load caused by the mass of goods and passengers，as well as the air resistance and inertia force while driving. The frame bears the other loads. Non-load-bearing body is widely used in buses and trucks，and it is also used in some high-end cars(Fig. 4. 1. 2).

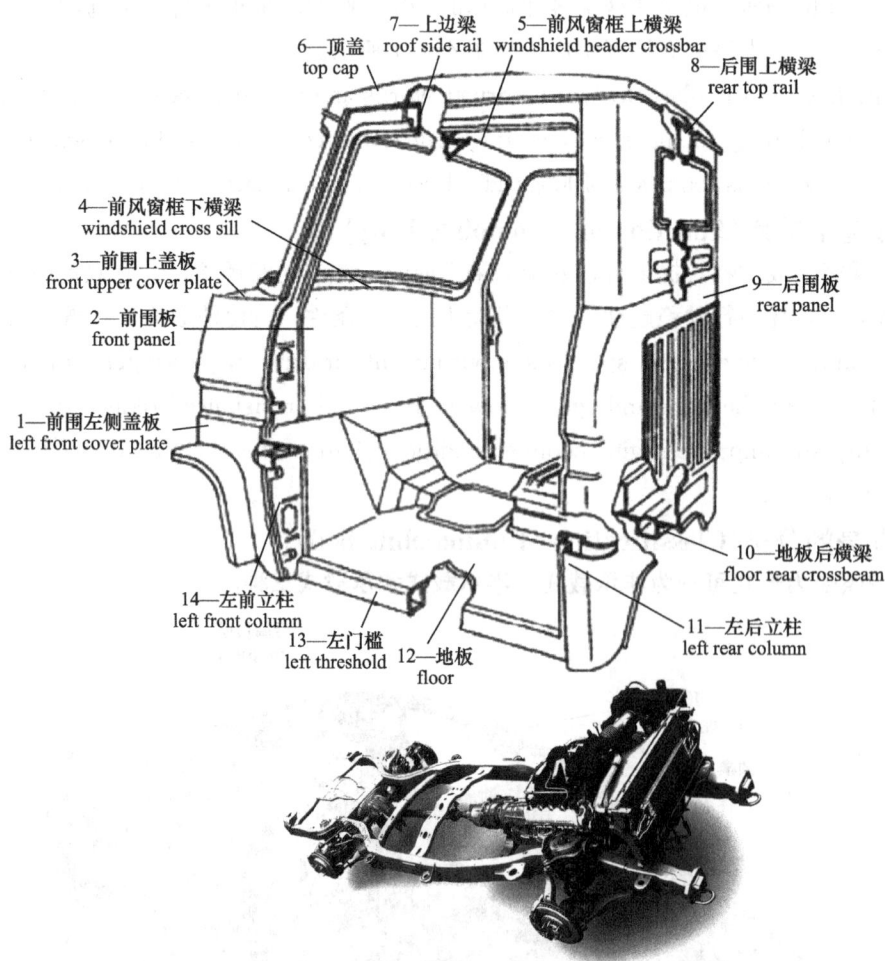

图4.1.2　非承载式车身
Figure 4. 1. 2　Non-load-bearing body

绝大多数货车驾驶室都是非承载式的结构，因为驾驶室只占汽车长度的一小部分，不可能采用承载式结构。驾驶室没有明显的骨架，由外部覆盖件和内部板件焊合成壳体，通过3点或4点弹性悬置与车架连接。

Most of the truck cabs are non-load-bearing structures，because the cabs only account for a small part of the length of the trucks. It is impossible to adopt load-bearing structures. The cab has no obvious framework，which is welded with external panels and internal plates to form the shell，which is connected to the frame by three or four-point elastic mounting.

（2）半承载式车身（Semi-load-bearing body）

与非承载式车身一样，半承载式车身下面保留有车架，但车身与车架刚性连接成一体，车身壳体承受部分载荷。半承载式车身骨架（立柱）与车架纵梁两侧悬伸的横梁焊接在一起，所以不像非承载式车身可以与车架分开（图4.1.3）。

Like the non-load-bearing body, there is a frame under the semi-load-bearing body, but the body is rigidly connected with the frame, and the body shell bears part of the loads. Semi-load-bearing body frame (column) is welded together with the overhanging beams on both sides of the frame longitudinal beam. So unlike the non-load-bearing body, it can be separated from the frame(Fig. 4.1.3).

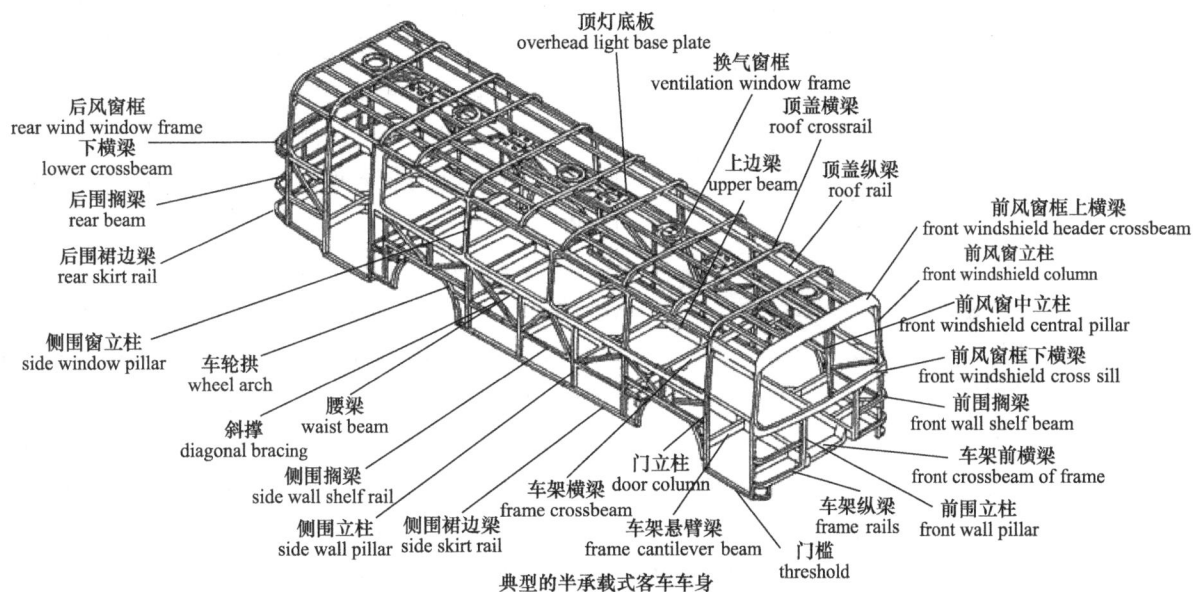

图4.1.3　半承载式车身

Figure 4.1.3　Semi-load-bearing body

（3）承载式车身（Load bearing body）

全部载荷由车身承受，底盘各部件直接与车身相连，将薄钢板压制成形状各异的板件然后再点焊成一个整体（图4.1.4）。

The body bears all the loads, and the chassis components are directly connected with the body. The sheet steels are pressed into different shapes and they are jointed into a whole by spot welding(Fig. 4. 1. 4).

图4.1.4　承载式车身

Figure 4.1.4　Load bearing body

2. 根据车身结构分类（Classification according to body structure）

小客车车身按车身结构分为两大类。一是大梁式车身，其大梁与主车身是分开的，大梁式车身结构本书将不详细讨论；二是整体式车身，其最大特征是将乘客舱和车架焊接成一体。

The minibus body can be divided into two categories according to the body structure. The first is the girder body, whose girder is separated from the main body, and the structure of the girder body will not be discussed in detail in this book. The second is the integral body, whose greatest feature is that the passenger compartment and the frame are welded into one.

（1）大梁式车身（Girder body）

大梁式车身的汽车有刚性车架，又称底盘大梁架，车身本体悬置于车架上，用弹性元件连接（图 4.1.5）。

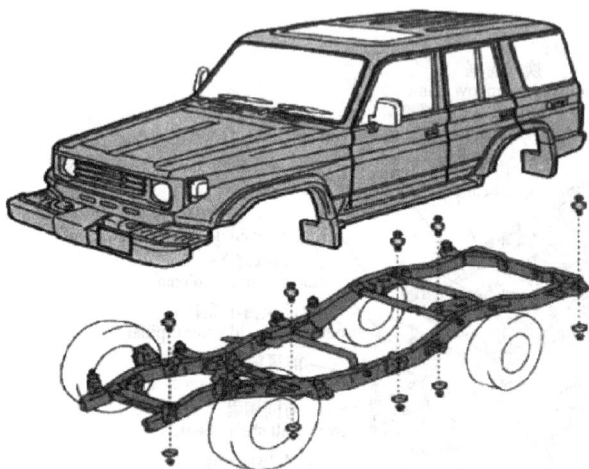

图 4.1.5 大梁式车身

Figure 4.1.5 Girder body

车架的振动通过弹性元件传到车身上，大部分振动被减弱或消除。当车辆发生碰撞时车架能吸收大部分冲击力，另外四个车轮受力由车架承担，不会传递到车身上，因此车厢变形小，抗颠簸性和安全性好，厢内噪声低。但大梁式车身较笨重，汽车质心高，高速行驶稳定性较差。

The automobile with girder body has rigid frame, which is also called chassis girder frame. The body is suspended on the frame and connected with elastic elements(Fig. 4.1.5).

The vibration of the frame is transmitted to the body through elastic elements, and most of the vibration is weakened or eliminated. When the vehicle collision occurs, the frame can absorb most of the impact force. The frame bears the force from the four wheels, which will not be transferred to the body. Therefore, the deformation of the carriage is small, the anti-bumpiness and safety are good, and the noise in the carriage is low. But the girder body is heavy, and has a high center of mass and poor high-speed driving stability.

（2）整体式车身（Integral body）

整体式车身没有独立的车架，发动机和底盘各总成安装在车身上，全部载荷由车身承受。整体式车身的构想是源自现代飞机机身设计，是将车身视为一个应力壳结构，因此作用在车身上的载荷不是集中于某一位置，而是分散至整个车身上。

整体式车身为目前轿车车身的主流，没有刚性车架，只是加强了车头、侧围、车尾、底板等部位，发动机、前后悬架和传动系统的一部分总成部件装配在车身上设计要求的位置，车身负载通过悬架装置传给车轮，其优点是公路行驶非常平稳，整个车身为一体，固有频率震动低，噪声小，整体式车身比较安全。缺点是当四个车轮受力不均匀时，车身会发生变形，制造成本和修理成本偏高。

"FF" 车辆是指前置发动机前轮驱动的车辆，是目前市面上整体式车身中最常见的类型。由于不需要后轮驱动的组件，所以 FF 车辆可以降低车底板中间位置拱起的高度，能提供较大的乘客舱空间。

The integral body has no independent frame. The engine and chassis assembly are installed on the body, and the body bears all the loads. The concept of integral body is derived from modern aircraft fuselage design, which regards the automobile body as a stress shell structure. Therefore, the loads acting on the body are not concentrated on a certain position, but distributed to the whole body.

Integral body is the mainstream of car body at present. It has no rigid frame, but strengthens the parts of front, side, rear and bottom. The engine, front and rear suspensions and some assembly parts of transmission system are assembled in the required position of the body design. The vehicle body load is transmitted to the wheel through the suspension device, whose advantages are that it runs very smoothly on highways. Due to its integral body, the natural frequency vibration is low, and the noise is small. The integral body is relatively safe. The disadvantage is that when the four wheels are not evenly loaded, the body will be deformed, and the manufacturing cost and repair cost are higher.

"FF" vehicle refers to the front-wheel drive vehicle with front engine, which is the most common type of integral body on the market at present. Because the rear wheel drive components are not required, FF vehicles can reduce the height of the mid-floor arch and provide larger passenger compartment space.

思考与练习

（Reflection and Exercises）

1. 汽车车身的功用。

2. 车身结构按照受力形式可分为？

1. The functions of automobile body.

2. The body structure can be divided into three parts according to the stress form?

任务二 汽车车身壳体

Task 2 Automobile Body Shell

教学目标

1. 知识目标

（1）了解汽车车身壳体主要组成；

（2）了解汽车车身壳体组成的作用。

2. 能力目标

培养学生能识别汽车车身壳体各部件。

3. 情感和素养目标

培养学生的爱国情感、良好的职业素养和精益求精的工匠精神。

Teaching objectives

1. Knowledge objectives

（1）Understand the main components of the car body shell;

（2）Understand the role of the car body shell composition.

2. Ability objectives

Cultivate students to identify the parts of the car body shell.

3. Emotion and quality goals

Cultivate students' patriotism, professional quality, and the craftsmanship spirit of striving for excellence.

车身壳体是一切车身部件的安装基础，通常指纵、横梁和立柱等主要承力元件以及与它们相连接的板件共同组成的空间结构，还包括在其上敷设的隔声、隔热、防振、防腐、密封等材料及涂层。车身还包括车门、车窗、车锁、内外饰件、附件、座椅及钣金件等。

通常整个车身壳体按强度等级分为三段，如图 4.2.1 所示，图中 A、B、C 分别代表车身前部、中部及后部。车身设计时，使中部乘客室尽可能具有最大的刚度，而相对于乘客室的前、后室则应具有较大的韧性。

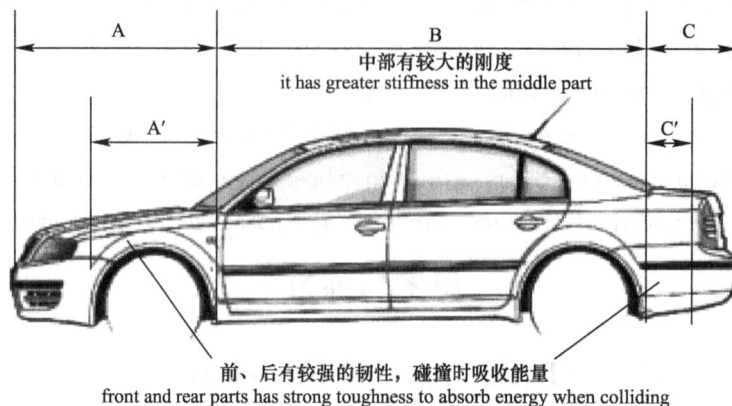

图 4.2.1 汽车车身壳体

Figure 4.2.1 The automobile body shell

汽车车身壳体的组成通常分为三段，即由前车身、中间车身和后车身三大部分及相关构件组成。

Body shell is the installation foundation of all body parts. It usually refers to the space structure consisting of main forced elements such as longitudinal beam, cross beam and column, and the plates connected with them. It also includes sound insulation, heat insulation, antivibration, anti-corrosion, sealing and other materials and coatings laid on it. The body also includes doors, windows, locks, interior and exterior decorations, accessories, seats and sheet metal parts, etc.

Usually the whole body shell is divided into three sections according to the strength grade. As shown in the figure, A, B and C represent the front, middle and rear parts of the body respectively. In body design, the middle passenger compartment should have the maximum stiffness as much as possible, while the front and rear rooms relative to the passenger compartment should have greater toughness.

The automobile body shell usually consists of three parts, namely, the front body, the middle body and the rear body and their related components.

2.1 前车身(Front body)

前车身主要由前翼子板、前纵梁、前围板及发动机罩、前轮罩、发动机安装支撑架以及保险杠等构件组成。

The front body is mainly composed of front fender, front longitudinal beam, front panel and engine hood, front wheel cover, engine mounting support frame and bumper, etc.

1. 前保险杠(Front bumper)

前保险杠位于车辆的最前端，是车身外部装饰体，主要部件一般由非金属面罩与金属加强筋相连而成（图 4.2.2）。

前保险杠在车辆行驶过程中经常发生刮蹭、碰撞等情况，前保险杠外皮、支架、装饰条等零件比较容易受到损坏，这些部件损坏后一般直接更换新件。

The front bumper is located at the front end of the vehicle and is the exterior decoration of the automobile body, whose main components are usually made of the nonmetal mask connecting with metal strengthening ribs(Fig. 4.2.2).

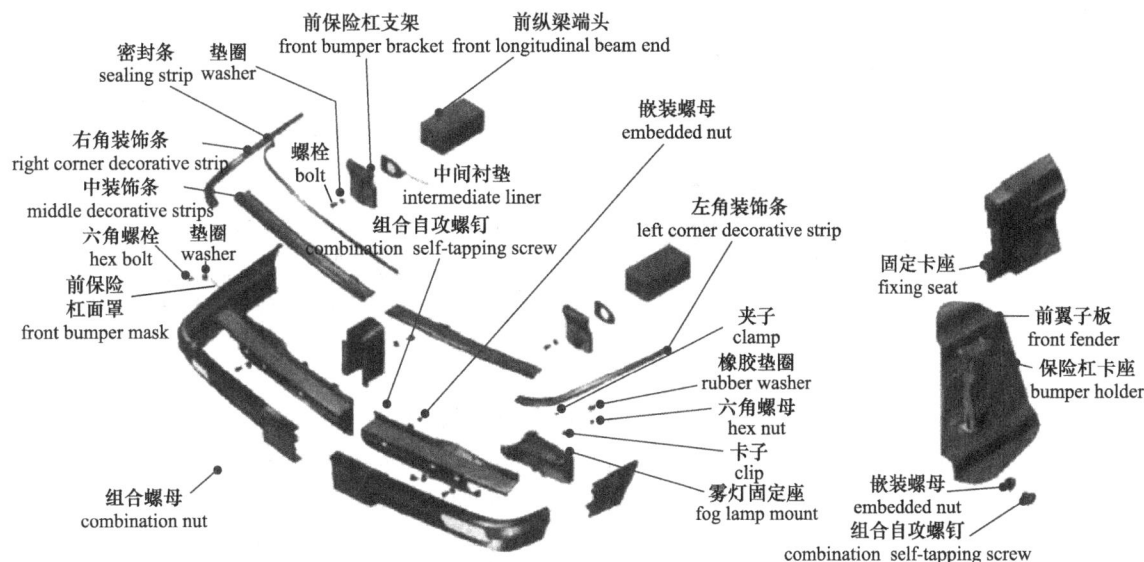

图 4.2.2 前保险杠
Figure 4.2.2 Front bumper

Scraping and collision often happens for the front bumper in the course of vehicle running. The front bumper skin, bracket, decorative strip and other parts are more easily to be damaged. When these parts are damaged, they are usually replaced by new ones directly.

2. 前翼子板(Front fender)

前翼子板位于汽车发动机罩侧下部，前轮上部，是重要车身装饰件，主要部件一般采用薄钢板冲压制造。

The front fender is located at the lower side of the automobile engine hood and the upper side of the front wheel. It is an important body decoration. The main parts are usually made of stamped thin steel sheet.

3. 发动机罩(Engine hood)

发动机罩位于车辆前上部，是发动机舱的维护盖板。

The engine hood is located in the front and upper part of the vehicle, which is the maintenance cover of the engine compartment.

4. 前围板(Front panel)

前围板位于乘客室前部，使发动机室与乘客室分开。

The front panel is located in the front of the passenger compartment to separate the engine compartment from the passenger compartment.

5. 前纵梁(Front longitudinal member)

前纵梁是前车身的主要强度件，直接焊接在车身下部（图 4.2.3）。

The front longitudinal member is the main strength part of the front body, which is directly welded to the lower part of the body Fig. 4.2.3.

2.2 中间车身(Middle body)

中间车身设有车门、侧体门框、门槛及箱型断面车顶、车底和立柱等构件，均以焊接方式组合在一起。

The middle body is composed of door, side door frame, threshold, box section roof, bottom and column, all of which are welded together.

1. 立柱/门槛板/地板(Column/Threshold/Floor)

立柱、门槛板是构成车身侧框架的钣金结构件，是车身非常重要的支撑件（图 4.2.4）。

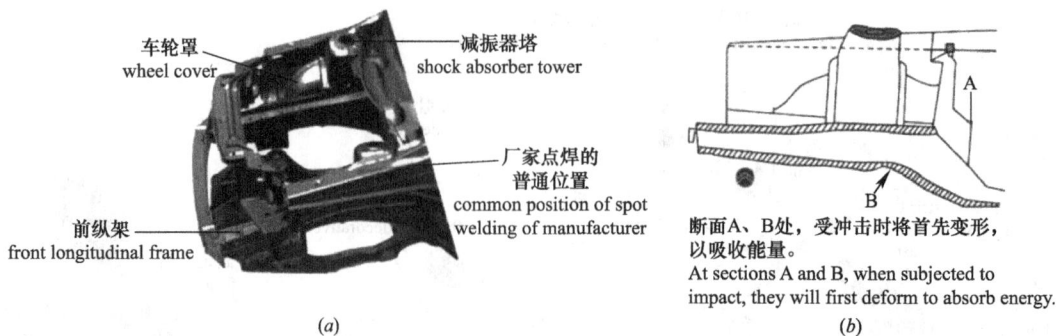

车轮罩
wheel cover

减振器塔
shock absorber tower

厂家点焊的
普通位置
common position of spot
welding of manufacturer

前纵架
front longitudinal frame

断面A、B处，受冲击时将首先变形，
以吸收能量。
At sections A and B, when subjected to
impact, they will first deform to absorb energy.

(a)

(b)

图 4.2.3　前纵梁

Figure 4.2.3　Front longitudinal member

(a) 前纵梁与轮罩的连接（Connection of Front Longitudinal Beam and Wheel Cover）；

(b) 纵梁断面的变化（Change of Longitudinal Beam Section）

Columns and Threshold plate are sheet metal structure parts which constitute the side frame of the body, and they are very important supports of the body(Fig. 4. 2. 4).

2. 车顶（Vehicle roof）

车顶是指车身车厢顶部的盖板，其上可能装备有天窗、换气窗或天线等，主要由车顶板、车顶内衬、横梁，有的车型还备有车顶行李架组成（图 4.2.5）。

The roof refers to the cover plate on the top of the body compartment，which may be equipped with a skylight，ventilation window or antenna, etc. It is mainly composed of the roof，roof lining，crossbeams，and some types has roof luggage racks as well(Fig. 4. 2. 5).

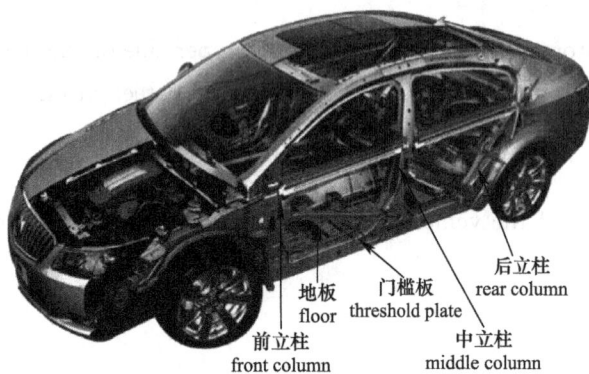

地板
floor

门槛板
threshold plate

后立柱
rear column

前立柱
front column

中立柱
middle column

图 4.2.4　立柱/门槛板/地板

Figure 4.2.4　Column/Threshold/Floor

图 4.2.5　车顶

Figure 4.2.5　Vehicle roof

3. 车门（Vehicle doors）

车门及附件主要包括车门板、车门内饰板、车门密封条、车门铰链、车门锁总成等零件组成。车门总成的零件中，车门板在损坏不严重的情况下一般采取钣金修复。其他零件属于易损件，在损坏时只要更换新件即可（图 4.2.6）。

Door and its accessories mainly include door panels，interior trim panels，door seals，door hinges，door lock assembly and other parts. In the parts of the door assembly，sheet metal is usually used to repair the door panels when the damage is not serious. Other parts belong to wearing parts. When damaged，they will be replaced by the new ones(Fig. 4. 2. 6).

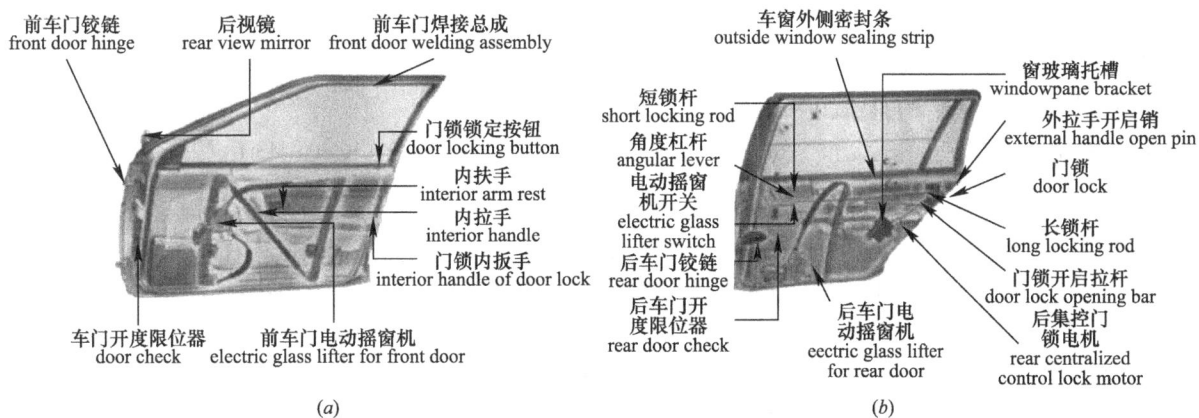

图 4.2.6　车门

Figure 4.2.6　Vehicle doors

(a) 前车门(front door)；(b) 后车门(rear door)

2.3　后车身(Rear body)

汽车后车身是用于放置物品的部分，可以说是中间车身侧体的延长部分。三厢式车的乘客室与行李舱是分开的，而两厢车的行李舱则与乘客室合二为一（图 4.2.7）。

The rear body of the vehicle is the part used for placing goods, which can be regard as the extension part of the side body of the middle body. The passenger compartment of a three-compartment vehicle is separated from the luggage compartment, while the luggage compartment of a two-compartment vehicle is combined with the passenger compartment(Fig. 4.2.7).

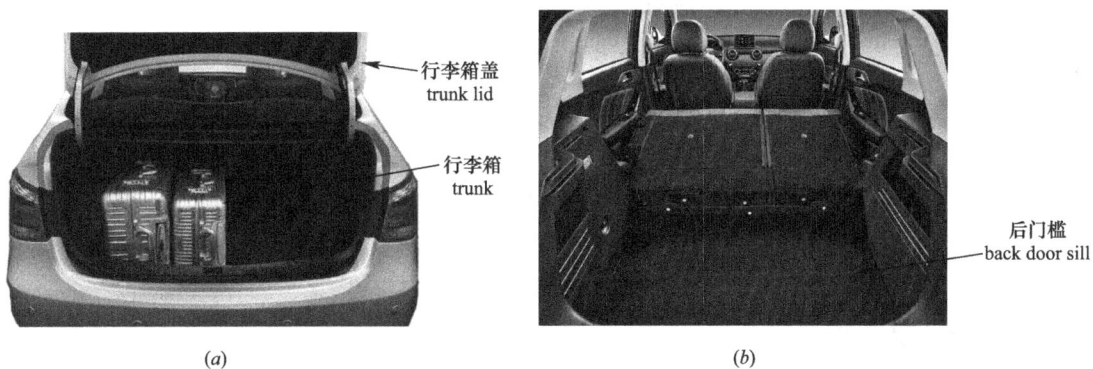

图 4.2.7　后车身

Figure 4.2.7　Rear body

(a) 三厢轿车后车身(The Rear Body of a three-compartment vehicle)；

(b) 两厢轿车后车身(Rear body of a two-compartment vehicle)

1. 行李舱和行李舱盖(Baggage compartment and trunk deck)

行李舱是由行李舱组件与车身地板钣金件构成。

行李舱盖主要由行李舱盖板、行李舱盖衬板、行李舱铰链、行李舱支撑、行李舱密封条等零件组成。

The luggage compartment is composed of the luggage compartment components and the sheet metal parts of the body floor.

The trunk deck mainly consists of baggage compartment cover plate, baggage compartment cover liner plate, baggage compartment hinge, baggage compartment support, baggage compartment sealing strip and other parts.

2. 后侧板(Rear side panel)

后侧板是指后门框以后的遮盖、后车轮及后侧车身的车身钣金件。

The rear side panel refers to the cover behind the rear door frame, body panels for rear wheels and rear body panels.

3. 后保险杠(Rear bumper)

后保险杠主要包括保险杠外皮、保险杠杠体、保险杠加强件、保险杠固定支架以及保险杠装饰条。起到装饰、防护车辆后部零件的作用（图4.2.8）。

The rear bumper mainly includes the bumper skin, the bumper body, the bumper reinforcement, the bumper fixing bracket and the bumper decorative strips. It plays the roles of decorating and protecting the rear parts of the vehicle(Figure 4.2.8).

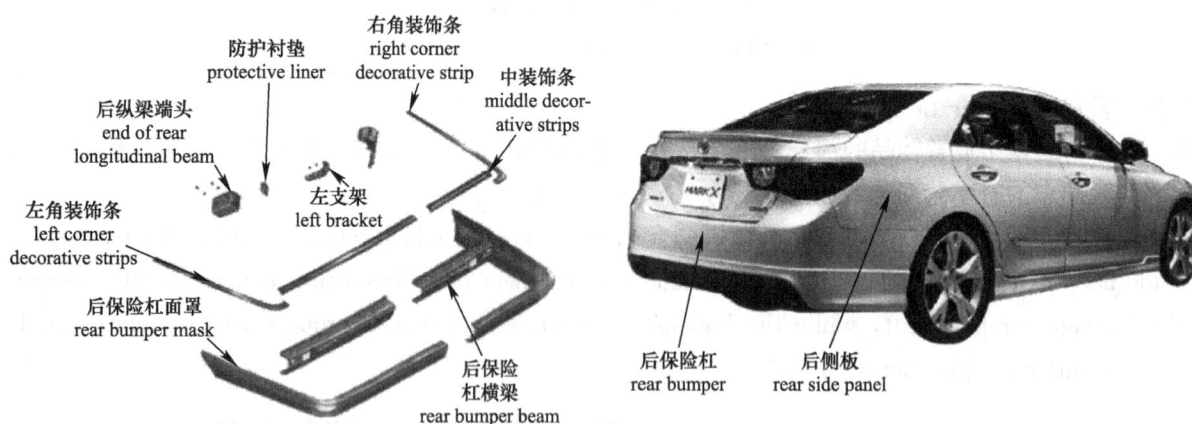

图4.2.8　后保险杠

Figure 4.2.8　Rear bumper

思考与练习

(Reflection and Exercises)

1. 汽车车身壳体主要组成?

2. 汽车前车身由什么组成?

1. Main components of car body shell?

2. What is the composition of car front body?

任务三　汽车车身主要附件及内饰

Task 3　Main Accessories and Interiors of Automobile Body

教学目标

1. 知识目标

（1）了解汽车车身主要附件;

（2）了解汽车车身内饰部件。

2. 能力目标

培养学生能识别汽车车身各部件。

3. 情感和素养目标

（1）培养学生勤奋学习的态度，严谨求实、创新的工作作风；

（2）培养学生良好的心理素质、职业道德素质以及高度责任心和良好的团队合作精神。

Teaching objectives

1. Knowledge objectives

（1）Understanding the main accessories of automobile body；

（2）Understanding interior parts of automobile body.

2. Ability objectives

To train students to recognize various parts of automobile body.

3. Emotion and quality goals

（1）Cultivate students′ attitude to learn diligently and to work rigorously, realistically and innovatively；

（2）Cultivate students′ psychological quality, professional ethics, high sense of responsibility and good team spirit.

3.1 汽车车身主要附件(Main accessories of automobile body)

汽车车身主要附件有：汽车玻璃、座椅、灯光、仪表、空调器、暖风机、风窗刮水器、车窗玻璃升降器、玻璃洗涤器械、音响设备、通信设备、仪表板、座椅及安全带、安全气囊、车内后视镜、遮阳顶窗及车门等。

The main accessories of automobile body are：automobile glass, seat, light, instrument, air conditioner, heater, windshield wiper, window glass lifter, glass washing equipment, audio equipment, communication devices, dashboard, seat and safety belt, airbag, interior rear-view mirror, sunshade roof window and door, etc.

1. 车门(Vehicle doors)

车门是车身上重要的部件之一，按其开启方法可分为顺开式、逆开式、水平滑移式、上掀式、折叠式和外摆式等，如图 4.3.1 所示。顺开式车门即使在汽车行驶时仍可借气流的压力关上，比较安全，故被广泛采用。逆开式车门在汽车行驶时若关闭不严就可能被迎面气流冲开，因而很少采用。水平滑移式车门的优点是：当车身侧壁与障碍物距离很小时仍能全部开启。上掀式车门广泛用于轿车及轻型客车的背门，有时也用于低矮的汽车。折叠式和外摆式车门广泛应用于大、中型客车。在有些大型客车上，还备有加速乘客撤离事故现场以及便于救援人员进入的安全门。

The door is one of the most important parts of the vehicle body. According to its opening method, it can be divided into forward opening, reverse opening, horizontal sliding, lifting folding and outward swinging, as shown in the following Figure 4.3.1. Forward door can be closed by the pressure of airflow even when the car is running. It is safe, so it is widely used. Reverse door is seldom used because it may be opened by oncoming air flow if it is not closed tightly. The advantage of the horizontal sliding door is that it can be opened completely when the distance between the side wall and the obstacle is very small. Lifting doors are widely used in the back doors of cars and light buses, and sometimes in low vehicles. Folding and outward swinging doors are widely used in large and medium buses. Some large buses are equipped with safety doors to speed up passenger evacuation from the accident site and be access for rescue workers.

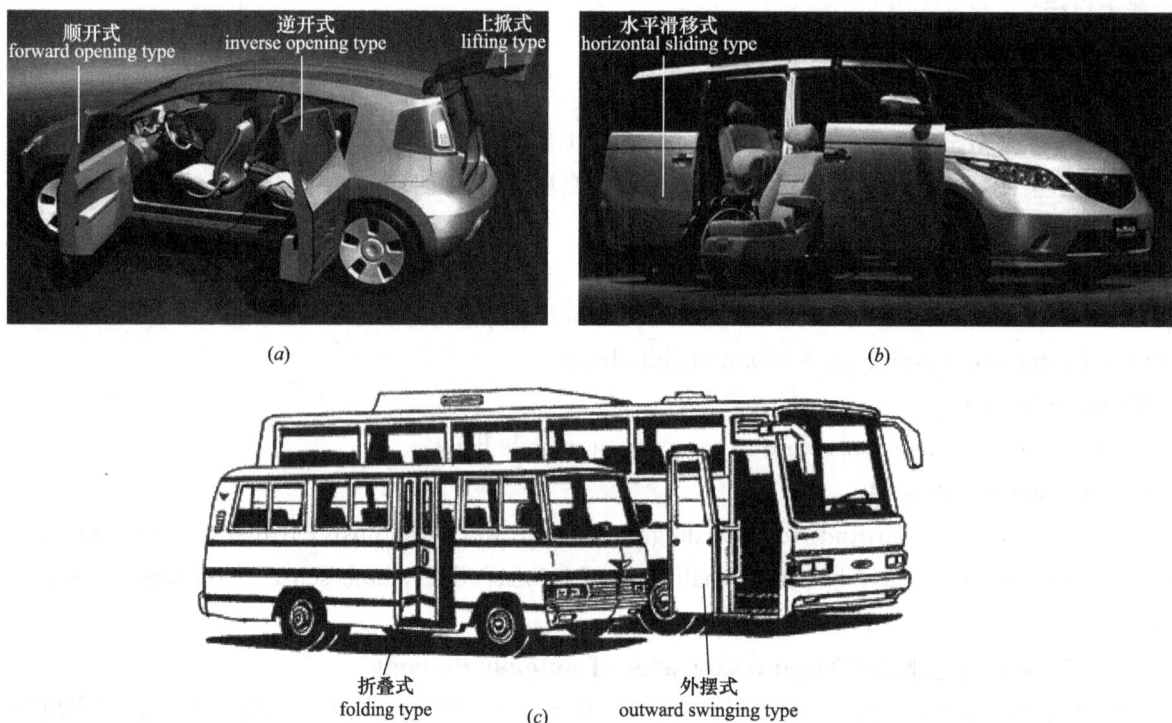

图 4.3.1　车门

Figure 4.3.1　Vehicle doors

(a) 顺开式、逆开式和上掀式车门(Forward, Reverse and lifting Doors)；

(b) 水平滑移式车门(Horizontal Sliding Door)；(c) 折叠式和外摆式车门(Folding and outward swinging doors)

2. 空调(Air conditioner)

现代汽车上都装有通风、暖气、冷气联合装置，或称四季空调系统。在风机的作用下，室外空气经由进风口进入系统，并经由过滤进口而流经制冷装置的蒸发器和暖气装置的散热器。系统的控制器可根据所需的温度指令控制分配箱内部各个阀门的开度，分别调节经由蒸发器和散热器的空气流量，然后将冷、热空气混合，以获得温度适宜的气流，再经由出风口导入室内。在寒冷季节还可将热空气经由热空气出口导向风窗除霜（图4.3.2）。

暖气装置的散热器与发动机水冷却系统的管道连接，可将流过的新鲜空气加热。

汽车空调系统的组成　The Composition of Vehicle Air Conditioning System

Modern automobiles are equipped with ventilation, heating, air-conditioning combination unit, or four seasons air-conditioning system. Under the action of the fan, the outdoor air enters the system through the air inlet, and flows through the filter inlet, the evaporator of the refrigeration device and the radiator of the heating device. The controller of the system can control the open degree of each valve in the distribution box according to the required temperature instructions, and adjust the air flow through the evaporator and radiator respectively, and then mix the cold and hot air to obtain the air flow with suitable temperature, and then lead it into the room through the air outlet. In the cold season, hot air can defrost the windshield through the guidance of hot air outlet(Fig. 4.3.2).

The radiator of the heating device is connected with the pipeline of the water cooling system of the engine to heat the fresh air flowing through.

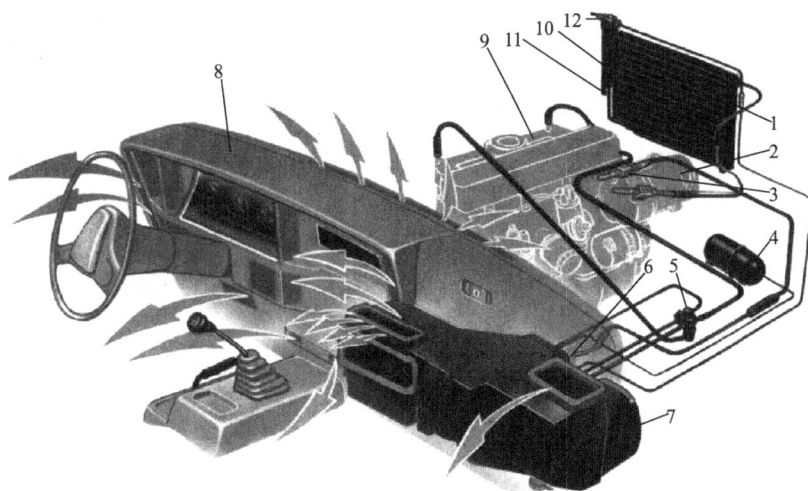

图 4.3.2　空调

Figure 4.3.2　Air conditioner

3. 座椅(Seat)

座椅是车身内部的重要装置。座椅的作用是支撑人体，使驾驶员操作方便和乘坐舒适。座椅由骨架、坐垫、靠背和调节机构等部分组成（图 4.3.3）。

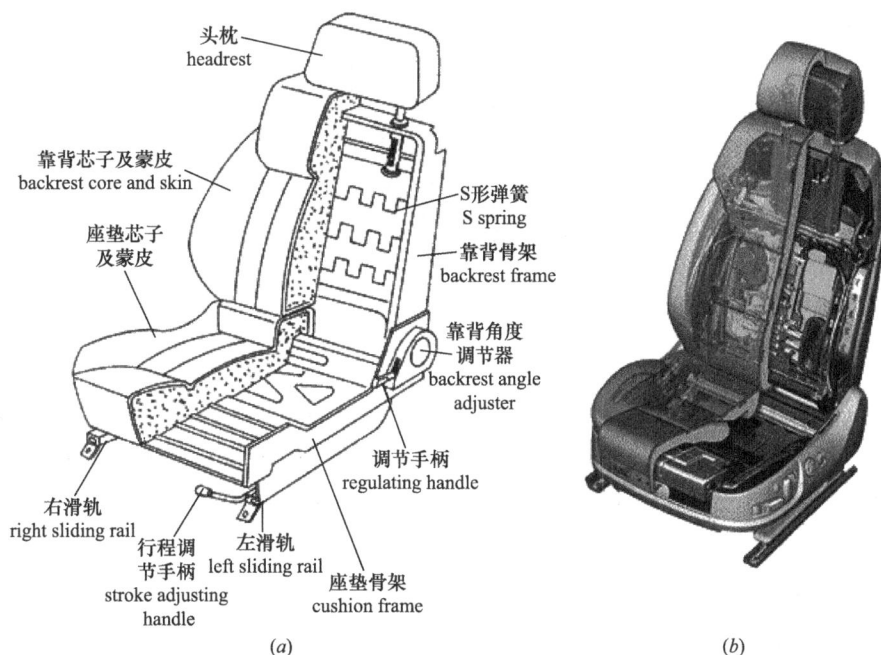

图 4.3.3　座椅

Figure 4.3.3　Seat

(a) 驾驶员手动调节座椅 (driver's manually adjusted seat)；(b) 驾驶员电动调节座椅(driver's electric regulating seat)

（1）普通座椅——为提高操作方便性和乘坐舒适性，现代轿车及高档客车的驾驶人座椅及乘客座椅大多用由钢管或型钢冲压成型的座椅骨架、与人体相适应的弹性坐垫和弹性靠背以及座椅调节机构等组成。

（2）电动座椅及电控座椅——为进一步提高驾驶人的操作方便性和乘客的乘坐舒适性，座椅的前后及高低位置应该因人而异地通过电动机调整到最舒适的位置，这种由电动机调节的汽车座椅称为电动座椅。

The seat is an important device in the body. The function of the seat is to support the human body, so that the driver can operate easily and ride comfortably. The seat is composed of frame, cushion, backrest and adjusting mechanism, etc(Fig. 4. 3. 3).

(1) Ordinary seats - In order to improve operation convenience and ride comfort, drivers' seats and passenger seats of modern cars and high-end buses are mostly composed of seat frame stamped with steel tubes or profile steels, elastic seat cushion and elastic backrest adapted to human body, and seat adjusting mechanism, etc.

(2) Power seat and electronic control seat - In order to further improve the driver's operation convenience and passenger's ride comfort, the front, back, high and low positions of the seat should be adjusted to the most comfortable positions by the motors from person to person. This kind of vehicle seat regulated by the motors is called power seat.

4. 安全带(Safety belt)

安全带是极有效的防护装置，可大幅度降低碰撞事故时车内乘员的受伤率和死亡率，其效能已被国外大量使用实践所证明。图 4. 3. 4 为最常用的三点式安全带的组成部分。

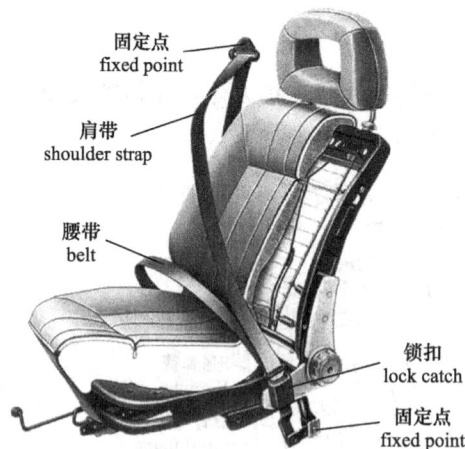

固定点
fixed point

肩带
shoulder strap

腰带
belt

锁扣
lock catch

固定点
fixed point

图 4. 3. 4　安全带
Figure 4. 3. 4　Safety belt

Safety belt is a very effective protective device, which can greatly reduce the injury rate and death rate of passengers in collision accidents. Its effectiveness has been proved by a large number of foreign practices.

The following figure shows the components of three-point seat belt which is the most commonly used one.

5. 安全气囊(Air bag)

气囊系统通常称为辅助约束系统（SRS），可与安全带一起对前排乘员提供有效的保护。对于未佩戴安全带的乘员，气囊系统的防护作用是极为有效的；而对于佩戴安全带的乘员，气囊系统可以有效地减轻头部受到的伤害。近年来，有些汽车为了提高其安全性，还设置了侧面气囊系统。

The airbag system, commonly known as the supplemental restraint system（SRS）, provides effective protection for the front passengers along with the safety belt.

For the passengers without seat belts, the protective effect of the airbag system is extremely effective. While for the passengers wearing seat belt, the airbag system can effectively reduce the head injury. In recent years, in order to improve the safety, some automobiles adopt side airbag system.

6. 音响设备(Audio equipment)

现代轿车已经使用高级音响及影视系统，其中包括数字调谐的 FM 立体声收音机、能自动换片的 CD/

VCD/DVD 影碟机以及由 USB 存储或移动硬盘存储的 MP3/MP4/MP5、投影机及液晶电视等。

Modern cars have used advanced audio and video systems，including digital tuning FM stereo radios，CD/VCD/DVD playerS that can automatically change film，MP3/MP4/MP5，projectors and LCD televisions stored by USB or mobile hard disks，etc.

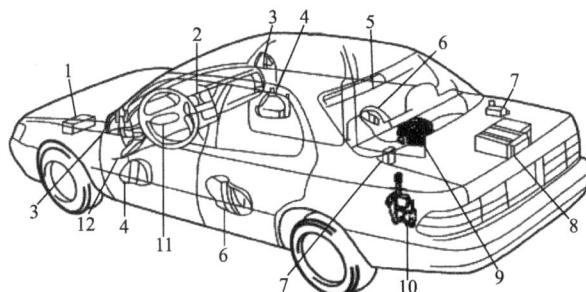

图 4.3.5　国外汽车音响的系统布置

Figure 4.3.5　System layout of foreign automobile audio

1—2 号接线盒（主熔断丝、ALT 熔断丝、AM 熔断丝、DOME 熔断丝、1 号收音机熔断丝）(No. 2 junction box（Main fuse、ALT Fuse、AM Fuse、DOME Fuse、No. 1 Radio Fuse））；2—收音机（radio）；3—高音扬声器（tweeter）；4—前门扬声器（front door speaker）；5—印刷天线（printed antenna）；6—后门扬声器（backdoor speaker）；7—低音扬声器及功放（woofer and power amplifier）；8—自动换片激光唱机（compact disc player of automatially change film）；9—低音扬声器（woofer）；10—自动天线（automatic antenna）；11—点火开关（the ignition switch）；12—1 号接线盒（2 号收音机熔断丝、EFI-ECU 点火熔断丝）(No. 1 junction box（No. 2 radio fuse，EFI-ECU ignition fuse））

7. 汽车仪表（Automobile instrument）

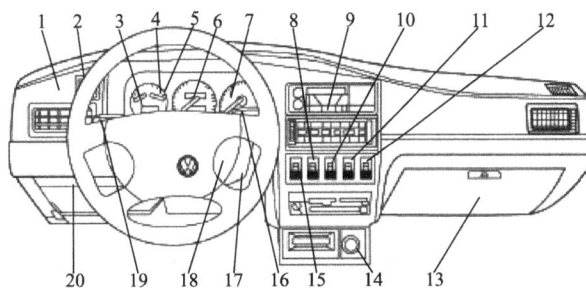

图 4.3.6　上海桑塔纳 2000 轿车的仪表板

Figure 4.3.6　Dashboard of the Santana 2000 car

1—出风口（air outlet）；2—灯光及仪表板照明调节器（light and dashboard lighting regulator）；3—电子钟（electronic clock）；4—冷却液温度表（coolant thermometer）；5—信号灯（signal lamp）；6—车速-里程表（speedometer）；7—发动机转速表（engine speed meter）；8—后窗加热开关（rear window heating switch）；9—收放机（radio）；10—危险报警闪光开关（danger alarm flash switch）；11—防盗报警设置（anti-theft alarm settings）；12—ABS 指示灯（ABS indicator light）；13—杂物箱（glove box）；14—点烟器（the cigarette lighter）；15—雾灯开关（fog lamp switch）；16—风窗刮水器及风窗洗涤器开关（windshield wiper and windshield washer switch）；17—转向器与点火开关（steering gear and ignition switch）；18—喇叭按钮（horn button）；19—转向灯及变光开关（turn signaldimmer switches）；20—熔断器护壳（fuse shell）

3.2 汽车车身内饰部件(Automobile body interiors)

车身内部装饰件：车门内护板、车顶顶篷、仪表板、侧壁、座椅等表面覆饰物，以及窗帘和地毯。在轿车上广泛采用天然纤维或合成纤维的纺织品、人造革或多层复合材料、连皮泡沫塑料等表面覆饰材料；在客车上则大量采用纤维板、纸板、工程塑料板、铝板、花纹橡胶板以及复合装饰板等覆饰材料。

Body interior decorations include interior guard panels of doors, ceiling, dashboards, side walls, seat and other surface decorations, as well as curtains and carpets. Textiles made of natural or synthetic fibers, artificial leather or multi-layer composite materials, integral skin foam and other surface decorative materials are widely used in cars. While in buses, fiberboard, cardboard, engineering plastic board, aluminium sheet, patterned rubber sheet and composite decorative board are widely used.

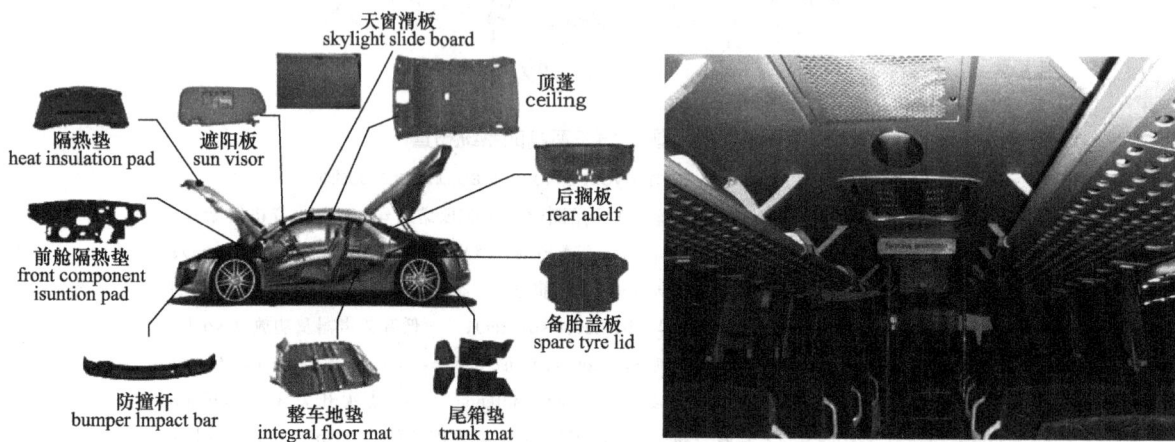

图 4.3.7　汽车车身内饰部件

Figure 4.3.7　Automobile body interiors

1. 车门内护板(Interior guard panels of doors)

车门内护板一般是塑料件，其结构复杂，主要有凸台、加强筋、卡角、预埋件、螺纹、花纹、标记等复杂塑料结构在车门护板上都有体现，并且它们的设计都很有技巧性（图4.3.8）。车门内护板的功能包括以下：

（1）它的立体艺术造型提高了汽车室内造型效果，给人以美感；

（2）使车门开关方便、支承肘腕、隔声、吸声、防尘、防水；

（3）采用触感好的非金属材料，提高乘坐舒适性，车辆冲撞时能吸收大量的碰撞能量，有效保护驾驶员和乘员的安全；

（4）结合其立体造型，还可设置杂物斗，为烟灰盒、门锁内手开手柄等功能部件提供固定条件。

Interior guard panels of doors are generally plastic parts, whose structure is complex. Complex plastic structures such as boss, reinforcing ribs, fastening angle, embedded parts, threads, patterns, markings and so on can be seen on the door guard plate(Figure 4.3.8). The functions of the interior guard panels of doors include the followings:

（1）Its three-dimensional artistic modelling improves the effect of car interior modelling and brings aesthetic feeling to people;

（2）It is easy to open and close the doors. It also has functions such assupporting elbow and wrist, sound insulation, sound absorption, dust-proof, waterproof;

（3）The adoption of non-metallic materials with good touch can improve ride amenity, ans absorb a large amount of collision energy when the vehicle collides, so as to effectively protect the safety of drivers and passengers.

（4）Combining with its three-dimensional shape, it can also set up sundries container to provide fixed conditions for functional components such as ash pan, interior handle of door lock, etc.

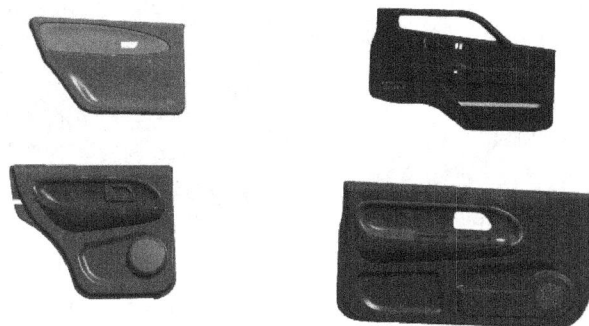

图 4.3.8 车门内护板

Figure 4.3.8 Interior guard panels of doors

2. 汽车顶棚(Automobile ceiling)

顶棚是汽车内饰的重要组成部分，体现车身内造型设计与外界的隔热、隔声和吸声，阻燃、降噪对乘员头部的保护（图 4.3.9）。

The ceiling is an important part of automobile interior decorations, which reflects the interior design of automobile body and the functions such as heat and sound insulations with outside, sound absorption, flame retard, noise reduction and the protection for passengers' heads(Figure 4.3.9).

图 4.3.9 汽车顶棚

Figure 4.3.9 Automobile ceiling

3. 仪表板(Dashboard)

仪表板总成是汽车内部饰件中最重要的组成部分，也是车厢内最吸引人注意的地方。

作用：仪表板的造型设计也体现了汽车的个性，可以将其作为衡量不同生产厂家的工艺水平及艺术风格的标准之一，软化的表面在撞车时对乘员起保护作用，减少对光线的反射率或产生反射光对驾驶员的视觉能起保护作用。

The dashboard assembly is the most important part of the interiors of the vehicle, and it is also the most attractive part inside the vehicle. Its functions are described next. The modelling design of the dashboard also reflects the personality of the vehicle, which can be used as one of the criteria to measure the technological level and artistic style of different manufacturers. The softened surface protects the passengers when crashing, reducing the reflectivity of light or producing reflective light to protect the driver's vision.

4. 汽车座椅(Car seat)

汽车座椅作为汽车重要的内部部件，具有支撑乘员质量、缓和衰减由车身传来的冲击和振动的作用；保证乘员乘坐舒适性，减轻乘员疲劳并且提供良好的工作条件；保护乘员避免和减少伤亡等重要作用。

As an important interior component of automobile, automobile seat can support the occupants' mass and mitigate the impact and vibration from the body. It also protects passengers' ride comfort, alleviating passengers' fatigue and providing good working conditions, protecting passengers to avoid and reduce casualties and other important roles.

图 4.3.10　汽车仪表板

Figure 4.3.10　Automobile dashboard

图 4.3.11　汽车座椅

Figure 4.3.11　Automobile seat

思考与练习

（Reflection and Exercises）

1. 汽车车身的功用。

2. 汽车车身的壳体有哪些？

3. 汽车车身的附件有哪些？

1. The functions of automobile body.

2. What are the parts of the body shell?

3. What are the accessories of the vehicle body?

项目五　汽车电气系统
Item 5　Automobile Electrical System

任务一　汽车电气系统概述
Task 1　Overview

教学目标

1. 知识目标

（1）能叙述汽车电气系统的特点；

（2）能叙述汽车蓄电池的作用、结构和工作原理；

（3）能叙述汽车发电机的作用、结构和工作原理。

2. 能力目标

（1）能识别汽车电气系统的基础元件；

（2）能掌握汽车电器供电设备。

3. 情感和素养目标

（1）培养学生的团队精神和协作精神；

（2）培养学生良好的心理素质和克服困难的能力。

Teaching objectives

1. Knowledge objectives

（1）Capable of describing the characteristics of automotive electrical system;

（2）Capable of describing the function, structure and working principle of automobile battery;

（3）Capable of describing the function, structure and working principle of automobile generator.

2. Ability objectives

（1）Recognition of basic components of automotive electrical system;

（2）Master the power supply equipment of automotive electrical appliances.

3. Emotion and quality goals

（1）Cultivate students' team spirit and cooperation spirit;

（2）Cultivate students' psychological quality and the ability to overcome difficulties.

汽车电气系统是汽车的重要组成部分，其性能的好坏直接影响到汽车的动力性、经济性、可靠性、安全性和尾气排放等各个方面。汽车电气系统的特点：

Automobile electrical system is an important part of the automobile. Its performance directly affects the power, economy, reliability, safety, exhaust emissions and other properties of the automobile. Characteristics of automotive electric system:

(1) 单线制（Single-wire system）

所谓单线制，就是利用汽车发动机和底盘、车身等金属机件作为各种用电设备的共用连线（俗称搭铁），而用电设备到电源只需另设一根导线。任何一个电路中的电流都是从电源的正极出发，经导线流入到用电设备后，通过金属车架流回电源负极而形成回路。

The single-wire system is the use of automobile engine, chassis, car body and other metal parts as a common wiring of various electrical equipment (commonly known as Put up iron), and only one additional wireway is needed to connect the electrical equipment to the power supply. The current in any circuit starts from the positive pole of the power supply, flows into the electrical equipment through the conductor, and flows back to the negative pole of the power supply through the metal frame to form a circuit.

采用单线制不仅可以节省材料（铜导线），使电路简化，而且便于安装和检修，降低故障率。但在一些不能形成可靠的电气回路或需要精确电子信号的回路，采用双线。

The single wire system can not only save material (copper wire), simplify the circuit, but also facilitate installation and overhaul, and reduce the failure rate. But in some circuits which can not form reliable electrical circuit or need precise electronic signal, double-wire is adopted.

(2) 负极搭铁（Negative put up iron）

所谓搭铁，就是采用单线制时，将蓄电池的一个电极用导线连接到发动机或底盘等金属车体上。若蓄电池的负极连接到金属车体上，称为负极搭铁；反之，若蓄电池的正极连接到金属车体上，称为正极搭铁。我国标准中规定汽车电器必须采用负极搭铁。目前世界各国生产的汽车也大多采用负极搭铁方式。

Put up iron is to connect one of the electrodes of the battery to the metal car body such as the engine or chassis with a wire when the single-wire system is adopted. If the negative pole of the battery is connected to the metal car body, it is called the negative put up iron; otherwise, if the positive pole of the battery is connected to the metal car body, it is called the positive put up iron. The standard of our country stipulates that the negative pole tapping iron must be used in automobile electrical appliances. At present, most of the automobiles manufactured in the world adopt the negative put up iron method.

(3) 两个电源（Two power sources）

所谓两个电源，就是指蓄电池和发电机两个供电电源。蓄电池是辅助电源，在汽车未运转时向有关用电设备供电；发电机是主电源，当发动机运转到一定转速后，发电机转速达到规定的发电转速，开始向有关用电设备供电，同时对蓄电池进行充电。两者互补可以有效地使用电设备在不同的情况下都能正常地工作，同时也延长了蓄电池的供电时间。

The so-called two power supply refers to the storage battery and generator these two power supplies. Battery is an auxiliary power supply, which supplies power to the relevant electrical equipment when the car is not running; generator is the main power supply. When the engine runs to a certain speed, the speed of generator reaches the specified power generation speed, the engine starts to supply power to the relevant electrical equipment, while charging the battery. They can effectively make the electrical equipment to work normally under different conditions, at the same time, it also prolongs the power supply time of the storage battery.

(4) 用电设备并联（Parallel connection of electrical equipment）

所谓用电设备并联，就是指汽车上的各种用电设备都采用并联方式与电源连接，每个用电设备都由各自串联在其支路中的专用开关控制，互不产生干扰。

The so-called parallel connection of electric equipment means that all kinds of electric equipment on automobiles are connected with power supply in parallel mode, and each electrical equipment is controlled by a special switch connected in series in its branch circuit, without interference from each other.

（5）低压直流供电（Low Voltage DC Power Supply）

汽车电气设备采用低压直流供电，柴油车大多采用24V直流供电，汽油车大都采用12V直流电压供电。

Low-voltage DC power supply is used for automotive electrical equipment, 24 V DC power supply for diesel vehicles and 12 V DC power supply for gasoline vehicles.

1.1 汽车电气系统的基础元件（Basic components of automotive electrical system）

1. 保险装置（Safety devices）

保险装置主要指的是保护电气线路或用电设备（用电器）的易熔线和熔断器（保险丝）。

Safety devices mainly refer to fusible wires and fuses (fuse wire) that protect electrical lines or electrical equipment (electrical appliances).

（1）易熔线（Fusible wire）

易熔线通常用来保护电源和大电流干线，它在5s内熔断的电流和普通熔丝相比，相当于有200～300A电流通过，因此绝对不允许换用比规定容量大的易熔线（图5.1.1）。

Fusible wires are usually used to protect power supply and high current trunk lines. Compared with ordinary fuses, the current it fuses in five seconds are equivalent to 200 A to 300 A. Therefore, it is absolutely not allowed to replace fusible wires with larger capacity than the stipulated ones(Fig. 5. 1. 1).

（2）熔断器（Fuse）

熔断器（保险丝）一般安装在仪表盘附近或发动机罩下面的熔断器盒内，常与继电器组装在一起，构成全车电路的中央接线盒。熔断器外观与熔值标注如图5.1.2所示。

Fuses (fuse wire) are usually installed in the fuse box near the dashboard or under the hood of the engine. They are often assembled with relays to form the central junction box of the whole vehicle circuit. The fuse appearance and fusing value as shown in Fig. 5. 1. 2.

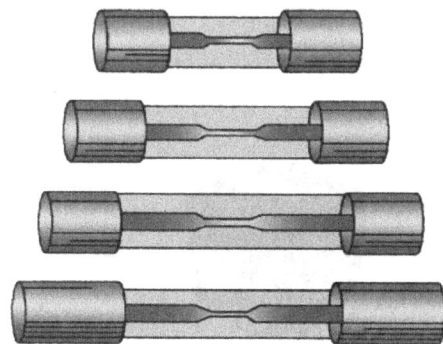

图 5.1.1 易熔线
Figure 5. 1. 1 Fusible wire

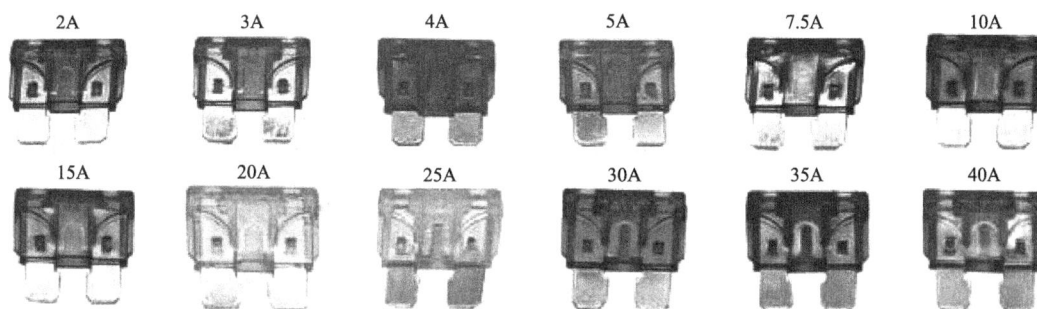

图 5.1.2 熔断器及熔值
Figure 5. 1. 2 Fuse appearance and fusing value

2. 继电器（Relay）

（1）继电器的概念（The concept of relay）

继电器是自动控制电路中常用的一种元件，它是利用电磁感应原理以较小的电流来控制较大电流的自动开关，在电路中起着自动操作、自动调节、安全保护等作用。

Relay is a common component in automatic control circuit. It is an automatic switch that uses electromagnetic induction principle to control larger current with smaller current. It plays an automatic operation, automatic regulation and safety protection role in the circuit.

（2）继电器的作用（The role of relays）

继电器是一种常用的控制器件，它可以用较小的电流来控制较大的电流，以保护开关。

Relay is a commonly used control device, which can use smaller current to control larger current to protect the switch.

（3）继电器符号（Relay symbols）

继电器的文字符号为"K"，常开式继电器的符号表示如图5.1.3所示。

The character number of the relay is "K", Symbolic Representation of Normally Open Relay as shown in Fig. 5.1.3.

（4）继电器的结构（Relay structure）

电磁继电器一般由铁芯、电磁线圈、衔铁、复位弹簧、触点（3、4、5）、支座及引脚（1、2）等组成（图5.1.4）。

Electromagnetic relay is generally composed of iron core, electromagnetic coil, armature, reset spring, contact (3, 4, 5), support and pins (1, 2), etc (Fig. 5.1.4).

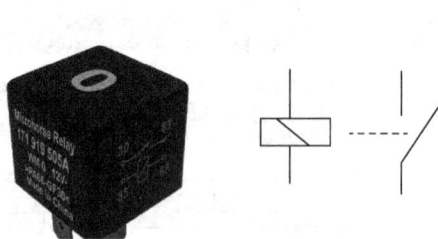

图5.1.3 继电器及符号
Figure 5.1.3 Relays and symbols

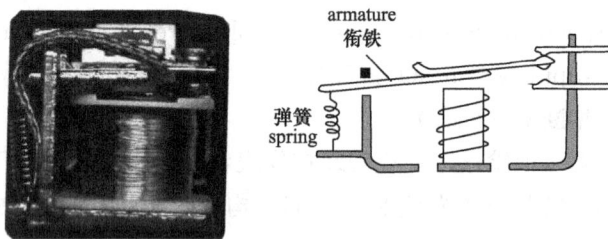

图5.1.4 继电器结构
Figure 5.1.4 Relay structure

（5）继电器的工作原理（Working principle of relay）

电磁继电器主要是利用电磁感应原理而工作的。

The work of electromagnetic relay is based on the principle of electromagnetic induction.

（6）继电器的种类（Types of relays）

1）继电器按触点状态来分有常开触点和常闭触点。

1) The relay has normal open contacts and normal closed contacts according to the state of contacts.

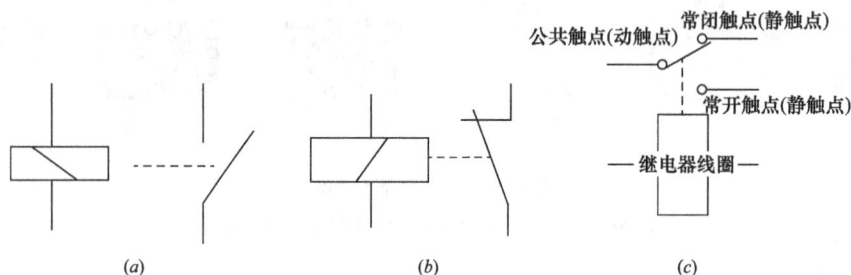

图5.1.5 继电器种类
Figure 5.1.5 Types of relays
（a）常开（normal open）；（b）常闭（normal closed）；（c）混合型（mix）

2）按引脚数目来分有三脚式、四脚式、七脚式等。

2）According to the number of pins, there are three-legged, four-legged, seven-legged and so on.

3）按触点数目有单组触点、多组触点继电器等。

3）According to the number of contacts, there are single group contacts, multiple groups of contacts relays, etc.

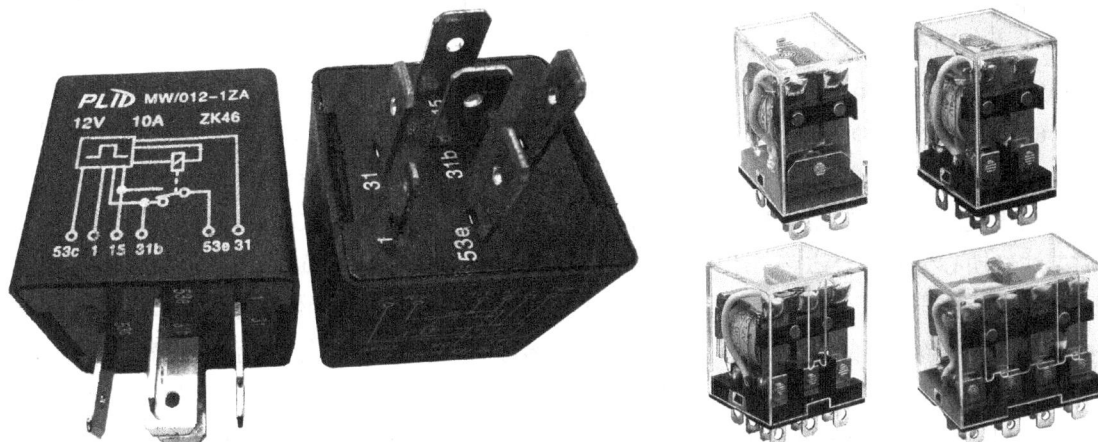

图 5.1.6 多脚和多触点继电器

Figure 5.1.6 Multi-foot and multi-contact relays

3. 点火开关(Ignition switch)

汽车的点火开关装在转向柱上，通常有 5 个不同的挡位，如图 5.1.7 所示。

The automobile ignition switch is mounted on the steering column and usually has five different gears, as shown in Figure 5.1.7.

（1）锁止（LOCK）。钥匙在此位置才可拔出并锁住转向盘，以防汽车无钥匙被移动。

（2）关闭（OFF）。钥匙在此位置全车电路不通，但转向盘可以转动。

（3）附件（ACC）。钥匙在此位置汽车附属电器的电路接通，如点烟器、收音机等，但点火系统不通。

（4）运转（ON）。钥匙在此位置时点火系统及汽车各电器均接通，一般汽车行驶均在此位置。

（5）启动（START）。由运转位置顺时针方向扭转钥匙即为启动位置，手放松时，钥匙又可回到运转位置。在启动位置，点火系统及启动系统均接通以启动发动机。

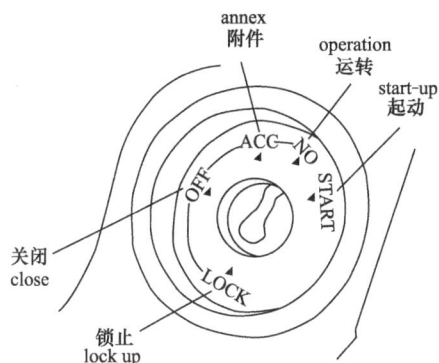

图 5.1.7 点火开关各挡位表示

Figure 5.1.7 Indication of each gear of ignition switch

（1）Lock up(LOCK). Only in this position can the key be pulled out and the steering wheel be locked to prevent from moving when the car is keyless.

（2）Close (OFF). When the key is in this position, the whole car circuit will not work, but the steering wheel can turn.

（3）Annex (ACC). When the key is in this position, the circuit of automobile accessory appliances is connected, such as cigarette lighter, radio, etc. , but the ignition system is not working.

（4）Operation (ON). When the key is in this position, the ignition system and all the electrical appliances of the car are connected. Generally, the car runs in this position.

(5) Start-up(START). Turning the key clockwise from the running position is the starting position. When the hand is relaxed, the key can return to the running position. In the starting position, the ignition system and the starting system are connected to start the engine.

4. 点火线圈(Ignition coil)

点火线圈能将汽车电源系统提供的低压电，变为高达几千伏甚至上万伏的高压电，用于点燃发动机内的汽油混合气。点火线圈分为开磁路式和闭磁路式两类。

The ignition coil can turn the low voltage electricity provided by the automotive power supply system into high voltage up to several kilovolts or even tens of thousands of volts, which can be used to ignite the gasoline mixture in the engine. Ignition coils can be divided into open circuit and closed circuit.

闭磁路式点火线圈的结构如图 5.1.8 所示。在"日"字形铁心内绕有一次绕组，在一次绕组的外面绕有二次绕组，磁感线经铁心构成闭合磁路。闭磁路式点火线圈的优点是漏磁少，磁路的磁阻小，因而能量损失小，能量变换率高，可达 75%（开磁路式点火线圈只有 60%）。闭磁路式点火线圈体积小，可直接装在分电器盖上，省去了点火线圈与分电器之间的高压导线，并可使二次电容减小，所以在电子点火系统中得到了广泛使用。

The structure of closed magnetic circuit type ignition coil is shown in Fig. 5.1.8. There is a primary winding in the "日" shaped core and a secondary winding outside the primary winding, the magnetic induction line through the core constitutes a closed magnetic circuit. The advantages of closed circuit ignition coil are less leakage of magnetic field and less reluctance of magnetic circuit, so the energy loss is small and the energy conversion rate is high, up to 75% (open circuit ignition coil is only 60%). The closed-circuit ignition coil is small in size and can be directly mounted on the distributor cover, eliminating the high-voltage wire between the ignition coil and the distributor, and reducing the secondary capacitance, so it is widely used in the electronic ignition system.

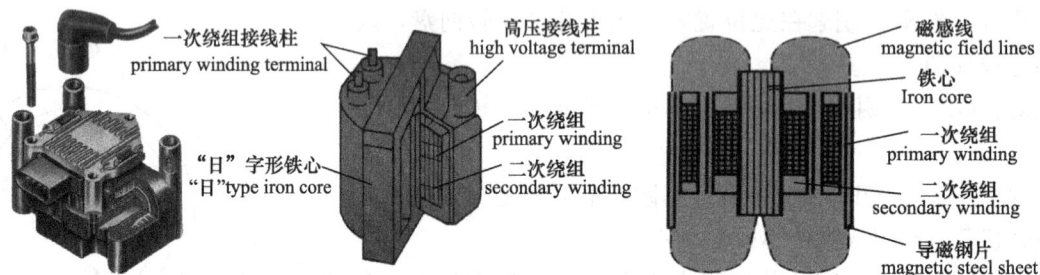

图 5.1.8 闭磁路式点火线圈结构图
Figure 5.1.8 The structure of closed magnetic circuit type ignition coil

5. 直流电动机(DC motor)

直流电动机是利用磁场的相互作用将电能转化成机械能，在磁场内通电导线受到磁场力的作用而产生移动的倾向。

DC motor uses the interaction of magnetic field to convert electrical energy into mechanical energy. In the magnetic field, the electrified conductor is affected by magnetic field force and tends to move.

直流电动机的原理如图 5.1.9 所示，在磁场中放置一个线圈，线圈的两点分别与两片换向片连接，两只电刷分别与两片换向片接触，并与蓄电池的正极或负极接通。

The principle of DC motor is as shown in the Figure 5.1.9. A coil is placed in the magnetic field. The two points of the coil are connected with two commutators respectively. The two brushes are in contact with two commutators respectively, and are connected with the positive or negative poles of the battery.

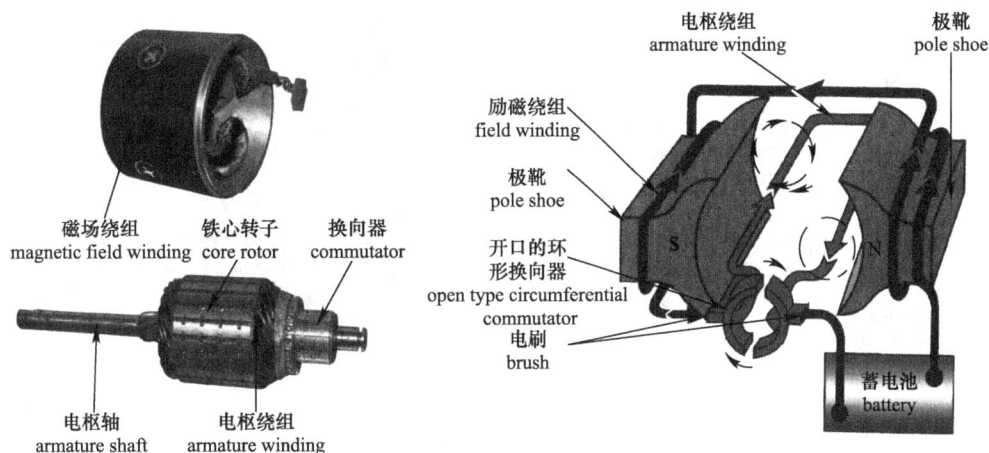

图 5.1.9　直流电动机

Figure 5.1.9　DC motor

1.2　汽车电器系统的供电设备(Power supply equipment for automotive electrical system)

蓄电池和发电机是汽车上的两大电源。发电机是主要电源,在正常工作时,对除起动机以外的所有用电器供电,并向蓄电池充电。现代汽车上普遍使用三相交流发电机,利用硅二极管组成的整流器,把定子绕组产生的三相交流电整流成直流电(图 5.1.10)。

Batteries and generators are two major power sources in automobiles. Generator is the main power supply. In normal operation, it not only supplies power to all electrical appliances except starter, but also charges batteries. Three-phase alternator is widely used in modern automobiles. The rectifier composed of silicon diodes rectifies the three-phase alternating current generated by stator winding into direct current.

1.2.1　蓄电池(Battery)

汽车蓄电池是一种储能装置,是低压直流电源,它是一种可逆直流电源,在汽车上与发电机并联。轿车一般使用电压 12V 的蓄电池。

Automotive battery is a kind of energy storage device, low-voltage DC power sources, it is a reversible DC power supply, in parallel with the generator on the car. Cars generally use 12 V batteries.

(1)蓄电池的作用 (The role of batteries)

1)发动机起动时,向起动机和点火系统供电。

2)发电机不发电或电压较低时,向用电设备供电。

图 5.1.10　汽车电源系统

Figure 5.1.10　Automobile power system

3)当用电设备同时接入较多使得发电机超载时,协助发电机供电。

4)当发电机的端电压高于蓄电池的电动势时,它可将电能转变为化学能储存起来(即充电)。

1) When the engine starts, it supplies power to the starter and ignition system.

2) When the generator does not generate electricity or the voltage is low, it supplies power to the electric equipment.

3) Assist the generator to supply power when more electrical equipment is connected at the same time, which results in overload of the generator.

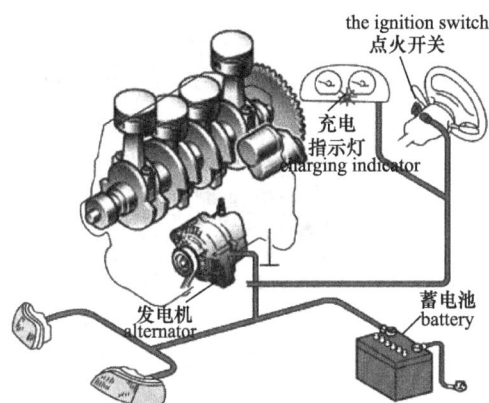

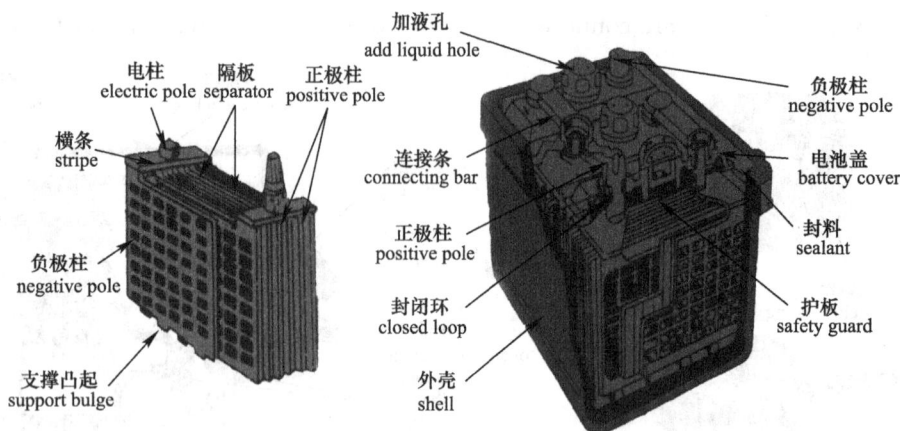

图 5.1.11　蓄电池

Figure 5.1.11　Battery

4) When the terminal voltage of the generator is higher than the electromotive force of the battery, it can convert the electric energy into chemical energy for storage (charging).

（2）蓄电池的组成（Composition of battery）

蓄电池一般由外壳、盖板、极板组、电解液、隔板与桩头等组成。如图 5.1.12 所示。

Batteries are generally composed of shell, cover plate, plate group, electrolyte, separator and pile head. As shown in the Figure 5.1.12.

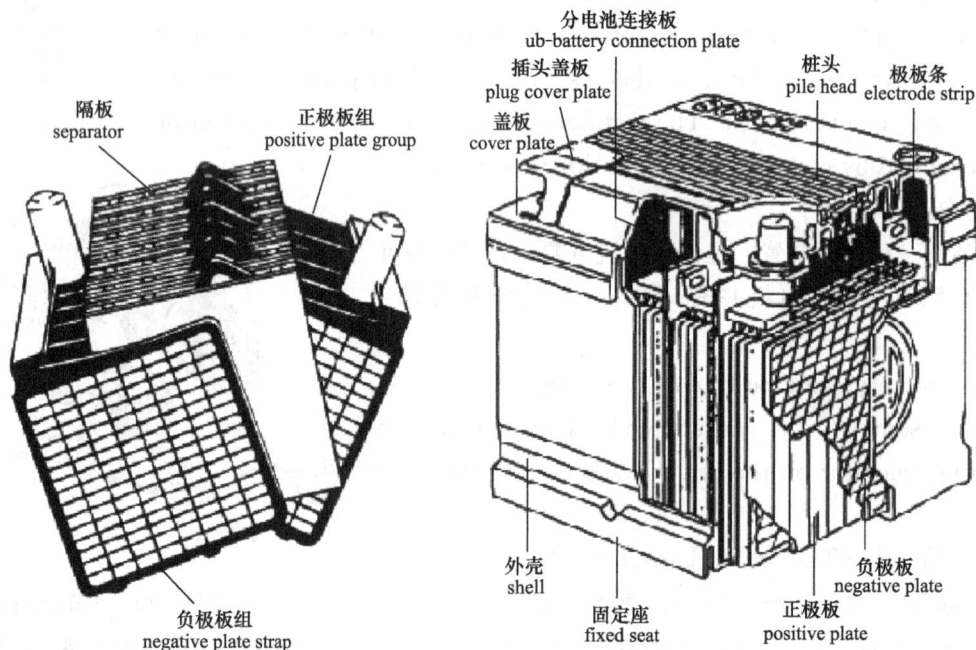

图 5.1.12　蓄电池的组成

Figure 5.1.12　Composition of battery

1）极板组（Plate group）

正极板是将红铅粉（Pb_3O_4）以稀硫酸调成糊状，加入硫酸铵作为胶合剂，涂在栅架（铅（Pb）和 5%～12% 的锑（Sb）制成）上，干燥后形成的。负极板是将黄铅粉（PbO）以稀硫酸调成糊状，加入硫酸钡或硫酸镁作为膨胀剂，涂在栅架上，干燥形成的。

The positive plate is made by mixing red lead powder (Pb_3O_4) with dilute sulfuric acid into paste, adding ammonium sulfate as cementing agent, and coating it on grid (lead Pb and antimony Sb of 5%~12%). It is formed after drying. The negative plate is formed by mixing yellow lead powder (PbO) with dilute sulfuric acid into paste, adding barium sulfate or magnesium sulfate as expansion agent, coating on the grid and drying.

2）电解液（Electrolyte）

蓄电池中的电解液，是以蒸馏水或精制水与硫酸配合而成的稀硫酸，一般密度为 $1.260 \sim 1.280 \mathrm{g/cm^3}$，并保持高出极板 $10 \sim 12 \mathrm{mm}$。

The electrolyte in the battery is dilute sulfuric acid, which is composed of distilled water or refined water and sulfuric acid. Its general density is $1.260 \text{-} 1.280 \mathrm{g/cm^3}$, and it keeps 10-12mm higher than the plate.

（3）蓄电池的工作原理（The working principle of storage battery）

铅蓄电池内的阳极（PbO_2）及阴极（Pb）浸到电解液（稀硫酸）中，两极间会产生 2V 的电力，这是根据铅蓄电池原理，经由充放电，则阴阳极及电解液即会发生如下的变化。

The anode (PbO_2) and cathode (Pb) in lead-acid batteries are immersed in electrolyte (dilute sulphuric acid), which generates 2V electric power between the two poles. According to the principle of lead-acid batteries, the cathode, anode and electrolyte will undergo the following changes through charging and discharging.

1）放电中的化学变化（Chemical changes in discharge）

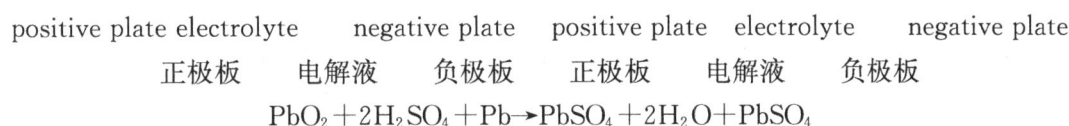

positive plate electrolyte　　negative plate　　positive plate　　electrolyte　　negative plate

正极板　　电解液　　负极板　　正极板　　电解液　　负极板

$$PbO_2 + 2H_2SO_4 + Pb \rightarrow PbSO_4 + 2H_2O + PbSO_4$$

2）充电中的化学变化（Chemical changes in charging）

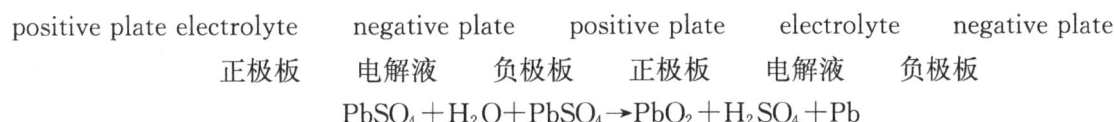

positive plate electrolyte　　negative plate　　positive plate　　electrolyte　　negative plate

正极板　　电解液　　负极板　　正极板　　电解液　　负极板

$$PbSO_4 + H_2O + PbSO_4 \rightarrow PbO_2 + H_2SO_4 + Pb$$

（4）蓄电池的容量与型号（Capacity and type of battery）

蓄电池型号的表示方法及含义　　　　　　　　　　　表 5.1.1

第一部分	串联的单格电池数		数字
第二部分	蓄电池的类型		Q—启动型蓄电池；T—拖动型蓄电池
	特征代号		A—干荷电式；W—免维护型；J—胶体电解液
第三部分	蓄电池的额定容量和特殊性能		数字，单位为 A·h（安培·小时），特殊性能用字母表示

the Expression Method and Meaning of Battery Model　　　　　　**Table 5.1.1**

Part Ⅰ	Number of single cell batteries in series		number
Part Ⅱ	Types of Batteries		Q-Start-up battery；T-Traction battery
	Feature code		A—Dry charge potential；W—Maintenance free；J— Gel electrolyte
Part Ⅲ	Rated Capacity and Special Performance of Batteries		Number, unit：A·h，Special properties are represented by letters

下面以型号"6-QAW-100"为例来说明蓄电池型号的表示方法及含义。

The following is an example of model "6-QAW-100" to illustrate the expression method and meaning of battery model.

第一部分：表示串联的单格电池数，用阿拉伯数字表示。其额定电压为这个数字的两倍。

Part Ⅰ：Indicate the number of single cell batteries in series, expressed in Arabic numerals. Its rated voltage is twice that.

第二部分：表示蓄电池的类型和特征，用两个汉语拼音字母表示。一般第一个字母是 Q，表示起动型蓄电池。第二个字母表示蓄电池的特征代号，如：A——干荷电式，W——免维护型，J——胶体电解液等。

Part Ⅱ：The types and characteristics of storage batteries, which are expressed by two Chinese phonetic alphabets. Generally, the first letter is Q, which means starting battery. The second letter denotes the characteristic code of the battery, such as A - dry charge type, W - maintenance free type, J - colloidal electrolyte, etc.

第三部分：表示蓄电池的额定容量和特殊性能，我国目前采用 20h 放电率的额定容量，单位是 A·h（安培·小时），用数字表示，特殊性能用字母表示。

Part Ⅲ：The rated capacity and special performance of storage battery are expressed. At present, the rated capacity of 20h discharge rate is adopted in our country. The unit is A. h (ampere. hour). It is expressed by numbers, and the special performance is expressed by letters.

因此"6-QAW-100"表示由 6 个单格电池串联而成，额定电压 12V，额定容量为 100A·h 的起动型干电荷免维护蓄电池。

Therefore, "6-QAW-100" means a start-up dry-charge maintenance-free battery with a rated voltage of 12V and a rated capacity of 100A·h, which consists of six cells in series.

1.2.2 发电机（Power generation）

启动发动机时需利用蓄电池供应启动机及点火系统等各种电器所需的电流。发动机启动后，必须由充电装置来提供点火系及其他电器的用电，并补充蓄电池在启动发动机时所消耗的电能，如此发动机才能维持运转，熄火后才能再起动。

When starting the engine, it is necessary to use the battery to supply the current needed by various electrical appliances such as the starter and the ignition system. After starting the engine, the charging device must supply power for the ignition system and other electrical appliances, and supplement the energy consumed by the battery when starting the engine, so that the engine can maintain operation and start again after flameout.

（1）交流发电机的功用（The functions of alternators）

发电机是汽车的主要电源，其功用是在发动机正常运转时（怠速以上），向所有用电设备（起动机除外）供电，同时向蓄电池充电。

Generator is the main power supply for automobiles. Its function is to supply power to all electrical equipment (except starter) when the engine is running normally (idle speed above), and charge the battery at the same time.

（2）交流发电机的分类（Classification of alternators）

按照调节器是否单独安装分为：

1）普通硅整流发电机：调节器单独安装，多用于中低档车型，如解放 CA1092 等。

2）整体式硅整流发电机：调节器安装于发电机内部，广泛用于中高档车型，如奥迪轿车。

Depending on whether the regulator is installed separately：

1）Ordinary silicon rectifier generator：regulator installed separately, mostly for medium and low-grade vehicles, such asJiefang CA1092, etc.

2）Integral silicon rectifier generator：The regulator is installed inside the generator and is widely used in medium and high-grade vehicles, such as Audi cars.

（3）交流发电机的组成（Composition of alternator）

一般交流发电机由转子、定子、整流器、端盖和电刷总成和调节器等组成。

The general alternator consists of rotor, stator, rectifier, end cover, brush assembly and regulator, etc.

1) 转子（Rotor）

转子由转子轴、励磁绕组、两块爪形磁极、滑环等组成。它的作用是当通过电刷给励磁绕组供电时，励磁绕组产生磁场。其电器符号一般用电磁线圈加文字标注表达（图 5.1.14）。

The rotor consists of a rotor shaft, an excitation winding, two claw-shaped poles and a sliding ring. Its function is when the excitation winding is powered by a brush, the excitation winding generates a magnetic field. Its electrical symbols are usually expressed by electromagnetic coils and text labels (Fig. 5.1.14).

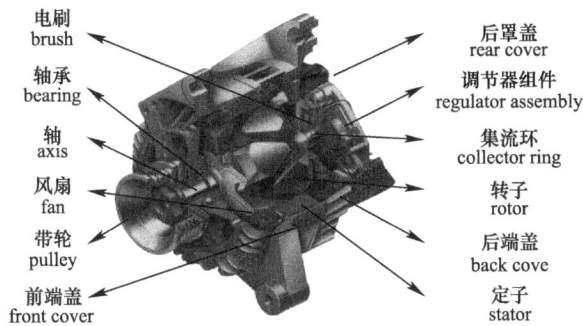

图 5.1.13　交流发电机

Figure 5.1.13　Composition of alternator

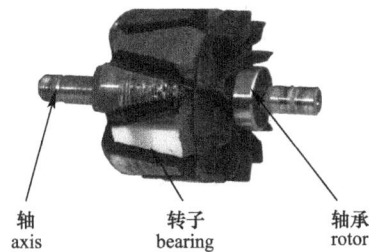

图 5.1.14　转子

Figure 5.1.14　Rotor

2) 定子（Stator）

定子又叫电枢，由铁心和三相绕组组成，其功用是产生感应电动势。定子绕组有星形连接和三角形连接两种形式。在星形连接形式中，三相绕组的公共接点称为中性点，一般用"N"表示（图 5.1.15）。

The stator, also known as armature, is composed of iron core and three-phase windings. Its function is to generate inductive electromotive force. There are two types of stator windings: star connection and triangular connection. In the form of star connection, the common contact of three-phase winding is called neutral point, which is generally expressed as "N" (Fig. 5.1.15).

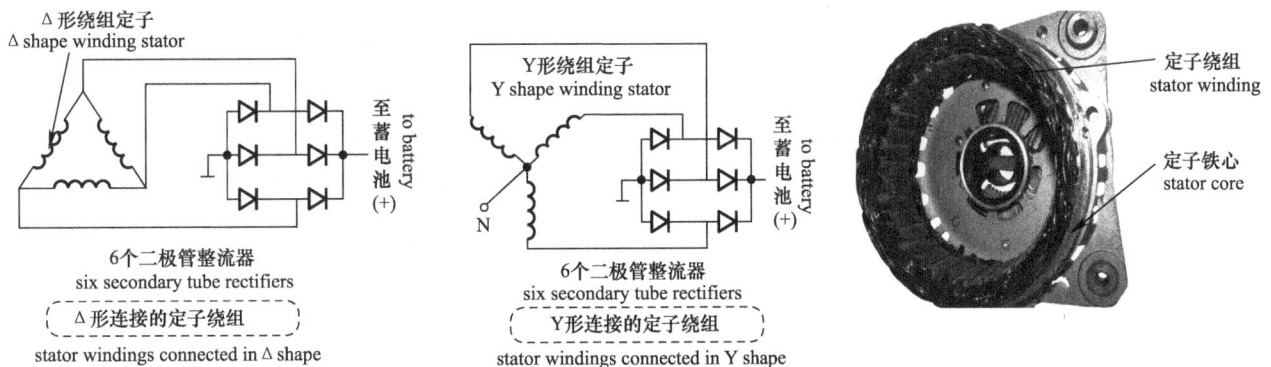

图 5.1.15　定子

Figure 5.1.15　Stator

3) 整流器（Rectifier）

整流器的功用是将发电机定子绕组产生的交流电变换为直流电。一般由 6 只整流硅二极管和安装二极管的散热板组成。目前国内外采用的硅整流发电机均为负极搭铁（图 5.1.16）。

The function of rectifier is to convert alternating current generated by generator stator winding into direct current. Generally, it consists of six rectifier silicon diodes and heat sink plates with diodes installed. At present, all silicon rectifier generators used at home and abroad are negative pole mounted iron(Fig. 5.1.16).

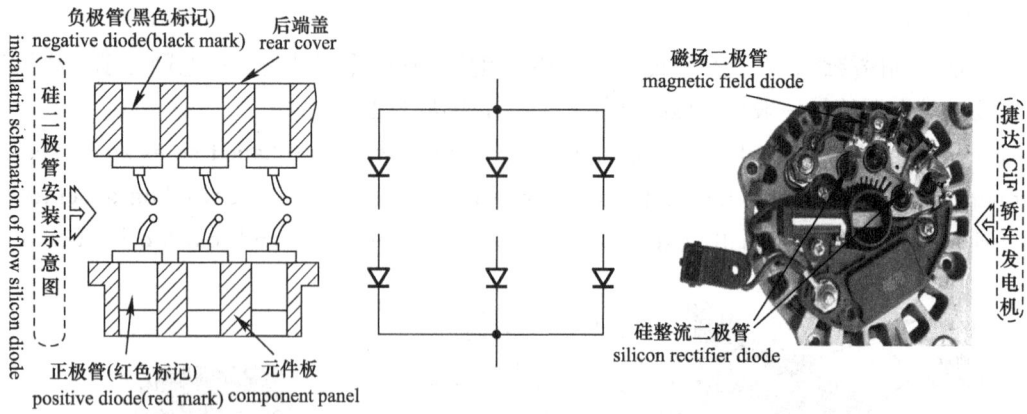

图 5.1.16　整流器

Figure 5.1.16　Rectifier

4）端盖和电刷总成（End cap and brush assembly）

前后端盖均由铝合金压铸或砂模铸造而成，这是因为铝合金为非导磁性材料，可减少磁化并具有轻便、散热性能良好的优点。

电刷总成由两只电刷、电刷弹簧和电刷架组成。电刷装在电刷架的孔内，借电刷弹簧的压力与转子总成上的滑环保持接触，用于给转子绕组提供磁场电流（图 5.1.17）。

The front and rear end caps are made of aluminium alloy by die casting or sand casting. This is because a-luminium alloy is a non-magnetic material, which can reduce magnetization and has the advantages of light weight and good heat dissipation.

The brush assembly consists of two brushes, a brush spring and a brush holder. The brush is mounted in the hole of the brush holder, and contacts the slip ring of the rotor assembly by the pressure of the brush spring, which is used to provide the magnetic field current to the rotor winding (Fig. 5.1.17).

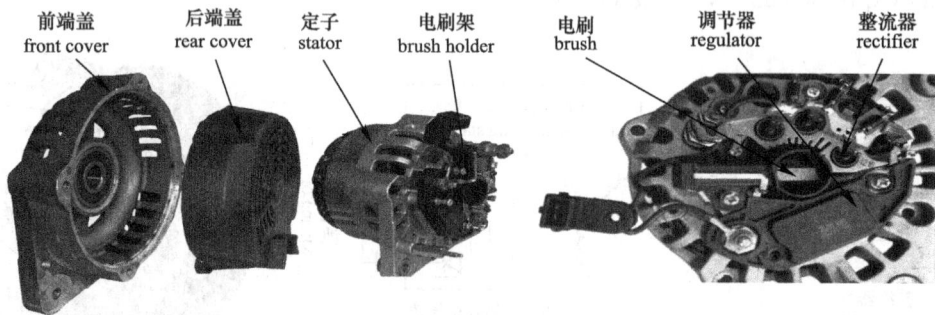

图 5.1.17　电刷总成

Figure 5.1.17　The brush assembly

5）电子调节器（Electronic regulator）

电子调节器是利用晶体三极管的开关特性，使磁场电路接通和断开来调节磁场绕组的平均电流。电子式电压调节器利用三极管的开关特性，在发电机转速变化时，通过改变励磁绕组电路的接通和断开的时间比来调节励磁电路的平均电流。各种电子式电压调节器的工作原理基本相同（图 5.1.18）。

The electronic regulator uses the switching characteristics of crystal triode to adjust the average current of magnetic field winding by switching on and off the magnetic field circuit. Electronic Voltage Regulator who utilizing the switching characteristics of the transistor, When the generator speed changes, the average current of the excitation circuit is adjusted by changing the time ratio of turn-on and turn-off of the excitation winding circuit. The working principle of various electronic voltage regulators is basically the same(Fig. 5. 1. 18).

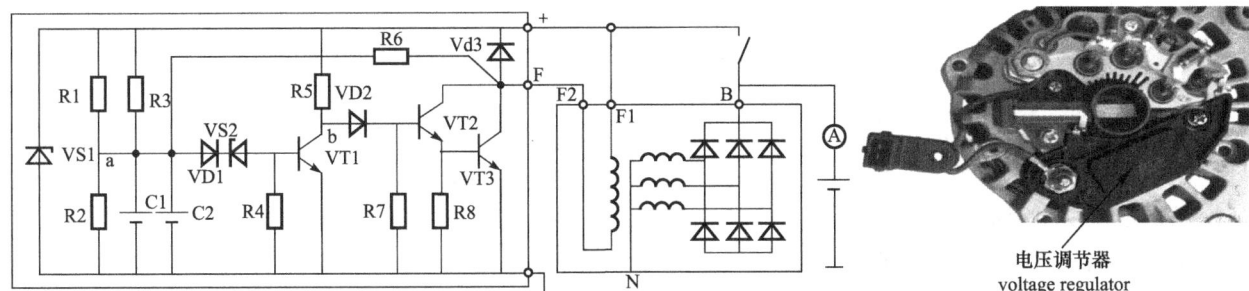

图 5. 1. 18　电子调节器

Figure 5. 1. 18　Electronic regulator

（4）交流发电机的工作原理（Working principle of AC generator）

1）工作原理（Working principle）

随着发电机三相定子绕组导线不断地切割转子爪极的旋转磁场而输出三相感应电动势。

As the three-phase stator winding wire of the generator continuously cuts the rotating magnetic field of the rotor claw pole，the three-phase induction electromotive force is output.

2）整流过程（Rectification process）

整流器用来将三相定子绕组中产生的三相交流电动势整流为直流电。整流器由 6 个硅二极管组成三相桥式全波整流电路。

The rectifier is used to rectify the three-phase AC electromotive force generated in the three-phase stator winding into direct current. The rectifier consists of six silicon diodes and a three-phase bridge full-wave rectifier circuit.

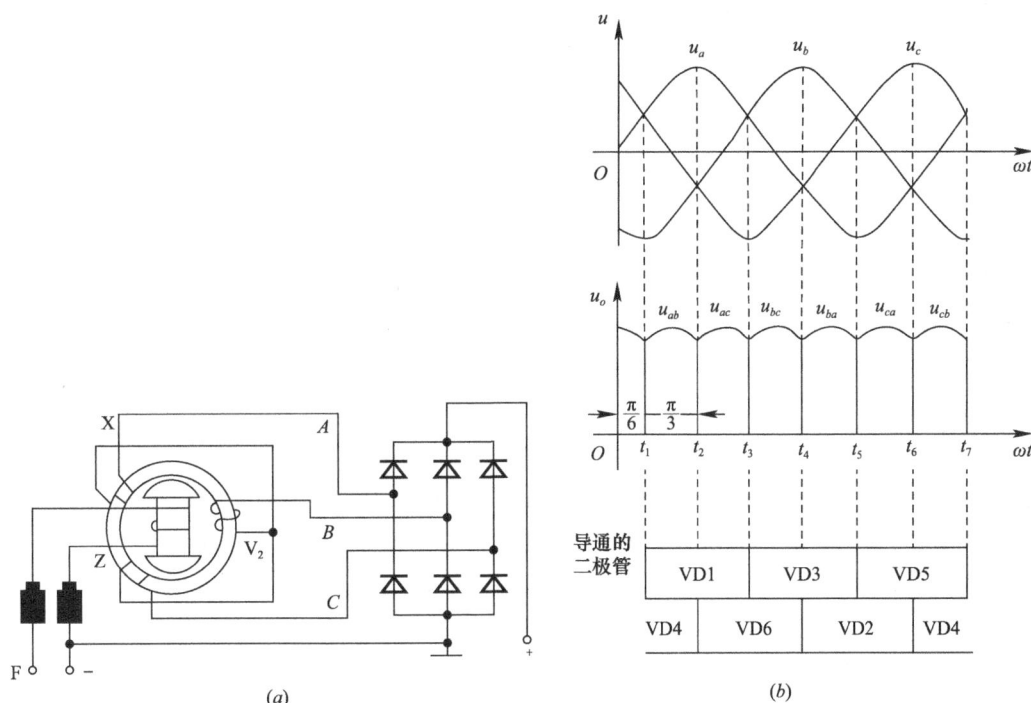

图 5. 1. 19　整流过程

Figure 5. 1. 19　Rectification process

（a）交流发电机工作原理（working principle of alternator）；

（b）三相桥式整流电路的电压波形（voltage waveform of three-phase bridge rectifier circuit）

思考与练习

Reflection and Exercises

1. 汽车电气的系统的特点是什么？

2. 继电器的工作原理是什么？

3. 蓄电池及发电机的工作原理是什么？

4. 交流发电机的组成和工作原理是什么？

1. What are the characteristics of automobile electrical system?

2. What is the working principle of the relay?

3. What is the working principle of battery and generator?

4. What is the composition and working principle of the alternator?

任务二　主要电气设备

Task 2　Main Electrical Equipment

教学目标

1. 知识目标

（1）能叙述汽车照明信号系统的作用与组成；

（2）能叙述汽车信号信号系统的作用与组成；

（3）能叙述仪表与报警装置的组成；

（4）能叙述暖风空调系统的工作过程；

（5）能叙述风窗刮水器与洗涤器的工作过程；

（6）能叙述中控门锁与电动座椅的工作过程。

2. 能力目标

（1）能掌握汽车电气系统用电设备的功能；

（2）能掌握汽车电气设备的组成。

3. 情感和素养目标

（1）培养学生团结协作、踏实、诚实、苦干的素质；

（2）培养学生安全用电意识，严格执行安全用电操作规范的能力。

Teaching objectives

1. Knowledge objectives

（1）The function and composition of automobile lighting signal system can be described；

（2）The function and composition of automobile signal system can be described；

（3）Describe the composition of instruments and alarm devices；

（4）Describe the working process of the heating air conditioning system；

（5）Describe the working process of windshield wipers and scrubbers；

（6）Describe the working process of the central control door lock and the power seat.

2. Competence objectives

（1）To be able to master the functions of electrical equipment in automotive electrical system；

（2）Be able to master the composition of automotive electrical equipment.

3. Emotion and quality goals

(1) Cultivate students′ quality of being united, cooperative, practical, honest and hard-working;

(2) Cultivate students′ awareness to use electricity safely and the ability to follow the operation norms of electricity use.

2.1 照明系统(Lighting system)

照明系统由电源、照明装置及其控制部分等组成。控制部分包括各种灯光开关、继电器等。照明装置包括车外照明、车内照明和工作照明三部分:

(1) 车外照明装置包括:前照灯、雾灯、倒车灯、牌照灯等。

(2) 车内照明装置包括:仪表灯、顶灯、阅读灯等。

(3) 工作照明装置包括:行李箱灯、发动机罩灯等。

汽车灯光的分类与组成 The Classification and Composition of Vehicle Lighting

The lighting system is composed of power supply, lighting device and its control part. The control part includes various light switches, relays and so on. The illumination device includes three parts: outside illumination, inside illumination and working illumination.

(1) Outside lighting devices include headlamp, fog lamp, reversing lamp, license plate lamp, etc.

(2) The interior lighting device includes instrument lamp, ceiling lamp, reading lamp, etc.

(3) Working lighting devices include trunk lamp, engine hood lamp, etc.

1. 前照灯(Headlights)

汽车在夜间,尤其在夜间高速行驶时,照明是必不可少的。汽车前照灯有近光、远光、闪光(会车)三种工作模式,在城市复杂交通路况行驶时采用近光模式,要求照射距离短、范围广、防眩目,实现驾驶人视线广阔的要求,便于其处理突发状况;在高速行驶时采用远光模式,要求明亮、照射距离远,150~200m 甚至更远;闪光模式是在提醒前方的车辆或行人被超越或避让。前照灯的类型有:

Lighting is indispensable for automobiles at night, especially when driving at high speed at night. There are three working modes of automobile headlamp: near-light, far-light and flash. Near-light mode is used when driving in complex urban traffic conditions. It requires short lighting distance, wide range and anti-glare, which meets the requirement of wide sight of drivers and is convenient for dealing with emergencies. Far-light mode is used when driving at high speed. It is required to be bright and to have a long irradiation distance of 150-200 m or more. Flash mode is to remind the vehicle or pedestrian ahead to be surpassed or avoided. Type of headlamp have:

(1) 封闭式前照灯 (Closed headlamp)

在这种类型中,灯泡、反光镜和灯罩制为一体。

In this type, the bulb, the reflector and the lampshade are integrated.

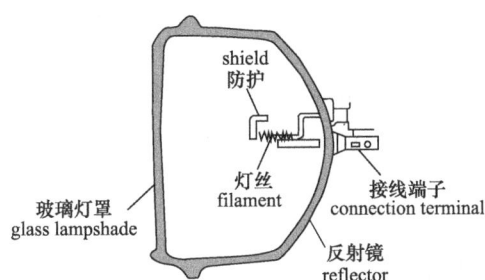

图 5.2.1 封闭式前照灯结构

Figure 5.2.1 Closed headlamp structure

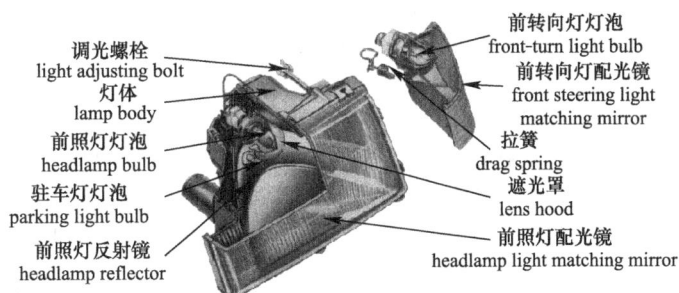

图 5.2.2 组合前照灯结构图

Figure 5.2.2 Structural chart of combination headlamp

（2）半封闭式前照灯（Semi-enclosed headlamp）

在这种类型中，灯泡可单独更换，分为常规型、多反射镜式、投射式等。

1）常规型前照灯。这是一种可替换灯泡的形式，使用普通白炽灯和卤素灯两种形式的前照灯。

2）多反射镜式前照灯。它有一个无色灯罩和形状复杂（混合抛物线形状）的反光镜。

3）投射式前照灯。这种前照灯能够通过玻璃透镜将灯泡发出的光汇聚到一个小的区域来有效利用光源。

In this type, the bulb can be replaced separately, which can be divided into conventional type, multi-reflector type, projection type, etc.

1）Conventional headlamp. This is a form of replaceable light bulb, using two forms of headlamp, common incandescent lamp and halogen lamp.

2）Multi-reflector headlamp. It has a colorless lampshade and a complex (mixed parabolic shape) reflector.

3）Projective headlamp. The headlamp can focus the light emitted by the bulb into a small area through a glass lens to achieve high light efficiency.

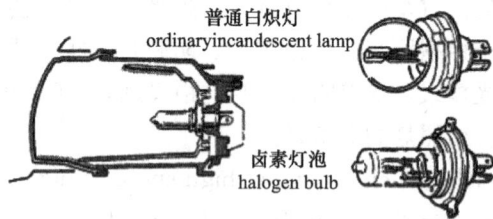

图 5.2.3　常规型半封闭前照灯

Figure 5.2.3　Conventional semi-enclosed headlamp

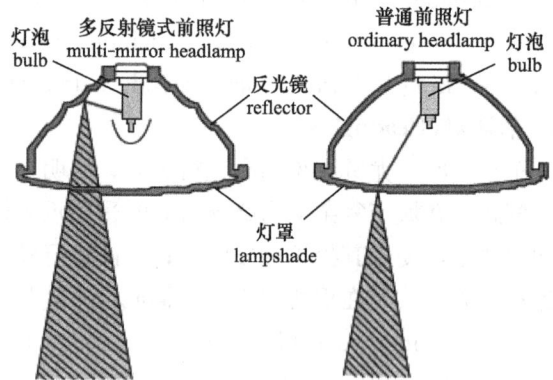

图 5.2.4　多反射镜式前照灯

Figure 5.2.4　Multi-reflector headlamp

2. 雾灯（Fog lamps）

采用黄色灯泡，其穿透功能好，雾天用来照明道路和发出警示。

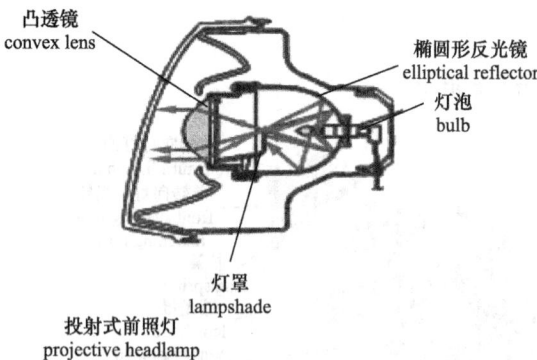

图 5.2.5　投射式前照灯

Figure 5.2.5　Projective headlamp

Fog lamp uses yellow light bulb with good penetration function to illuminate road and give warning in fog.

3. 牌照灯（License plate lamp）

装在汽车尾部用以照明牌照，并作为汽车尾部的灯光标志。桑塔纳轿车的牌照灯有两只，受车灯开关控制。

It is installed at the rear of the car to illuminate the license plate and as a light sign at the rear of the car. There are two license plate lamps for Santana, which are controlled by the lamp switch.

4. 行李箱灯（Luggage light）

行李箱灯在夜间行李箱门打开时照亮行李箱，桑塔纳轿车的行李箱灯由车灯开关和行李箱灯门控开关共同控制。

Luggage light illuminates the suitcase when the suitcase door opens at night. The suitcase light of Santana car is controlled by both the light switch and the suitcase light gate control switch.

5. 顶灯（Ceiling lamp）

顶灯装于驾驶室顶部照明驾驶室，有的车辆顶灯还具有门灯的作用，当车门关闭不严时灯亮，提醒驾驶员注意。桑塔纳轿车的顶灯开关和门控开关共同控制。

The headlights are installed on the top of the cab to illuminate the cab. In some vehicles, the headlights also have the function of door lights. When the doors are not closed properly, the lights are on to remind drivers to pay attention. The top light switch and gate switch of Santana car are controlled together.

6. 车灯开关（Car light switch）

车灯开关用来控制前照灯、雾灯、仪表灯、顶灯等电路。常见的灯开关有拉杆式、摇转式、组合式。在桑塔纳轿车的转向柱上装有一套，包括点火开关、前风窗刮水及清洗开关、转向灯开关及变光开关的组合开关，组合开关结构如图5.2.6所示。

The car lamp switch is used to control the circuit of headlamp, fog lamp, instrument lamp, top lamp, etc. Common light switches are pull rod type, swing type and combination type. The steering column of Santana car is equipped with a set of combined switches, including ignition switch, front windshield wiping and cleaning switch, steering light switch and dimmer switch. The combined switch structure is shown in the Figure 5.2.6.

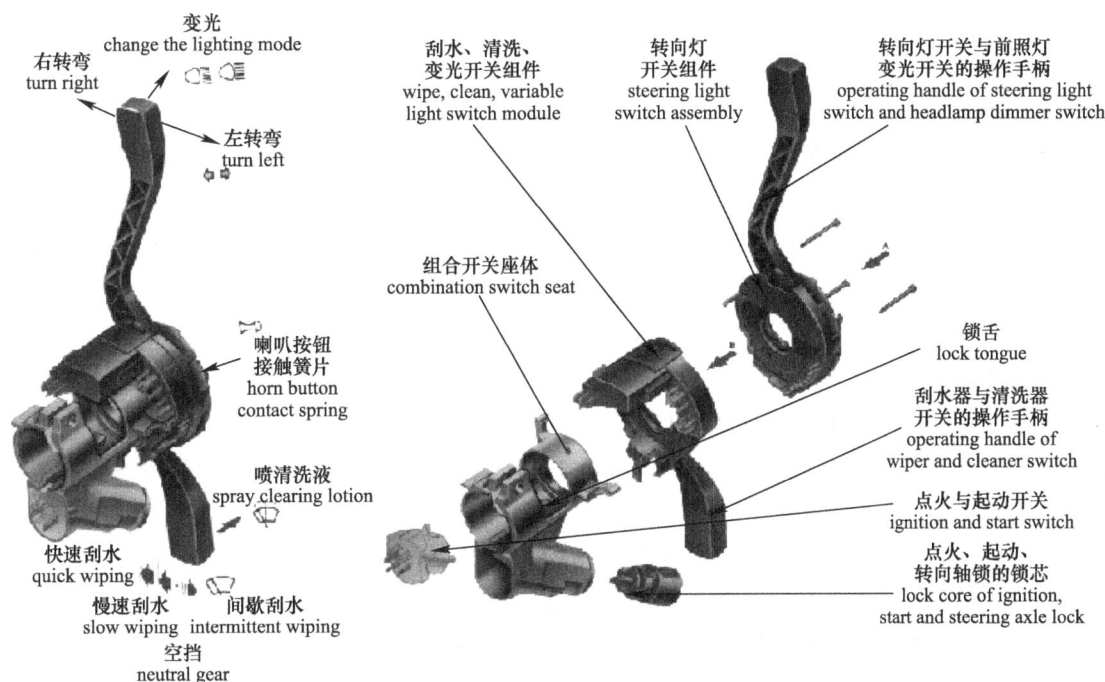

图 5.2.6　车灯开关

Figure 5.2.6　Car light switch

2.2　信号系统（Signal system）

汽车的信号系统主要包括各种信号灯和喇叭。

灯光信号是用来告知其他车辆驾驶人和行人本车的行驶路线及状况，提醒其避让。灯光信号包括前示宽灯、制动灯、倒车灯、雾灯、电喇叭等。

The signal system of automobile mainly includes various kinds of signal lights and horns.

Lighting signals are used to inform drivers and pedestrians of other vehicles, the route and condition of the car, and to remind them to avoid. Lighting signals include the front width lights, brake lamp, reversing lamp, fog lamp, electric horn, etc.

1. 示宽灯及尾灯(Width lights and taillights)

示宽灯（或称小灯和尾灯）分别安置在车头和车尾侧面。前示宽灯颜色一般为黄色或白色，后示宽灯（尾灯）颜色为红色，夜间行驶打开示宽灯开关时，仪表灯、牌照灯等同时点亮，显示车辆的形状与位置，警示前后车辆。

Width lights (or small lights) and taillights are placed on the front and rear sides of the car respectively. The color of the front width lights is usually yellow or white. The color of the rear width lights (taillight) is red. When the switch of the width lights is turned on at night, the instrument light and license plate light are simultaneously lit to show the shape and position of the vehicle and to warn vehicles in front and behind.

2. 制动灯(Brake lights)

制动灯安装在车辆尾部，颜色为红色，车尾部两侧各设一个。后风窗玻璃上加装一高位制动灯，能更好地避免追尾事故的危险。随着灯光照明技术的发展，LED 制动灯已普遍使用。它不是普通的灯泡，而是由多个发光二极管连接在一起组成的。

The brake lamp is installed at the rear of the vehicle, the color is red, and there is one on each side of the rear. A high brake lamp installed on the rear windshield can better avoid the danger of rear-end collision. With the development of lighting technology, LED brake lamp has been widely used. It's not an ordinary light bulb, but is composed of several light-emitting diodes connected together.

3. 倒车灯(Reversing lights)

倒车灯安装在车辆尾部，颜色为白色。当变速器挂入倒挡时点亮，照明车身后方的视野，并提醒后方车辆、行人避让。

The reversing lamp is installed at the rear of the vehicle and the color is white. When the transmission is in reverse, the reversing lamp lights up and illuminates the vision behind the body to remind the rear vehicles and pedestrians to avoid.

4. 雾灯(Fog lamps)

雾灯安装在车辆头部和尾部，分为前雾灯和后雾灯。前雾灯为橙黄色，光波长，透雾性好。在雾天、雨天、尘埃弥漫的能见度低的天气情况下使用，能够明显改善道路照明情况。后雾灯为红色，提醒尾随车辆保持车距。

Fog lamp is installed in the head and tail of the vehicle, which is divided into front fog lamp and rear fog lamp. The color of the front fog lamp is orange and yellow. It has the characteristics of light wavelength and good fog permeability. The use of fog lamps in foggy, rainy and dusty weather with low visibility can significantly improve road lighting. The rear fog lamp is red, which reminds the following vehicles to keep their distance.

5. 转向及危险警报装置(Steering and danger alarm devices)

转向灯安装在车辆头部、尾部的左右两侧，以指示车辆的行驶趋势。为增强提醒效果，很多车型在车身两侧的倒车镜或车身上也装有转向灯。另外，在车辆紧急遇险状态时，打开危险警报装置，所有转向灯全部开始闪烁，提醒其他车辆避让。

The steering lights are installed on the left and right sides of the head and tail of the vehicle to indicate the driving trend of the vehicle. In order to enhance the reminder effect, many vehicles are equipped with steering lights on both sides of the body. In addition, when the vehicle is in emergency, turn on the danger alarm device, and all the turning lights start flashing to remind other vehicles to avoid.

6. 喇叭(Horn)

为了警告行人和其他车辆，以引起注意并保证安全，汽车上都装有喇叭。汽车喇叭按发音动力划分有气喇叭和电喇叭两种。气喇叭是利用气流使金属膜片振动产生声响，多用在具有压缩空气气源的载货汽车上。电喇叭使利用电磁力使金属膜片振动产生声响，广泛应用于各种类型的汽车。

电喇叭按有无触点可分为普通电喇叭和电子喇叭。

In order to warn pedestrians and other vehicles to attract attention and ensure safety, cars are equipped with horns. The power of automobile horn is divided into air horn and electric horn. Air horn is used in trucks with compressed air source to make metal diaphragm vibrate and produce sound. Electric horn makes use of electromagnetic force to make metal diaphragm vibration produce sound, which is widely used in various types of automobiles.

Electric horn with or without contact can be divided into ordinary electric horn and electronic horn.

(1) 普通电喇叭 (General electric horn)

当按下喇叭按钮时，电流通过喇叭线圈产生磁场，从而使山形铁芯吸下衔铁；同时触点断开，线圈的电磁力则消失，振动膜片在其自身的弹性和弹簧钢片的作用下，同衔铁一道返回原位，触点重新闭合，电路又重新接通。如此反复循环，膜片不断振动，从而发出一定频率的声波，共鸣盘与膜片刚性连接，目的是使膜片振动时发出的声音更加悦耳。

When the horn button is pressed, the current generates a magnetic field through the horn coil, which makes the hill-shaped iron core pull down the armature. At the same time, when the contact is disconnected, the electromagnetic force of the coil disappears. Under the action of its own elasticity and spring steel plate, the vibration diaphragm returns to its original position with the armature-track. The contacts are re-closed and the circuit is re-connected. In this way, the diaphragm oscillates continuously, thus generating a certain frequency of sound waves. The resonant disc is rigidly connected with the diaphragm in order to make the sound produced by the diaphragm more pleasant when it vibrates.

(2) 电子喇叭 (Electronic horn)

电子喇叭的结构如图 5.2.7 所示。电子喇叭发声原理与普通电喇叭相同，但其用晶体管开关电路替代普通电喇叭的触点。

The structure of the electronic horn is shown in the Figure 5.2.7. The principle of electronic horn is the same as the ordinary electric horn, but it uses transistor switching circuit to replace the contact of ordinary electric horn.

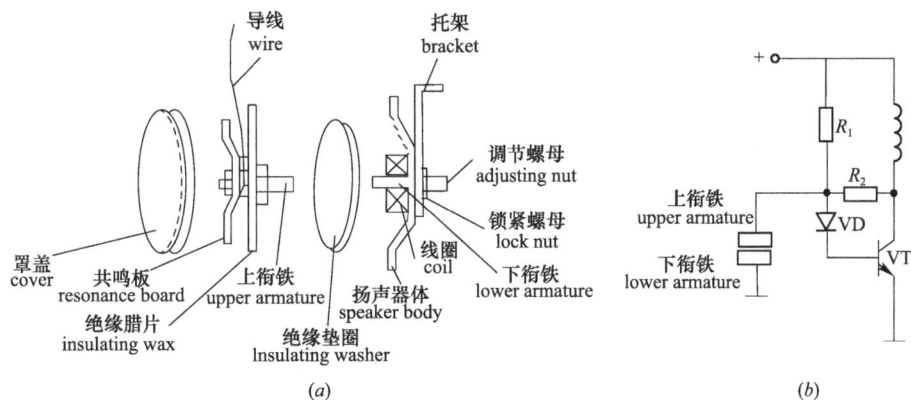

图 5.2.7 电子喇叭的结构与电路

Figure 5.2.7 Structure of Electronic Horn in Circuit

(a) 电子喇叭的结构(Structure and Circuit of Electronic Horn); (b) 电子喇叭电路(Electronic Horn Circuit)

2.3 仪表与报警装置(Instruments and alarm devices)
1. 汽车仪表的作用(The function of automotive instruments)

为了便于驾驶员随时了解汽车各个主要系统的工作情况，正确使用汽车，及时发现问题、采取措施，防止发生人身和机械事故，保证汽车可靠而安全的行驶，汽车上安装了一些仪表，用来反映汽车和发动机的一些重要运行状态参数的大小。

In order to facilitate drivers to keep abreast of the working conditions of the main automotive systems at any time, Correct use of automobiles, timely detection of problems, take measures to prevent personal and mechanical accidents, to ensure reliable and safe driving of automobiles, automobiles are equipped with some instruments to reflect the size of some important operating state parameters of automobiles and engines.

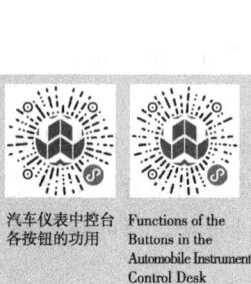

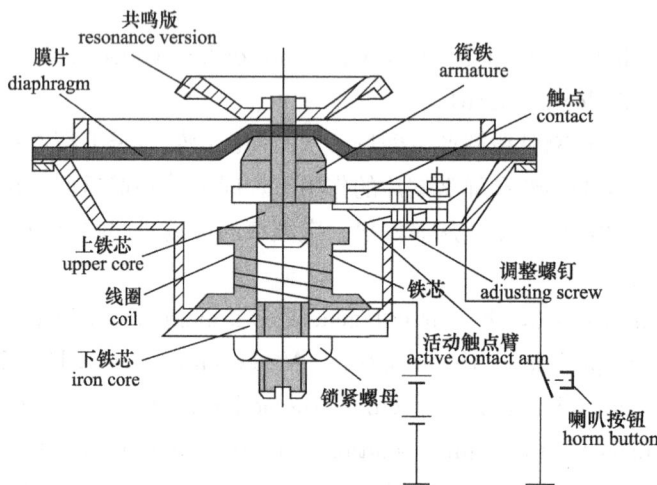

汽车仪表中控台各按钮的功用
Functions of the Buttons in the Automobile Instrument Control Desk

图 5.2.8 普通电喇叭结构
Figure 5.2.8 General electric horn structure

2. 汽车仪表的分类与特点(Classification and characteristics of automotive instruments)

汽车仪表按其安装方式可划分组合式与分装式两种。

按作用原理不同，指示表分为电热式（双金属片式）和电磁式两种。

汽车仪表按工作原理可划分机械式、电气式、模拟电路式和数字式等种类。

According to its installation mode, automobile instrument can be divided into two types: combined type and separate type. According to the principle of action, the indicator can be divided into two types: electrothermal (bimetallic) and electromagnetic. According to the working principle, automotive instruments can be divided into mechanical, electrical, analog and digital types.

3. 数字式仪表的组成(Composition of digital instruments)

当今主流汽车普遍使用数字式组合仪表。由仪表、警告灯、指示灯和行车电脑信息显示屏组成。

Nowadays, digital combination instrument is widely used in mainstream automobiles. It is composed of instrument, warning light, indicator light and computer information display screen.

（1）仪表 （Instrument）

常见的汽车仪表有机油压力表、发动机冷却液温度表、燃油表、车速里程表、发动机转速表等。

Common automotive instruments include oil pressure gauges, engine coolant thermometers, fuel meters, speedometers, engine speed meters, etc.

1）机油压力表（Oil pressure gauge）

机油压力表用来检测和显示发动机主油道的机油压力值，该装置由装在发动机主油道中或滤清器上的机油压力传感器和仪表板上的机油压力指示表组成。常用的电热式机油压力表配双金属片式机油压力传感器，电磁式机油压力表配可变电阻式机油压力传感器。

The oil pressure gauge is used to detect and display the oil pressure value of the main oil channel of the engine. The device consists of the oil pressure sensor installed in the main oil channel of the engine or on the filter and the oil pressure indicator on the dashboard. The commonly used electrothermal oil pressure gauge is equipped with bimetal sheet oil pressure sensor, and the electromagnetic oil pressure gauge is equipped with variable resistance oil pressure sensor.

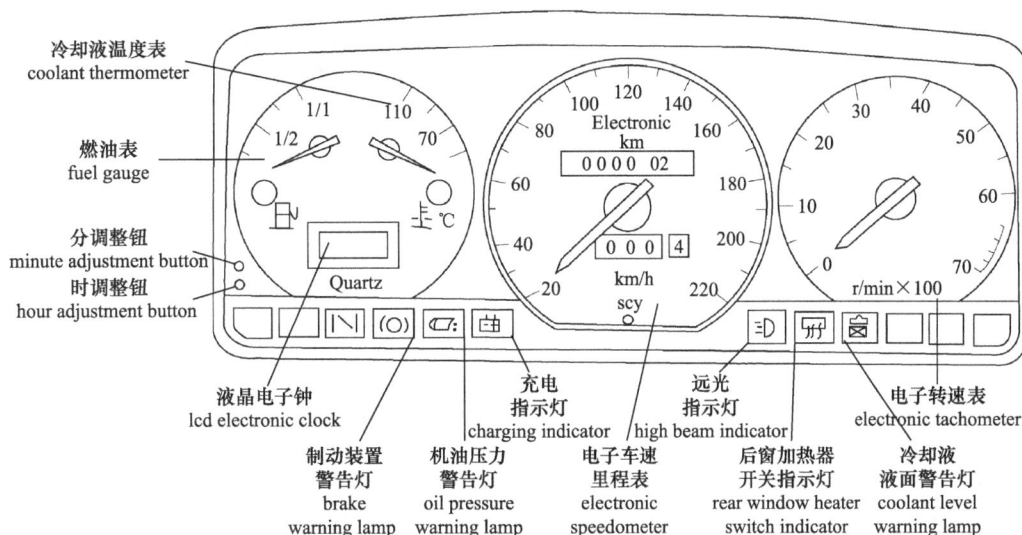

图 5.2.9　仪表
Figure 5.2.9　Instrument

① 电热式机油压力表与电热式机油压力传感器（Electrothermal oil pressure gauge and electrothermal oil pressure sensor）

当油压很低时，只要流过加热线圈较小的电流，温度略升高，触点就会分开。这样使触点打开的时间长，闭合的时间短，因而电路中电流的有效值小，使指示表中双金属片因温度较低而弯曲程度小，指针（图 5.2.10）向右偏移角度就小，即指示较低的油压值。

When the oil pressure is very low, as long as the current flowing through the heating coil is small, the temperature rises slightly, and the contacts will be separated. In this way, the contact opens for a long time and closes for a short time. Therefore, the current value in the circuit is small, which makes the bimetal sheet in the indicator less bent due to lower temperature, and the angle of the pointer shifting to the right is small, that is to say, indicating the lower oil pressure value (Figure 5.2.10).

当油压增高时，膜片向上拱曲，加在触点上的压力增大，双金属片向上弯曲程度增大，这样，只有在双金属片温度较高时，也就是要加热线圈通过较大的电流，经过较长的时间后，触点才能分开，而且当触点分开不久，双金属片稍一冷却触点又很快闭合。因此当油压高时，触点断开状态的时间缩短，频率增高，指针偏摆角度大，指向高油压值。

When the oil pressure increases, the diaphragm arches upward, the pressure added to the contact increases, and the upward bending degree of the bimetallic sheet increases. In this way, the contact can be separated only when the temperature of the bimetal sheet is higher, that is, when the heating coil passes through a larger current, after a longer period of time. And soon after the contacts are separated, when the bimetal

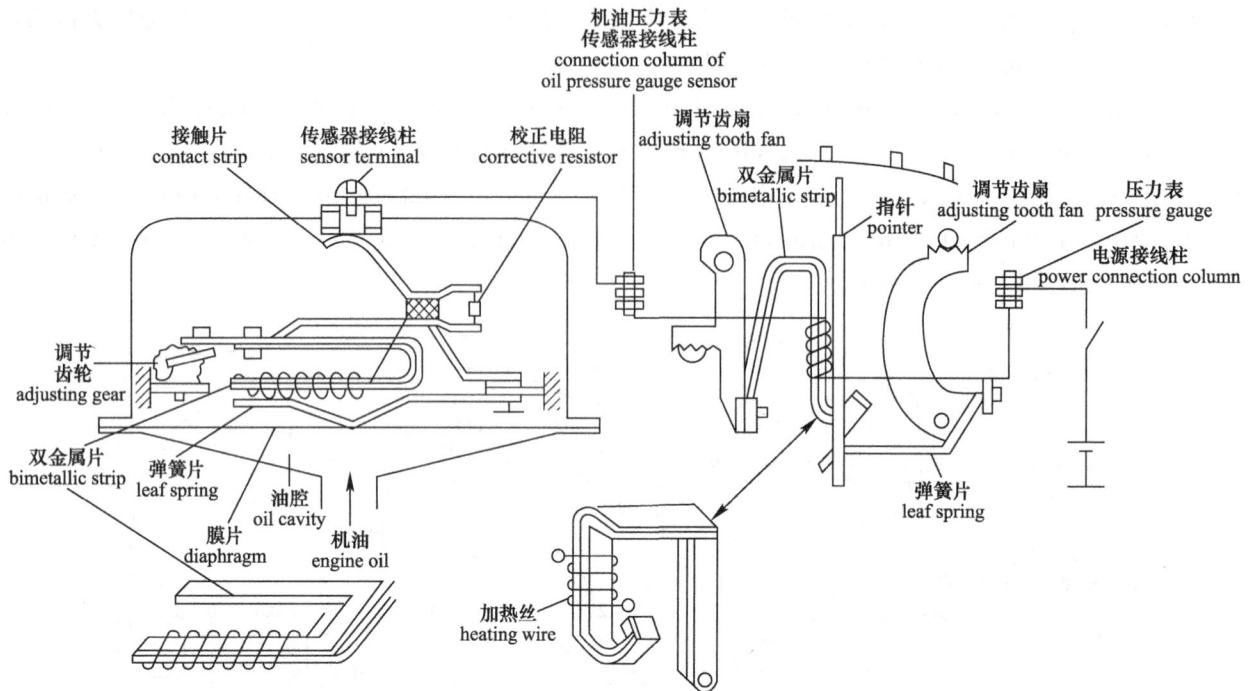

图 5.2.10　电热式机油压力表与电热式传感器

Figure 5.2.10　Electrothermal oil pressure gauge and electrothermal oil pressure sensor

sheet is cooled slightly, the contacts will close quickly. Therefore, when the oil pressure is high, the time of contact disconnection is shortened, the frequency is increased, and the angle of pointer swing is large, pointing to the high oil pressure value.

② 电磁式机油压力表与可变电阻式机油压力传感器（Electromagnetic oil pressure gauge and variable resistance oil pressure sensor）

当油压降低时，机油压力传感器的电阻值增大，线圈 L1 中的电流减小，线圈 L2 中的电流增大，转子带动指针随合成磁场的方向逆时针转动，指向低油压值；当油压升高时，传感器的电阻值减小，线圈 L1 中的电流增大，线圈 L2 中的电流减小，转子带动指针随合成磁场的方向顺时针转动，指向高油压值。

When oil pressure decreased, the resistance value of the oil pressure sensor increased. Then the current in coil L1 decreased, and the current in coil L2 increases. The rotor-driven pointer rotates counterclockwise with the direction of the synthetic magnetic field, pointing to the low oil pressure value. When the oil pressure increased, the resistance of the sensor decreases, then the current in coil L1 increased, and the current in coil L2 decreases. The rotor-driven pointer rotates clockwise along the direction of the synthetic magnetic field, pointing to the high oil pressure.

2）发动机冷却液温度表（Engine coolant thermometer）

冷却液温度表用来检测和显示发动机水套中冷却液的温度，以防因冷却液温度过高而使发动机过热。它由装在仪表板上的水温指示表和装在发动机气缸盖上水套的水温传感器两部分组成。

Coolant thermometer is used to detect and display the temperature of the coolant in the engine water jacket to prevent the engine from overheating due to the excessive temperature of the coolant. It consists of a water temperature indicator mounted on the dashboard and a water temperature sensor mounted on the water jacket of the engine cylinder head.

常用冷却液温度表有：电热式冷却液温度指示表配双金属片式传感器、电热式冷却液温度指示表配热敏电阻式传感器和电磁式冷却液温度指示表配热敏电阻式传感器三种形式。

Commonly used coolant thermometers are: electrothermal coolant temperature indicator with bimetal plate sensor, electrothermal coolant temperature indicator with thermistor sensor and electromagnetic coolant temperature indicator with thermistor sensor.

① 电热式冷却液温度表配双金属片式传感器 (Electrothermal coolant thermometer with bimetal plate sensor)

当冷却液温度较低时, 双金属片变形小, 触点压力大, 闭合时间长, 打开时间短, 电路中电流的平均值大, 该电流流过指示表加热线圈, 温度表的双金属片变形大, 指针偏摆角度大, 指向低温区域。高温反之。

When the coolant temperature is low, the deformation of bimetallic sheet is small, the contact pressure is high, the closing time is long, the opening time is short, and the average current in the circuit is large. The current flows through the heating coil of the indicator. The bimetallic sheet of the thermometer is deformed greatly, and the angle of the pointer is large, pointing to the low temperature region. On the contrary, it points to the high temperature zone.

② 电磁式冷却液温度表配热敏电阻式温度传感器 (Electromagnetic coolant thermometer with thermistor temperature sensor)

热敏电阻为负温度系数, 当水温较低时, 热敏电阻值大, 右线圈中电流变小, 磁场减弱, 合成磁场主要取决于左线圈, 使指针指在低温处。当冷却液温度升高时, 传感器的电阻减小, 右线圈中的电流增大, 磁场增强, 合成磁场偏移, 转子便带动指针转动指向高温。

Thermistor is negative temperature coefficient. When the water temperature is low, the value of thermistor is large, theelectrorheological change in the right coil is small, and the magnetic field is weakened. The synthetic magnetic field mainly depends on the left coil, which makes the pointer point at low temperature. When the coolant temperature increased, the resistance of the sensor was decreased, the current in the right coil increases, the magnetic field increases, and the synthetic magnetic field shifts. The rotor drives the pointer to turn to high temperature.

3) 燃油表 (Fuel gauge)

① 电磁式燃油表配可变电阻式传感器 (Electromagnetic fuel meter with variable resistance sensor)

当油箱无油时, 浮子下沉, 可变电阻上的滑片移至最右端, 可变电阻被短路, 右线圈也被短路, 左线圈的电流达最大值, 产生的电磁吸力最强, 吸引转子, 使指针停在最左面的 "0" 位。随着油箱中油量的增加, 浮子上浮, 带动滑片沿可变电阻滑动。可变电阻部分接入电路, 左线圈电流相应减小, 而右线圈中电流增大。转子在合成磁场的作用下向右偏转, 带动指针指示油箱中的燃油量。

When there is no oil in the tank, the float sinks, the slider on the variable resistance moves to the right end, the variable resistance is short-circuited, the right coil is short-circuited, the current of the left coil reaches the maximum value, the electromagnetic attraction is the strongest, attracting the rotor, so that the pointer stops at the "0" position on the left. With the increase of oil content in the tank, the float floats and drives the slider to slide along the variable resistance. When the variable resistance part was connected to the circuit, the current in the left coil decreased correspondingly, while the current in the right coil increases. The rotor deflects to the right under the action of the synthetic magnetic field, and drives the pointer to indicate the fuel quantity in the fuel tank.

② 动磁式燃油表配可变电阻式燃油量传感器 (Magneto-dynamic fuel meter with variable resistance fuel sensor)

③ 电热式燃油表配可变电阻式燃油量传感器 (Electric-thermal fuel meter with variable resistance fuel sensor)

当油箱无油时, 浮子下沉, 滑片处于可变电阻的最右端, 传感器的电阻全部串入电路中, 此时电路中电流最小, 燃油表加热线圈发热量小, 双金属片变形小, 带动指针指在 "0" 位。当油箱内油量增加时, 浮子上升，滑片向左移动，串入电路中的电阻减小，电路中的电流增大，燃油表加热线圈发热量大，双金属片变形增大，带动指针向右偏转。

When there is no oil in the tank, the float sinks, the slider is at the right end of the variable resistance, and the resistance of the sensor is all connected into the circuit. At this time, the current in the circuit is the smallest, the heating coil of the fuel meter has little heat, the deformation of the bimetal sheet is small, and the pointer is at the "0" position. When the oil volume in the tank increased, the float rises, the slider moves to the left, the resistance in the series circuit decreases, the current in the circuit increases, the heating coil of the fuel meter heats up, the deformation of the bimetallic sheet increases, and the pointer moves to the right.

④ 交叉线圈型燃油表配传感器（Cross-coil fuel meter with sensor）

表针与一磁性转子相连，在磁性转子的外面按 4 个方向绕上线圈，相邻两线圈之间的夹角为 90°。当线圈有电流通过时，4 个线圈在 4 个方向上产生磁场，合成为某一方向的磁场，使磁性转子转动至一定的位置。当电流发生变化时，合成磁场的方向也发生变化，从而使得磁性转子的转动位置发生变化。

The needle is connected with a magnetic rotor and coils are wound in four directions outside the magnetic rotor. The angle between the two adjacent coils is 90 degrees. When the coil passes through with current, four coils generate magnetic fields in four directions, which are synthesized into magnetic fields in a certain direction, so that the magnetic rotor rotates to a certain position. When the current changes, the direction of the synthetic magnetic field also changes, which makes the rotational position of the magnetic rotor change.

4）车速里程表（Speed odometer）

车速里程表是用来指示汽车行驶速度和累计行驶里程数的仪表。车速里程表有磁感应式、电子式两种类型。

Speed odometer is an instrument used to indicate the speed of a car and the cumulative mileage. Speed odometer has magnetic induction type and electronic type.

电子式车速里程表主要由车速传感器、电子电路、车速表和里程表四部分组成。

The electronic speedometer is mainly composed of four parts: speed sensor, electronic circuit, speedometer and odometer.

① 车速传感器（Vehicle speed sensor）

车速传感器由变速器驱动。它由一个舌簧开关和一个含有 4 对磁极的转子组成。变速器驱动转子旋转，转子每转一周，舌簧开关中的触点闭合、打开 8 次，产生 8 个脉冲信号，汽车每行驶 1km，车速传感器将输出 4127 个脉冲。

The speed sensor is driven by a transmission. It consists of a tongue spring switch and a rotor with four pairs of magnetic poles. The transmission drives the rotor to rotate. The contact points in the tongue spring switch are closed and opened eight times per revolution. Eight pulse signals are generated. The speed sensor will output 4127 pulses per km of the vehicle.

② 电子电路（Electronic circuits）

电子电路的作用是将车速传感器送来的电信号整形、触发，输出一个电流大小与车速成正比的电流信号。其基本组成主要包括稳压电路、单稳态触发电路、恒流源驱动电路、64 分频电路和功率放大电路

The function of the electronic circuit is to shape and trigger the electric signal sent by the speed sensor, and output a current signal whose magnitude is proportional to the speed of the vehicle. Its basic components include voltage stabilization circuit, monostable trigger circuit, constant current source drive circuit, 64-frequency divider circuit and power amplifier circuit.

③ 车速表（Speedometer）

车速表是一个电磁式电流表，当汽车以不同车速行驶时，与车速成正比的电流信号便驱动车速表指针偏

转，即可指示相应的车速。

Speedometer is an electromagnetic ammeter. When a car travels at different speeds, the current signal proportional to the speed drives the pointer of the speedometer to deflect, indicating the corresponding speed.

④ 里程表（Odometer）

里程表由一个步进电动机和六位数字的十进制数字轮组成。

The odometer consists of a stepping motor and a six-digit decimal digital wheel.

5）发动机转速表（Engine tachometer）

发动机转速表用于指示发动机的运转速度，电子式转速表获取转速信号有三种方式，即：取自点火系、发动机的转速传感器和发电机。

The engine tachometer is used to indicate the speed of the engine. There are three ways for the electronic tachometer to obtain the speed signal, obtained from ignition system, the engine speed sensor and the generator.

① 磁感应式电子转速表（Electromagnetic induction electronic tachometer）

② 电容器充放电式电子转速表（Capacitor charging and discharging electronic speed meter）

（2）警告灯（Warning lights）

警告灯在用来提醒驾驶人，系统发生故障或需要充电或需要维修，以确保行车安全。根据紧急情况或信息的优先等级，警告灯显示时使用红灯和黄灯。

常用的警告灯有：ABS 警告灯、制动液位警告灯、发动机故障指示灯、放电警告灯、座椅安全带警告灯、开门警告灯、安全气囊警告灯、燃油低位警告灯、机油低油压警告灯、燃油沉淀器警告灯（仅用于柴油机车辆）、电热塞警告灯（仅用于柴油机车辆）等。

Warning lights are used to warn drivers that the system is malfunctioning or needs to be recharged or repaired to ensure driving safety. According to the priority level of emergency or information, red and yellow lights are used when warning lights are displayed.

Commonly used warning lights are: ABS warning lamp, brake fluid level warning lamp, engine failure indicator lamp, discharge warning lamp, seat belt warning lamp, door warning lamp, airbag warning lamp, fuel low warning lamp, oil low pressure warning lamp, fuel precipitator warning lamp (only for diesel engine vehicles), electric plug warning lamp (only for diesel engine vehicles), etc.

（3）指示灯（Indicator lamp）

仪表盘上的指示灯点亮会告诉驾驶人，其操作的设备开始工作。

这些指示灯用蓝、绿和黄灯表示不同的含义。常用的指示灯有：转向信号灯、危险警告指示灯、自动变速器（AT）挡位指示灯、远光灯指示灯、轮胎气压异常指示灯、车身稳定系统指示灯和牵引力控制系统指示灯等。

The light on the dashboard tells the driver that the equipment it operates is working.

These lights use blue, green and yellow lights to indicate different meanings. Commonly used indicators are steering lights, danger warning lights, automatic transmission (AT) gear indicator lights, high-light indicator lights, tire pressure abnormal indicator lights, body stability system indicator lights and traction control system indicator lights.

4. 普通仪表构造与原理(Structure and principle of common instruments)

除了机械转鼓计数式里程表和磁感应式车速表外，其他传统仪表都是利用电流的热效应或磁场和电流（或磁场）之间的作用，通过指示表的机械指针和刻度盘将电流、电压、发动机转速及传感器输出的模拟信号直接显示出来。

In addition to mechanical drum counting odometer and magnetic induction speedometer, other traditional instruments use the thermal effect of current or the interaction between magnetic field and current (or magnetic field).

The analog signals of current, voltage, engine speed and sensor output are displayed directly by mechanical pointer and dial of indicator.

5. 报警指示装置(Alarm indicator)

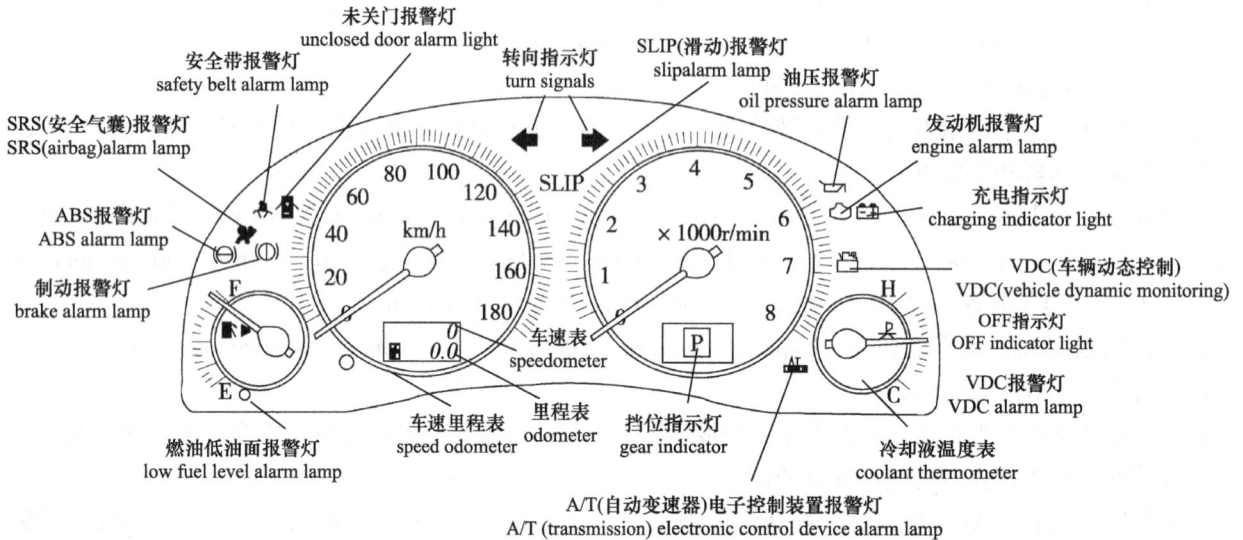

未关门报警灯
unclosed door alarm light

安全带报警灯
safety belt alarm lamp

SRS(安全气囊)报警灯
SRS(airbag)alarm lamp

ABS报警灯
ABS alarm lamp

制动报警灯
brake alarm lamp

转向指示灯
turn signals

SLIP(滑动)报警灯
slipalarm lamp

油压报警灯
oil pressure alarm lamp

发动机报警灯
engine alarm lamp

充电指示灯
charging indicator light

VDC(车辆动态控制)
VDC(vehicle dynamic monitoring)

OFF指示灯
OFF indicator light

VDC报警灯
VDC alarm lamp

燃油低油面报警灯
low fuel level alarm lamp

车速里程表
speed odometer

里程表
odometer

车速表
speedometer

挡位指示灯
gear indicator

冷却液温度表
coolant thermometer

A/T(自动变速器)电子控制装置报警灯
A/T (transmission) electronic control device alarm lamp

图 5.2.11　报警指示装置
Figure 5.2.11　Alarm indicator

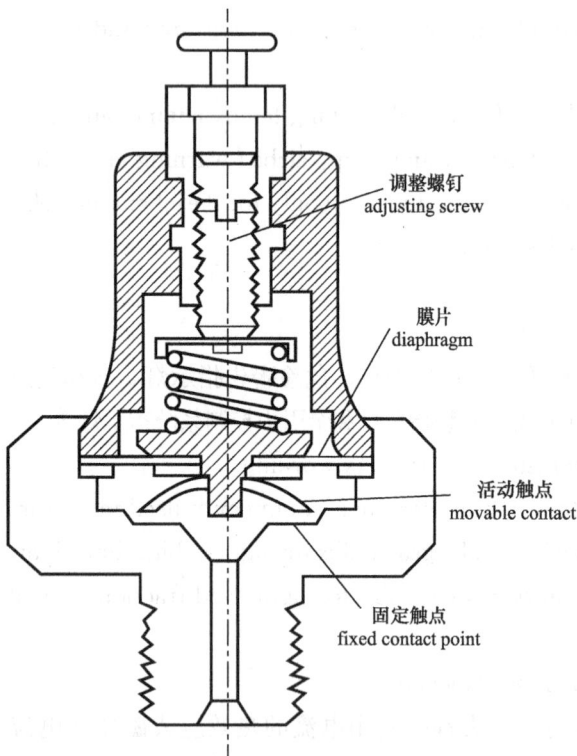

调整螺钉
adjusting screw

膜片
diaphragm

活动触点
movable contact

固定触点
fixed contact point

图 5.2.12　膜片式油压力警告灯传感器结构
Figure 5.2.12　Structure of diaphragm oil pressure warning sensor

（1）机油压力报警装置（Oil pressure alarm device）

传感器的活动触点固定在膜片上，固定触点设置在传感器的壳体上。无油压或油压低于某一数值时，弹簧压合触点，接通电路，使警告灯发亮。当油压达到某一定值时，膜片上凸触点分开，警告灯熄灭（图 5.2.12）。

The movable contact of the sensor is fixed on the diaphragm, and the fixed contact is arranged on the shell of the sensor. When there is no oil pressure or the oil pressure is lower than a certain value, the spring closes the contact, the circuit is connected, and the warning lamp is lit. When the oil pressure reaches a certain value, the convex contacts on the diaphragm are separated and the warning lamp is turned off (Fig. 5.2.12).

（2）冷却液温度报警装置（Coolant temperature alarm device）

在传感器的密封套管内装有条形双金属片，双金属片自由端焊有动触点，而静触点直接搭铁。当温度升高到95～98℃时，双金属片向静触点方向弯曲，使两触点接触，红色警告灯便通电发亮（图 5.2.13）。

A strip bimetal sheet is installed in the sealed sleeve of the sensor. The free end of the bimetal sheet is welded with a moving contact, and the static contact is directly put up iron. When the temperature rises to 95~98℃, the bimetal sheet bends toward the static contact, which makes the two contacts contact, and the red warning lamp turns on and lights up(Fig. 5. 2. 13).

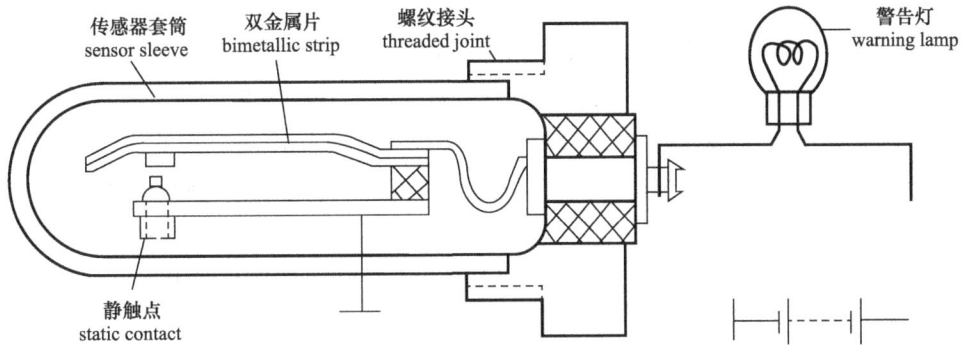

图 5. 2. 13 冷却液温度警告灯电路图

Figure 5. 2. 13 Coolant temperature warning circuit diagram

（3）燃油油量报警装置（Fuel oil alarm device）

当燃油箱内燃油量多时，负温度系数的热敏电阻元件浸没在燃油中散热快，其温度较低，电阻值大，所以电路中电流很小，警告灯处于熄灭状态。当燃油减少到规定值以下时，热敏电阻元件露出油面，散热慢，温度升高，电阻值减小，电路中电流增大，则警告灯发亮，以示警告（图 5. 2. 14）。

When the amount of fuel in the fuel tank is large, the thermistor with negative temperature coefficient is submerged in the fuel, which has fast heat dissipation, low temperature and high resistance value, so the current in the circuit is very small and the warning lamp is in the state of extinction. When the fuel is reduced below the prescribed value, the thermistor element appears on the oil surface, the heat dissipates slowly, the temperature rises, the resistance value decreases, the current in the circuit increases, and the warning lamp lights up to show the warning(Fig. 5. 2. 14).

（4）制动液液面报警装置（Brake fluid level alarm device）

当浮子随着制动液面下降到规定值以下时，永久磁铁的吸力吸动舌簧开关，使之闭合，接通警告灯点亮，发出警告。制动液液面在规定值以上时，浮子上升，吸力不足，舌簧开关在自身弹力的作用下，断开警告灯电路（图 5. 2. 15）。

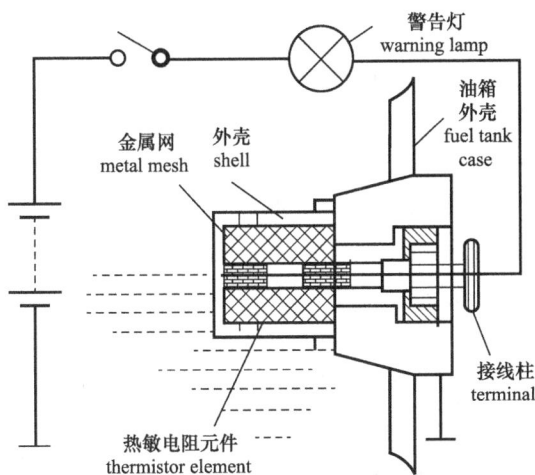

图 5. 2. 14 燃油油量报警装置工作原理

Figure 5. 2. 14 Working principle of fuel alarm device

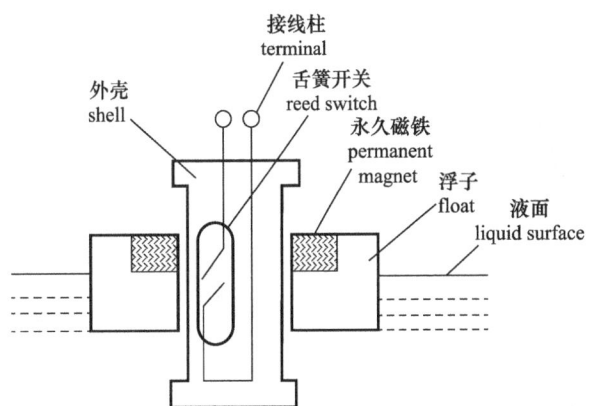

图 5. 2. 15 制动液液面报警开关结构

Figure 5. 2. 15 Structure of brake fluid level alarm switch

When the float drops below the specified value along with the brake fluid level, the permanent magnet attracts the tongue spring switch, which makes it closed. The warning lamp light up and gives a warning. When the brake fluid level is above the specified value, the float rises and the permanent magnet suction is insufficient. Under the action of its own elasticity, the tongue spring switch disconnects the warning lamp circuit(Figure 5.2.15).

2.4 暖风空调系统 (Heating air conditioning system)

对车内空气或进入车内的外部空气进行加热的装置，称为汽车暖风装置。近代汽车空调是全年性的冷暖一体化的装置。通过冷热风的混合，人为设定冷热风量的比例，通过风门开闭和调节，满足人们对舒适性的要求。因此，暖风是汽车空调的重要组成部分。

汽车空调暖通系统的工作原理
Working Principles of Automobile Air Conditioner Heating System and Ventilation System

The device that heats the air inside the car or the outside air entering the car is called the automobile warm air device. Modern automotive air conditioning is a year-round integrated device of heating and cooling. Through the mixing of hot and cold air, the ratio of hot and cold air is set artificially, and the adjustment of the opening and closing of the air door meets people's requirements for comfort. Therefore, warm air is an important part of automobile air conditioning.

1. 暖风系统的分类 (Classification of warm air system)

按所使用的热源不同可分为：

（1）水暖式暖风系统，利用发动机的冷却液热量，多用于轿车。

（2）独立热源式，装有专门的暖风装置，多用于客车和载货车。

（3）综合预热式，既利用发动机的冷却液热量，又装有燃烧预热的综合加热装置暖风，多用于大客车。

According to the different heat sources used, it can be divided into:

(1) Water-heated warm air system, using the engine coolant heat heating. It is mostly used in cars.

(2) Independent heat source type, equipped with special heater, mostly used for buses and trucks.

(3) Comprehensive preheating. It not only uses the heat of engine coolant to heat, but also equips a comprehensive heating device for combustion preheating. It is mostly used in buses.

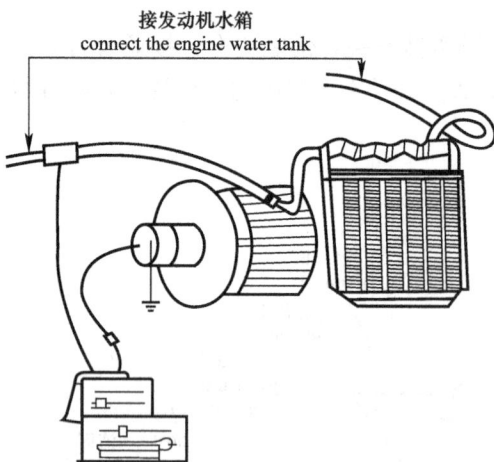

接发动机水箱
connect the engine water tank

图 5.2.16　水暖式暖风系统组成
Figure 5.2.16　Composition of water-heated warm air system

2. 暖风系统的作用(The function of warm air system)

（1）冬季天气寒冷，在运动的汽车内人们感觉更寒冷。这时，汽车空调可以向车内提供暖风，提高车室内的温度，使乘员不再感觉到寒冷。

（2）冬季或者初春，室内外温差较大，车窗玻璃会结霜或起雾，影响司机和乘客的视线，不利于安全行车，这时可以用暖风来除霜和除雾。

(1) Winter weather is cold, people feel colder in sports cars. At this time, the car air conditioning system can provide warm air to the car and improve the temperature in the car room, so that the passengers no longer feel cold.

(2) In winter or early spring, the temperature difference between indoor and outdoor is large, and the window glass will frost or fog, which affects the sight of drivers and passengers, and is not conducive to safe driving. At this time, warm air can be used to defrost and defrost.

3. 水暖式暖风系统组成 (Composition of water-heated warm air system)

水暖式暖风系统一般由控制开关、鼓风机、暖风水箱、循环水控制开关及相应的管路组成，这种暖风装置结构简单、耗能少、成本低、操作维修方便，所以各种汽车一般都采用这种暖风装置（图5.2.16）。

Water-heated warm air system is generally composed of control switch, blower, heater water tank, circulating water control switch and corresponding pipeline. This kind of warm air device has simple structure, less energy consume, low cost, easy operation and maintenance, so all kinds of automobiles generally use this kind of warm air device. As shown in the figure(Figure 5.2.16).

4. 水暖式暖风系统原理(Principle of water-heated warm air system)

利用水冷式发动机冷却系统中的循环热水作为热源，在制热过程中并将其引入车内换热器，再用鼓风机将被加热的空气送入车内取暖（图5.2.17）。

The circulating hot water in the cooling system of water-cooled engine is used as the heat source, which is introduced into the heat exchanger in the car during the heating process, and then the heated air is fed into the car by a blower for heating(Figure 5.2.17).

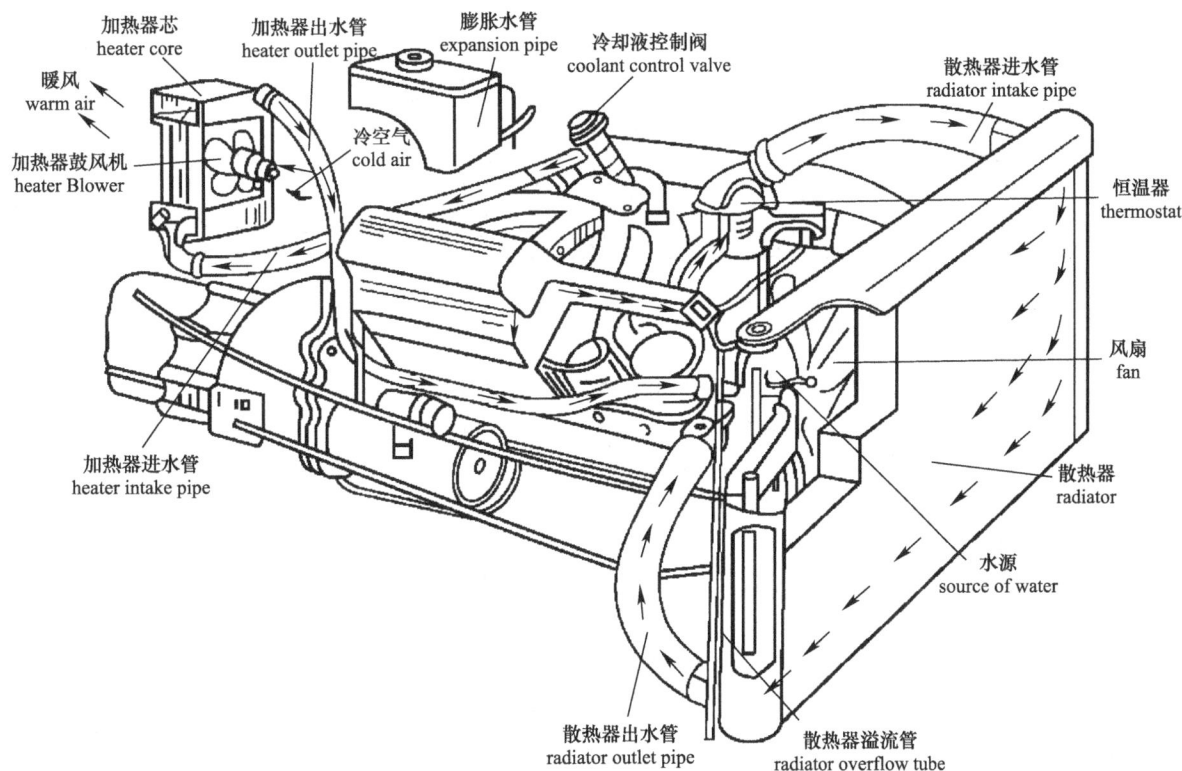

图 5.2.17　水暖式暖风系统原理

Figure 5.2.17　Principle of water-heated warm air system

5. 车内空气的通风系统(Ventilation system of vehicle air)

车内空气的通风换气通常采用自然通风，只有在自然通风不足时才采用强制通风。而所谓强制通风，则是采用鼓风机或换气扇将车外空气强制抽入车内（图5.2.18）。

Natural ventilation is usually used for ventilation and ventilation of the air in the car, and forced ventilation is only used when natural ventilation is insufficient. The so-called forced ventilation is the use of blowers or ventilation fans to force the outside air into the car(Figure 5.2.18).

2.5　风窗刮水器与洗涤器(Windshield wipers and scrubbers)

1. 刮水器和洗涤器系统作用(The function of wiper and scrubber system)

刮水器的作用是用来清除风窗玻璃上的雨水、雪或尘土，以确保驾驶人有良好的视野。在行驶中，由于泥土的飞溅或其他原因污染风窗玻璃，所以刮水器还设有洗涤装置。有些乘用车还装备有前照灯冲洗系统。刮水器和洗涤器系统在车上的布置如图 5.2.19 所示。

The function of the wiper is to remove rain, snow or dust from the windshield to ensure that the driver has a good vision. During driving, the windshield is contaminated by soil splash or other reasons, so the wiper also has a washing device. Some passenger cars are also equipped with headlamp flushing systems. The wiper and scrubber systems are arranged on the car as shown in the Figure 5.2.19.

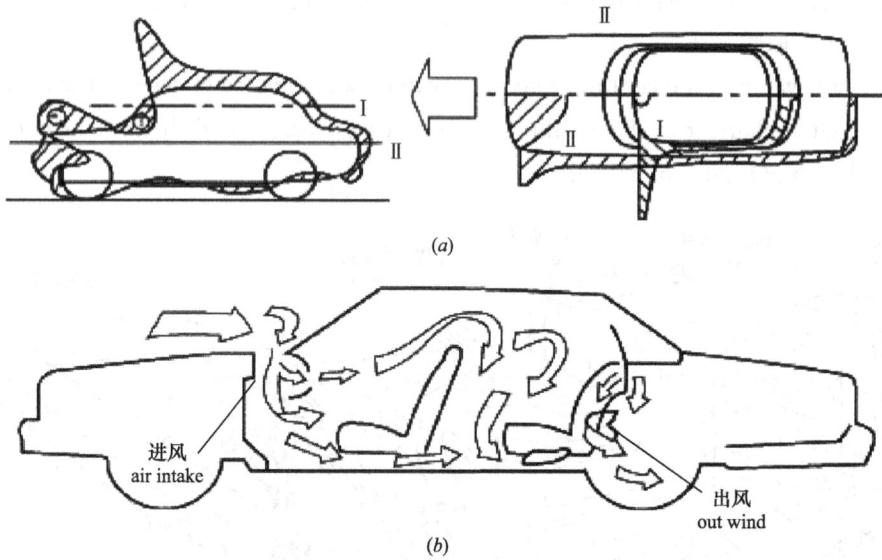

(a)

(b)

图 5.2.18　轿车的自然通风

Figure 5.2.18　Natural ventilation of car

(a) 车身表面风压（wind pressure on body surface）；(b) 车内空气流动（air flow in vehicle）

画于车身内的为正压区，画于车身外的为负压区

The positive pressure area painted in the body and the negative pressure area painted outside the body.

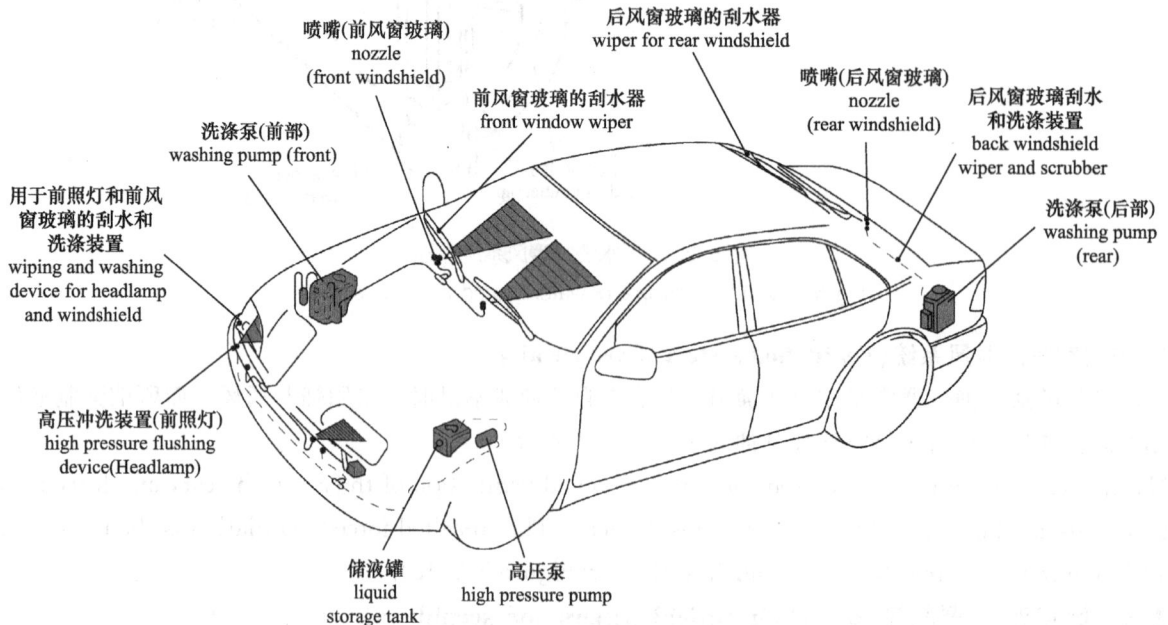

图 5.2.19　刮水器和洗涤器系统

Figure 5.2.19　Windshield wipers and scrubbers

2. 电动刮水器的分类（Types of electric wipers）

现代汽车均使用电动机驱动刮水器，这样可以保持一定速度摆动，不受发动机转速与负荷变动的影响，且可以随驾驶人的需要，视雨势大小调整动作速度。电动刮水器更可以做1～30s/次一次间歇动作的无级变速调整。根据刮水片的联动方式（图5.2.20），刮水器可分为：

Modern automobiles use motors to drive wipers, so that they can not be affected by engine speed and load changes, maintain a certain swing speed, and adjust the action speed according to the driver's needs and the size of rain. Electric wiper can make intermittent and continuously variable speed adjustment from once per second to 30 seconds. According to the linkage mode of the wiper(Figure 5.2.20), the wiper can be divided into:

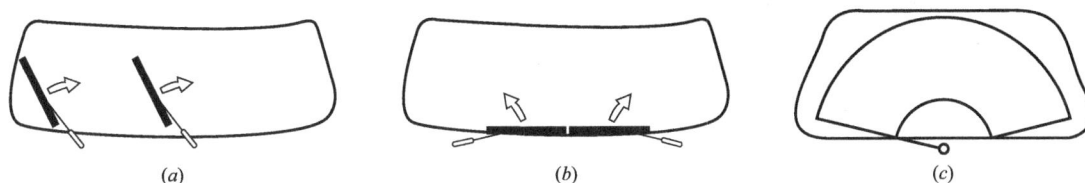

图5.2.20 电动刮水器的分类

Figure 5.2.20 Types of electric wipers

(a) 平行连动式(parallel linkage type)；(b) 对向连动式(counter-directional linkage type)；

(c) 单臂式(single-arm type)

（1）平行连动式：一般小型车采用最多。

（2）对向连动式：大型车采用。

（3）单臂式：部分小型车采用。

目前使用的刮水器多数是平行连动式。

(1) Parallel linkage type: generally used for small cars.

(2) Counter-directional linkage type: large-scale vehicle.

(3) Single-arm type: some small cars are adopted.

At present, most of the wipers used are parallel connected.

3. 电动刮水器的组成（Composition of electric wiper）

为了保证雨雪天气行车时驾驶员有良好的视线，在汽车风窗玻璃上装有刮水器。一般汽车的前风窗玻璃上都装有两个刮水片，部分汽车在后风窗玻璃上还装有一个刮水片，一些豪华轿车还装有与风窗刮水器一起开动的前照灯刮水器。

In order to ensure that the driver has good sight when driving in snow and rain weather, a wiper is installed on the windshield of the car. Generally, there are two wipers on the front windshield of automobiles. Some cars also have a wiper on the rear windshield. Some luxury cars also have a headlamp wiper that operates with the windshield wiper.

电动刮水器主要由微型直流电动机、蜗轮、蜗杆、拉杆、摆杆、刷架和刮水片等组成（图5.2.21）。微型直流电动机是电动刮水器的动力源。通过传动机构，刮水片在风窗玻璃外表面上往复摆动，以扫除风窗玻璃上的雨水、积雪或灰尘。刮水器在使用中应能根据雨雪的大小来调整刮水片的刮水速度，在雨雪小时低速刮水，雨雪大时高速刮水，故需电动机能改变转速，以调整刮水片的刮水速度。

Electric wiper is mainly composed of micro DC motor, worm wheel, worm, pull rod, swing rod, brush frame and wiper blade(Figure 5.2.21). Micro DC motor is the power source of electric wiper. Through the transmission mechanism, the wipers oscillate to and fro on the outside surface of the windowpane to remove

215

rain, snow or dust on the windowpane. The wiper should adjust the wiping speed of the wiper according to the size of rain and snow. When the amount of rain and snow is small, it wipes at low speed, and when the amount of rain and snow is large, it wipes at high speed. Therefore, the motor is needed to change the speed to adjust the wiping speed of the wiper.

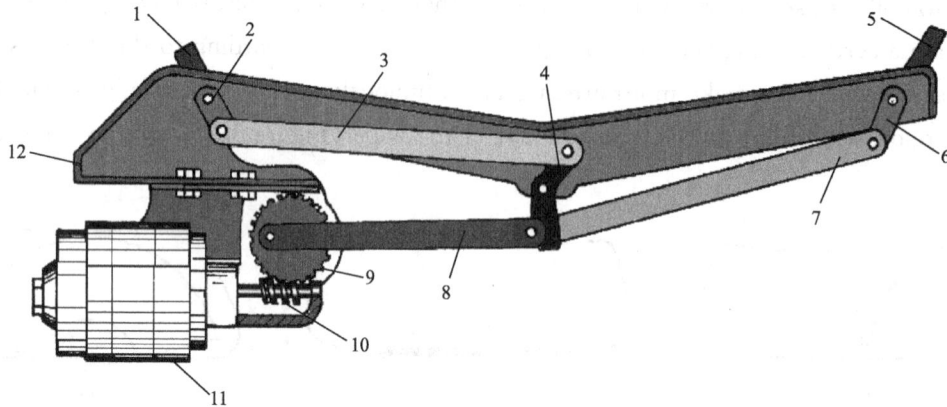

图 5.2.21　电动刮水器

Figure 5.2.21　Electric wiper

1、5—刷架（brush holder）；2、4、6—摆杆（swing rod）；3、7、8—拉杆（pull rod）；

9—蜗轮（worm gear）；10—蜗杆（worm）；11—电动机（motor）；12—底板（floor）

4. 永磁式刮水电动机的结构（Structure of permanent magnet wiper motor）

刮水电动机按其磁场结构不同分为有绕线式和永磁式两种。永磁式刮水电动机具有体积小、质量轻、噪声小、结构简单等优点，目前在国内外汽车上得到了广泛的应用。永磁式刮水电动机总成的结构如图 5.2.22 所示。

Wiper motor can be divided into winding type and permanent magnet type according to its magnetic field structure. Permanent magnet wiper motor has many advantages, such as small size, light weight, low noise and simple structure. It has been widely used in automobiles at home and abroad. The structure of permanent magnet wiper motor assembly is shown in the Figure 5.2.22.

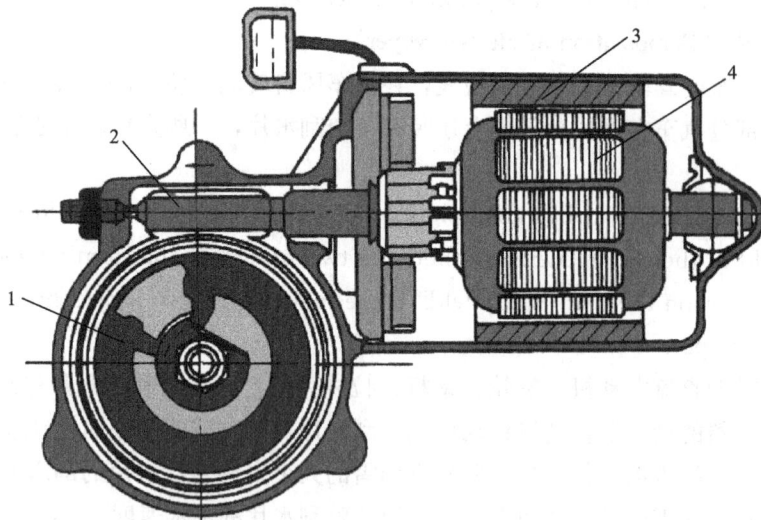

图 5.2.22　永磁式刮水电动机的结构

Figure 5.2.22　Structure of permanent magnet wiper motor

1—蜗轮（worm gear）；2—蜗杆（worm）；3—磁极（magnetic pole）；4—电枢（armature）

5. 永磁式刮水电动机的变速原理（Variable speed principle of permanent magnet wiper motor）

永磁刮水电动机是利用三个电刷来改变正、负电刷之间串联线圈的个数实现变速。高速电刷比低速电刷偏移 60°。$n=(E_x-I_s\sum R)/K_e\varphi$ 工作时产生的电枢磁通因歪曲使合成磁通减弱而使电动机转速增加。

Permanent magnet wiper motor uses three brushes to change the number of series coils between positive and negative brushes to achieve variable speed. The high-speed brush is 60 degrees offset from the low-speed brush. $n=(E_x-I_s\sum R)/K_e\varphi$. The armature flux produced during operation decreases the synthetic flux due to distortion and increases the motor speed.

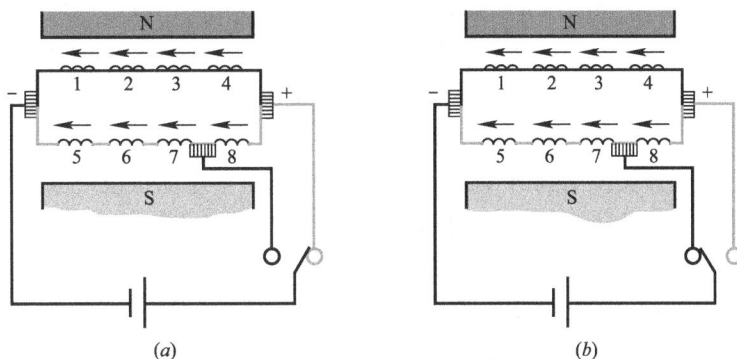

图 5.2.23　三刷式电动机变速原理

Figure 5.2.23　Variable speed principle of three brush motor

（a）低速（low speed）；（b）高速（high speed）

6. 刮水电动机的控制电路和自动复位装置（Control circuit and automatic reset device of wiper motor）

刮水电动机的刮水速度应能根据雨雪的大小由驾驶员进行控制。在停止刮水，动复位装置可在任何时刻切断刮水电动机电路时，都能使刮水片自动停止在风窗玻璃的下部，以免影响驾驶员的视线。

铜环式刮水器的控制电路和自动复位装置，用刮水器开关控制刮水器的刮水速度和复位。

The wiping speed of the wiper motor should be controlled by the driver according to the size of rain and snow. When the wiper is stopped and the wiper motor circuit can be cut off by the dynamic reset device at any time, the wiper can automatically stop at the lower part of the windowpane to avoid affecting the driver's sight.

The control circuit and automatic reset device of copper ring wiper are designed. The wiper switch is used to control the wiping speed and reset of the wiper.

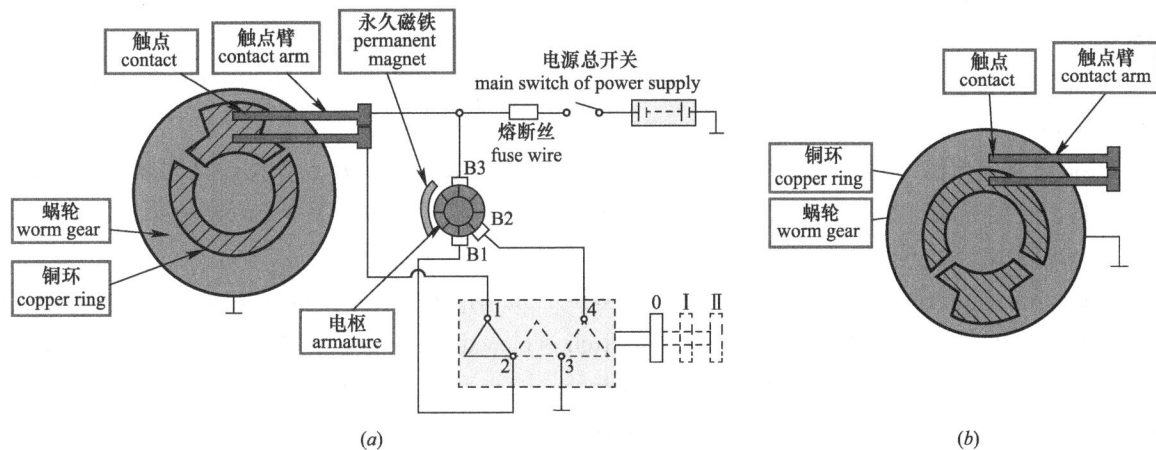

图 5.2.24　刮水电动机的控制电路和自动复位装置

Figure 5.2.24　Control circuit and automatic reset device of wiper motor

刮水器开关有 R（复位）、L（低速）、H（高速）三个挡位，四个接线柱，Ⅰ 接线柱接复位装置，Ⅱ 接线柱接电动机的低速电刷，Ⅲ 接线柱搭铁，Ⅳ 接线柱接电动机高速电刷。复位装置是在减速蜗轮 8（由塑料或尼龙材料制成）上，嵌有铜环 7 和 9。其中铜环 9 与电动机外壳相连（为搭铁）。触点臂 3 和 5 用磷铜片（弹性导电材料）制成，一端分别铆有触点 4 和 6，与铜环 7 和 9 保持接触。

The wiper switch has three gears, R (reset), L (low speed), H (high speed), four connection posts, Ⅰ connection reset device, Ⅱ connection post connection motor's low speed brush, Ⅲ connection post lapping iron, Ⅳ connection post connection motor's high speed brush. The reset device is mounted on the decelerating worm gear 8 (made of plastic or nylon material) with copper rings 7 and 9. The copper ring 9 is connected with the motor housing (as a tie-in). Contact arms 3 and 5 are made of phosphorus-copper sheets (elastic conductive materials). Contacts 4 and 6 are riveted at one end, respectively, to maintain contact with copper rings 7 and 9.

接通电源开关，将刮水器开关拉出到 L（低速）位时，电流从蓄电池正极→电源开关→熔丝→电刷 B3→电枢绕组→电刷 B1→接线柱 Ⅱ→接触片→接线柱Ⅲ→搭铁→蓄电池负极，构成回路，电动机以低速运转。

When switching on the power switch and pulling the wiper switch out to the L (low speed) position, the current from the battery positive pole→power switch →fuse brush B3 →armature →winding brush B1→wiring pole Ⅱ→contact piece→wiring poleⅢ →lapping iron →battery negative pole forms a circuit, and the motor runs at low speed.

7. 间歇式刮水器（Intermittent wiper）

汽车在小雨或雾天行驶时，若仍按上述刮水速度刮水，风窗上的微量水分和灰尘会形成一层发黏的表面，不能将风窗玻璃刮拭干净，却使玻璃模糊不清。为此现代汽车刮水器都装有电子间歇控制系统，使刮水器能按照一定的周期停止和刮水，即每动作一次停止 2～12s，以使驾驶员获得更好的视线。按照间歇时间是否可调分为可调节型和不可调节型。

When a car is driving in light rain or fog, if it still wipes at the above speed, the trace moisture and dust on the windowpane will form a layer of sticky surface, and the windowpane can not be wiped clean, resulting in blurred glass. For this reason, modern automobile wipers are equipped with electronic intermittent control system, so that wipers can stop and wipe in accordance with a certain period, i. e. every action stops for 2-12 seconds, so that drivers can get better sight. According to whether the interval time is adjustable, it can be divided into adjustable type and non-adjustable type.

（1）不可调节间歇控制电路（Non-adjustable intermittent control circuit）

刮水器的间歇控制是利用自动复位装置和电子振荡电路或集成电路实现。

The intermittent control of wiper is realized by automatic reset device and electronic oscillation circuit or integrated circuit.

1）同步间歇振荡电路。当刮水器开关置于间歇挡位置（刮水器开关处于 0 位，且间歇开关闭合）时，电源将通过自动复位开关向电容器 C 充电，其电路为：蓄电池正极→电源开关→熔断器→自动复位开关常闭触点（上）→电阻 R_1→C→搭铁→蓄电池负极。

1) Synchronized intermittent oscillation circuit. When the wiper switch is placed in the intermittent block position (wiper switch is at 0 and the intermittent switch is closed), the power supply will charge to capacitor C through the automatic reset switch. Its circuit is: battery positive pole →power switch →fuse →automatic reset switch →normal closed contact (top)→resistance R_1→C→Tie up→battery negative pole.

2）集成间歇振荡电路。当闭合间歇刮水器开关时，集成电路将输出高电位，使继电器磁化线圈通电，在电磁吸力的作用下，常闭触点打开，常开触点（虚线）闭合，刮水电动机运转，电路为：蓄电池正极→电源开关→熔断器→B_3→B_1→刮水器开关→继电器常开触点→搭铁→蓄电池负极。同时自动复位开关的常闭触点打开，常开触点（虚线）闭合。

2) Integrated intermittent oscillation circuit. When closing the intermittent wiper switch, the integrated circuit will output high potential to make the relay magnetization coil electrified. Under the action of electromagnetic attraction, the normally closed contact opens, the normally open contact (dotted line) closes, and the wiper motor runs. The circuit is as follows: battery positive pole →power switch→fuse→B_3→B_1→wiper switch→relay→normally open contact →Tie up→battery negative pole. At the same time, the normal closed contacts of the automatic reset switch are opened and the normal open contacts (dotted lines) are closed.

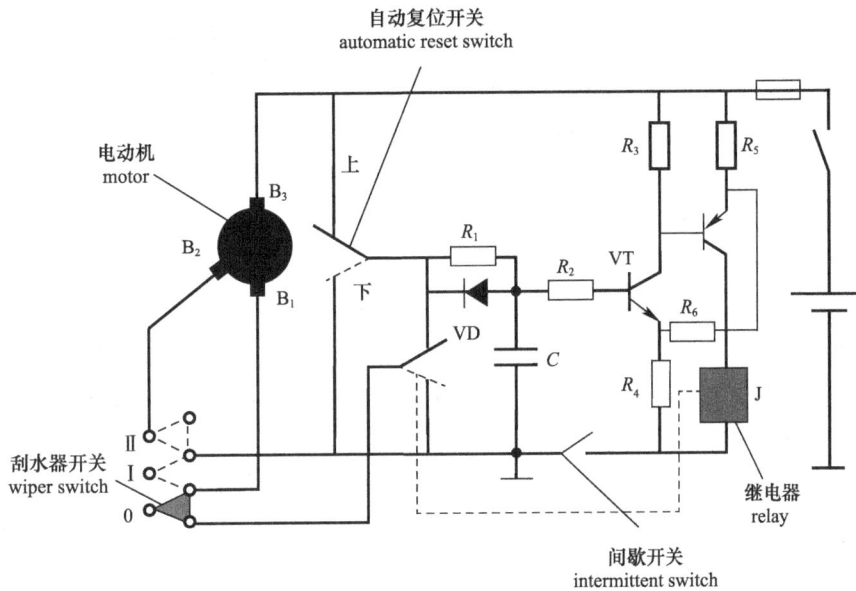

图 5.2.25　同步间歇震荡电路

Figure 5.2.25　Synchronized intermittent oscillation circuit

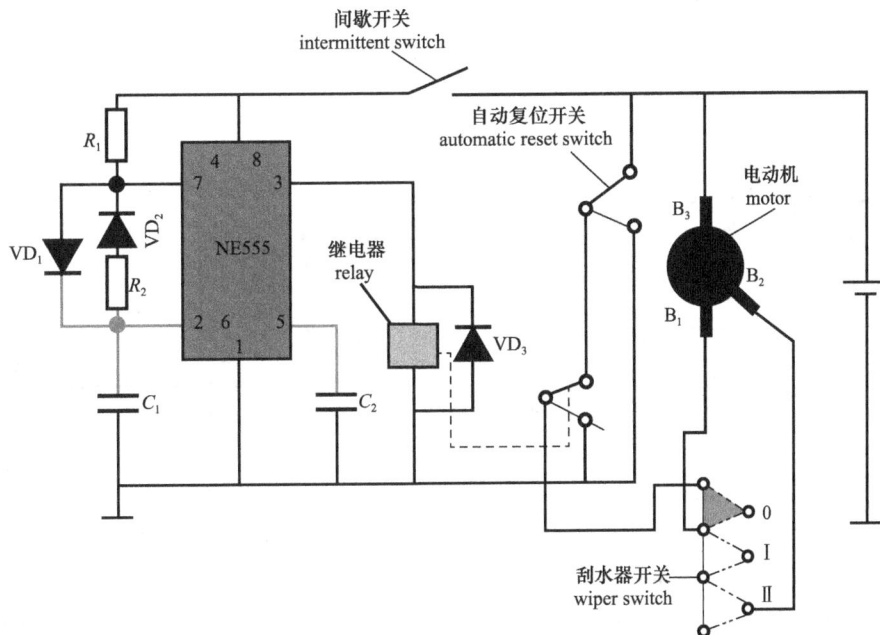

图 5.2.26　集成间歇振荡电路

Figure 5.2.26　Integrated intermittent oscillation circuit

（2）可调节间歇控制电路（Adjustable intermittent control circuit）

能使汽车刮水器根据雨量大小自动开启或关闭，并自动调节间歇时间。S_1、S_2 和 S_3 是安装在风窗玻璃外侧的流量检测电极，雨水落在两检测电极之间，使其阻值减小，水流量越大，其阻值越小。S_1 与 S_3 之间的距离较近（约 2.5cm），因此晶体管 VT_1 首先导通，继电器 J_1 通电，在电磁吸力的作用下，开关 P 闭合，刮水电动机低速旋转。

It can make the automobile wiper open or close automatically according to the rainfall and adjust the interval time automatically. S_1, S_2 and S_3 are the flow detection electrodes installed on the outside of windshield glass. Rainwater falls between the two detection electrodes, which reduces the resistance value. The larger the water flow, the smaller the resistance value. The distance between S_1 and S_3 is relatively close (about 2.5cm), so the transistor VT_1 is turned on first, and the relay J_1 is electrified. Under the action of electromagnetic attraction, the switch P closes and the wiper motor rotates at low speed.

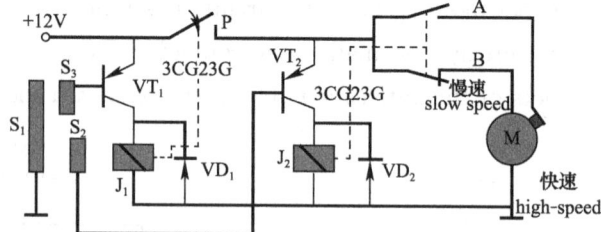

图 5.2.27　自动开关与调速控制电路

Figure 5.2.27　Automatic switch and speed control circuit

8. 风窗洗涤器的组成（Composition of windshield scrubber）

风窗洗涤器主要由贮液罐、电动洗涤泵、输液软管、三通接头、喷嘴等组成。

（1）洗涤泵一般永磁直流电动机和离心叶片泵组成，装在贮液罐上，也有安装在管路内，泵的进液口处有滤网。出水压力可达 70～88kPa。

（2）喷嘴在风窗玻璃下面，喷柱直径为 0.8～1.0mm，喷射方向可调。

The windshield scrubber is mainly composed of liquid storage tank, electric washing pump, infusion hose, tee joint, nozzle and so on.

（1）Washing pumps are generally composed of permanent magnet DC motors and centrifugal vane pumps, which are mounted on liquid storage tanks or in pipelines. There is a filter at the inlet of the washing pump, and the pressure of the effluent can reach 70～88kPa.

（2）The nozzle is installed under the windowpane, the diameter of the nozzle is 0.8～1.0 mm, and the direction of the nozzle is adjustable.

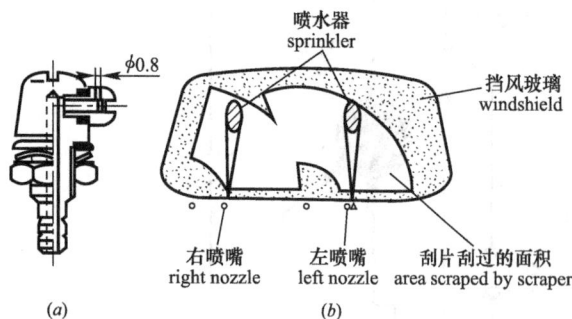

图 5.2.28　喷嘴的构造和调整位置

Figure 5.2.28　Structure and position adjustment of nozzle

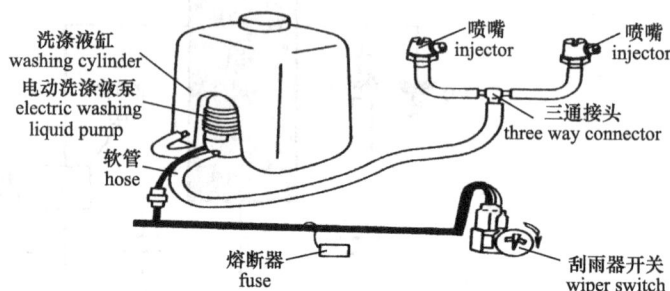

图 5.2.29　挡风玻璃洗涤设备

Figure 5.2.29　Windshield washing equipment

9. 风窗洗涤器工作原理（Working principle of windscreen washer）

接通洗涤器开关时（将刮水器开关向上扳动），洗涤泵工作：电源正极→中间继电器触点→熔断器 S_{11}→洗涤器开关→洗涤泵 V_s→搭铁→电源负极，喷嘴向风窗玻璃喷射清洗液，同时刮水器间歇继电器工作：电源正极→中间继电器触点→熔断器 S_{11}→洗涤器开关→刮水器间歇继电器→搭铁→电源负极。松开控制手柄时开关自动复位，喷嘴停喷，刮片复位。

When switching on the washer switch (pulling the wiper switch upward), the washer pump works: power supply positive pole→intermediate relay contact →fuse S_{11}→washer switch →washer pump V_s→lapping iron→power supply negative pole, The nozzle sprays cleaning fluid to the windshield glass while the wiper intermittent relay works: Positive pole of power supply→Intermediate relay contacts→Fuse S_{11}→Scrubber Switch→Wiper Intermittent Relay→Tie up→Power supply negative pole. When the control handle is loosened, the switch automatically resets, the nozzle stops spraying and the scraper resets.

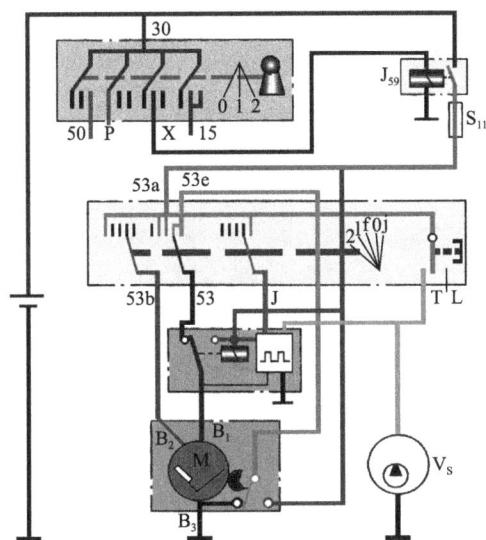

图 5.2.30　电动刮水器控制电路
Figure 5.2.30　Electric wiper control circuit

10. 风窗洗涤器的使用(Use of windshield scrubbers)

（1）洗涤泵连续工作时间不要超过 1min。

（2）对刮水与洗涤分别控制的汽车，应先开洗涤泵，再接通刮水器。

（3）喷水停止后，刮水器应继续刮动 3～5 次。

（4）洗涤液：硬度不超过 205ppm，添加少量的去垢剂、防锈剂。冬用洗涤剂应加甲醇、异丙醇、甘醇等防冻剂。

（5）冬季若不用洗涤器时，应将洗涤管中的水放掉。

（1）The continuous working time of the washing pump should not exceed 1 minute.

（2）For automobiles with separate control of wiping and washing, the washing pump should be turned on first, and then the wiper should be connected.

（3）The wiper should continue to scrape 3～5 times after the water spray stops.

（4）Detergent: Hardness not exceeding 205 ppm, adding a small amount of detergent and antirust agent. Winter detergent should be methanol, isopropanol, glycol and other antifreeze agents.

（5）If you do not use a washer in winter, you should release the water from the washing pipe.

思考与练习

(Reflection and Exercises)

1. 简述汽车照明信号系统的作用与组成。

2. 简述汽车信号信号系统的作用与组成。

3. 能叙述仪表与报警装置的组成。

4. 简述暖风空调系统的工作原理。

5. 简述风窗刮水器与洗涤器工作过程。

6. 简述中控门锁与电动座椅工作过程。

1. Describe the function and composition of automotive lighting signal system.

2. Describe the Function and Composition of Vehicle Signal System.

3. The composition of instrument and alarm device can be described.

4. Describe the working principle of the heating air conditioning system.

5. Describe the working process of windshield wiper and scrubber.

6. Describe the Working Process of Central Control Door Lock and Power seat.

参 考 文 献
References

［1］ 李亚，郭法宽，石岩. 汽车构造［M］. 沈阳：东北大学出版社，2013.

［2］ 陈家瑞. 汽车构造［M］. 5 版. 北京：人民交通出版社，2006.

［3］ 李丹，朱春龙，王怀强. 汽车底盘构造与维修［M］. 沈阳：东北大学出版社，2015.

［4］ 张柏荣，李宏亮，李亮. 汽车电气设备构造与维修［M］. 沈阳：东北大学出版社，2015.